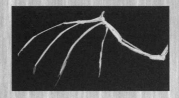

I'M ATTRACTED TO ANIMALS WITH WINGS.
IN PARTICULAR, I'M A BIG FAN OF BATS, SINCE
THEIR SKELETAL WINGS LOOK SO COOL.
- TAKESHI OBATA

Tsugumi Ohba
Born in Tokyo.
Hobby: Collecting teacups.
Day and night, develops manga plots
while holding knees on a chair.

Takeshi Obata was born in 1969 in Niigata, Japan, and
is the artist of the wildly popular SHONEN JUMP title
Hikaru no Go, which won the 2003 Tezuka Shinsei
"New Hope" award and the Shogakukan Manga award.
Obata is also the artist of **Arabian Majin Bokentan
Lamp Lamp, Ayatsuri Sakon,** and **Cyborg Jichan G.**

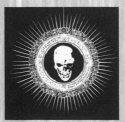

DEATH NOTE VOL 10
SHONEN JUMP ADVANCED Manga Edition

STORY BY TSUGUMI OHBA
ART BY TAKESHI OBATA

Translation & Adaptation/Tetsuichiro Miyaki
Touch-up Art & Lettering/Gia Cam Luc
Design/Sean Lee
Editor/Pancha Diaz

Published by VIZ Media, LLC
P.O. Box 77010
San Francisco, CA 94107

13
First printing, March 2007
Thirteenth printing, November 2015

SHONEN JUMP ADVANCED MANGA

DEATHNOTE

デスノート

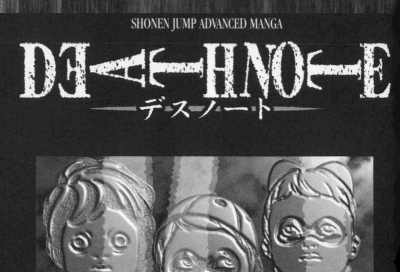

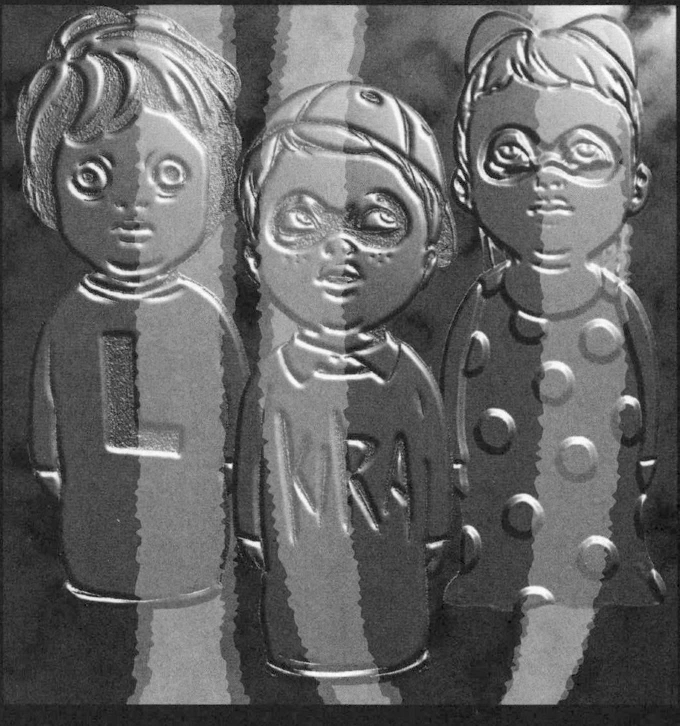

Vol. 10
Deletion

Story by Tsugumi Ohba
Art by Takeshi Obata

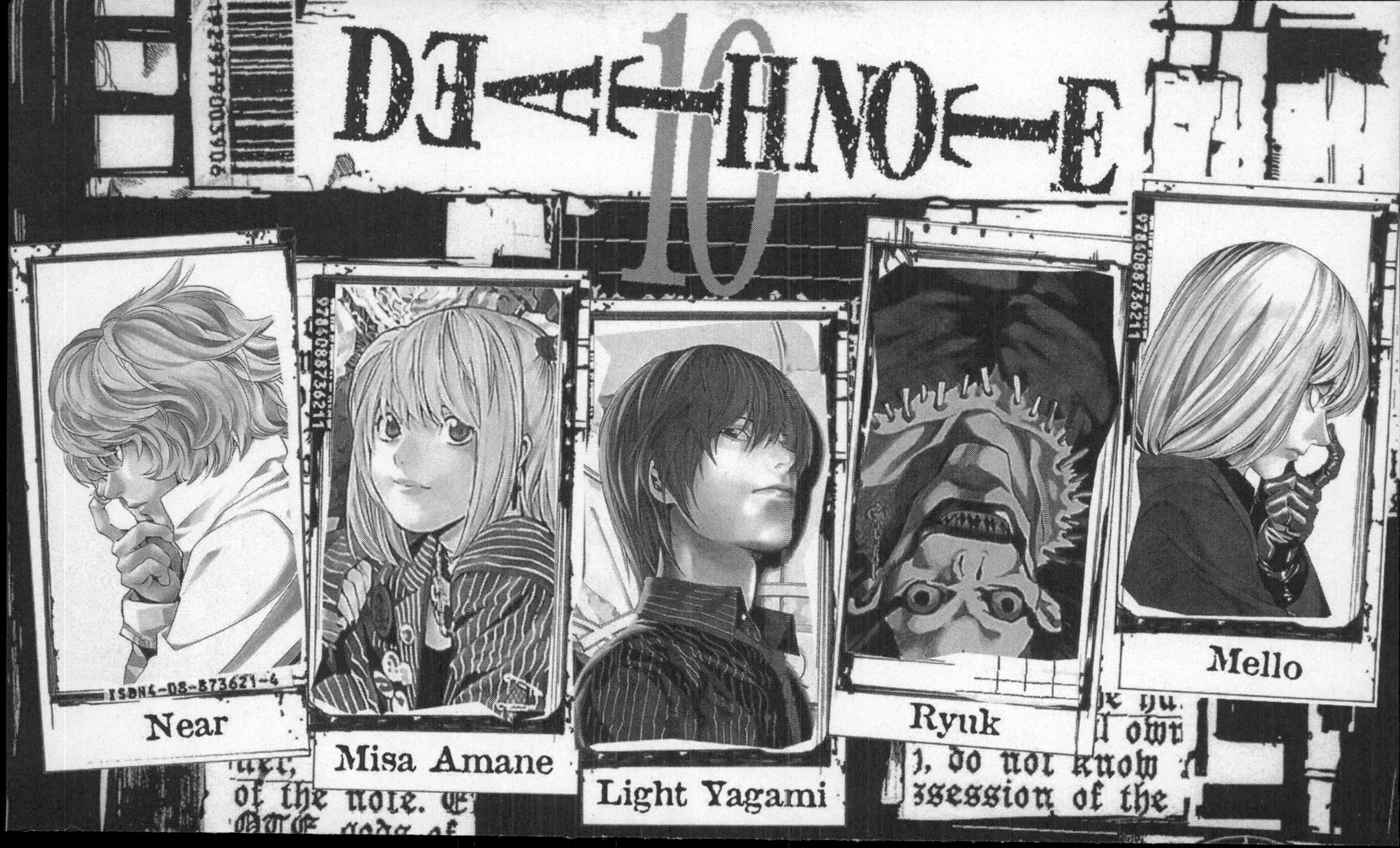
DEATH NOTE
10
Near
Misa Amane
Light Yagami
Ryuk
Mello
ISBN4-08-873621-4
9784088736211
of the note.
l, do not know
ossession of the
l own

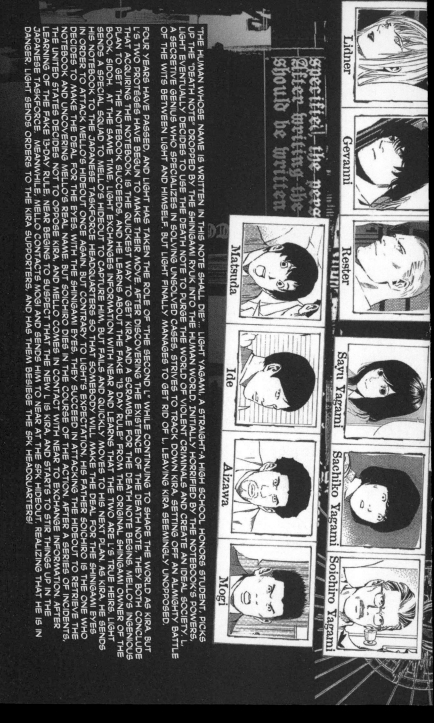

Soichiro Yagami
Sachiko Yagami
Sayu Yagami
Rester
Gevanni
Lidner
Mogi
Aizawa
Ide
Matsuda
specified, the pers
After writing the
should be written

"THE HUMAN WHOSE NAME IS WRITTEN IN THIS NOTE SHALL DIE"... LIGHT YAGAMI, A STRAIGHT-A HIGH SCHOOL HONORS STUDENT, PICKS UP THE "DEATH NOTE" DROPPED BY THE SHINIGAMI RYUK INTO THE HUMAN WORLD. INITIALLY HORRIFIED BY THE NOTEBOOK'S POWERS, LIGHT EVENTUALLY DECIDES TO USE THE DEATH NOTE TO PURGE THE WORLD OF VIOLENT CRIMINALS AND CREATE AN IDEAL SOCIETY. L, A SECRETIVE GENIUS WHO SPECIALIZES IN SOLVING UNSOLVED CASES, STRIVES TO TRACK DOWN KIRA, SETTING OFF AN ALMIGHTY BATTLE OF THE WITS BETWEEN LIGHT AND HIMSELF. BUT LIGHT FINALLY MANAGES TO GET RID OF L, LEAVING KIRA SEEMINGLY UNOPPOSED.

FOUR YEARS HAVE PASSED, AND LIGHT HAS TAKEN THE ROLE OF "THE SECOND L" WHILE CONTINUING TO SHAPE THE WORLD AS KIRA. BUT L'S TWO PROTÉGÉS HAVE BEGUN TO MAKE THEIR MOVE. AFTER DISCOVERING THE EXISTENCE OF THE DEATH NOTE, THEY BOTH CONCLUDE THAT ACQUIRING THE NOTEBOOK IS THE QUICKEST WAY TO GET KIRA, AND A SCRAMBLE FOR THE DEATH NOTE BEGINS. MELLO'S INGENIOUS PLAN TO GET THE NOTEBOOK SUCCEEDS, AND HE LEARNS ABOUT THE FAKE "13 DAY RULE" FROM THE ORIGINAL SHINIGAMI OWNER OF THE BOOK, SIDOH. AT THE SAME TIME, LIGHT EXCHANGES INFORMATION WITH NEAR AND LEARNS THAT THE TWO ARE L'S TRUE HEIRS. LIGHT SENDS A SPECIAL SQUAD TO MELLO'S HIDEOUT TO CAPTURE HIM, BUT FAILS AND QUICKLY MOVES TO HIS NEXT PLAN. AS KIRA, HE SENDS HIS NOTEBOOK TO THE JAPANESE TASKFORCE HEADQUARTERS SO THAT SOMEBODY WILL MAKE THE DEAL FOR THE SHINIGAMI EYES IN ORDER TO ATTACK MELLO'S HIDEOUT ONCE AGAIN. BUT CONTRARY TO LIGHT'S EXPECTATION, HIS FATHER SOICHIRO IS THE ONE WHO DECIDES TO MAKE THE DEAL FOR THE EYES. WITH THE SHINIGAMI EYES, THEY SUCCEED IN ATTACKING THE HIDEOUT TO RETRIEVE THE NOTEBOOK AND UNCOVERING MELLO'S REAL NAME. BUT SOICHIRO DIES IN THE COURSE OF THE ACTION. AFTER A SERIES OF INCIDENTS, THE UNITED STATES DECIDES NOT TO OPPOSE KIRA, AND MELLO COMES IN CONTACT WITH NEAR TO EXCHANGE INFORMATION. AFTER LEARNING OF THE FAKE 13-DAY RULE, NEAR BEGINS TO SUSPECT THAT THE NEW L IS KIRA, AND STARTS TO STIR THINGS UP IN THE JAPANESE TASKFORCE. MEANWHILE, MELLO CONTACTS MOGI AND SENDS HIM TO NEAR AT THE SPK HIDEOUT. REALIZING THAT HE IS IN DANGER, LIGHT SENDS ORDERS TO THE KIRA SUPPORTERS, AND HAS THEM BESIEGE THE SPK HEADQUARTERS!

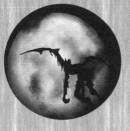

DEATH NOTE
Vol. 10

CONTENTS

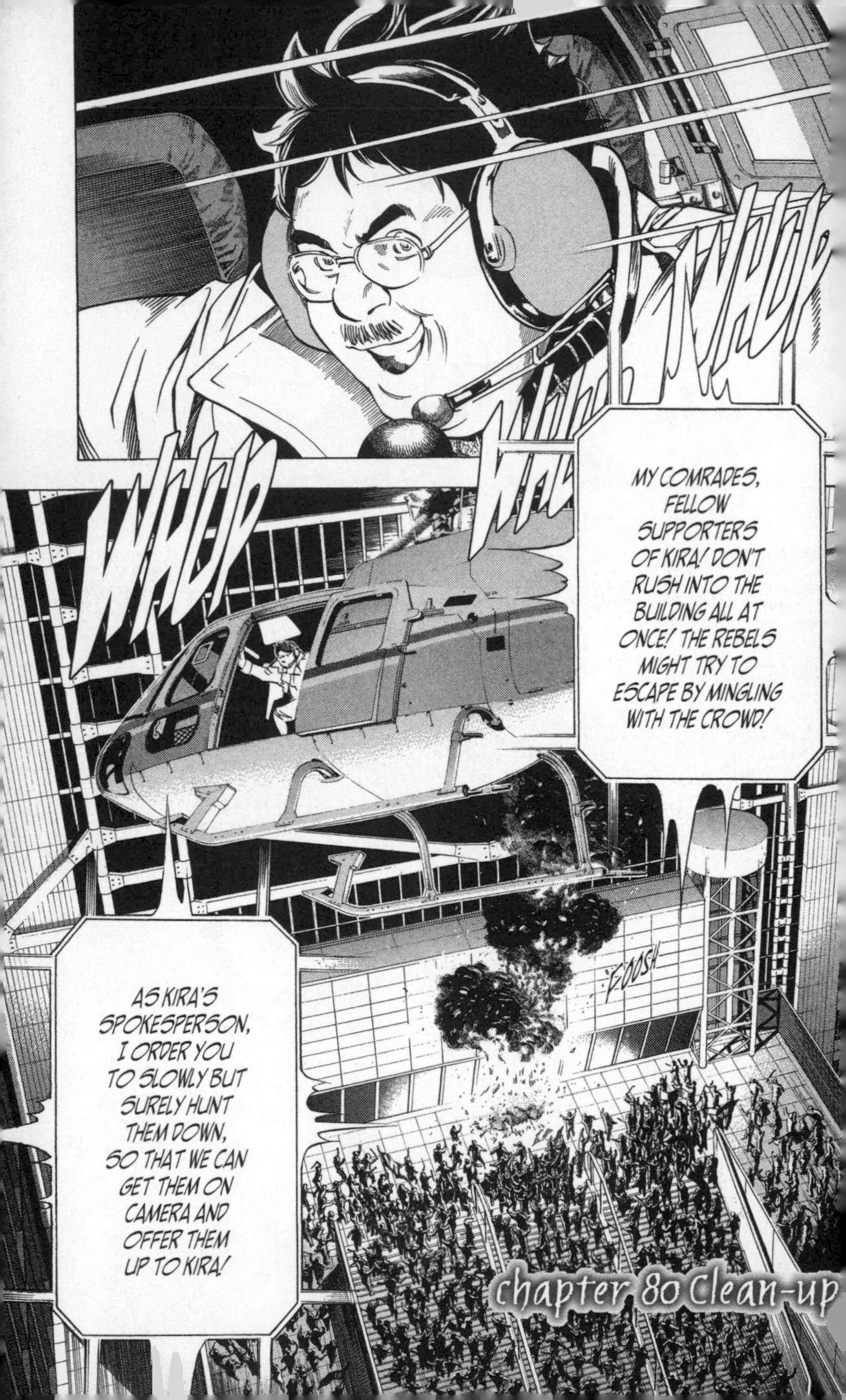
WHUP WHUP
WHUP
MY COMRADES, FELLOW SUPPORTERS OF KIRA! DON'T RUSH INTO THE BUILDING ALL AT ONCE! THE REBELS MIGHT TRY TO ESCAPE BY MINGLING WITH THE CROWD!
WHUP
GOOSH
AS KIRA'S SPOKESPERSON, I ORDER YOU TO SLOWLY BUT SURELY HUNT THEM DOWN, SO THAT WE CAN GET THEM ON CAMERA AND OFFER THEM UP TO KIRA!
chapter 80 Clean-up

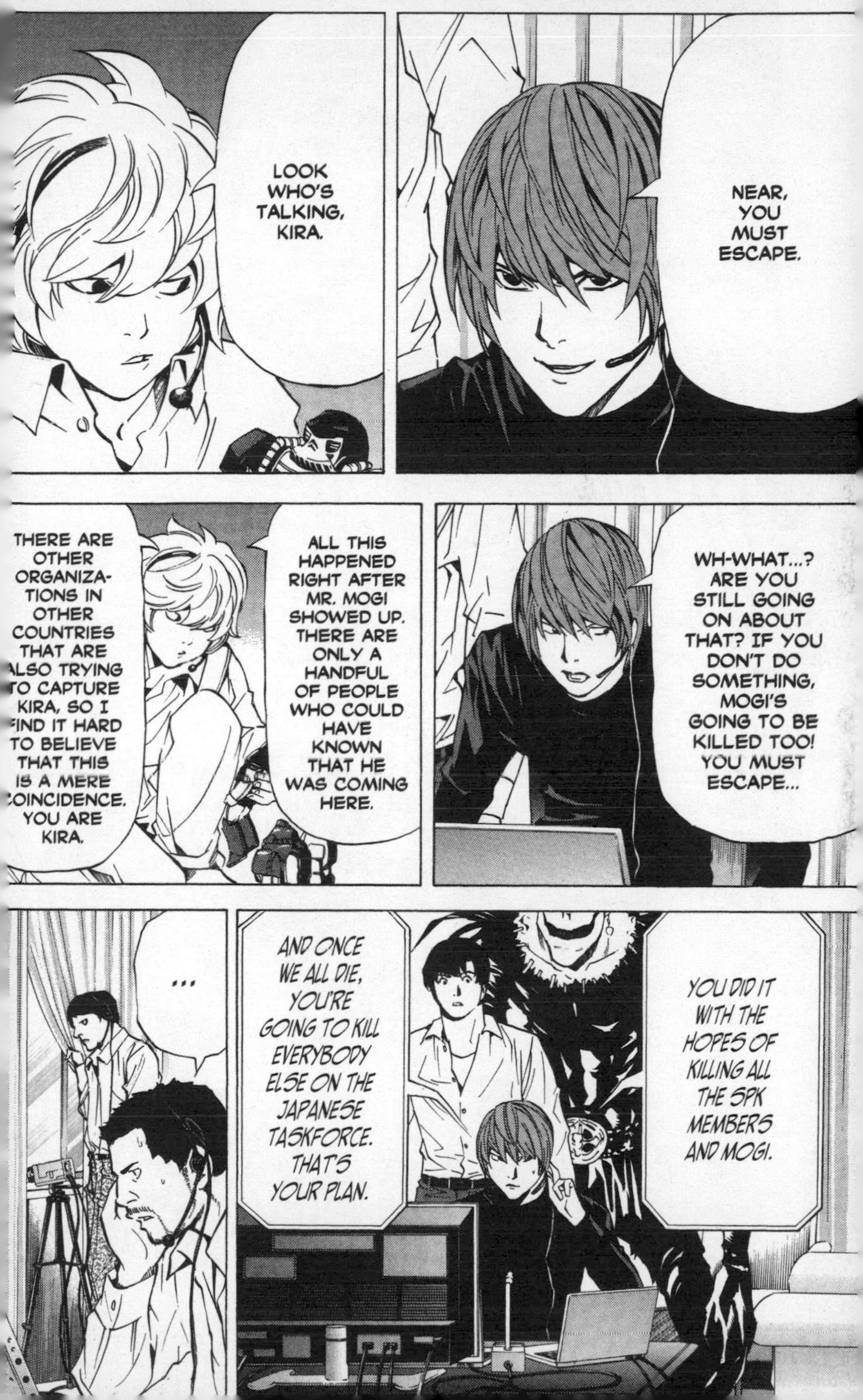
NEAR, YOU MUST ESCAPE.
LOOK WHO'S TALKING, KIRA.
WH-WHAT...? ARE YOU STILL GOING ON ABOUT THAT? IF YOU DON'T DO SOMETHING, MOGI'S GOING TO BE KILLED TOO! YOU MUST ESCAPE...
ALL THIS HAPPENED RIGHT AFTER MR. MOGI SHOWED UP. THERE ARE ONLY A HANDFUL OF PEOPLE WHO COULD HAVE KNOWN THAT HE WAS COMING HERE.
THERE ARE OTHER ORGANIZATIONS IN OTHER COUNTRIES THAT ARE ALSO TRYING TO CAPTURE KIRA, SO I FIND IT HARD TO BELIEVE THAT THIS IS A MERE COINCIDENCE. YOU ARE KIRA.
YOU DID IT WITH THE HOPES OF KILLING ALL THE SPK MEMBERS AND MOGI.
AND ONCE WE ALL DIE, YOU'RE GOING TO KILL EVERYBODY ELSE ON THE JAPANESE TASKFORCE. THAT'S YOUR PLAN.
...

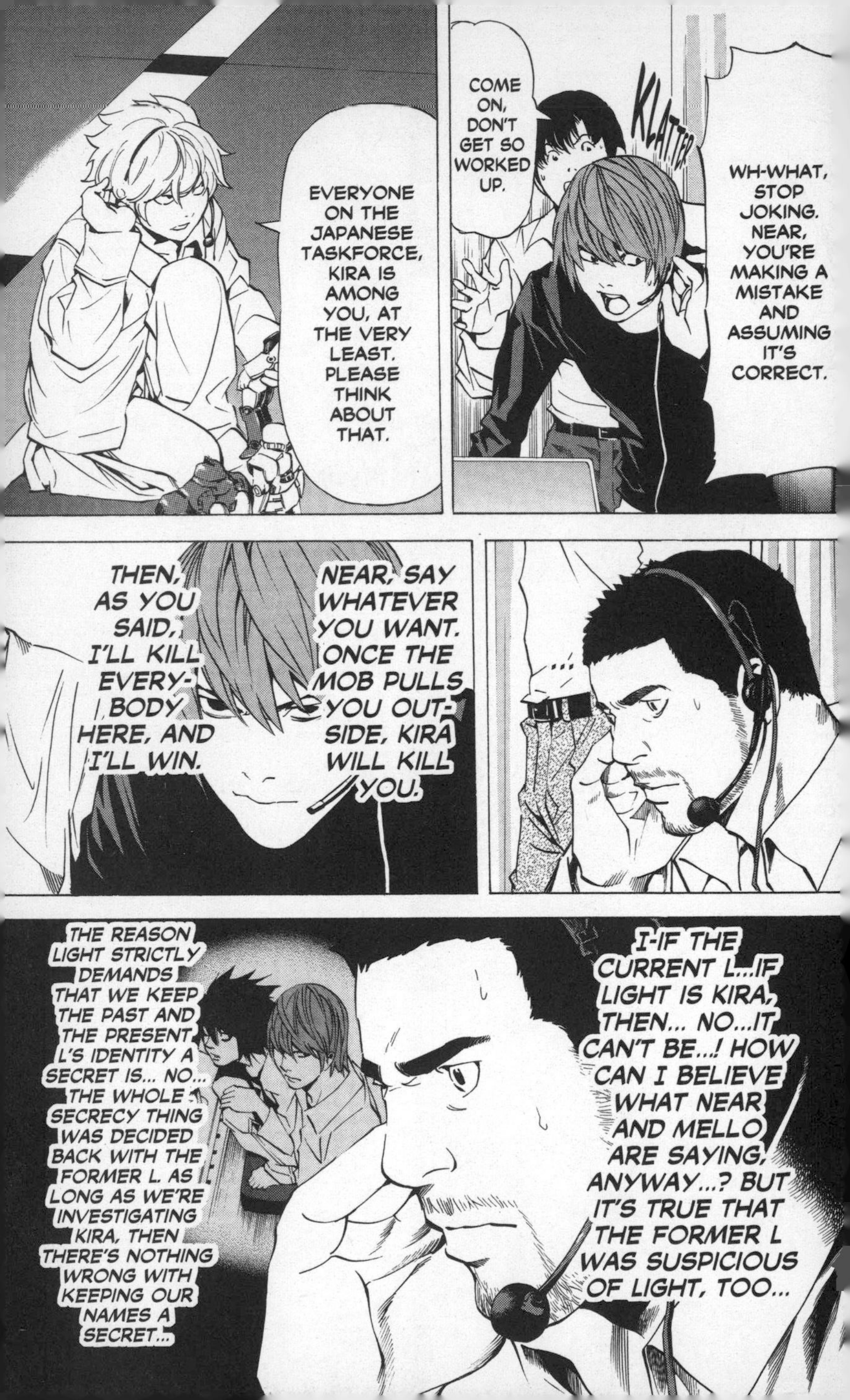
KLATTER
WH-WHAT, STOP JOKING. NEAR, YOU'RE MAKING A MISTAKE AND ASSUMING IT'S CORRECT.
COME ON, DON'T GET SO WORKED UP.
EVERYONE ON THE JAPANESE TASKFORCE, KIRA IS AMONG YOU, AT THE VERY LEAST. PLEASE THINK ABOUT THAT.
NEAR, SAY WHATEVER YOU WANT. ONCE THE MOB PULLS YOU OUT-SIDE, KIRA WILL KILL YOU.
THEN, AS YOU SAID, I'LL KILL EVERY-BODY HERE, AND I'LL WIN.
I-IF THE CURRENT L...IF LIGHT IS KIRA, THEN... NO...IT CAN'T BE...! HOW CAN I BELIEVE WHAT NEAR AND MELLO ARE SAYING, ANYWAY...? BUT IT'S TRUE THAT THE FORMER L WAS SUSPICIOUS OF LIGHT, TOO...
THE REASON LIGHT STRICTLY DEMANDS THAT WE KEEP THE PAST AND THE PRESENT L'S IDENTITY A SECRET IS... NO... THE WHOLE SECRECY THING WAS DECIDED BACK WITH THE FORMER L. AS LONG AS WE'RE INVESTIGATING KIRA, THEN THERE'S NOTHING WRONG WITH KEEPING OUR NAMES A SECRET...

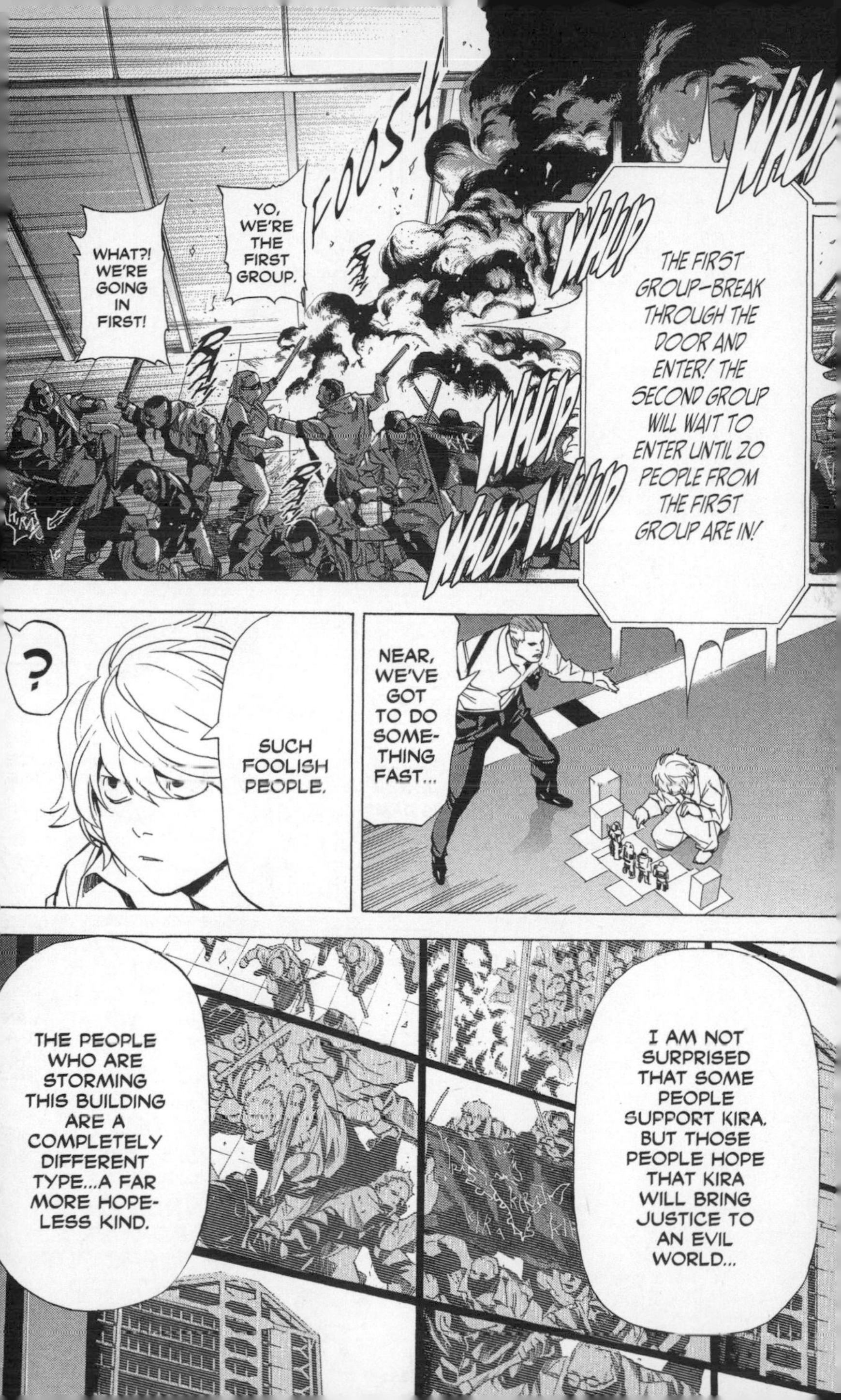
WHUP
THE FIRST GROUP-BREAK THROUGH THE DOOR AND ENTER! THE SECOND GROUP WILL WAIT TO ENTER UNTIL 20 PEOPLE FROM THE FIRST GROUP ARE IN!
WHUP
WHUP
WHUP WHUP
FOOSH
YO, WE'RE THE FIRST GROUP.
WHAT?! WE'RE GOING IN FIRST!
NEAR, WE'VE GOT TO DO SOMETHING FAST...
SUCH FOOLISH PEOPLE.
?
I AM NOT SURPRISED THAT SOME PEOPLE SUPPORT KIRA. BUT THOSE PEOPLE HOPE THAT KIRA WILL BRING JUSTICE TO AN EVIL WORLD...
THE PEOPLE WHO ARE STORMING THIS BUILDING ARE A COMPLETELY DIFFERENT TYPE...A FAR MORE HOPELESS KIND.

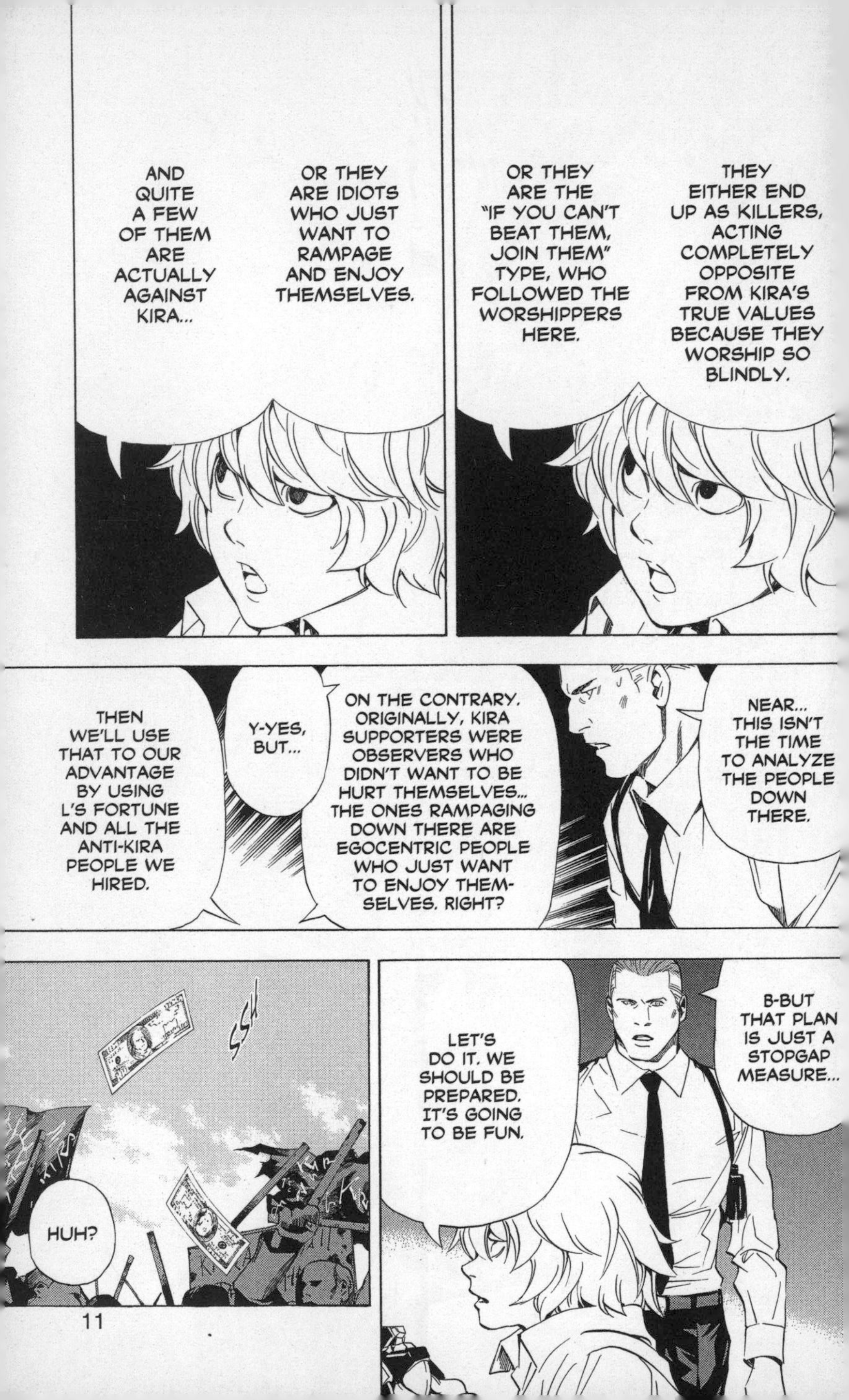
THEY EITHER END UP AS KILLERS, ACTING COMPLETELY OPPOSITE FROM KIRA'S TRUE VALUES BECAUSE THEY WORSHIP SO BLINDLY.
OR THEY ARE THE "IF YOU CAN'T BEAT THEM, JOIN THEM" TYPE, WHO FOLLOWED THE WORSHIPPERS HERE.
OR THEY ARE IDIOTS WHO JUST WANT TO RAMPAGE AND ENJOY THEMSELVES.
AND QUITE A FEW OF THEM ARE ACTUALLY AGAINST KIRA...
NEAR... THIS ISN'T THE TIME TO ANALYZE THE PEOPLE DOWN THERE.
ON THE CONTRARY. ORIGINALLY, KIRA SUPPORTERS WERE OBSERVERS WHO DIDN'T WANT TO BE HURT THEMSELVES... THE ONES RAMPAGING DOWN THERE ARE EGOCENTRIC PEOPLE WHO JUST WANT TO ENJOY THEMSELVES. RIGHT?
Y-YES, BUT...
THEN WE'LL USE THAT TO OUR ADVANTAGE BY USING L'S FORTUNE AND ALL THE ANTI-KIRA PEOPLE WE HIRED.
B-BUT THAT PLAN IS JUST A STOPGAP MEASURE...
LET'S DO IT. WE SHOULD BE PREPARED. IT'S GOING TO BE FUN.
SSH
HUH?

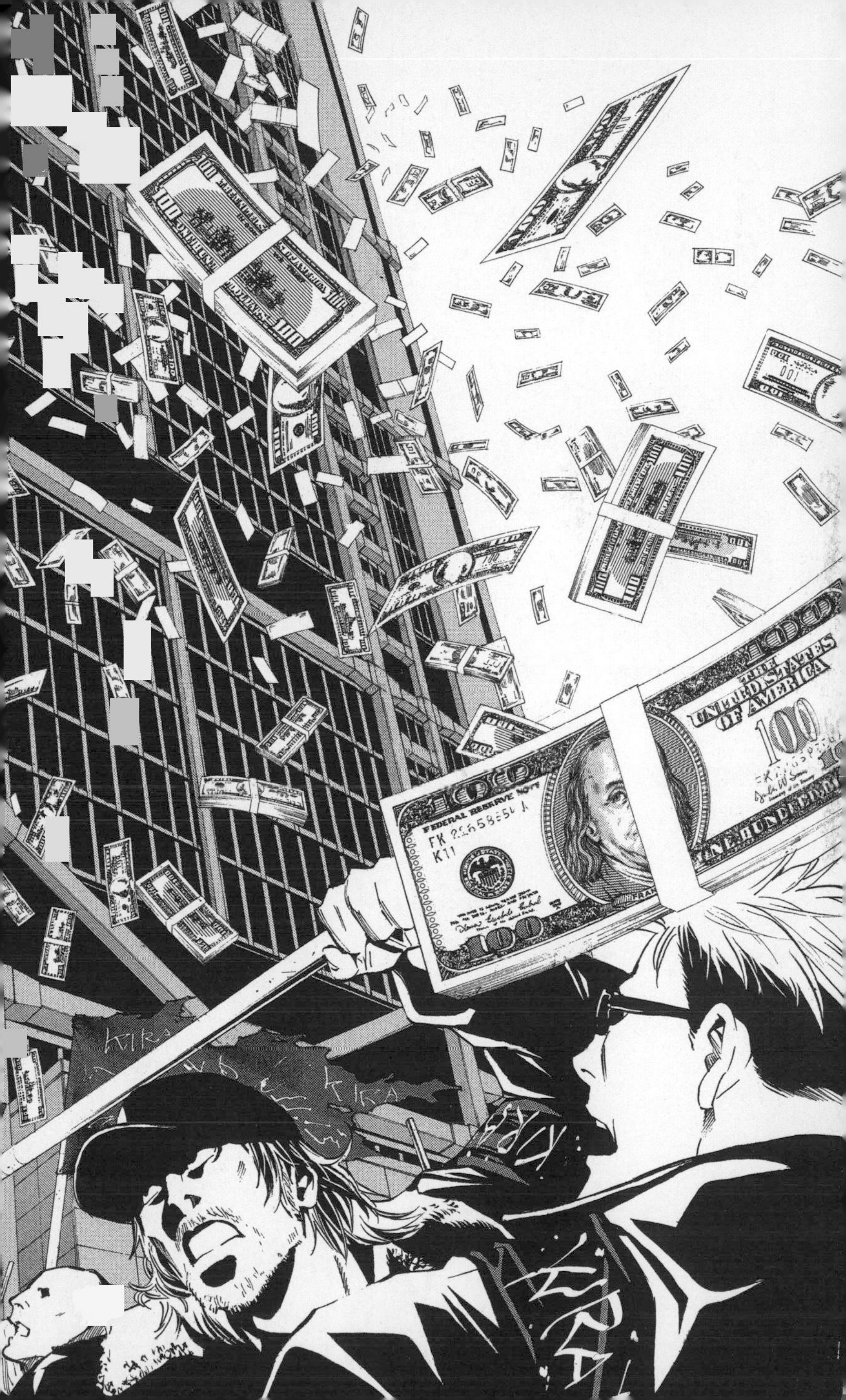

THE UNITED STATES OF AMERICA
FEDERAL RESERVE NOTE
KIRA
KIRA

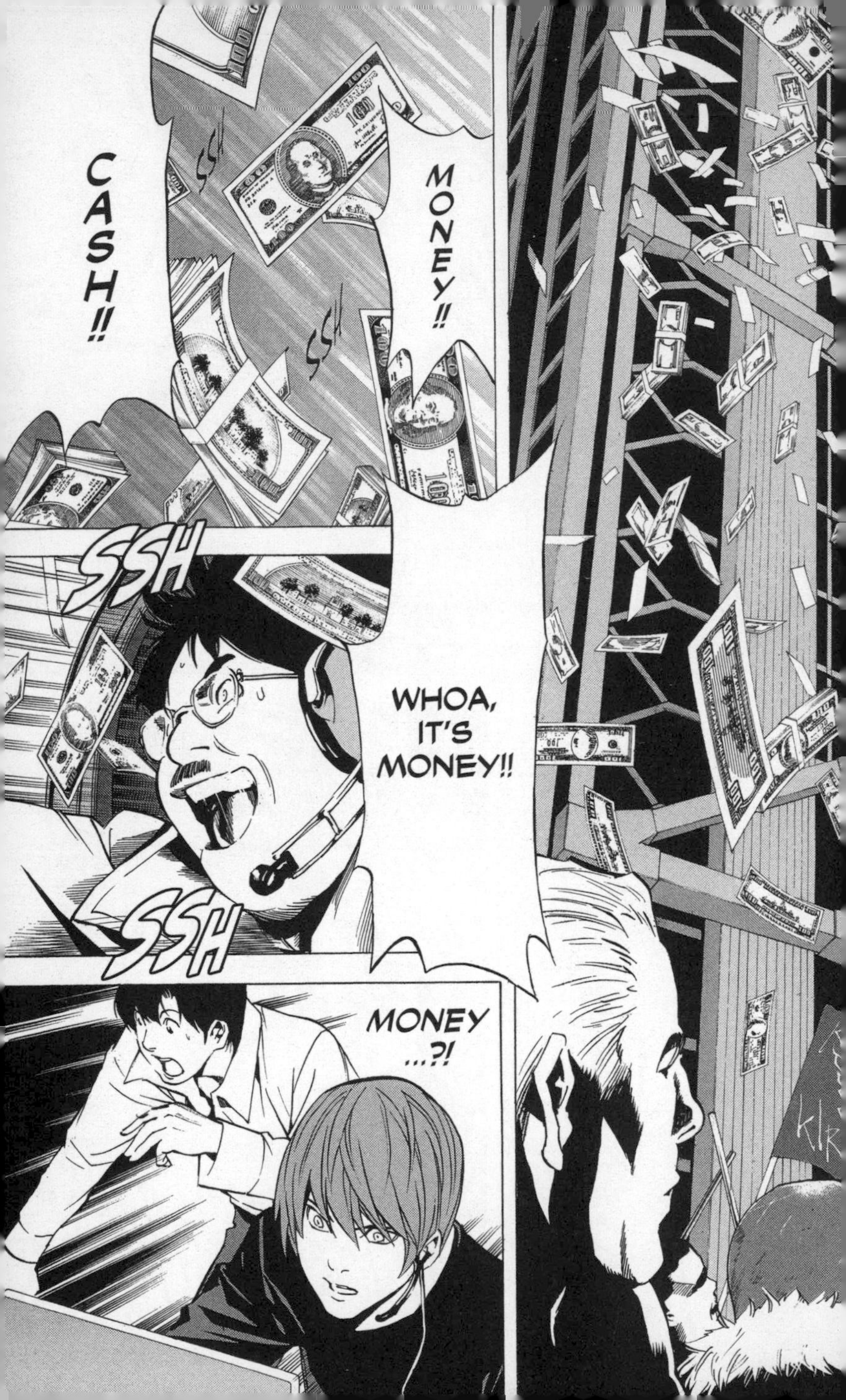
MONEY!!
CASH!!
WHOA, IT'S MONEY!!
SSH
SSH
MONEY ...?!

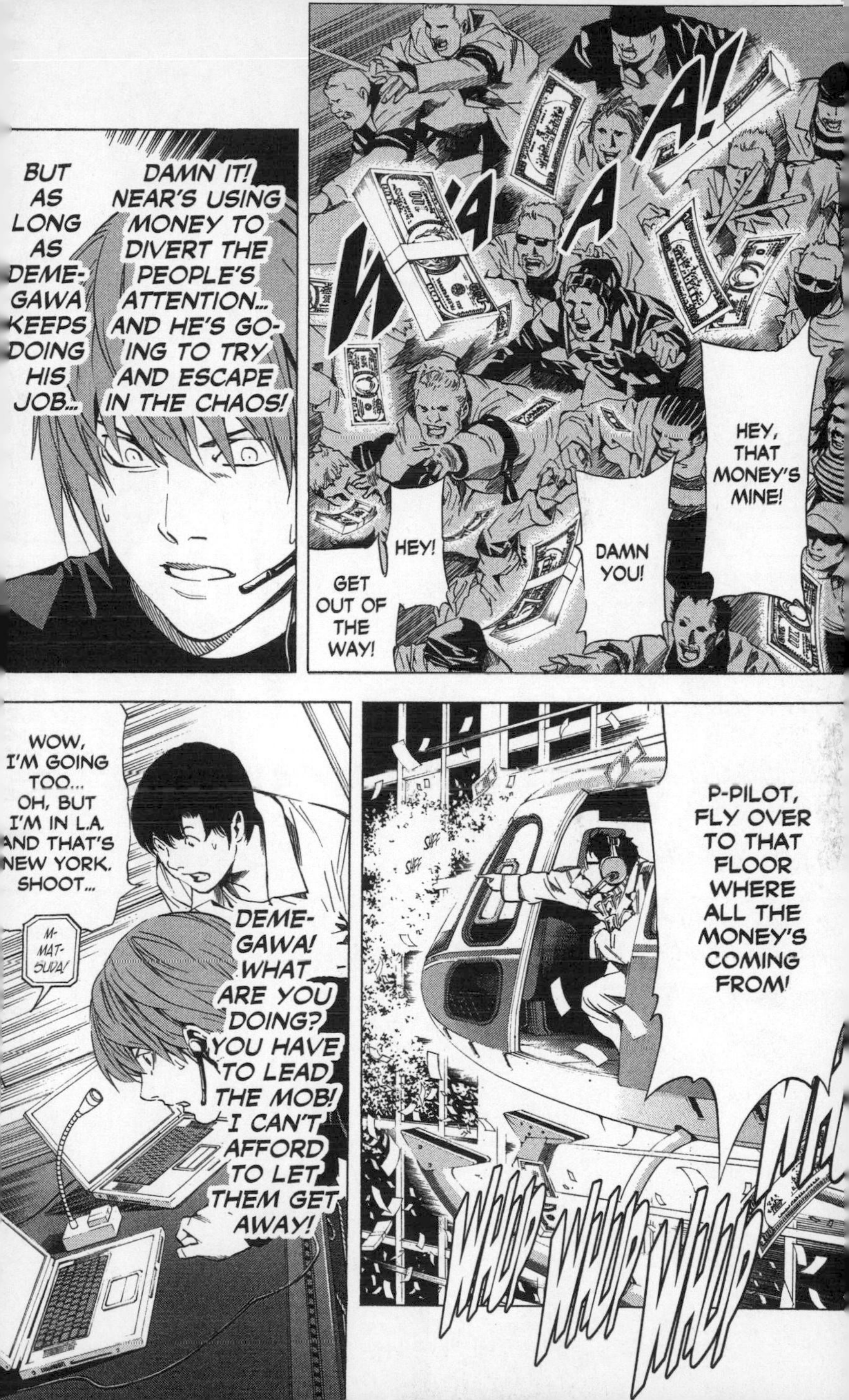
WAAA!
HEY, THAT MONEY'S MINE!
DAMN YOU!
HEY!
GET OUT OF THE WAY!
DAMN IT! NEAR'S USING MONEY TO DIVERT THE PEOPLE'S ATTENTION... AND HE'S GOING TO TRY AND ESCAPE IN THE CHAOS!
BUT AS LONG AS DEMEGAWA KEEPS DOING HIS JOB...
P-PILOT, FLY OVER TO THAT FLOOR WHERE ALL THE MONEY'S COMING FROM!
DEMEGAWA! WHAT ARE YOU DOING? YOU HAVE TO LEAD THE MOB! I CAN'T AFFORD TO LET THEM GET AWAY!
WOW, I'M GOING TOO... OH, BUT I'M IN L.A. AND THAT'S NEW YORK. SHOOT...
M-MATSUDA!

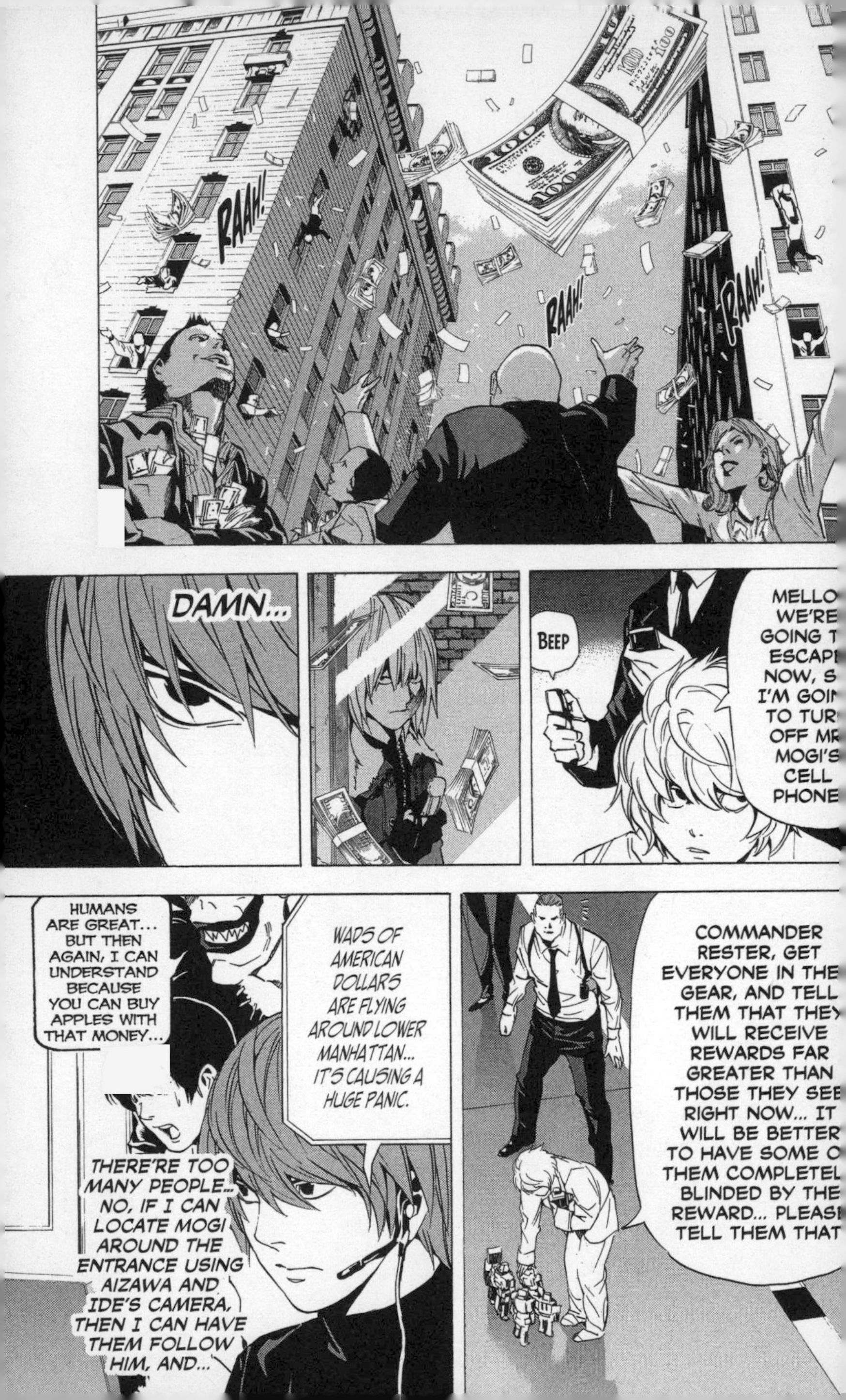
RAAH!
RAAH!
RAAH!
BEEP
MELLO WE'RE GOING T ESCAPE NOW, S I'M GOIN TO TUR OFF MR MOGI'S CELL PHONE
DAMN...
COMMANDER RESTER, GET EVERYONE IN THE GEAR, AND TELL THEM THAT THEY WILL RECEIVE REWARDS FAR GREATER THAN THOSE THEY SEE RIGHT NOW... IT WILL BE BETTER TO HAVE SOME O THEM COMPLETEL BLINDED BY THE REWARD... PLEAS TELL THEM THAT
WADS OF AMERICAN DOLLARS ARE FLYING AROUND LOWER MANHATTAN... IT'S CAUSING A HUGE PANIC.
HUMANS ARE GREAT... BUT THEN AGAIN, I CAN UNDERSTAND BECAUSE YOU CAN BUY APPLES WITH THAT MONEY...
THERE'RE TOO MANY PEOPLE... NO, IF I CAN LOCATE MOGI AROUND THE ENTRANCE USING AIZAWA AND IDE'S CAMERA, THEN I CAN HAVE THEM FOLLOW HIM, AND...

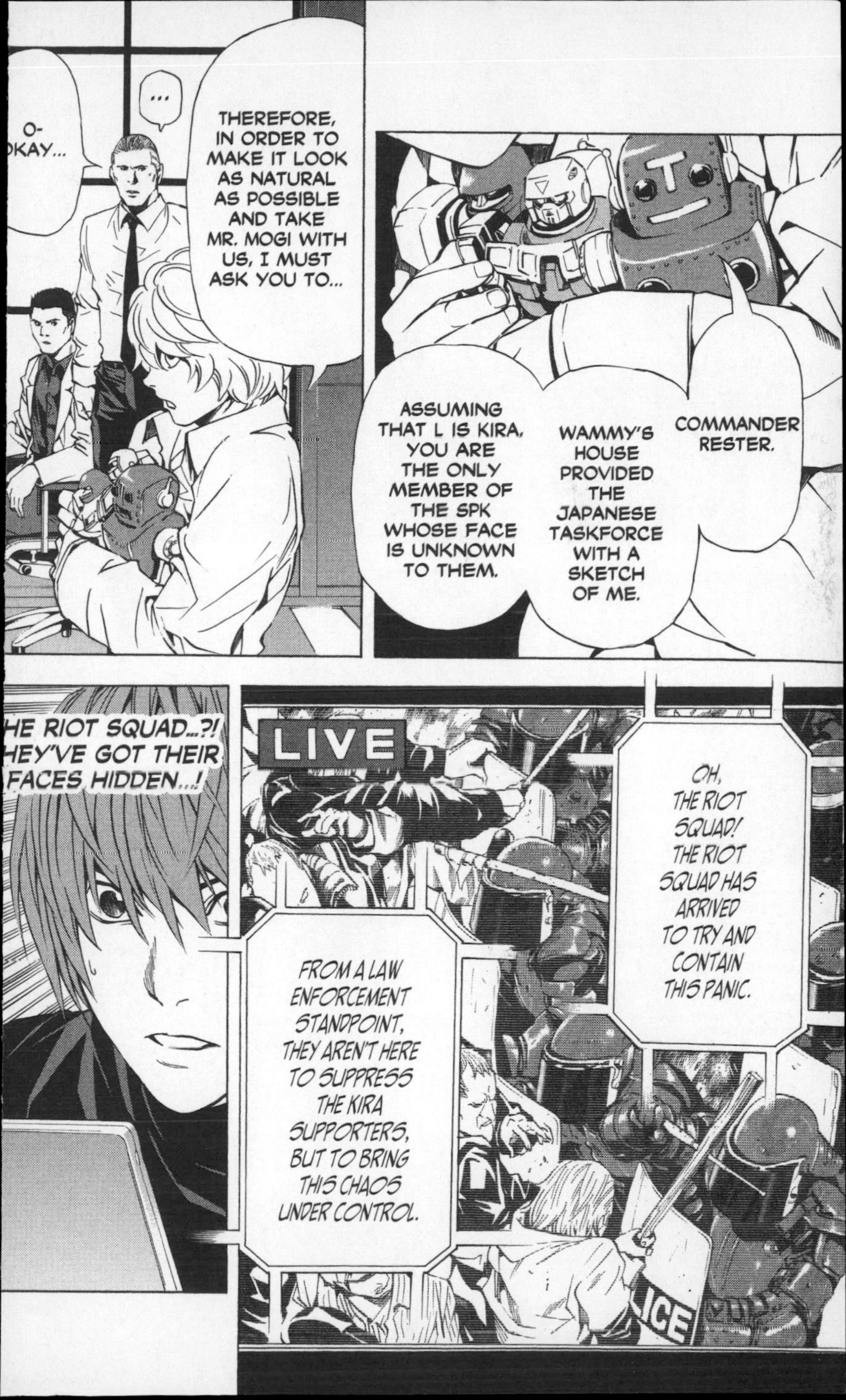
COMMANDER RESTER.
WAMMY'S HOUSE PROVIDED THE JAPANESE TASKFORCE WITH A SKETCH OF ME.
ASSUMING THAT L IS KIRA, YOU ARE THE ONLY MEMBER OF THE SPK WHOSE FACE IS UNKNOWN TO THEM.
THEREFORE, IN ORDER TO MAKE IT LOOK AS NATURAL AS POSSIBLE AND TAKE MR. MOGI WITH US, I MUST ASK YOU TO...
...
O- KAY...
LIVE
OH, THE RIOT SQUAD! THE RIOT SQUAD HAS ARRIVED TO TRY AND CONTAIN THIS PANIC.
FROM A LAW ENFORCEMENT STANDPOINT, THEY AREN'T HERE TO SUPPRESS THE KIRA SUPPORTERS, BUT TO BRING THIS CHAOS UNDER CONTROL.
ICE
HE RIOT SQUAD...?! HEY'VE GOT THEIR FACES HIDDEN...!

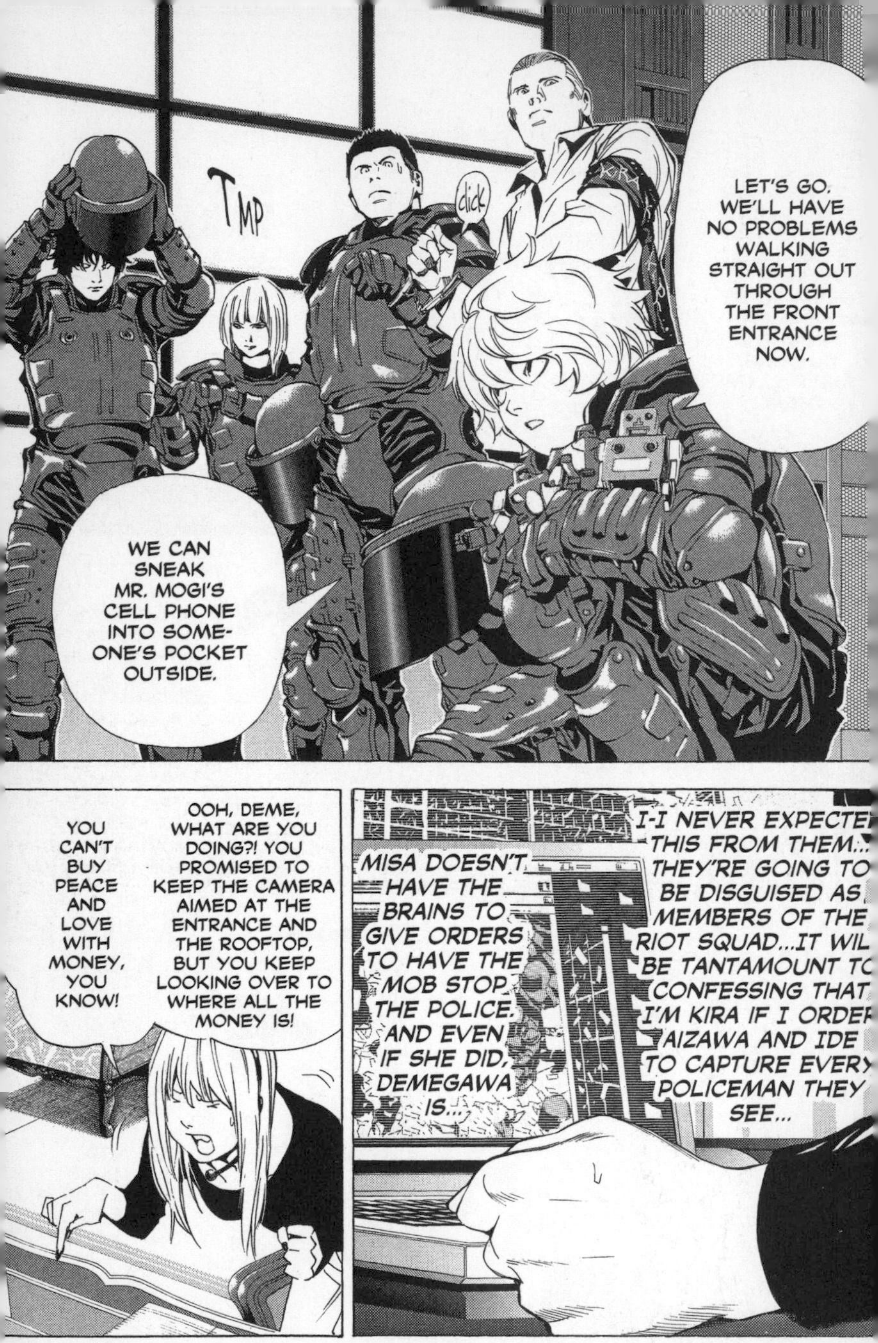
LET'S GO. WE'LL HAVE NO PROBLEMS WALKING STRAIGHT OUT THROUGH THE FRONT ENTRANCE NOW.
click
TMP
WE CAN SNEAK MR. MOGI'S CELL PHONE INTO SOME-ONE'S POCKET OUTSIDE.
I-I NEVER EXPECTE THIS FROM THEM... THEY'RE GOING TO BE DISGUISED AS MEMBERS OF THE RIOT SQUAD...IT WIL BE TANTAMOUNT TC CONFESSING THAT I'M KIRA IF I ORDEF AIZAWA AND IDE TO CAPTURE EVERY POLICEMAN THEY SEE...
MISA DOESN'T HAVE THE BRAINS TO GIVE ORDERS TO HAVE THE MOB STOP THE POLICE. AND EVEN IF SHE DID, DEMEGAWA IS...
OOH, DEME, WHAT ARE YOU DOING?! YOU PROMISED TO KEEP THE CAMERA AIMED AT THE ENTRANCE AND THE ROOFTOP, BUT YOU KEEP LOOKING OVER TO WHERE ALL THE MONEY IS!
YOU CAN'T BUY PEACE AND LOVE WITH MONEY, YOU KNOW!

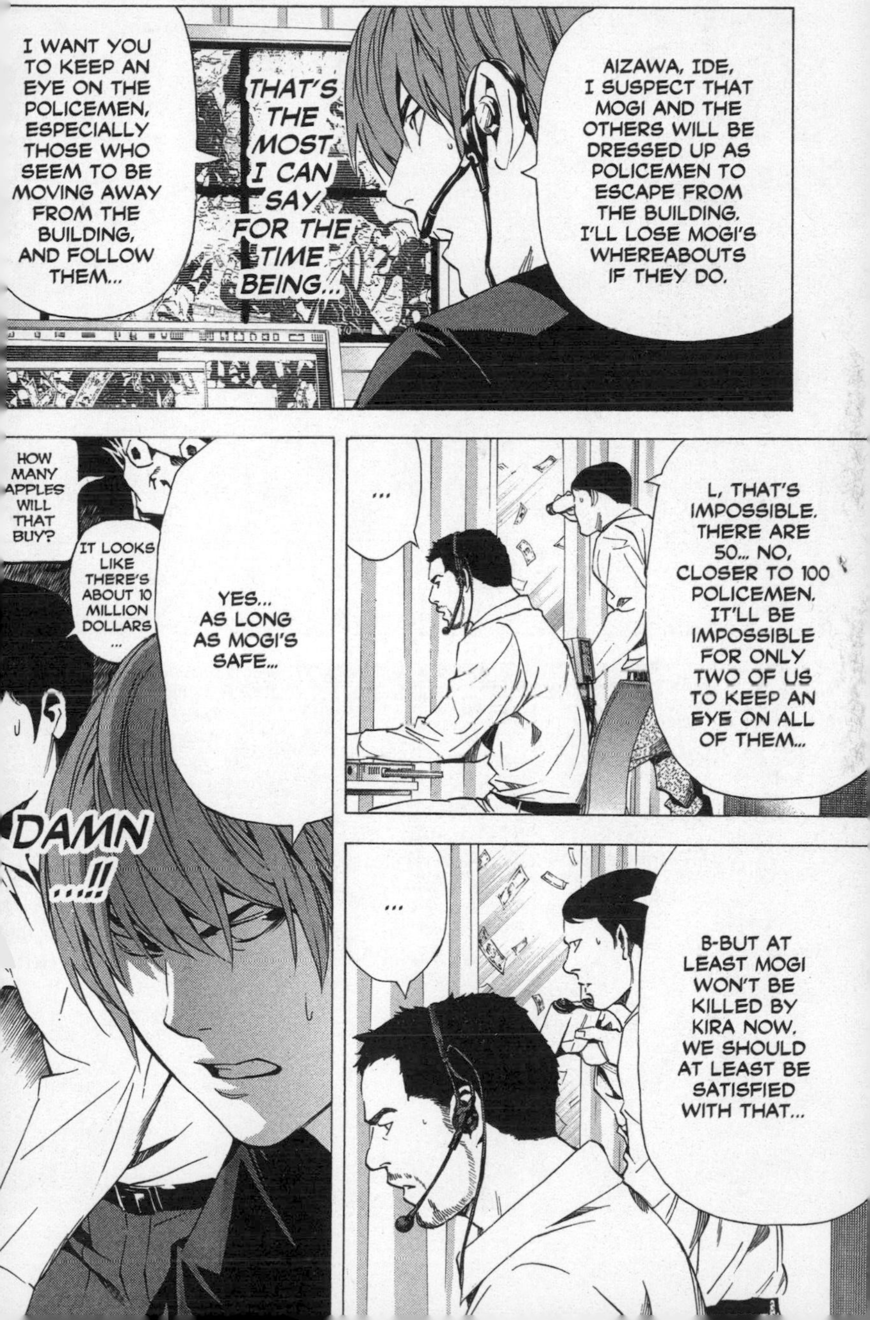
AIZAWA, IDE, I SUSPECT THAT MOGI AND THE OTHERS WILL BE DRESSED UP AS POLICEMEN TO ESCAPE FROM THE BUILDING. I'LL LOSE MOGI'S WHEREABOUTS IF THEY DO.
THAT'S THE MOST I CAN SAY FOR THE TIME BEING...
I WANT YOU TO KEEP AN EYE ON THE POLICEMEN, ESPECIALLY THOSE WHO SEEM TO BE MOVING AWAY FROM THE BUILDING, AND FOLLOW THEM...
L, THAT'S IMPOSSIBLE. THERE ARE 50... NO, CLOSER TO 100 POLICEMEN. IT'LL BE IMPOSSIBLE FOR ONLY TWO OF US TO KEEP AN EYE ON ALL OF THEM...
...
B-BUT AT LEAST MOGI WON'T BE KILLED BY KIRA NOW. WE SHOULD AT LEAST BE SATISFIED WITH THAT...
...
YES... AS LONG AS MOGI'S SAFE...
HOW MANY APPLES WILL THAT BUY?
IT LOOKS LIKE THERE'S ABOUT 10 MILLION DOLLARS...
DAMN ...!!

READ THIS WAY

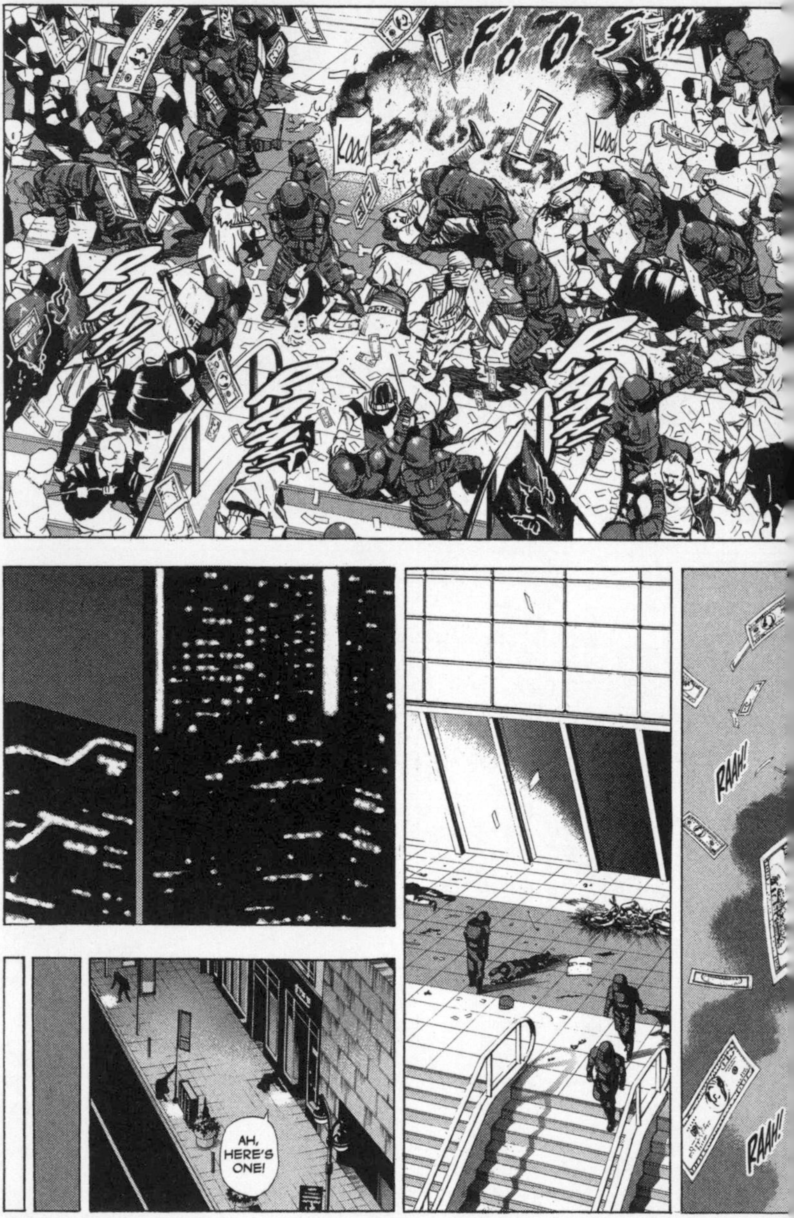
FOOOSH
KOOSH
KOOSH
RAAH!
RAAH!
AH, HERE'S ONE!

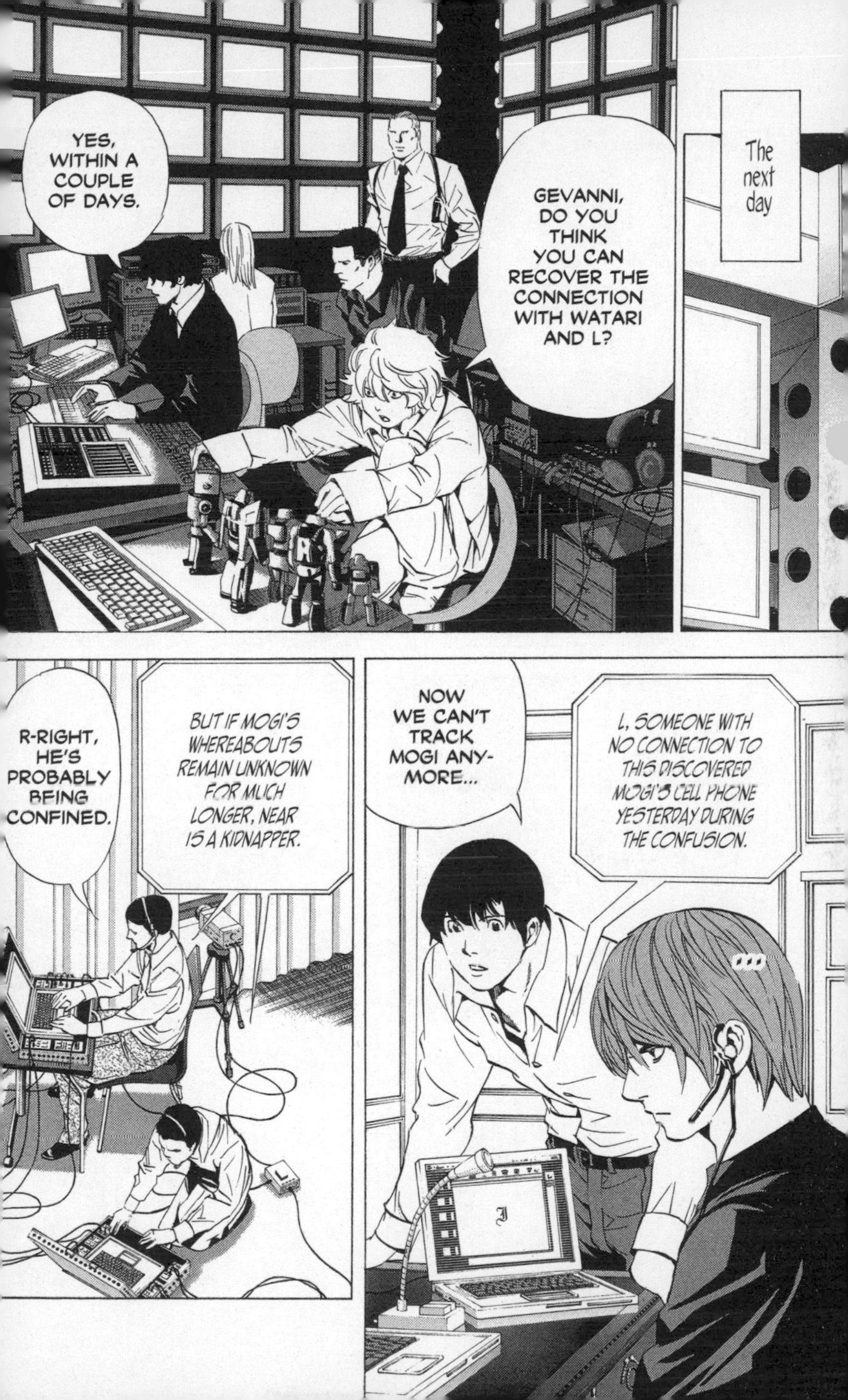
The next day
GEVANNI, DO YOU THINK YOU CAN RECOVER THE CONNECTION WITH WATARI AND L?
YES, WITHIN A COUPLE OF DAYS.
L, SOMEONE WITH NO CONNECTION TO THIS DISCOVERED MOGI'S CELL PHONE YESTERDAY DURING THE CONFUSION.
NOW WE CAN'T TRACK MOGI ANY-MORE...
...
BUT IF MOGI'S WHEREABOUTS REMAIN UNKNOWN FOR MUCH LONGER, NEAR IS A KIDNAPPER.
R-RIGHT, HE'S PROBABLY BEING CONFINED.

READ THIS WAY

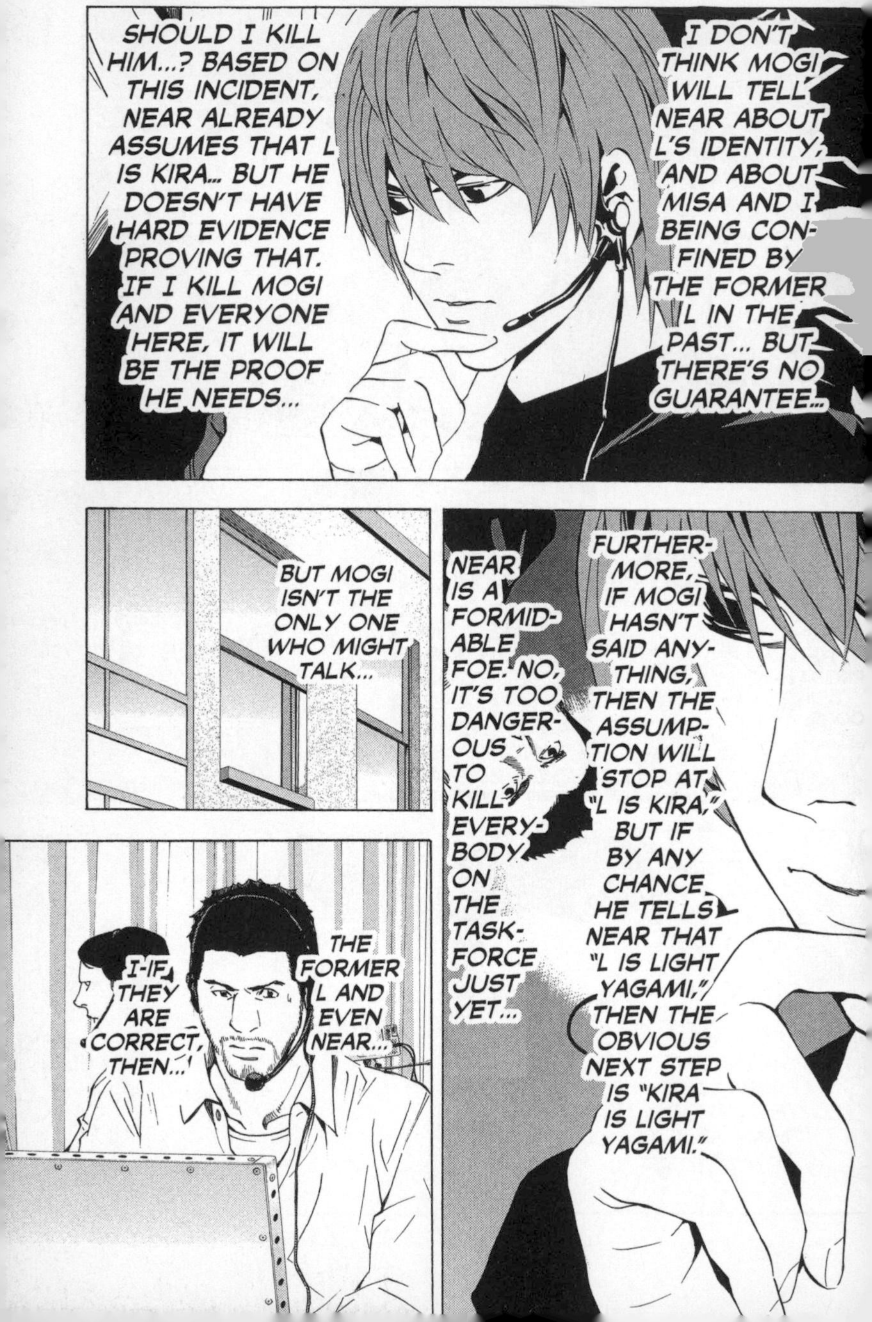
I DON'T THINK MOGI WILL TELL NEAR ABOUT L'S IDENTITY, AND ABOUT MISA AND I BEING CONFINED BY THE FORMER L IN THE PAST... BUT THERE'S NO GUARANTEE...
SHOULD I KILL HIM...? BASED ON THIS INCIDENT, NEAR ALREADY ASSUMES THAT L IS KIRA... BUT HE DOESN'T HAVE HARD EVIDENCE PROVING THAT. IF I KILL MOGI AND EVERYONE HERE, IT WILL BE THE PROOF HE NEEDS...
FURTHERMORE, IF MOGI HASN'T SAID ANYTHING, THEN THE ASSUMPTION WILL STOP AT "L IS KIRA," BUT IF BY ANY CHANCE HE TELLS NEAR THAT "L IS LIGHT YAGAMI," THEN THE OBVIOUS NEXT STEP IS "KIRA IS LIGHT YAGAMI."
NEAR IS A FORMIDABLE FOE. NO, IT'S TOO DANGEROUS TO KILL EVERYBODY ON THE TASKFORCE JUST YET...
BUT MOGI ISN'T THE ONLY ONE WHO MIGHT TALK...
THE FORMER L AND EVEN NEAR...
I-IF THEY ARE CORRECT, THEN...

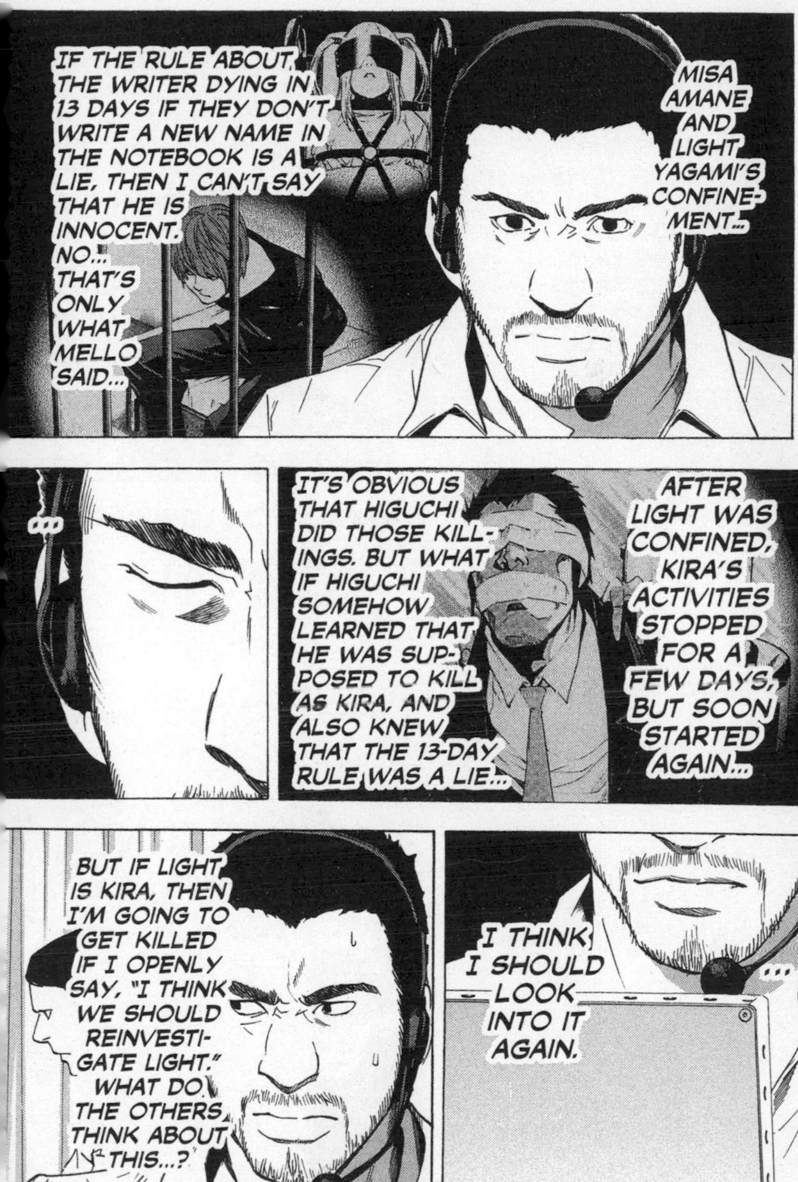
MISA AMANE AND LIGHT YAGAMI'S CONFINEMENT...
IF THE RULE ABOUT THE WRITER DYING IN 13 DAYS IF THEY DON'T WRITE A NEW NAME IN THE NOTEBOOK IS A LIE, THEN I CAN'T SAY THAT HE IS INNOCENT.
NO... THAT'S ONLY WHAT MELLO SAID...
AFTER LIGHT WAS CONFINED, KIRA'S ACTIVITIES STOPPED FOR A FEW DAYS, BUT SOON STARTED AGAIN...
IT'S OBVIOUS THAT HIGUCHI DID THOSE KILLINGS. BUT WHAT IF HIGUCHI SOMEHOW LEARNED THAT HE WAS SUPPOSED TO KILL AS KIRA, AND ALSO KNEW THAT THE 13-DAY RULE WAS A LIE...
...
...
I THINK I SHOULD LOOK INTO IT AGAIN.
BUT IF LIGHT IS KIRA, THEN I'M GOING TO GET KILLED IF I OPENLY SAY, "I THINK WE SHOULD REINVESTIGATE LIGHT." WHAT DO THE OTHERS THINK ABOUT THIS...?

READ THIS WAY

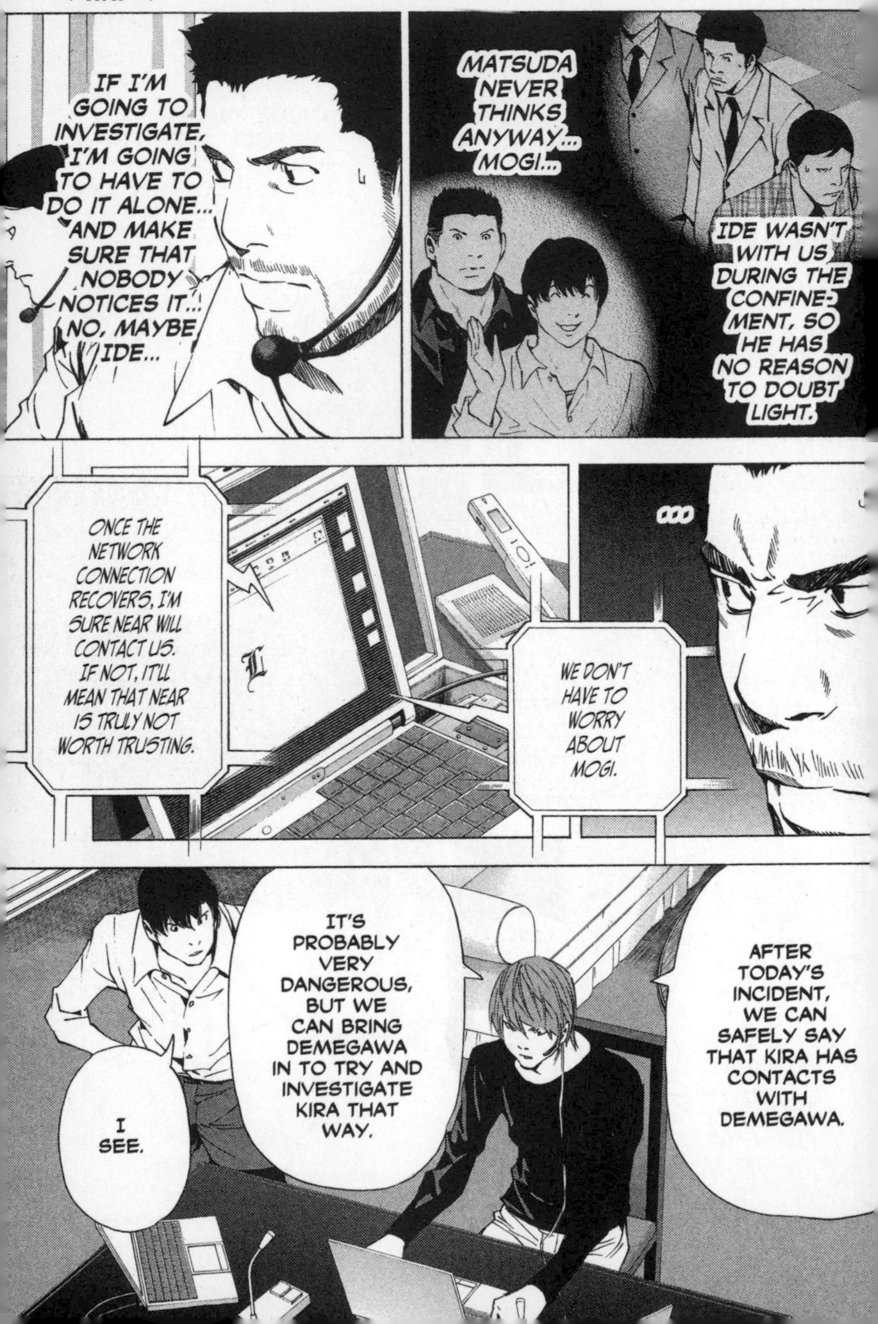
MATSUDA NEVER THINKS ANYWAY... MOGI...
IDE WASN'T WITH US DURING THE CONFINE-MENT, SO HE HAS NO REASON TO DOUBT LIGHT.
IF I'M GOING TO INVESTIGATE, I'M GOING TO HAVE TO DO IT ALONE... AND MAKE SURE THAT NOBODY NOTICES IT... NO, MAYBE IDE...
...
WE DON'T HAVE TO WORRY ABOUT MOGI.
ONCE THE NETWORK CONNECTION RECOVERS, I'M SURE NEAR WILL CONTACT US. IF NOT, IT'LL MEAN THAT NEAR IS TRULY NOT WORTH TRUSTING.
AFTER TODAY'S INCIDENT, WE CAN SAFELY SAY THAT KIRA HAS CONTACTS WITH DEMEGAWA.
IT'S PROBABLY VERY DANGEROUS, BUT WE CAN BRING DEMEGAWA IN TO TRY AND INVESTIGATE KIRA THAT WAY.
I SEE.

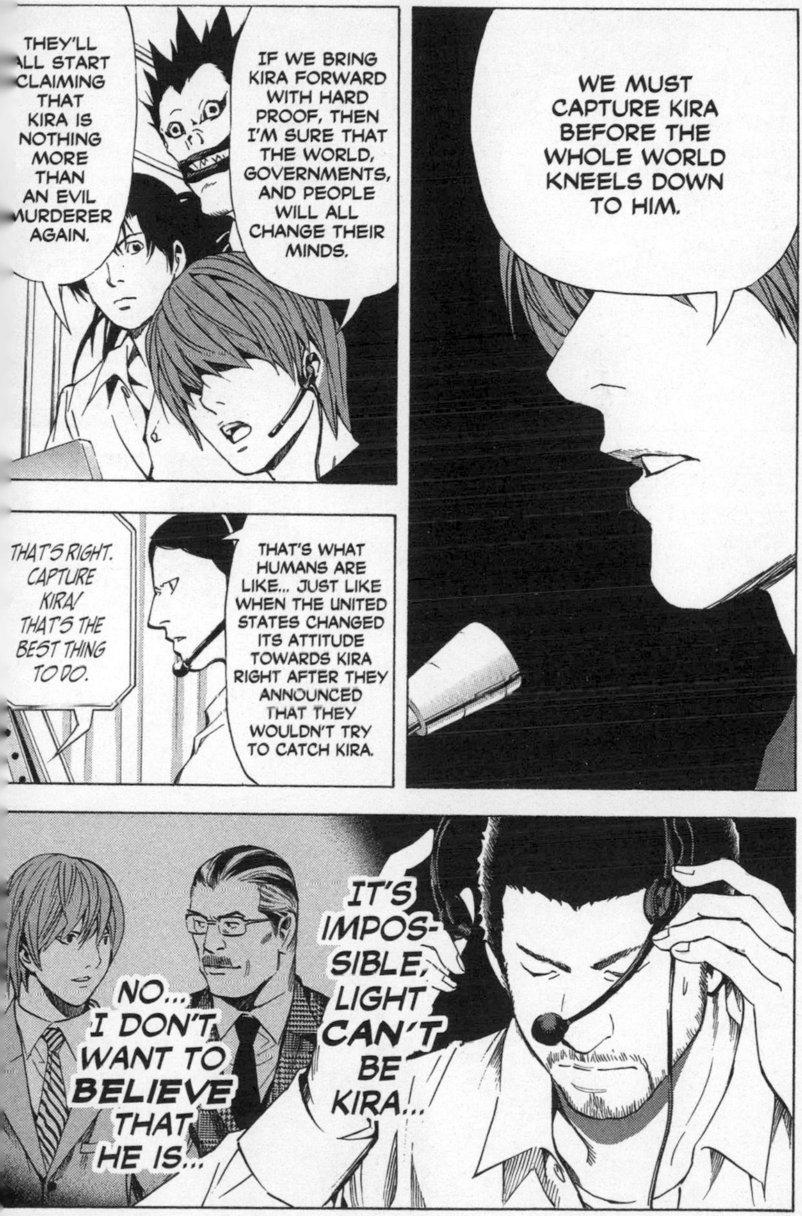
WE MUST CAPTURE KIRA BEFORE THE WHOLE WORLD KNEELS DOWN TO HIM.
IF WE BRING KIRA FORWARD WITH HARD PROOF, THEN I'M SURE THAT THE WORLD, GOVERNMENTS, AND PEOPLE WILL ALL CHANGE THEIR MINDS.
THEY'LL ALL START CLAIMING THAT KIRA IS NOTHING MORE THAN AN EVIL MURDERER AGAIN.
THAT'S WHAT HUMANS ARE LIKE... JUST LIKE WHEN THE UNITED STATES CHANGED ITS ATTITUDE TOWARDS KIRA RIGHT AFTER THEY ANNOUNCED THAT THEY WOULDN'T TRY TO CATCH KIRA.
THAT'S RIGHT. CAPTURE KIRA! THAT'S THE BEST THING TO DO.
IT'S IMPOSSIBLE, LIGHT CAN'T BE KIRA...
NO... I DON'T WANT TO BELIEVE THAT HE IS...

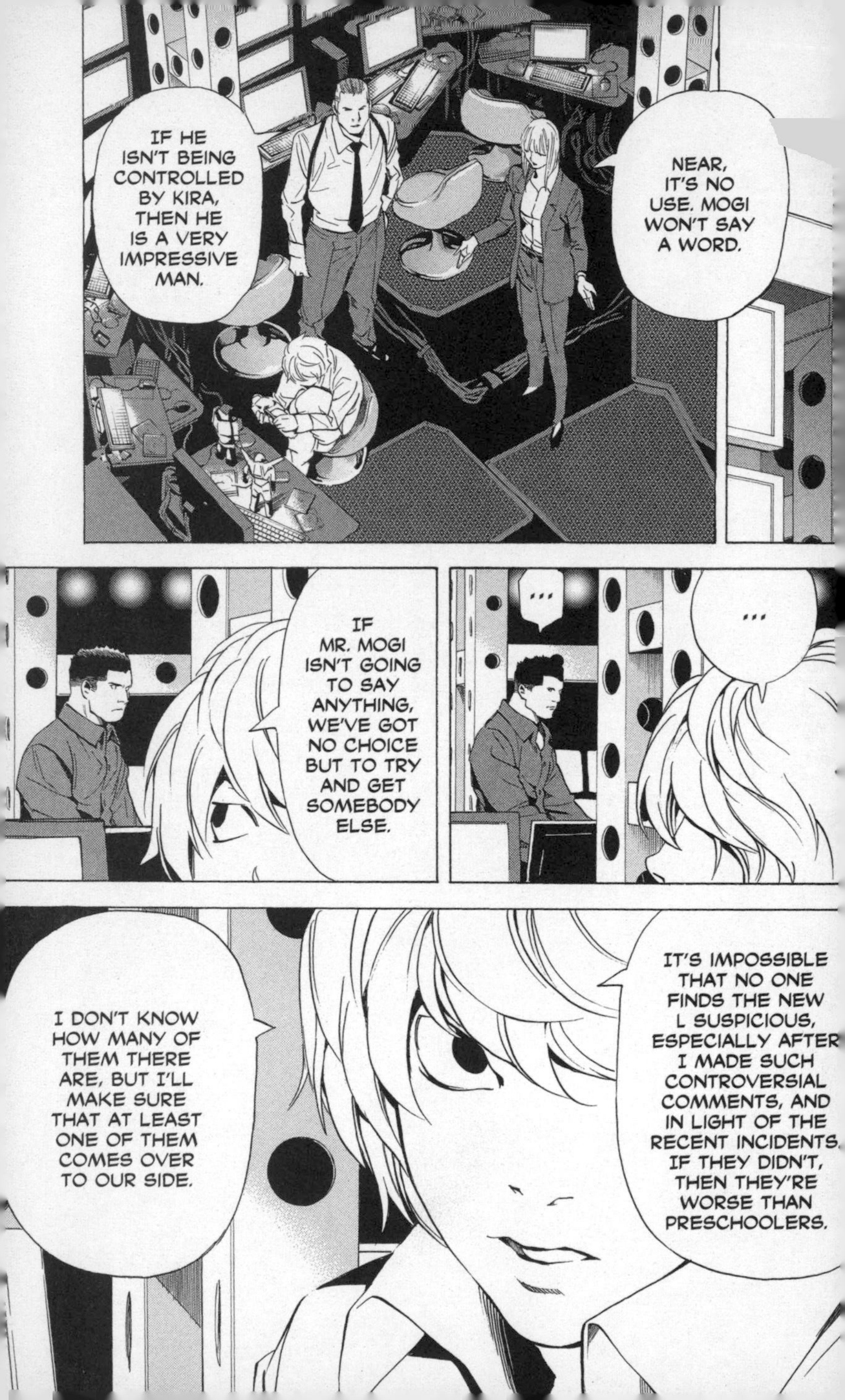
NEAR, IT'S NO USE. MOGI WON'T SAY A WORD.
IF HE ISN'T BEING CONTROLLED BY KIRA, THEN HE IS A VERY IMPRESSIVE MAN.
...
...
IF MR. MOGI ISN'T GOING TO SAY ANYTHING, WE'VE GOT NO CHOICE BUT TO TRY AND GET SOMEBODY ELSE.
IT'S IMPOSSIBLE THAT NO ONE FINDS THE NEW L SUSPICIOUS, ESPECIALLY AFTER I MADE SUCH CONTROVERSIAL COMMENTS, AND IN LIGHT OF THE RECENT INCIDENTS. IF THEY DIDN'T, THEN THEY'RE WORSE THAN PRESCHOOLERS.
I DON'T KNOW HOW MANY OF THEM THERE ARE, BUT I'LL MAKE SURE THAT AT LEAST ONE OF THEM COMES OVER TO OUR SIDE.

DEATH NOTE
HOW TO USE IT
LIII

° The DEATH NOTE will not take effect if you write a specific victim's name using several different pages.

デスノートの効力を得るには、
一人の名前を複数のページにまたがって記してはならない。

° But the front and back of a page is considered as one page. For example, the DEATH NOTE will still take effect even if you write the victim's surname on the front page and given name on the back.

ただし、そのページの表と裏は1ページとみなされ、
たとえば、表に苗字、裏に名前という書き方であれば、有効である。

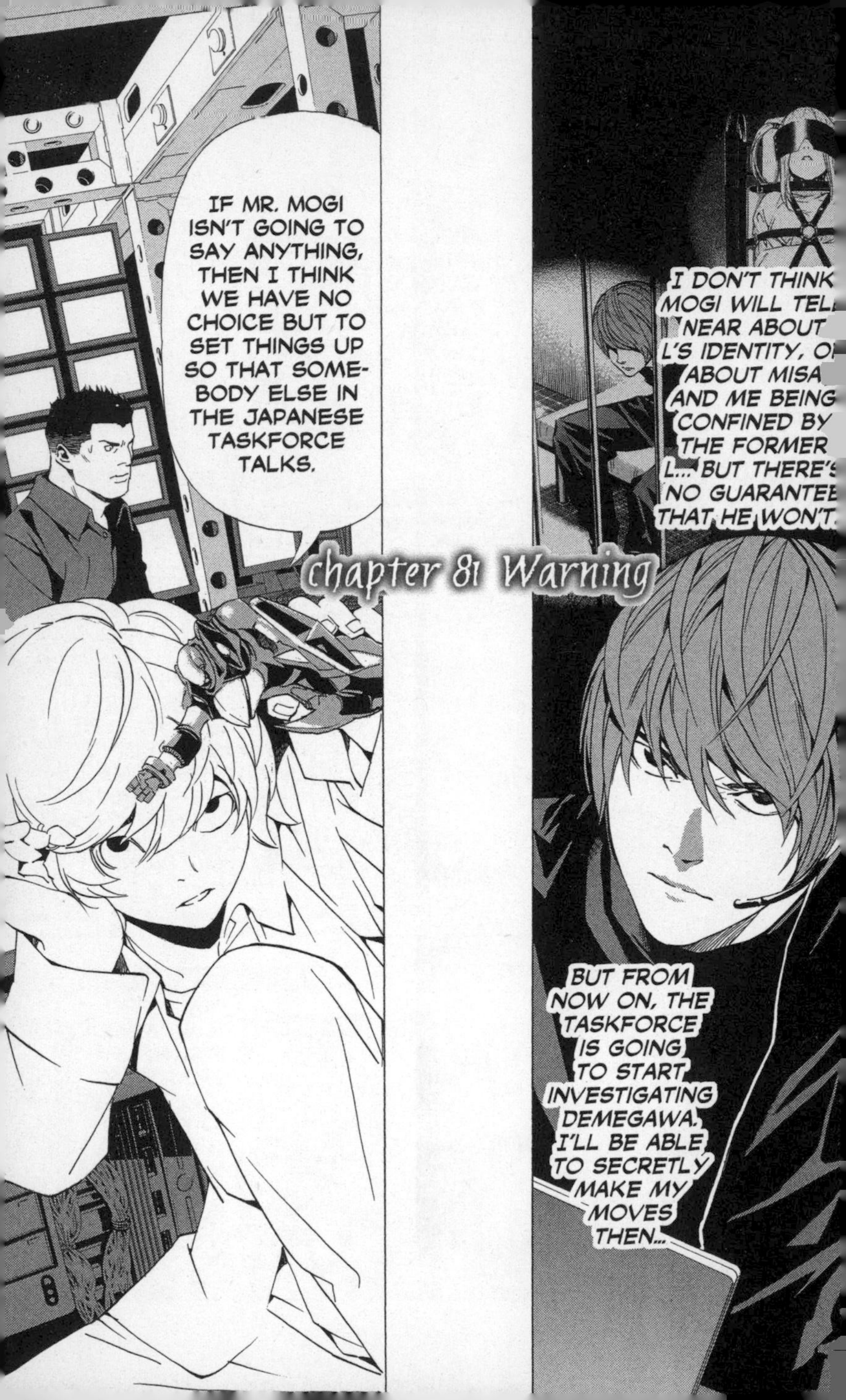
chapter 81 Warning
I DON'T THINK MOGI WILL TELL NEAR ABOUT L'S IDENTITY, OR ABOUT MISA AND ME BEING CONFINED BY THE FORMER L... BUT THERE'S NO GUARANTEE THAT HE WON'T.
BUT FROM NOW ON, THE TASKFORCE IS GOING TO START INVESTIGATING DEMEGAWA. I'LL BE ABLE TO SECRETLY MAKE MY MOVES THEN...
IF MR. MOGI ISN'T GOING TO SAY ANYTHING, THEN I THINK WE HAVE NO CHOICE BUT TO SET THINGS UP SO THAT SOMEBODY ELSE IN THE JAPANESE TASKFORCE TALKS.

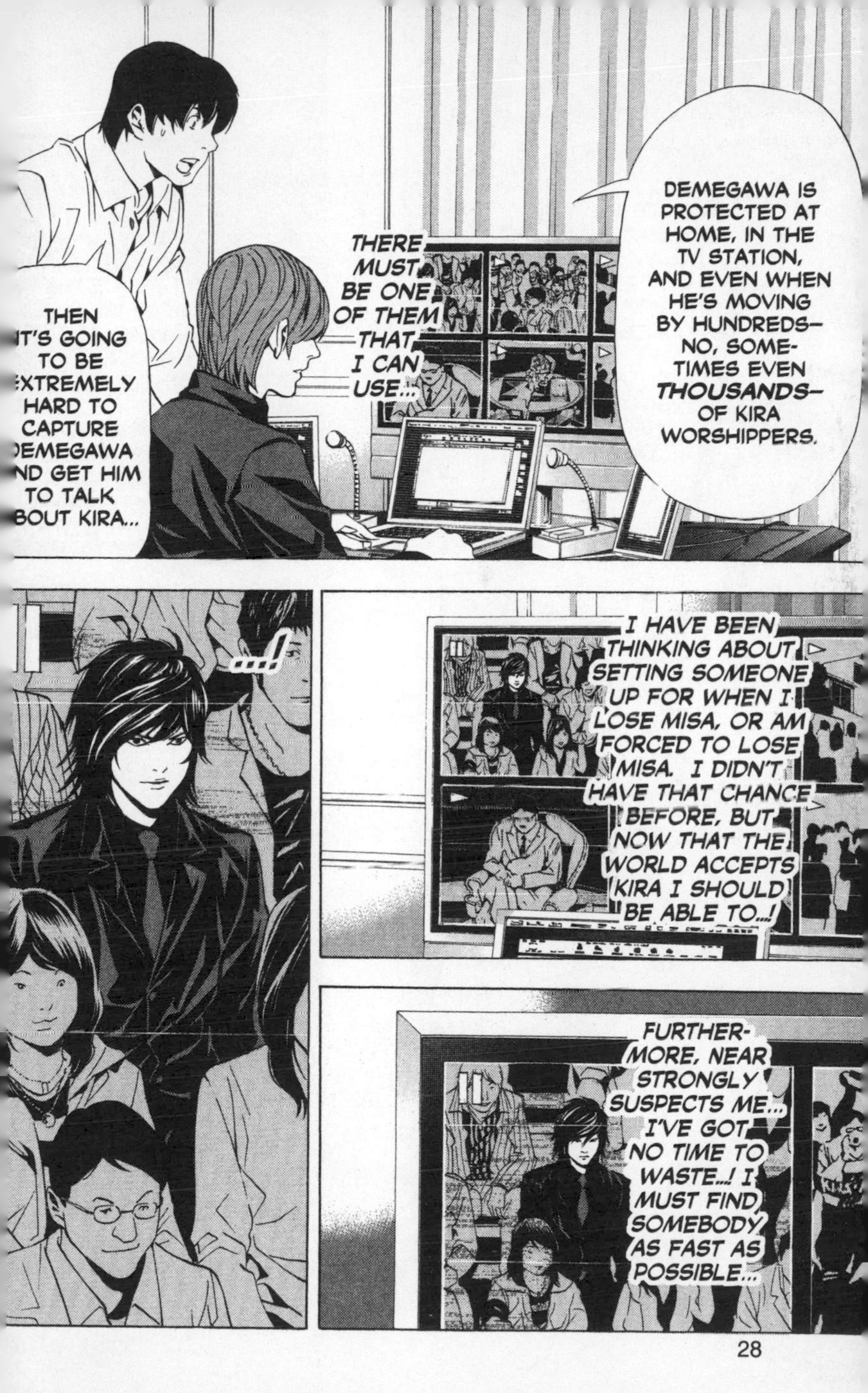
DEMEGAWA IS PROTECTED AT HOME, IN THE TV STATION, AND EVEN WHEN HE'S MOVING BY HUNDREDS— NO, SOMETIMES EVEN *THOUSANDS*— OF KIRA WORSHIPPERS.
THERE MUST BE ONE OF THEM THAT I CAN USE...
THEN IT'S GOING TO BE EXTREMELY HARD TO CAPTURE DEMEGAWA AND GET HIM TO TALK ABOUT KIRA...
I HAVE BEEN THINKING ABOUT SETTING SOMEONE UP FOR WHEN I LOSE MISA, OR AM FORCED TO LOSE MISA. I DIDN'T HAVE THAT CHANCE BEFORE, BUT NOW THAT THE WORLD ACCEPTS KIRA I SHOULD BE ABLE TO...!
FURTHERMORE, NEAR STRONGLY SUSPECTS ME... I'VE GOT NO TIME TO WASTE...! I MUST FIND SOMEBODY AS FAST AS POSSIBLE...
...!

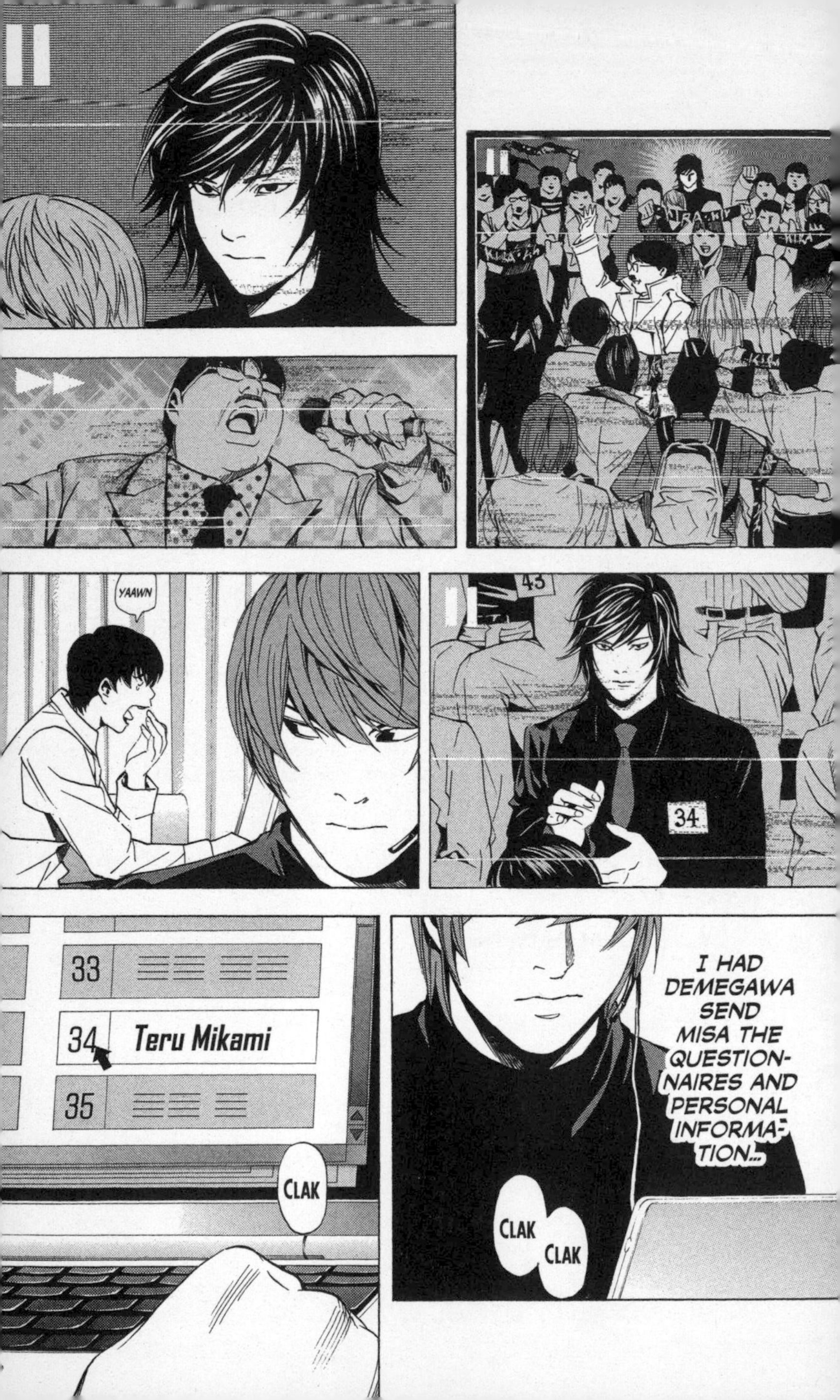
43
34
YAAWN
I HAD DEMEGAWA SEND MISA THE QUESTION-NAIRES AND PERSONAL INFORMA-TION...
CLAK
CLAK
33
34 Teru Mikami
35
CLAK

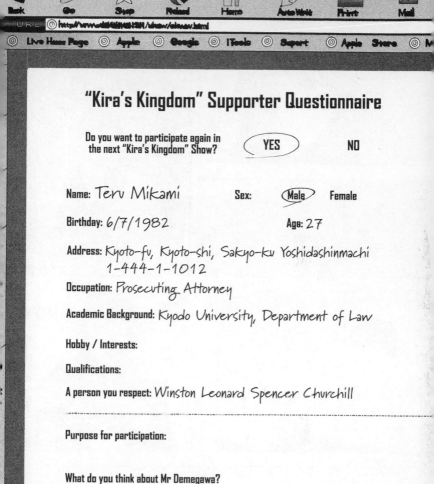

"Kira's Kingdom" Supporter Questionnaire

Do you want to participate again in the next "Kira's Kingdom" Show?   (YES)   NO

Name: Teru Mikami   Sex: (Male) Female

Birthday: 6/7/1982   Age: 27

Address: Kyoto-fu, Kyoto-shi, Sakyo-ku Yoshidashinmachi 1-444-1-1012

Occupation: Prosecuting Attorney

Academic Background: Kyodo University, Department of Law

Hobby / Interests:

Qualifications:

A person you respect: Winston Leonard Spencer Churchill

Purpose for participation:

What do you think about Mr Demegawa?

What do you think about Kira? God

Please tell us your ideas about the Kira Society in the future.

Comments and requests to the show:

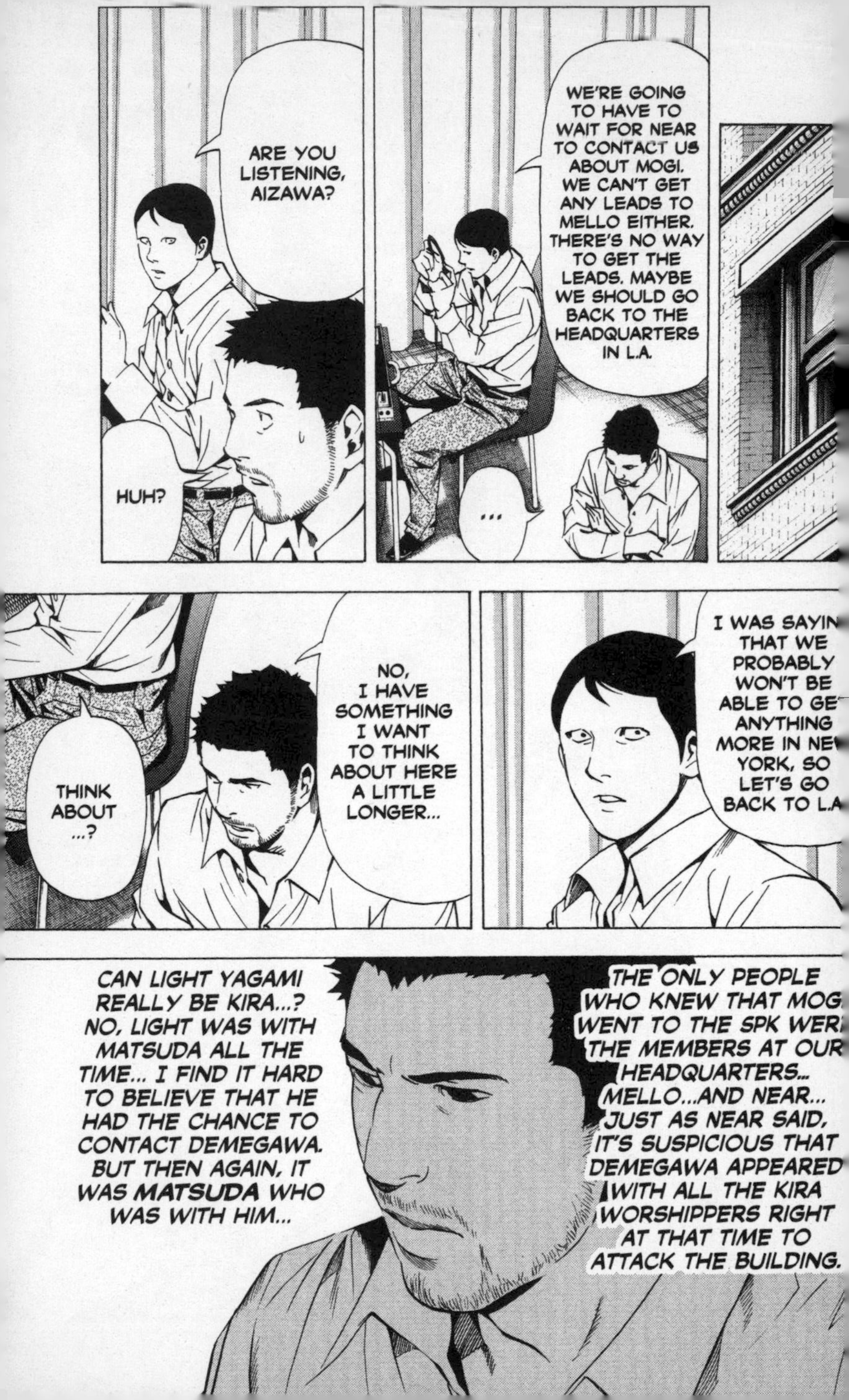
WE'RE GOING TO HAVE TO WAIT FOR NEAR TO CONTACT US ABOUT MOGI. WE CAN'T GET ANY LEADS TO MELLO EITHER. THERE'S NO WAY TO GET THE LEADS. MAYBE WE SHOULD GO BACK TO THE HEADQUARTERS IN L.A.
...
ARE YOU LISTENING, AIZAWA?
HUH?
I WAS SAYIN THAT WE PROBABLY WON'T BE ABLE TO GE ANYTHING MORE IN NE YORK, SO LET'S GO BACK TO L.A
NO, I HAVE SOMETHING I WANT TO THINK ABOUT HERE A LITTLE LONGER...
THINK ABOUT ...?
THE ONLY PEOPLE WHO KNEW THAT MOG WENT TO THE SPK WER THE MEMBERS AT OUR HEADQUARTERS... MELLO...AND NEAR... JUST AS NEAR SAID, IT'S SUSPICIOUS THAT DEMEGAWA APPEARED WITH ALL THE KIRA WORSHIPPERS RIGHT AT THAT TIME TO ATTACK THE BUILDING.
CAN LIGHT YAGAMI REALLY BE KIRA...? NO, LIGHT WAS WITH MATSUDA ALL THE TIME... I FIND IT HARD TO BELIEVE THAT HE HAD THE CHANCE TO CONTACT DEMEGAWA. BUT THEN AGAIN, IT WAS MATSUDA WHO WAS WITH HIM...

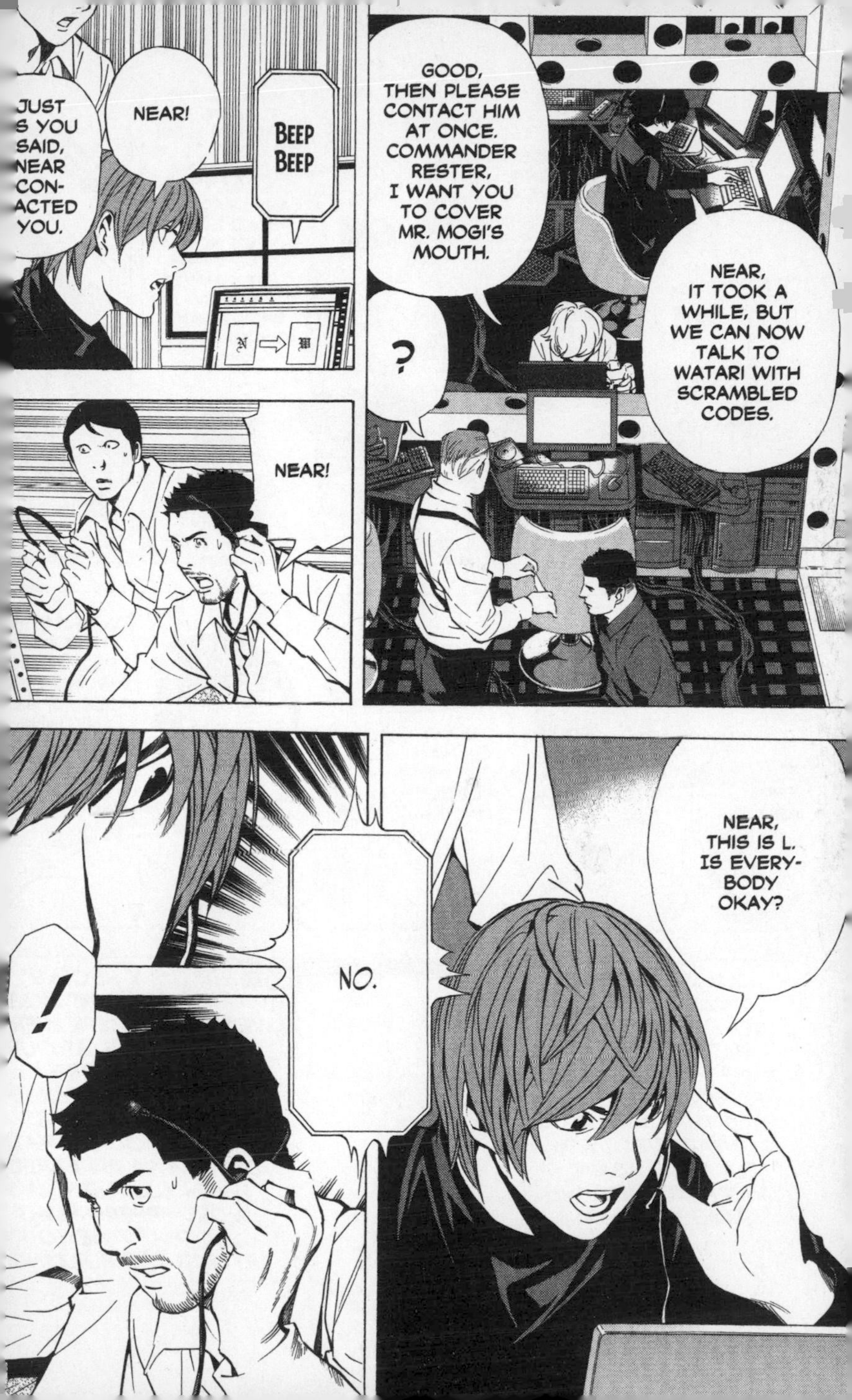

NEAR, IT TOOK A WHILE, BUT WE CAN NOW TALK TO WATARI WITH SCRAMBLED CODES.
GOOD, THEN PLEASE CONTACT HIM AT ONCE. COMMANDER RESTER, I WANT YOU TO COVER MR. MOGI'S MOUTH.
?
BEEP BEEP
NEAR!
JUST S YOU SAID, NEAR CON- ACTED YOU.
NEAR!
NEAR, THIS IS L. IS EVERY- BODY OKAY?
NO.
!

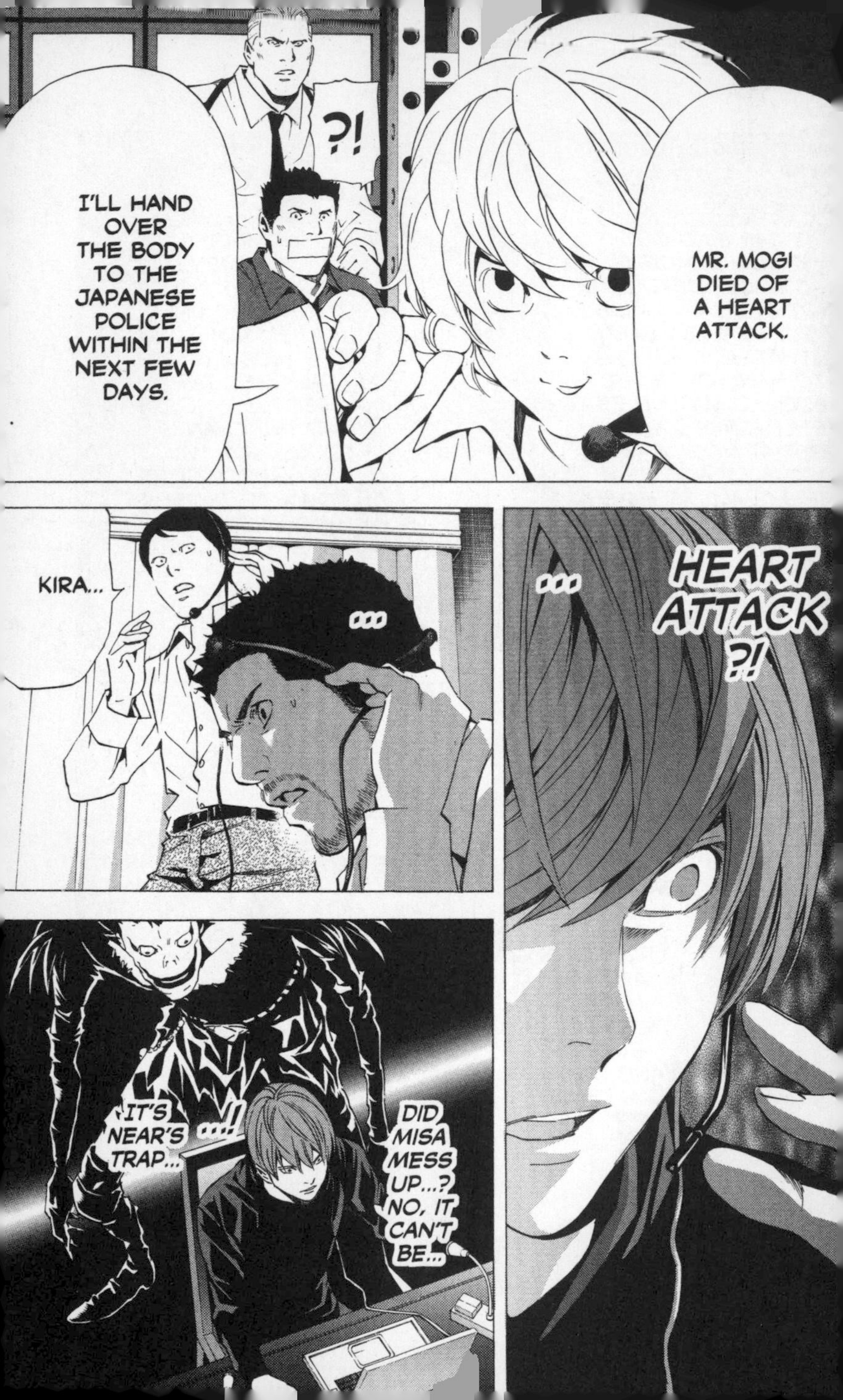
MR. MOGI DIED OF A HEART ATTACK.
?!
I'LL HAND OVER THE BODY TO THE JAPANESE POLICE WITHIN THE NEXT FEW DAYS.
HEART ATTACK ?!
...
...
KIRA...
DID MISA MESS UP...? NO, IT CAN'T BE...
...!!
IT'S NEAR'S TRAP...

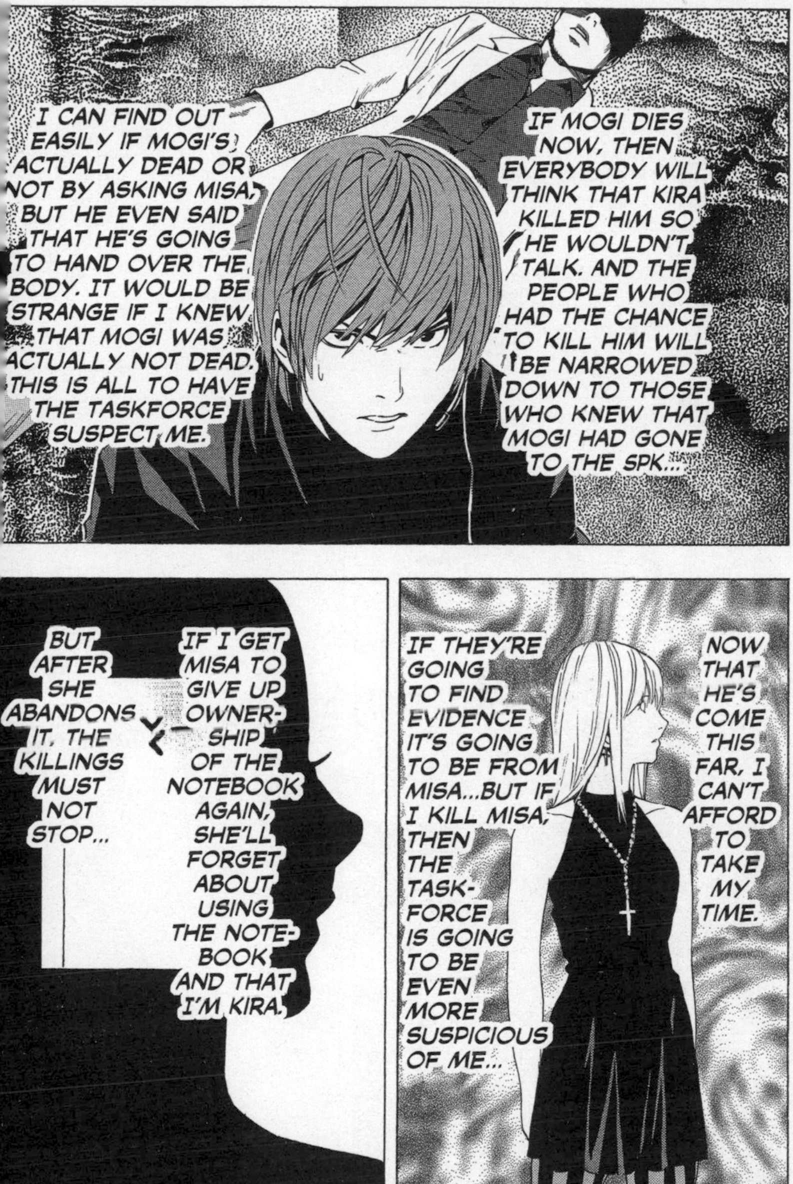
IF MOGI DIES NOW, THEN EVERYBODY WILL THINK THAT KIRA KILLED HIM SO HE WOULDN'T TALK. AND THE PEOPLE WHO HAD THE CHANCE TO KILL HIM WILL BE NARROWED DOWN TO THOSE WHO KNEW THAT MOGI HAD GONE TO THE SPK...
I CAN FIND OUT EASILY IF MOGI'S ACTUALLY DEAD OR NOT BY ASKING MISA, BUT HE EVEN SAID THAT HE'S GOING TO HAND OVER THE BODY. IT WOULD BE STRANGE IF I KNEW THAT MOGI WAS ACTUALLY NOT DEAD. THIS IS ALL TO HAVE THE TASKFORCE SUSPECT ME.
NOW THAT HE'S COME THIS FAR, I CAN'T AFFORD TO TAKE MY TIME.
IF THEY'RE GOING TO FIND EVIDENCE IT'S GOING TO BE FROM MISA...BUT IF I KILL MISA, THEN THE TASK-FORCE IS GOING TO BE EVEN MORE SUSPICIOUS OF ME...
IF I GET MISA TO GIVE UP OWNER-SHIP OF THE NOTEBOOK AGAIN, SHE'LL FORGET ABOUT USING THE NOTE-BOOK AND THAT I'M KIRA.
BUT AFTER SHE ABANDONS IT, THE KILLINGS MUST NOT STOP...

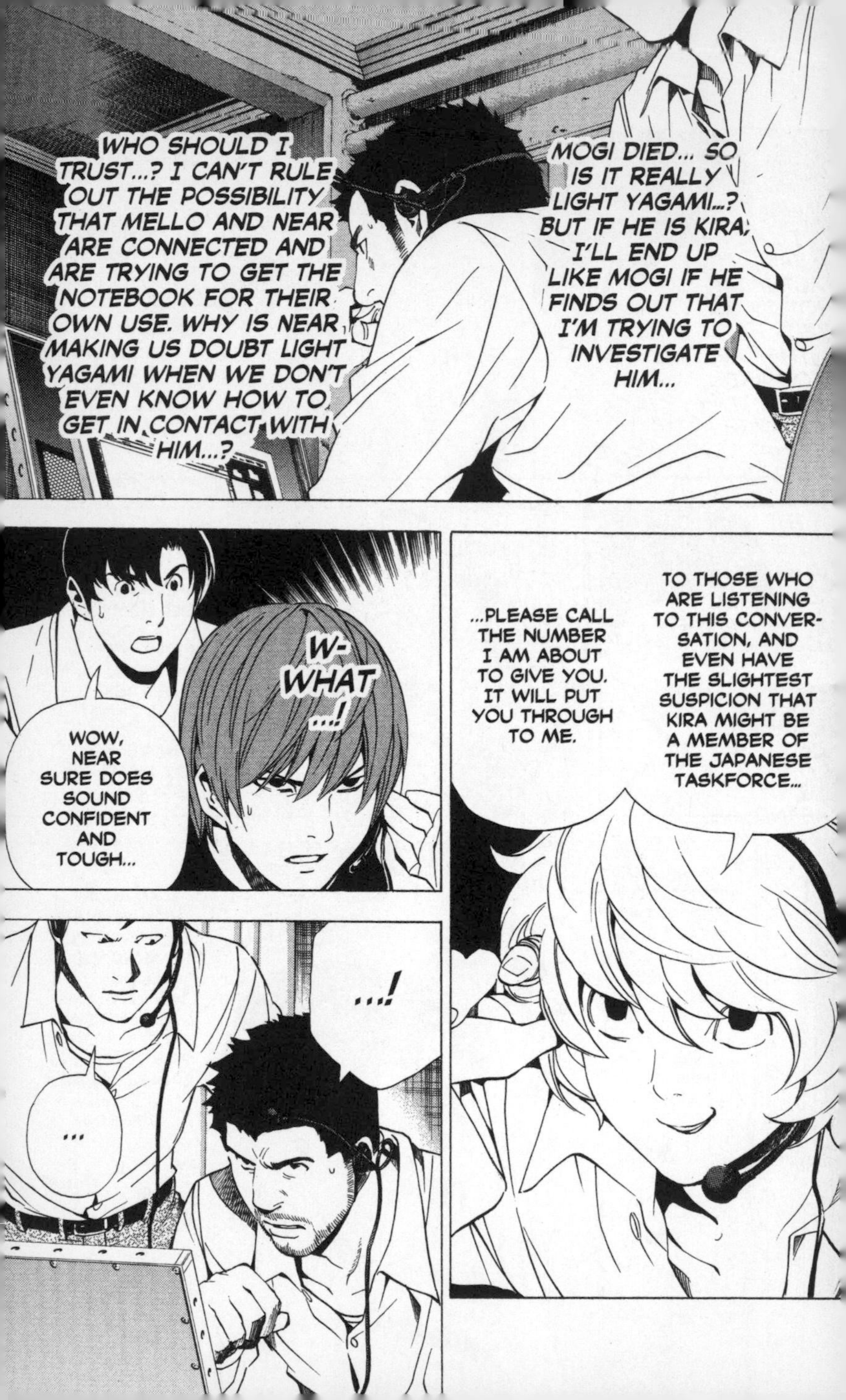
MOGI DIED... SO IS IT REALLY LIGHT YAGAMI...? BUT IF HE IS KIRA, I'LL END UP LIKE MOGI IF HE FINDS OUT THAT I'M TRYING TO INVESTIGATE HIM...
WHO SHOULD I TRUST...? I CAN'T RULE OUT THE POSSIBILITY THAT MELLO AND NEAR ARE CONNECTED AND ARE TRYING TO GET THE NOTEBOOK FOR THEIR OWN USE. WHY IS NEAR MAKING US DOUBT LIGHT YAGAMI WHEN WE DON'T EVEN KNOW HOW TO GET IN CONTACT WITH HIM...?
TO THOSE WHO ARE LISTENING TO THIS CONVERSATION, AND EVEN HAVE THE SLIGHTEST SUSPICION THAT KIRA MIGHT BE A MEMBER OF THE JAPANESE TASKFORCE...
...PLEASE CALL THE NUMBER I AM ABOUT TO GIVE YOU. IT WILL PUT YOU THROUGH TO ME.
W-WHAT ...!
WOW, NEAR SURE DOES SOUND CONFIDENT AND TOUGH...
...!
...

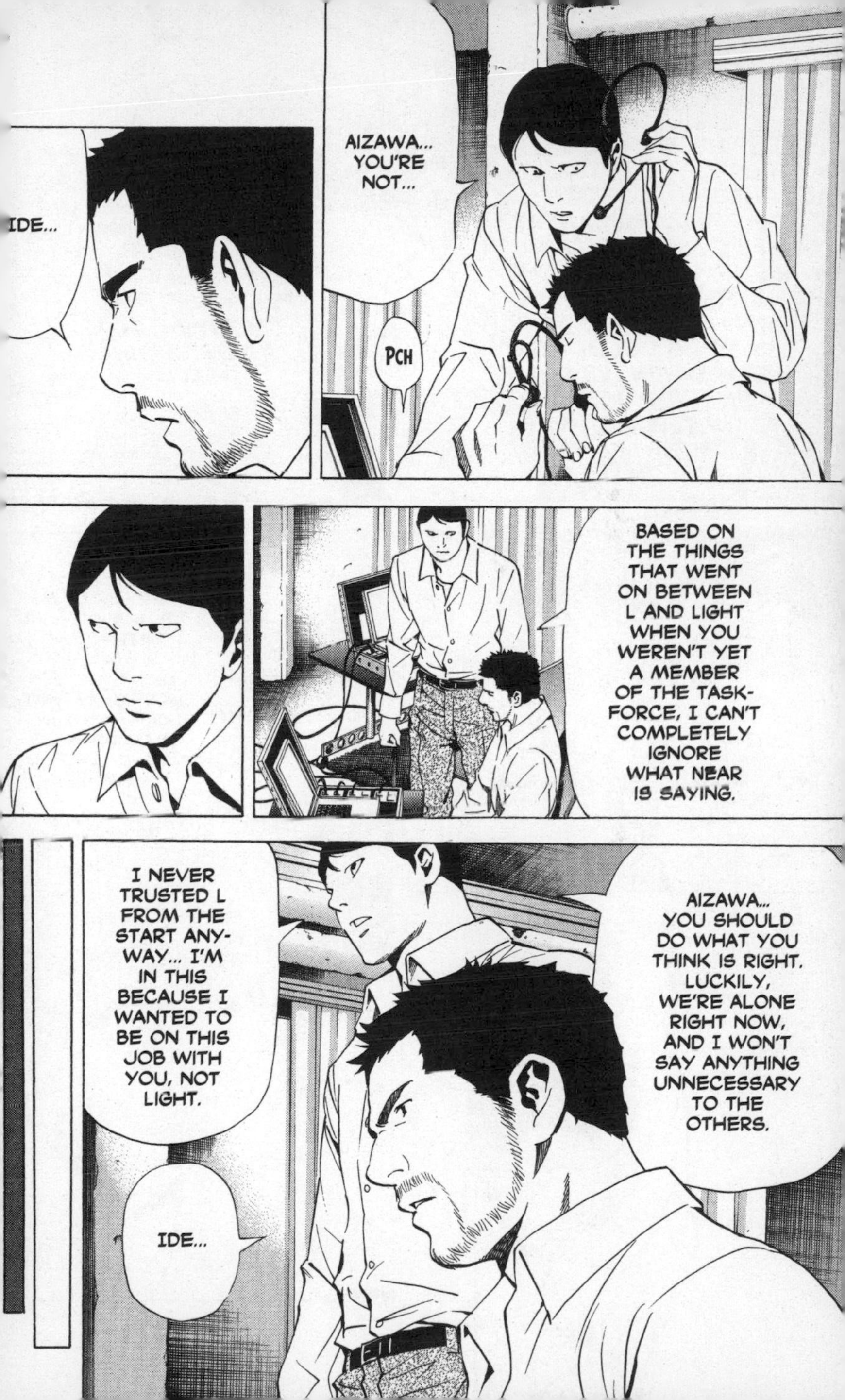
AIZAWA... YOU'RE NOT...
PCH
IDE...
BASED ON THE THINGS THAT WENT ON BETWEEN L AND LIGHT WHEN YOU WEREN'T YET A MEMBER OF THE TASK-FORCE, I CAN'T COMPLETELY IGNORE WHAT NEAR IS SAYING.
AIZAWA... YOU SHOULD DO WHAT YOU THINK IS RIGHT. LUCKILY, WE'RE ALONE RIGHT NOW, AND I WON'T SAY ANYTHING UNNECESSARY TO THE OTHERS.
I NEVER TRUSTED L FROM THE START ANY-WAY... I'M IN THIS BECAUSE I WANTED TO BE ON THIS JOB WITH YOU, NOT LIGHT.
IDE...

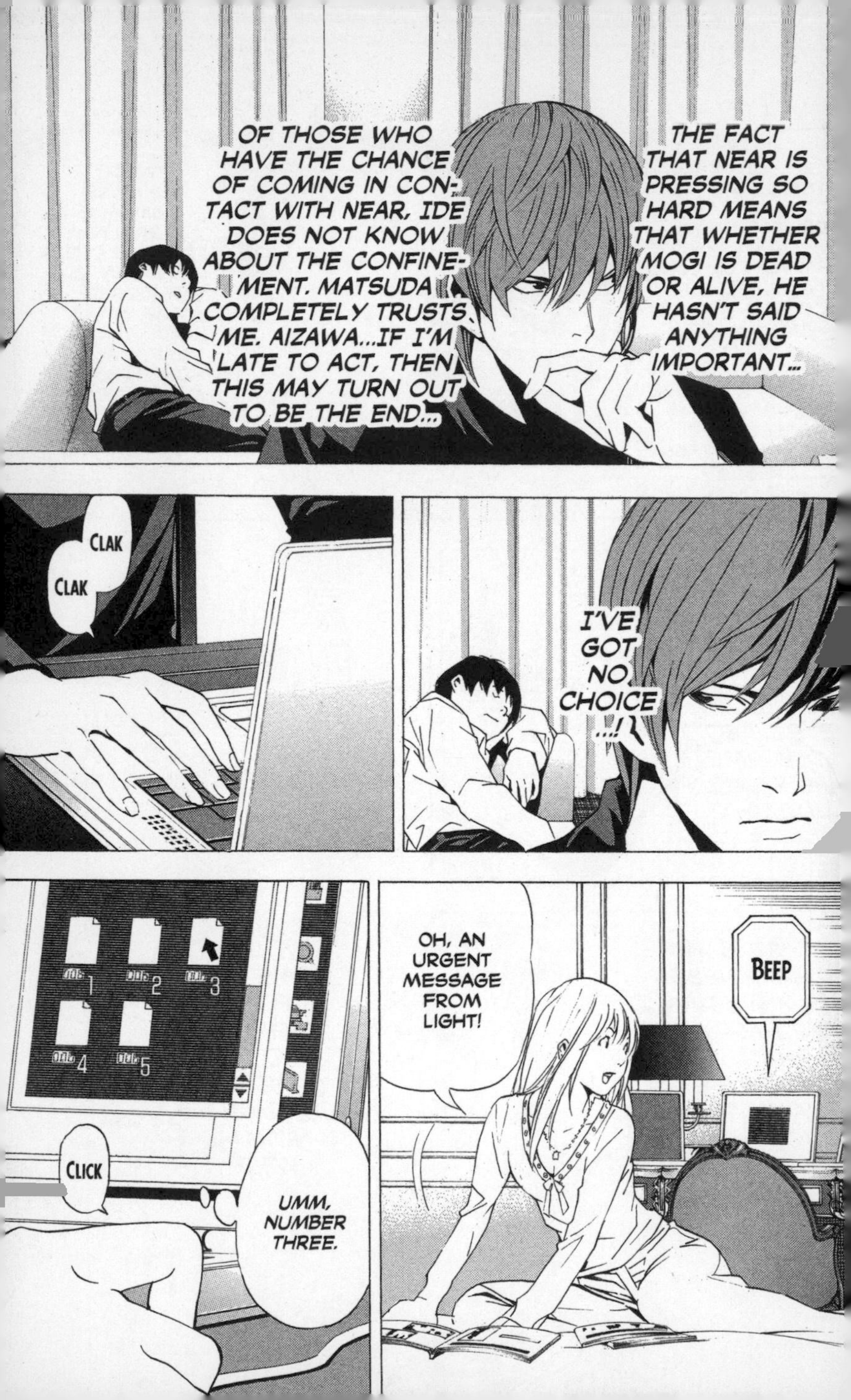
THE FACT THAT NEAR IS PRESSING SO HARD MEANS THAT WHETHER MOGI IS DEAD OR ALIVE, HE HASN'T SAID ANYTHING IMPORTANT...
OF THOSE WHO HAVE THE CHANCE OF COMING IN CONTACT WITH NEAR, IDE DOES NOT KNOW ABOUT THE CONFINEMENT. MATSUDA COMPLETELY TRUSTS ME. AIZAWA...IF I'M LATE TO ACT, THEN THIS MAY TURN OUT TO BE THE END...
I'VE GOT NO CHOICE ...!
CLAK
CLAK
BEEP
OH, AN URGENT MESSAGE FROM LIGHT!
UMM, NUMBER THREE.
CLICK

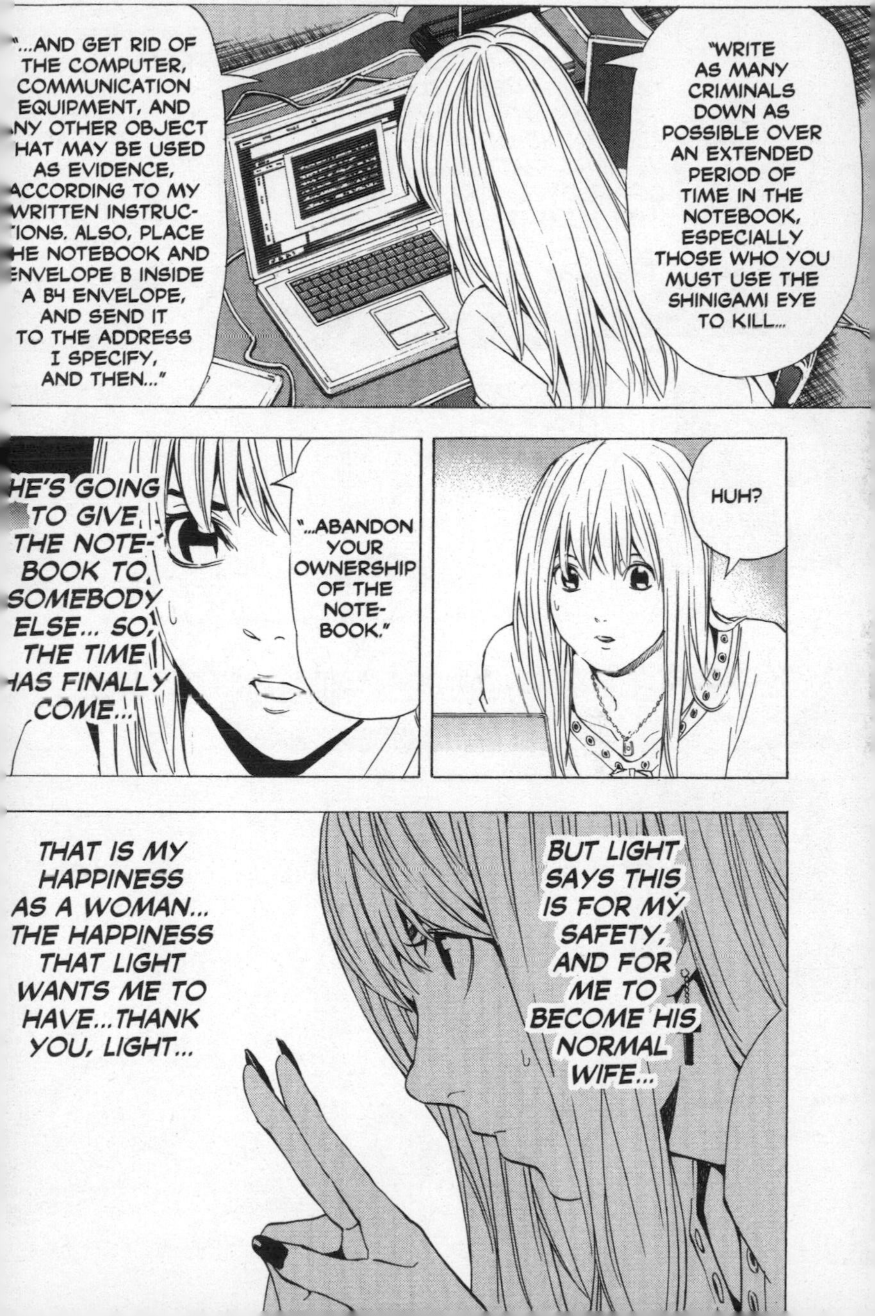
"WRITE AS MANY CRIMINALS DOWN AS POSSIBLE OVER AN EXTENDED PERIOD OF TIME IN THE NOTEBOOK, ESPECIALLY THOSE WHO YOU MUST USE THE SHINIGAMI EYE TO KILL...
"...AND GET RID OF THE COMPUTER, COMMUNICATION EQUIPMENT, AND NY OTHER OBJECT HAT MAY BE USED AS EVIDENCE, ACCORDING TO MY WRITTEN INSTRUC- IONS. ALSO, PLACE HE NOTEBOOK AND ENVELOPE B INSIDE A B4 ENVELOPE, AND SEND IT TO THE ADDRESS I SPECIFY, AND THEN..."
HUH?
"...ABANDON YOUR OWNERSHIP OF THE NOTE- BOOK."
HE'S GOING TO GIVE THE NOTE- BOOK TO SOMEBODY ELSE... SO, THE TIME HAS FINALLY COME...
BUT LIGHT SAYS THIS IS FOR MY SAFETY, AND FOR ME TO BECOME HIS NORMAL WIFE...
THAT IS MY HAPPINESS AS A WOMAN... THE HAPPINESS THAT LIGHT WANTS ME TO HAVE...THANK YOU, LIGHT...

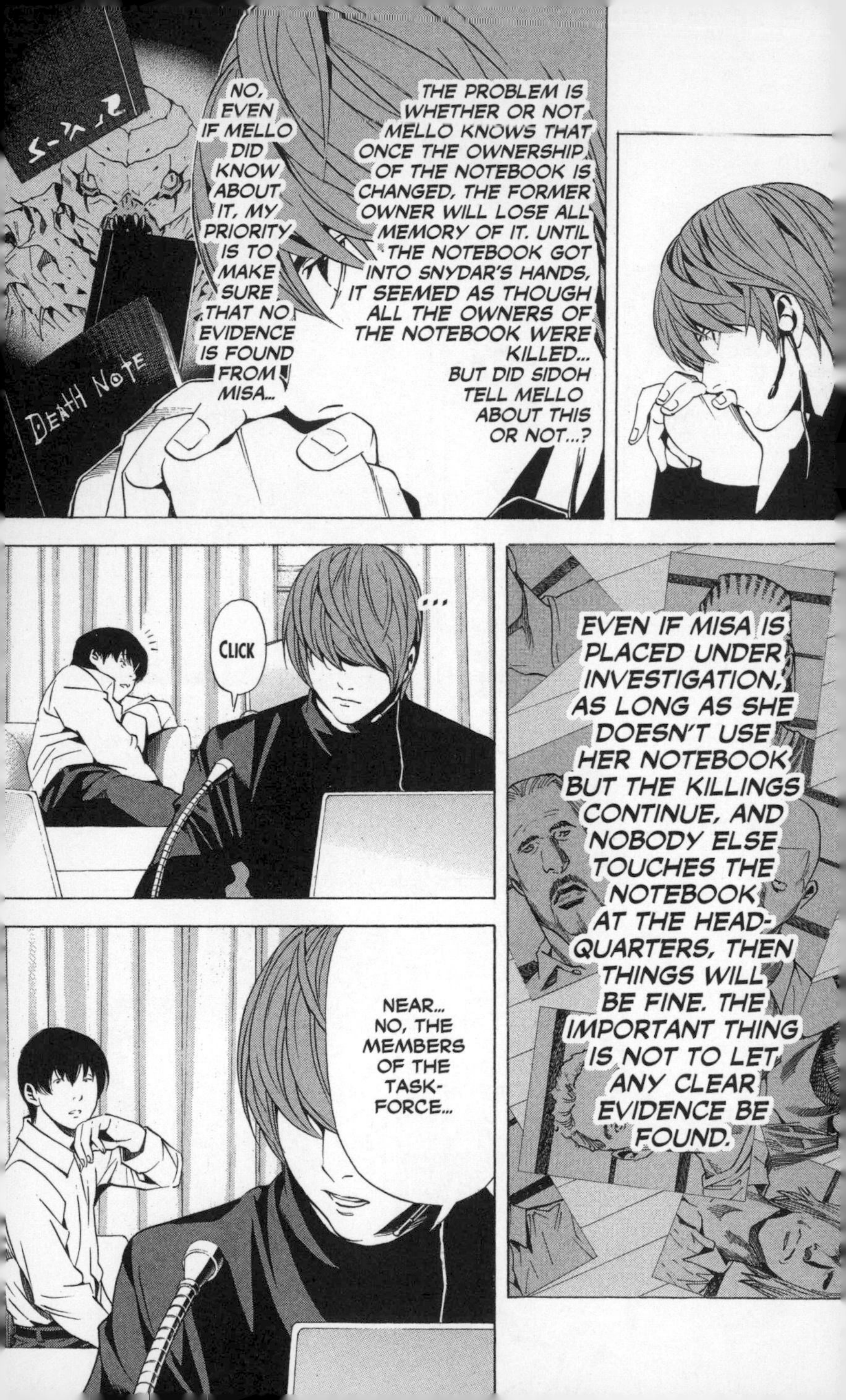
THE PROBLEM IS WHETHER OR NOT MELLO KNOWS THAT ONCE THE OWNERSHIP OF THE NOTEBOOK IS CHANGED, THE FORMER OWNER WILL LOSE ALL MEMORY OF IT. UNTIL THE NOTEBOOK GOT INTO SNYDAR'S HANDS, IT SEEMED AS THOUGH ALL THE OWNERS OF THE NOTEBOOK WERE KILLED... BUT DID SIDOH TELL MELLO ABOUT THIS OR NOT...?
NO, EVEN IF MELLO DID KNOW ABOUT IT, MY PRIORITY IS TO MAKE SURE THAT NO EVIDENCE IS FOUND FROM MISA...
DEATH NOTE
EVEN IF MISA IS PLACED UNDER INVESTIGATION, AS LONG AS SHE DOESN'T USE HER NOTEBOOK BUT THE KILLINGS CONTINUE, AND NOBODY ELSE TOUCHES THE NOTEBOOK AT THE HEAD-QUARTERS, THEN THINGS WILL BE FINE. THE IMPORTANT THING IS NOT TO LET ANY CLEAR EVIDENCE BE FOUND.
...
CLICK
NEAR... NO, THE MEMBERS OF THE TASK-FORCE...

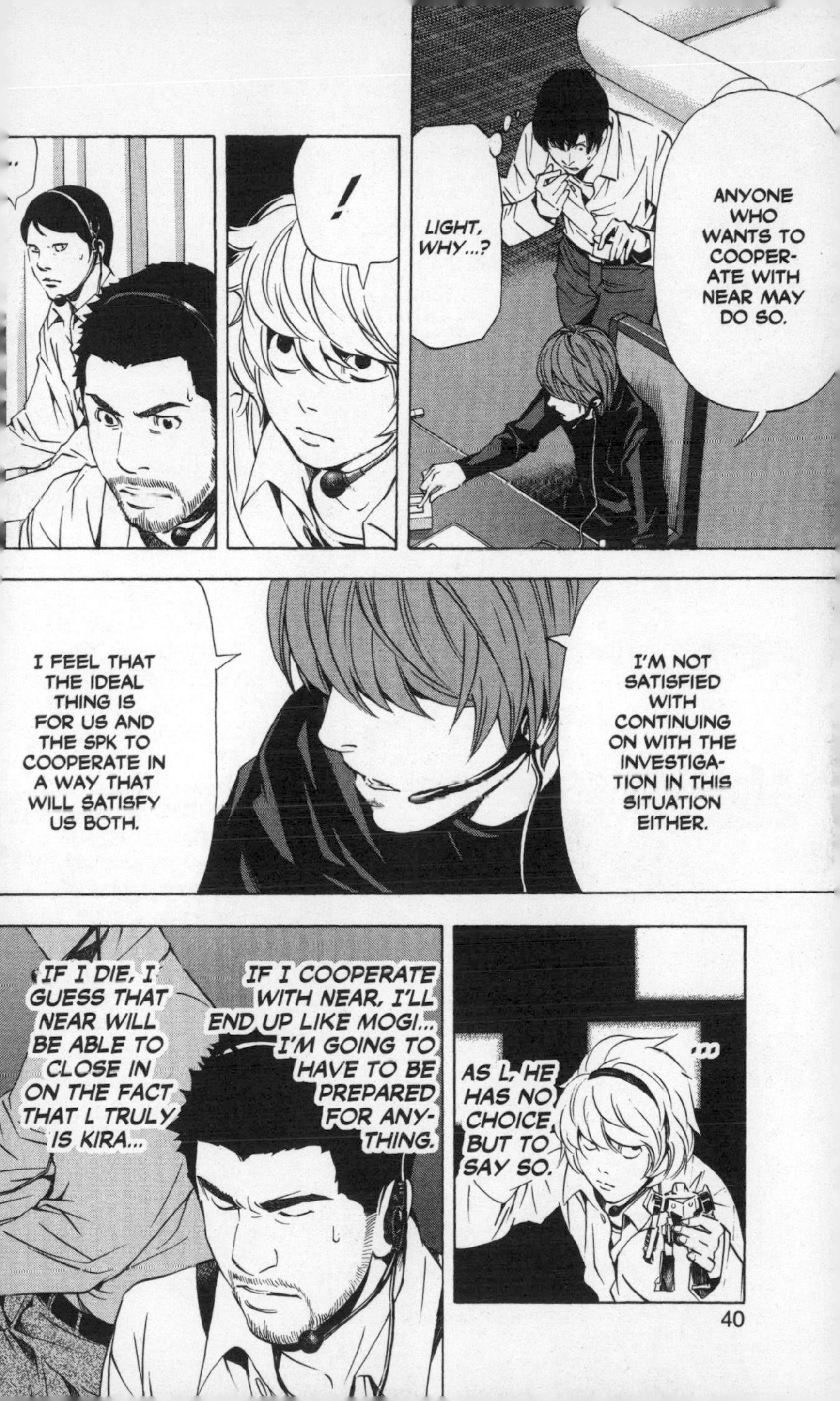
ANYONE WHO WANTS TO COOPERATE WITH NEAR MAY DO SO.
LIGHT, WHY...?
!
..
I'M NOT SATISFIED WITH CONTINUING ON WITH THE INVESTIGATION IN THIS SITUATION EITHER.
I FEEL THAT THE IDEAL THING IS FOR US AND THE SPK TO COOPERATE IN A WAY THAT WILL SATISFY US BOTH.
...
AS L, HE HAS NO CHOICE BUT TO SAY SO.
IF I COOPERATE WITH NEAR, I'LL END UP LIKE MOGI... I'M GOING TO HAVE TO BE PREPARED FOR ANYTHING.
IF I DIE, I GUESS THAT NEAR WILL BE ABLE TO CLOSE IN ON THE FACT THAT L TRULY IS KIRA...

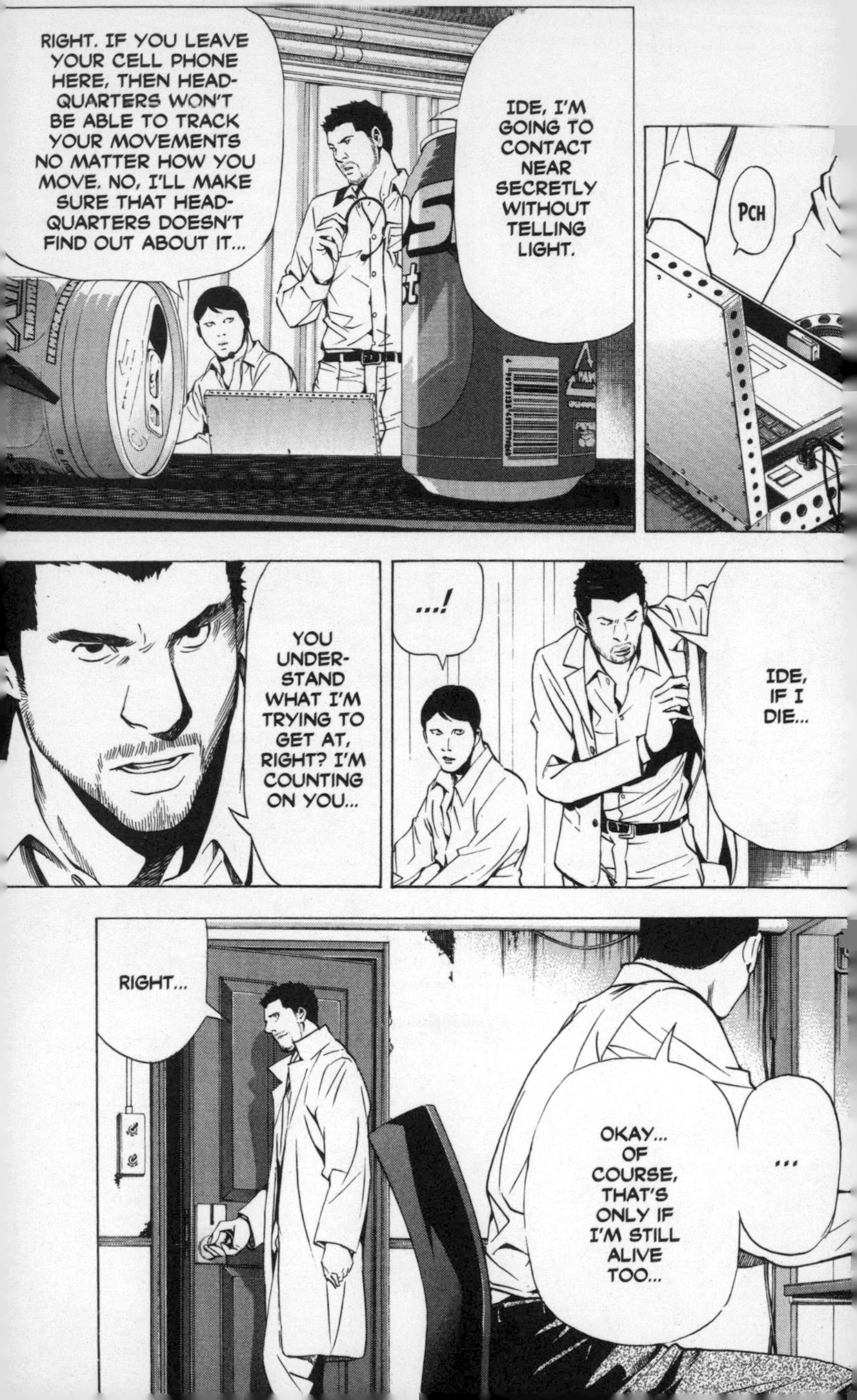
IDE, I'M GOING TO CONTACT NEAR SECRETLY WITHOUT TELLING LIGHT.
RIGHT. IF YOU LEAVE YOUR CELL PHONE HERE, THEN HEAD-QUARTERS WON'T BE ABLE TO TRACK YOUR MOVEMENTS NO MATTER HOW YOU MOVE. NO, I'LL MAKE SURE THAT HEAD-QUARTERS DOESN'T FIND OUT ABOUT IT...
PCH
IDE, IF I DIE...
...!
YOU UNDER-STAND WHAT I'M TRYING TO GET AT, RIGHT? I'M COUNTING ON YOU...
...
OKAY... OF COURSE, THAT'S ONLY IF I'M STILL ALIVE TOO...
RIGHT...

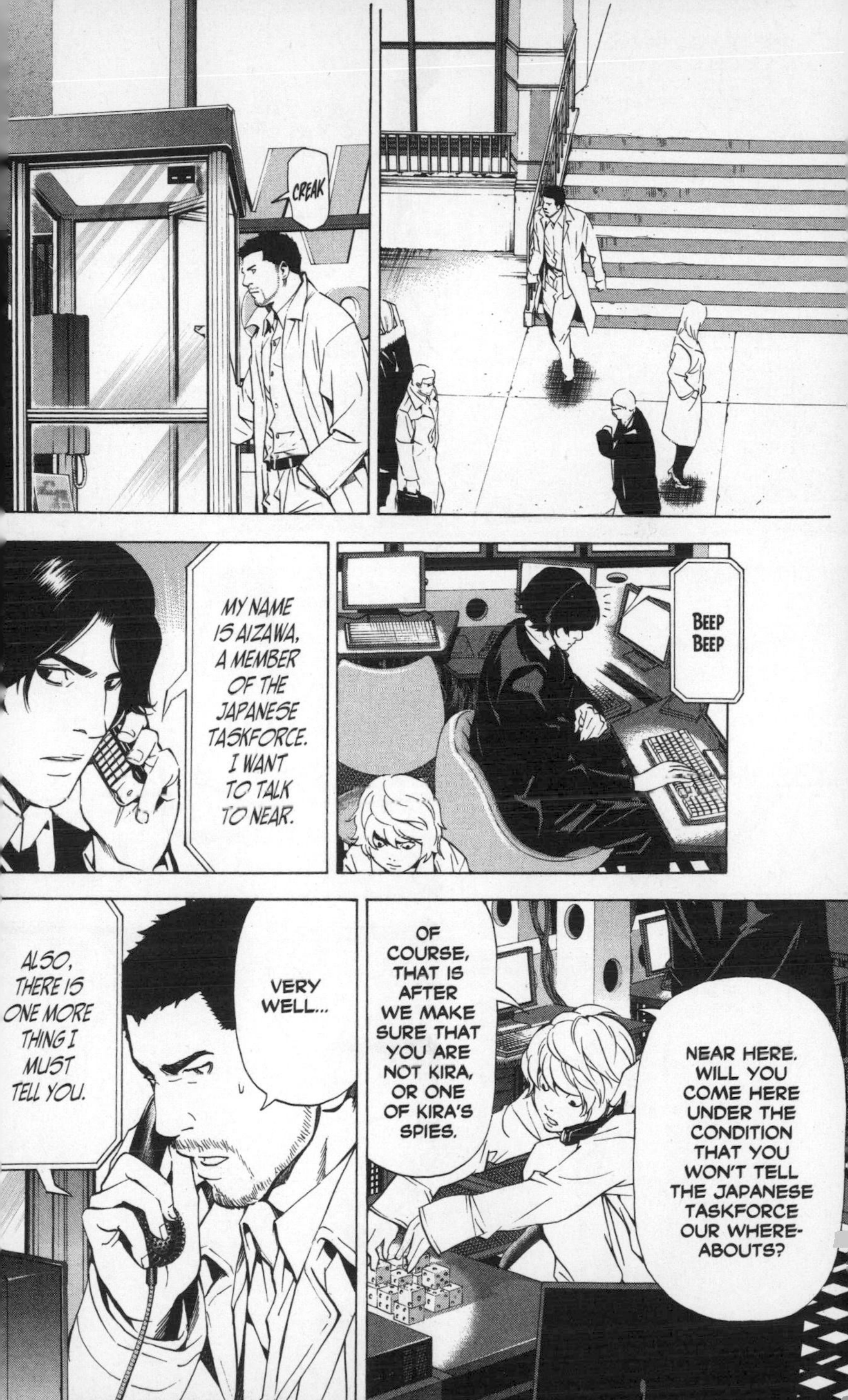
CREAK
BEEP BEEP
MY NAME IS AIZAWA, A MEMBER OF THE JAPANESE TASKFORCE. I WANT TO TALK TO NEAR.
NEAR HERE. WILL YOU COME HERE UNDER THE CONDITION THAT YOU WON'T TELL THE JAPANESE TASKFORCE OUR WHERE-ABOUTS?
OF COURSE, THAT IS AFTER WE MAKE SURE THAT YOU ARE NOT KIRA, OR ONE OF KIRA'S SPIES.
VERY WELL...
ALSO, THERE IS ONE MORE THING I MUST TELL YOU.

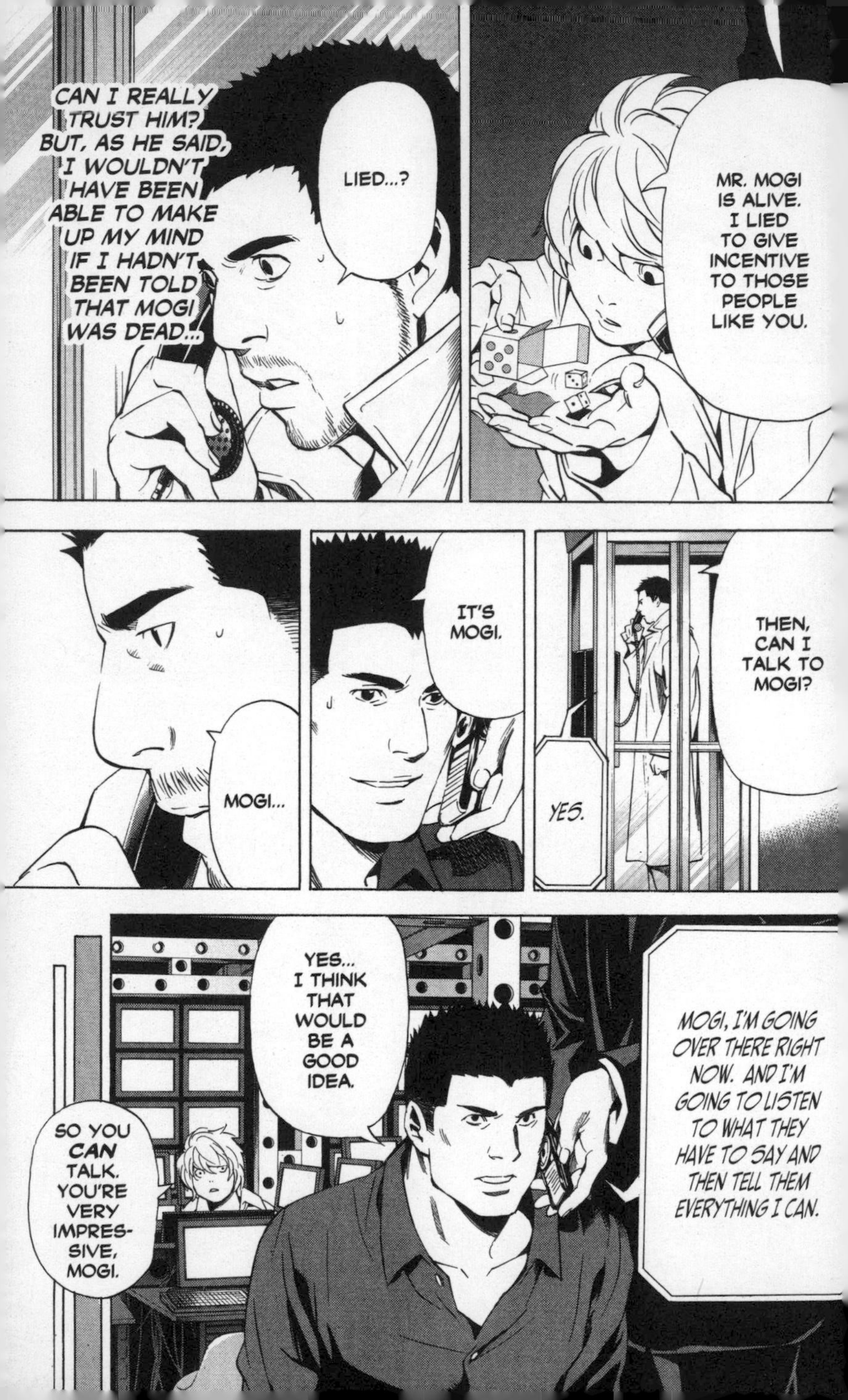
MR. MOGI IS ALIVE. I LIED TO GIVE INCENTIVE TO THOSE PEOPLE LIKE YOU.
LIED...?
CAN I REALLY TRUST HIM? BUT, AS HE SAID, I WOULDN'T HAVE BEEN ABLE TO MAKE UP MY MIND IF I HADN'T BEEN TOLD THAT MOGI WAS DEAD...
THEN, CAN I TALK TO MOGI?
YES.
IT'S MOGI.
MOGI...
MOGI, I'M GOING OVER THERE RIGHT NOW. AND I'M GOING TO LISTEN TO WHAT THEY HAVE TO SAY AND THEN TELL THEM EVERYTHING I CAN.
YES... I THINK THAT WOULD BE A GOOD IDEA.
SO YOU **CAN** TALK. YOU'RE VERY IMPRESSIVE, MOGI.

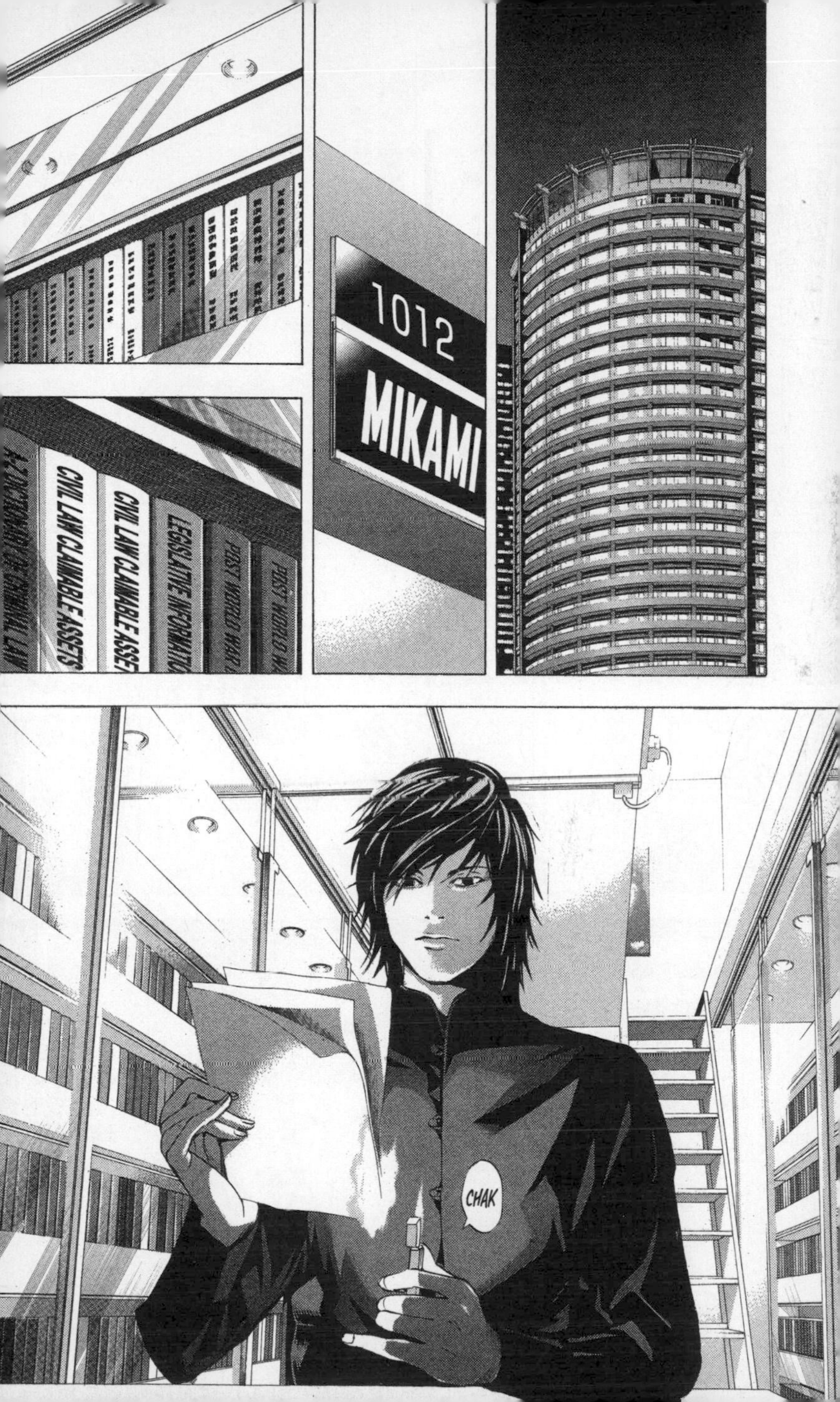
1012
MIKAMI
POST WORLD WA
POST WORLD WAR
LEGISLATIVE INFORMATIO
CIVIL LAW CLAIMABLE ASSET
CIVIL LAW CLAIMABLE ASSETS
A DICTIONARY OF CRIMINAL LAW
CHAK

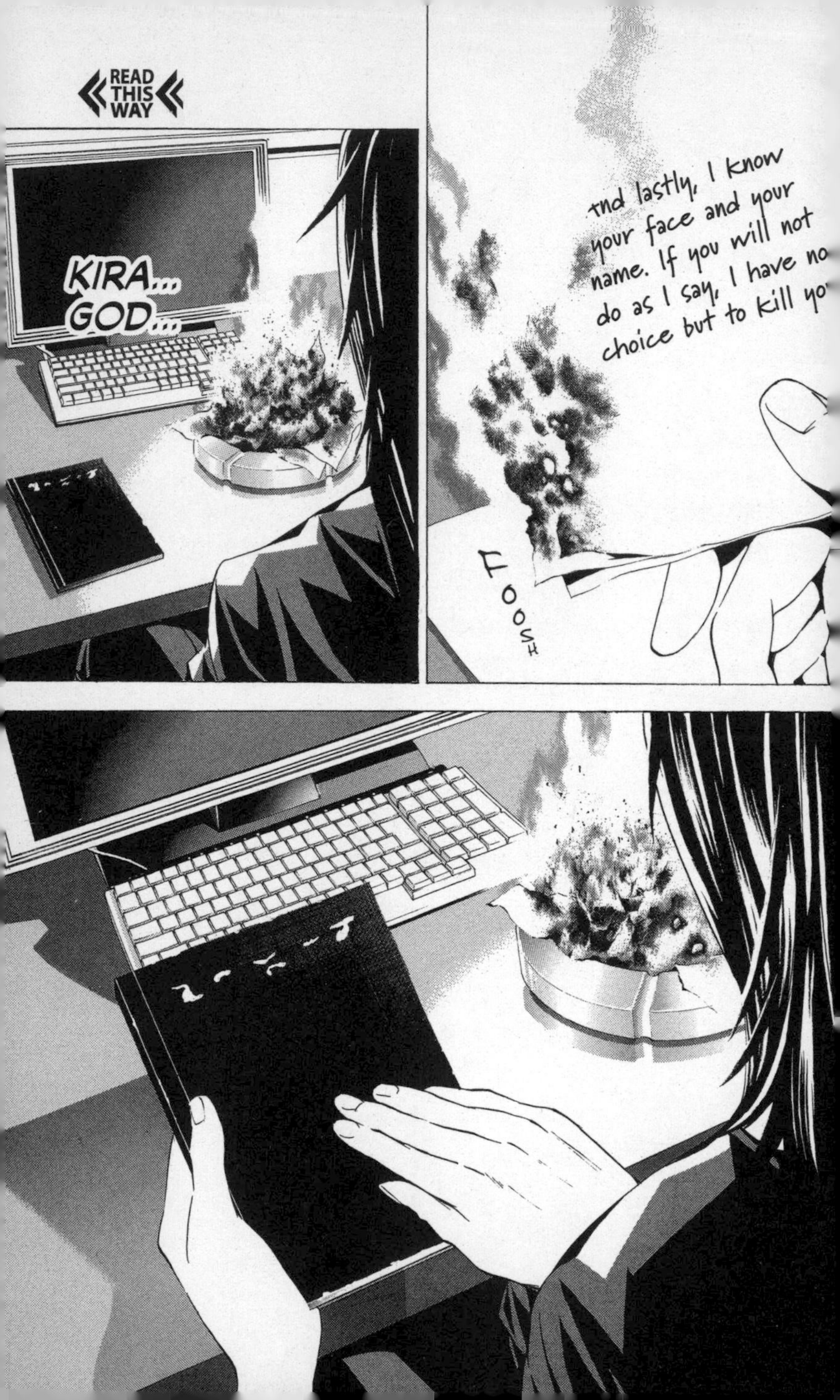

READ THIS WAY
And lastly, I know your face and your name. If you will not do as I say, I have no choice but to kill yo
FOOSH
KIRA... GOD...

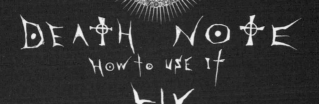

DEATH NOTE
How to use it
LIV

In order to make the DEATH NOTE take effect, the victims name must be written on the same page, but the cause of death and the situation around the death can be described in other pages of the DEATH NOTE. This will work as long as the person that writes the DEATH NOTE keeps the specific victims name in mind when writing the cause and situation of the death.

デスノートの効力を得るには、
一人の名前は同ページに記さなくてはならないが、
その名前に関する死因や死の状況は、
書き込む者がその記した名前に対する死因や状況と考えて記せば、
他のページに記しても有効である。

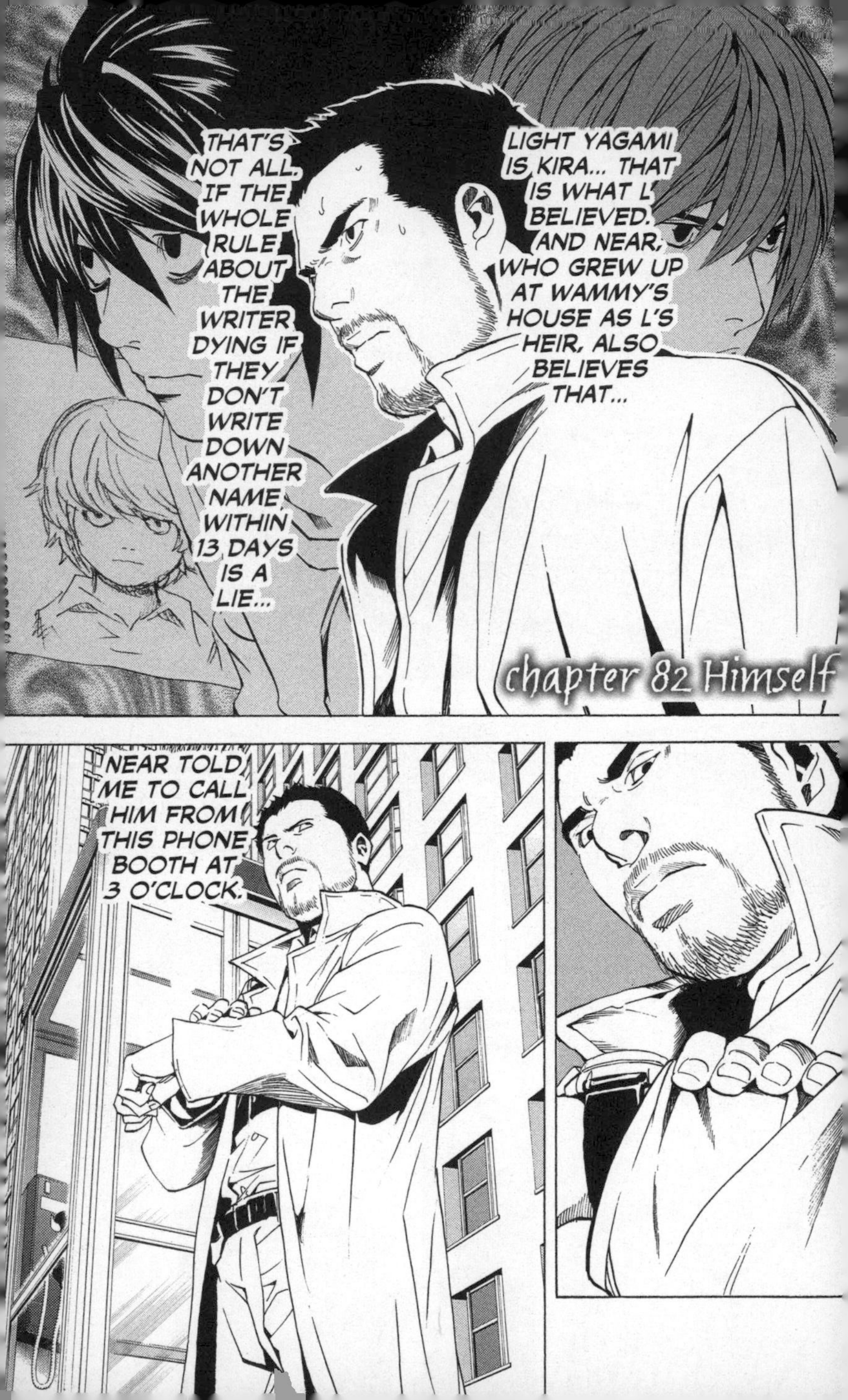
LIGHT YAGAMI IS KIRA... THAT IS WHAT L BELIEVED. AND NEAR, WHO GREW UP AT WAMMY'S HOUSE AS L'S HEIR, ALSO BELIEVES THAT...
THAT'S NOT ALL. IF THE WHOLE RULE ABOUT THE WRITER DYING IF THEY DON'T WRITE DOWN ANOTHER NAME WITHIN 13 DAYS IS A LIE...
chapter 82 Himself
NEAR TOLD ME TO CALL HIM FROM THIS PHONE BOOTH AT 3 O'CLOCK.

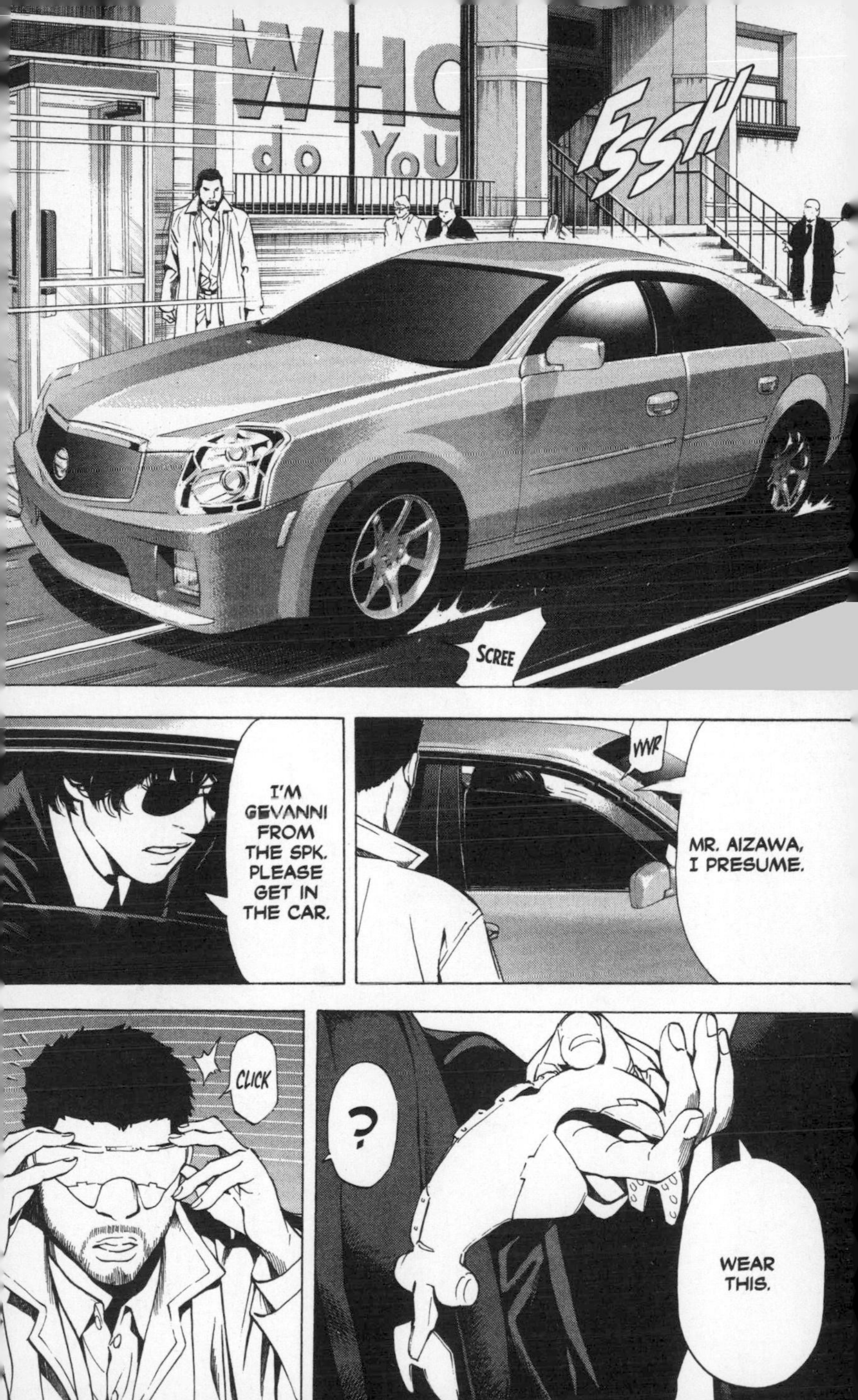
WHO
do YOU
FSSH
SCREE
VVVR
MR. AIZAWA, I PRESUME.
I'M GEVANNI FROM THE SPK. PLEASE GET IN THE CAR.
?
WEAR THIS.
CLICK

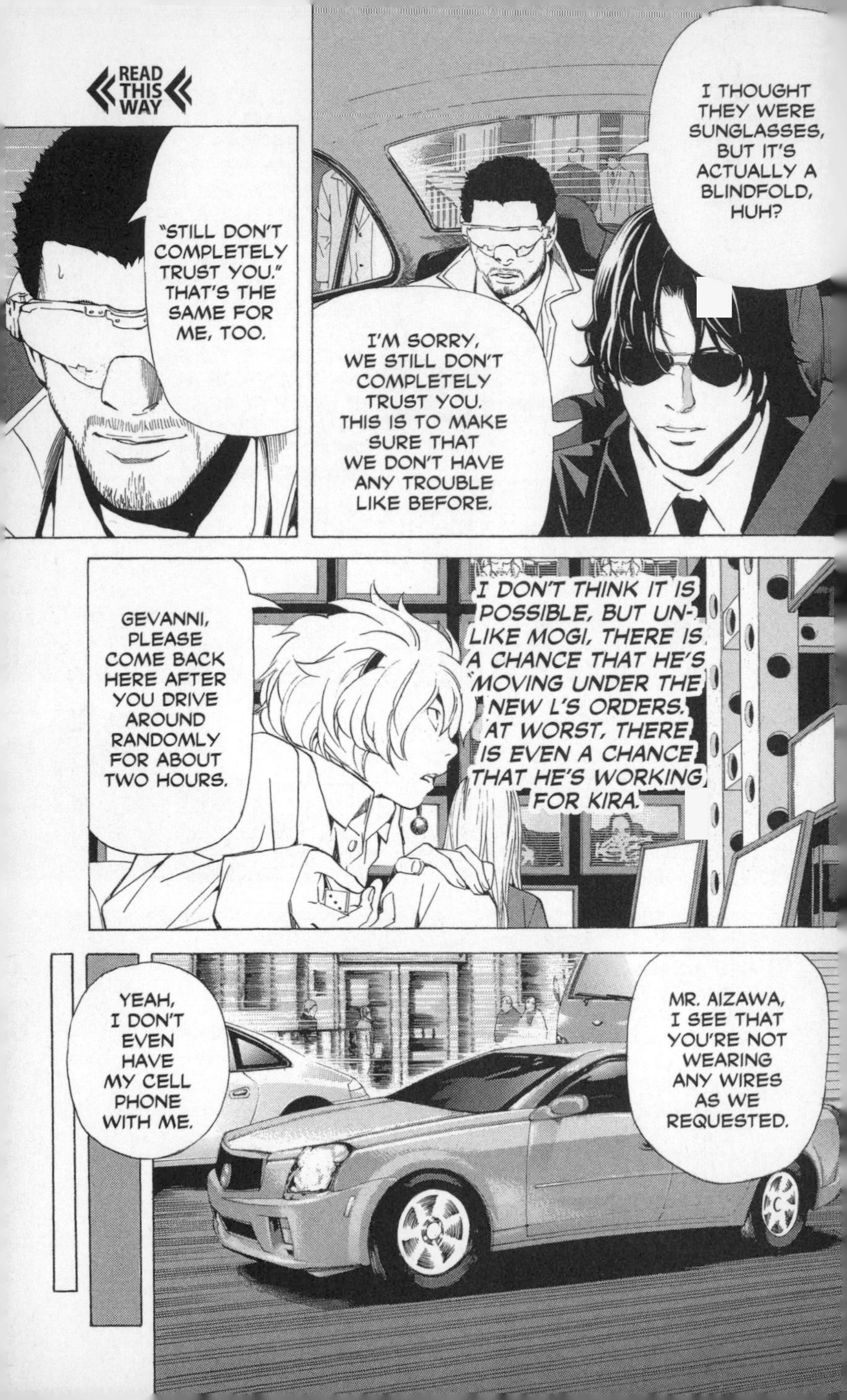
READ THIS WAY
I THOUGHT THEY WERE SUNGLASSES, BUT IT'S ACTUALLY A BLINDFOLD, HUH?
I'M SORRY, WE STILL DON'T COMPLETELY TRUST YOU. THIS IS TO MAKE SURE THAT WE DON'T HAVE ANY TROUBLE LIKE BEFORE.
"STILL DON'T COMPLETELY TRUST YOU." THAT'S THE SAME FOR ME, TOO.
I DON'T THINK IT IS POSSIBLE, BUT UN-LIKE MOGI, THERE IS A CHANCE THAT HE'S MOVING UNDER THE NEW L'S ORDERS. AT WORST, THERE IS EVEN A CHANCE THAT HE'S WORKING FOR KIRA.
GEVANNI, PLEASE COME BACK HERE AFTER YOU DRIVE AROUND RANDOMLY FOR ABOUT TWO HOURS.
MR. AIZAWA, I SEE THAT YOU'RE NOT WEARING ANY WIRES AS WE REQUESTED.
YEAH, I DON'T EVEN HAVE MY CELL PHONE WITH ME.

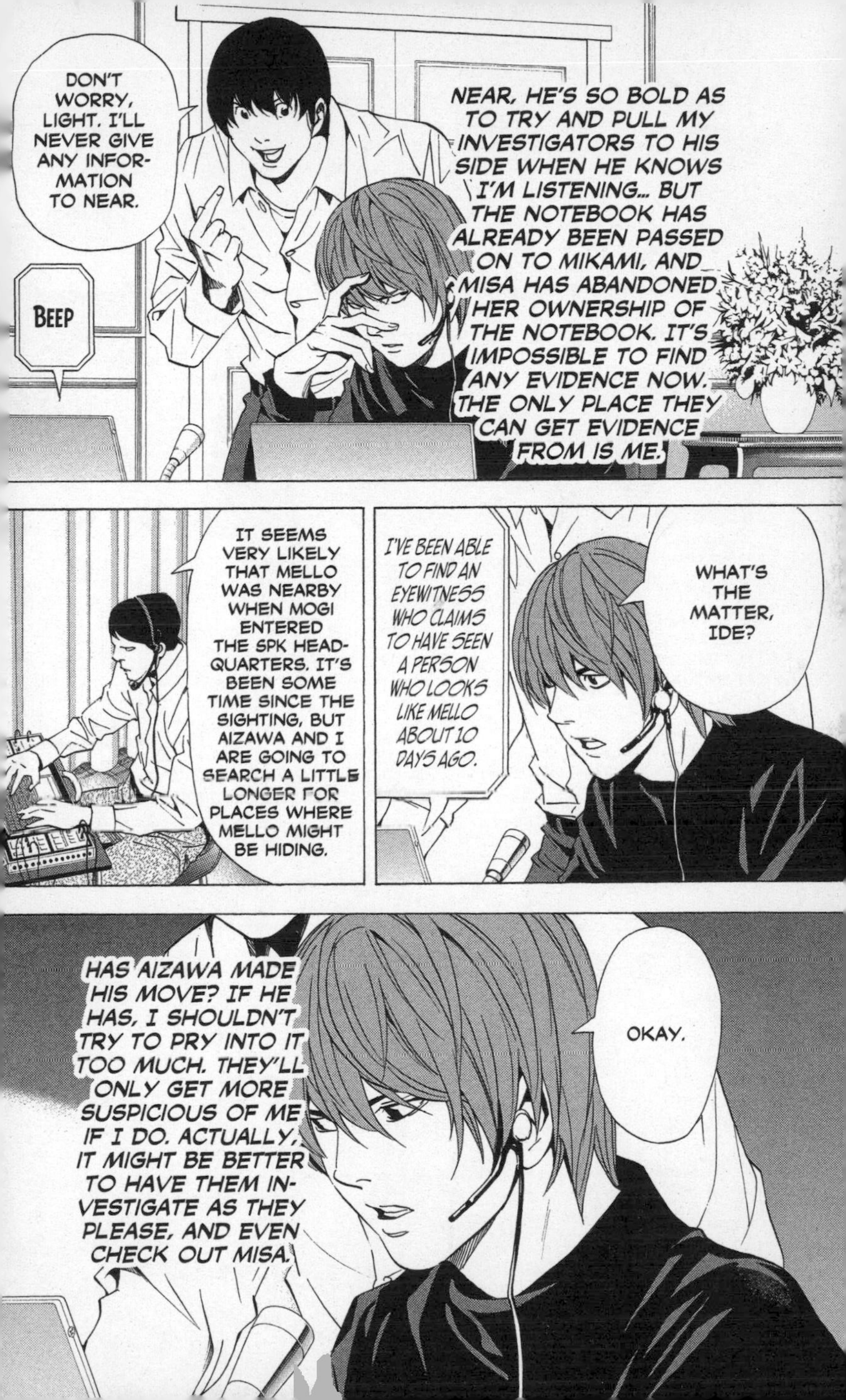
NEAR, HE'S SO BOLD AS TO TRY AND PULL MY INVESTIGATORS TO HIS SIDE WHEN HE KNOWS I'M LISTENING... BUT THE NOTEBOOK HAS ALREADY BEEN PASSED ON TO MIKAMI, AND MISA HAS ABANDONED HER OWNERSHIP OF THE NOTEBOOK. IT'S IMPOSSIBLE TO FIND ANY EVIDENCE NOW. THE ONLY PLACE THEY CAN GET EVIDENCE FROM IS ME.
DON'T WORRY, LIGHT. I'LL NEVER GIVE ANY INFORMATION TO NEAR.
BEEP
WHAT'S THE MATTER, IDE?
I'VE BEEN ABLE TO FIND AN EYEWITNESS WHO CLAIMS TO HAVE SEEN A PERSON WHO LOOKS LIKE MELLO ABOUT 10 DAYS AGO.
IT SEEMS VERY LIKELY THAT MELLO WAS NEARBY WHEN MOGI ENTERED THE SPK HEADQUARTERS. IT'S BEEN SOME TIME SINCE THE SIGHTING, BUT AIZAWA AND I ARE GOING TO SEARCH A LITTLE LONGER FOR PLACES WHERE MELLO MIGHT BE HIDING.
OKAY.
HAS AIZAWA MADE HIS MOVE? IF HE HAS, I SHOULDN'T TRY TO PRY INTO IT TOO MUCH. THEY'LL ONLY GET MORE SUSPICIOUS OF ME IF I DO. ACTUALLY, IT MIGHT BE BETTER TO HAVE THEM INVESTIGATE AS THEY PLEASE, AND EVEN CHECK OUT MISA.

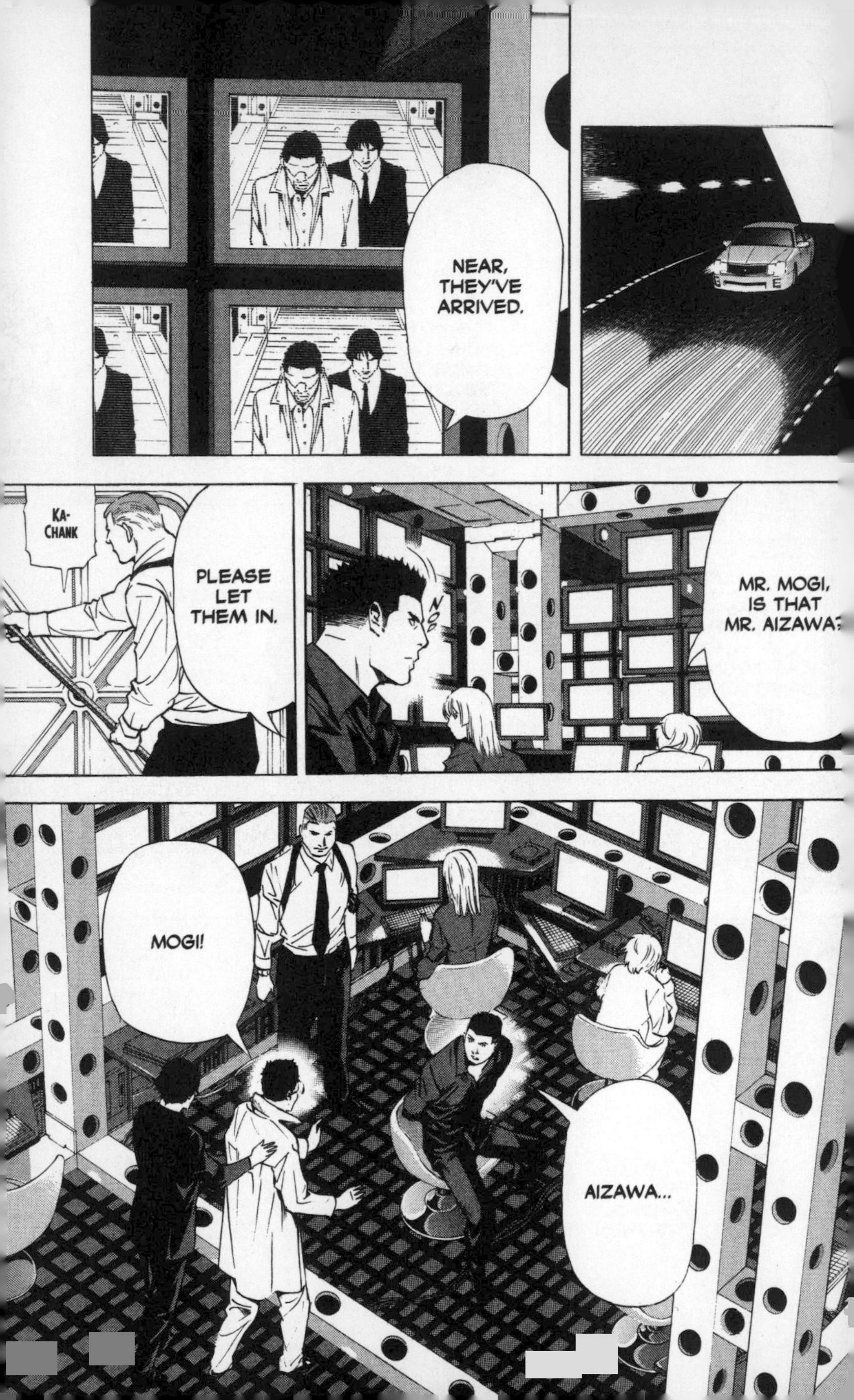
NEAR, THEY'VE ARRIVED.
MR. MOGI, IS THAT MR. AIZAWA?
NOD
PLEASE LET THEM IN.
KA-CHANK
AIZAWA...
MOGI!

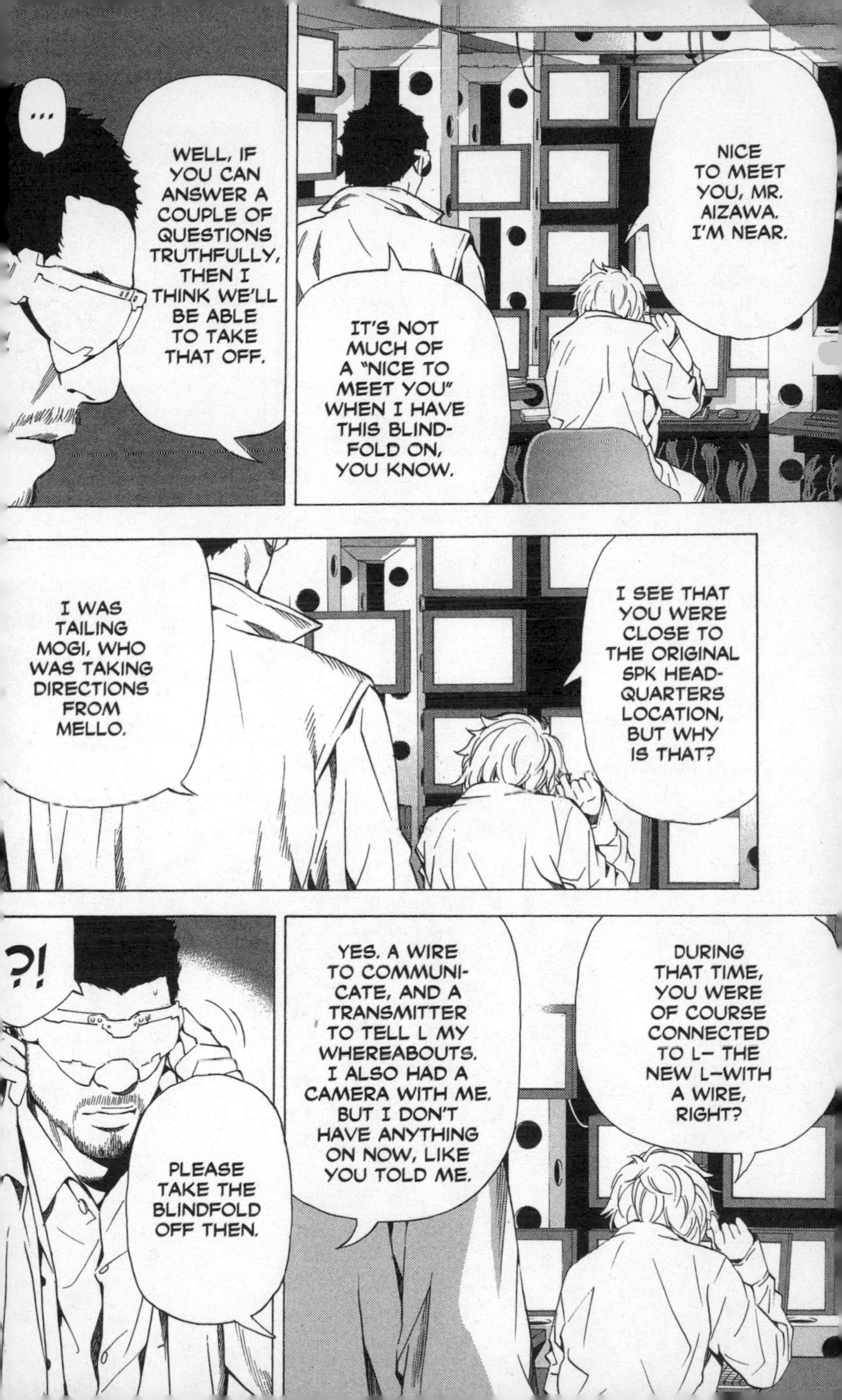
NICE TO MEET YOU, MR. AIZAWA. I'M NEAR.
IT'S NOT MUCH OF A "NICE TO MEET YOU" WHEN I HAVE THIS BLIND-FOLD ON, YOU KNOW.
WELL, IF YOU CAN ANSWER A COUPLE OF QUESTIONS TRUTHFULLY, THEN I THINK WE'LL BE ABLE TO TAKE THAT OFF.
...
I SEE THAT YOU WERE CLOSE TO THE ORIGINAL SPK HEAD-QUARTERS LOCATION, BUT WHY IS THAT?
I WAS TAILING MOGI, WHO WAS TAKING DIRECTIONS FROM MELLO.
DURING THAT TIME, YOU WERE OF COURSE CONNECTED TO L– THE NEW L–WITH A WIRE, RIGHT?
YES. A WIRE TO COMMUNI-CATE, AND A TRANSMITTER TO TELL L MY WHEREABOUTS. I ALSO HAD A CAMERA WITH ME. BUT I DON'T HAVE ANYTHING ON NOW, LIKE YOU TOLD ME.
?!
PLEASE TAKE THE BLINDFOLD OFF THEN.

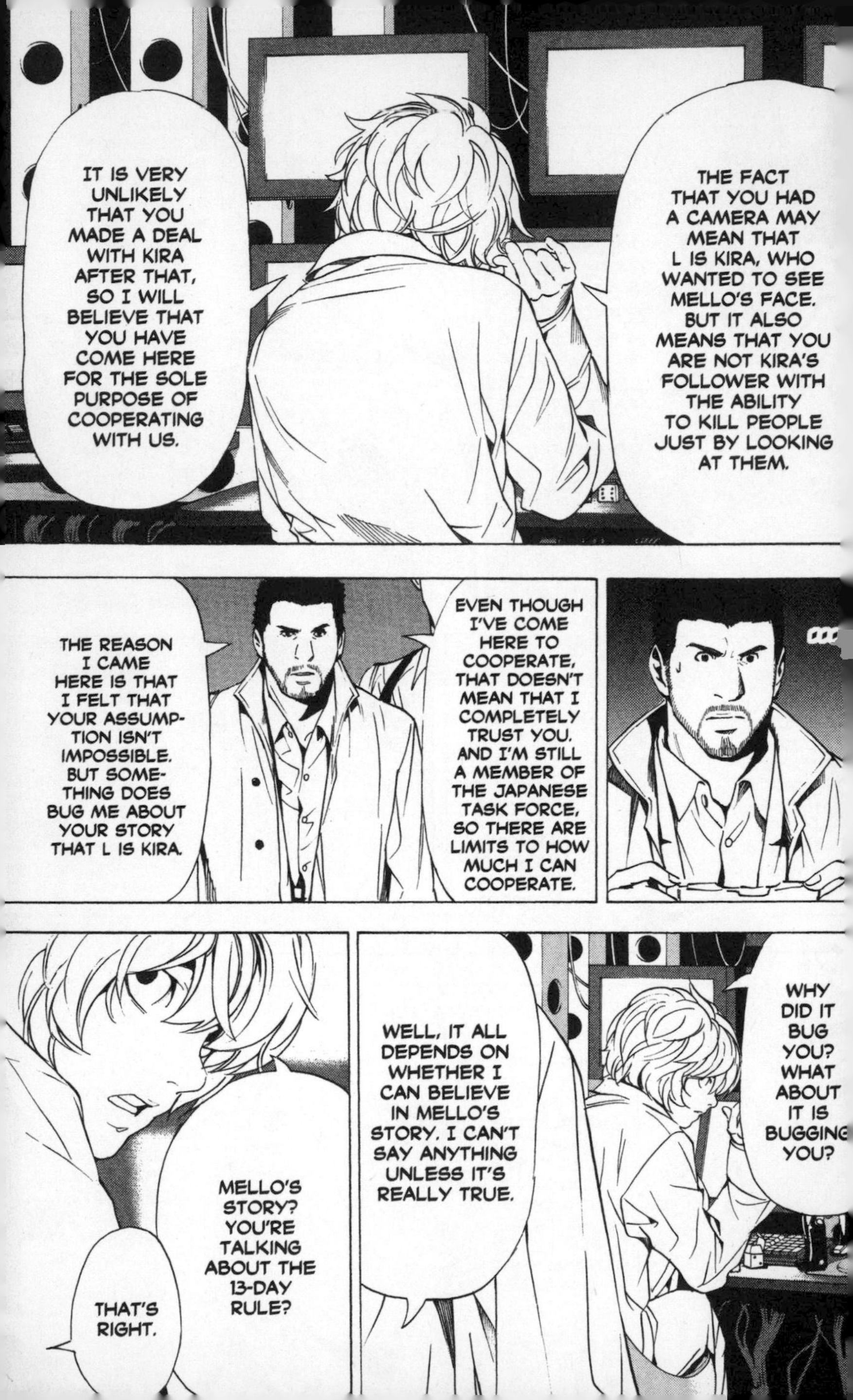
THE FACT THAT YOU HAD A CAMERA MAY MEAN THAT L IS KIRA, WHO WANTED TO SEE MELLO'S FACE. BUT IT ALSO MEANS THAT YOU ARE NOT KIRA'S FOLLOWER WITH THE ABILITY TO KILL PEOPLE JUST BY LOOKING AT THEM.
IT IS VERY UNLIKELY THAT YOU MADE A DEAL WITH KIRA AFTER THAT, SO I WILL BELIEVE THAT YOU HAVE COME HERE FOR THE SOLE PURPOSE OF COOPERATING WITH US.
...
EVEN THOUGH I'VE COME HERE TO COOPERATE, THAT DOESN'T MEAN THAT I COMPLETELY TRUST YOU. AND I'M STILL A MEMBER OF THE JAPANESE TASK FORCE, SO THERE ARE LIMITS TO HOW MUCH I CAN COOPERATE.
THE REASON I CAME HERE IS THAT I FELT THAT YOUR ASSUMPTION ISN'T IMPOSSIBLE. BUT SOMETHING DOES BUG ME ABOUT YOUR STORY THAT L IS KIRA.
WHY DID IT BUG YOU? WHAT ABOUT IT IS BUGGING YOU?
WELL, IT ALL DEPENDS ON WHETHER I CAN BELIEVE IN MELLO'S STORY. I CAN'T SAY ANYTHING UNLESS IT'S REALLY TRUE.
MELLO'S STORY? YOU'RE TALKING ABOUT THE 13-DAY RULE?
THAT'S RIGHT.

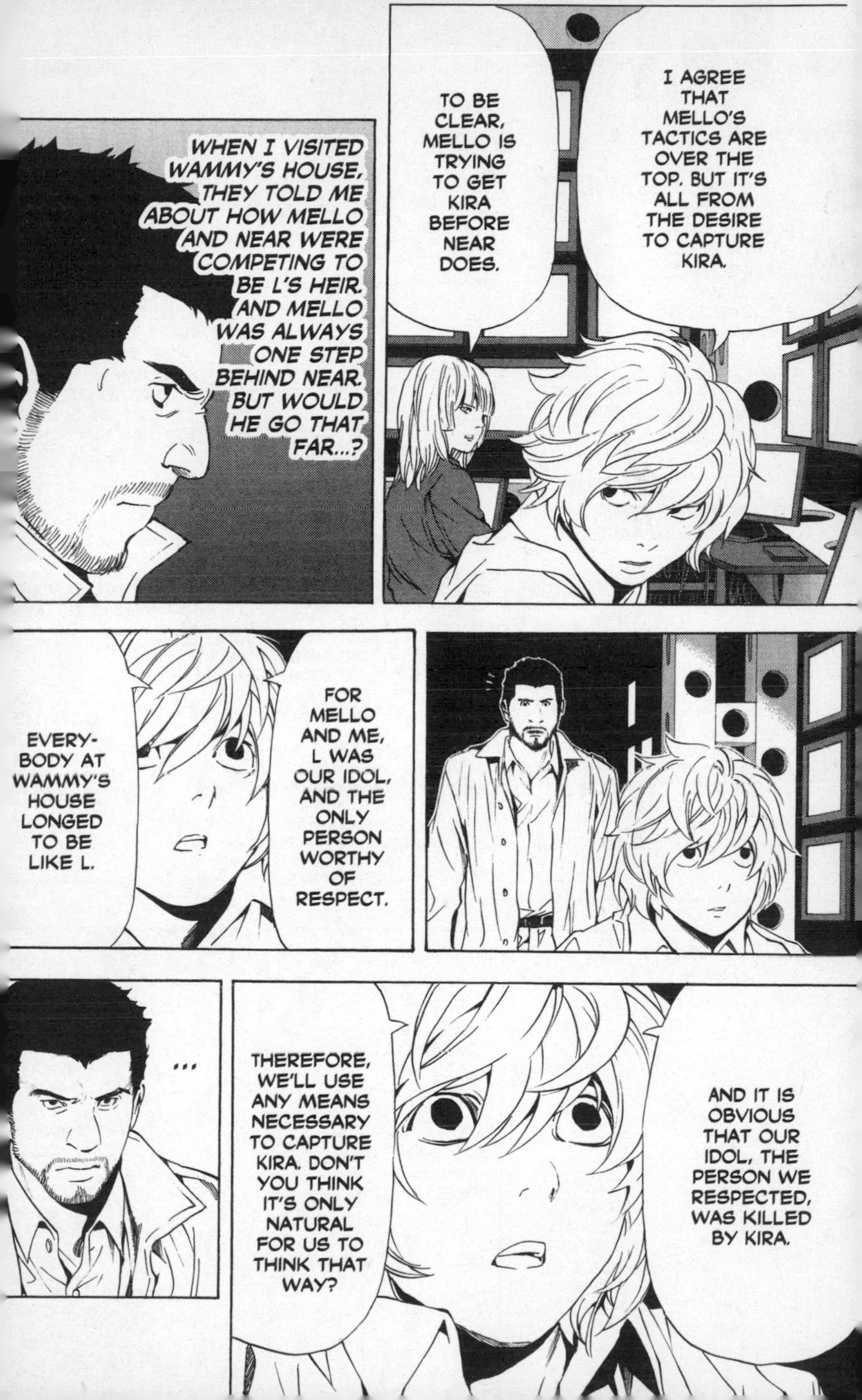

I AGREE THAT MELLO'S TACTICS ARE OVER THE TOP. BUT IT'S ALL FROM THE DESIRE TO CAPTURE KIRA.
TO BE CLEAR, MELLO IS TRYING TO GET KIRA BEFORE NEAR DOES.
WHEN I VISITED WAMMY'S HOUSE, THEY TOLD ME ABOUT HOW MELLO AND NEAR WERE COMPETING TO BE L'S HEIR. AND MELLO WAS ALWAYS ONE STEP BEHIND NEAR. BUT WOULD HE GO THAT FAR...?
FOR MELLO AND ME, L WAS OUR IDOL, AND THE ONLY PERSON WORTHY OF RESPECT.
EVERY-BODY AT WAMMY'S HOUSE LONGED TO BE LIKE L.
AND IT IS OBVIOUS THAT OUR IDOL, THE PERSON WE RESPECTED, WAS KILLED BY KIRA.
THEREFORE, WE'LL USE ANY MEANS NECESSARY TO CAPTURE KIRA. DON'T YOU THINK IT'S ONLY NATURAL FOR US TO THINK THAT WAY?
...

READ THIS WAY

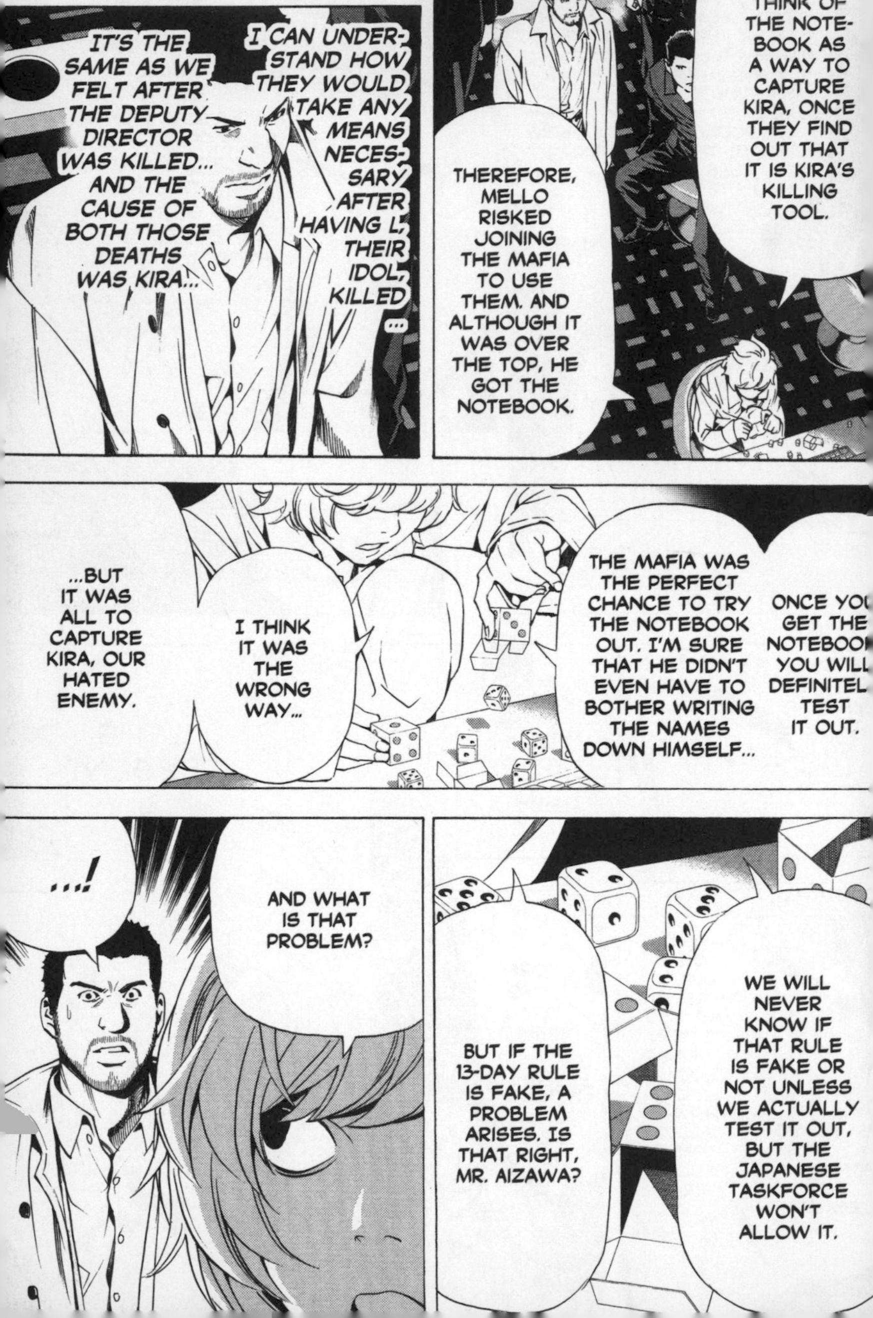
ANYBODY WOULD THINK OF THE NOTEBOOK AS A WAY TO CAPTURE KIRA, ONCE THEY FIND OUT THAT IT IS KIRA'S KILLING TOOL.
THEREFORE, MELLO RISKED JOINING THE MAFIA TO USE THEM. AND ALTHOUGH IT WAS OVER THE TOP, HE GOT THE NOTEBOOK.
I CAN UNDERSTAND HOW THEY WOULD TAKE ANY MEANS NECESSARY AFTER HAVING L, THEIR IDOL, KILLED...
IT'S THE SAME AS WE FELT AFTER THE DEPUTY DIRECTOR WAS KILLED... AND THE CAUSE OF BOTH THOSE DEATHS WAS KIRA...
ONCE YO GET THE NOTEBOO YOU WILL DEFINITEL TEST IT OUT.
THE MAFIA WAS THE PERFECT CHANCE TO TRY THE NOTEBOOK OUT. I'M SURE THAT HE DIDN'T EVEN HAVE TO BOTHER WRITING THE NAMES DOWN HIMSELF...
I THINK IT WAS THE WRONG WAY...
...BUT IT WAS ALL TO CAPTURE KIRA, OUR HATED ENEMY.
WE WILL NEVER KNOW IF THAT RULE IS FAKE OR NOT UNLESS WE ACTUALLY TEST IT OUT, BUT THE JAPANESE TASKFORCE WON'T ALLOW IT.
BUT IF THE 13-DAY RULE IS FAKE, A PROBLEM ARISES. IS THAT RIGHT, MR. AIZAWA?
AND WHAT IS THAT PROBLEM?
...!

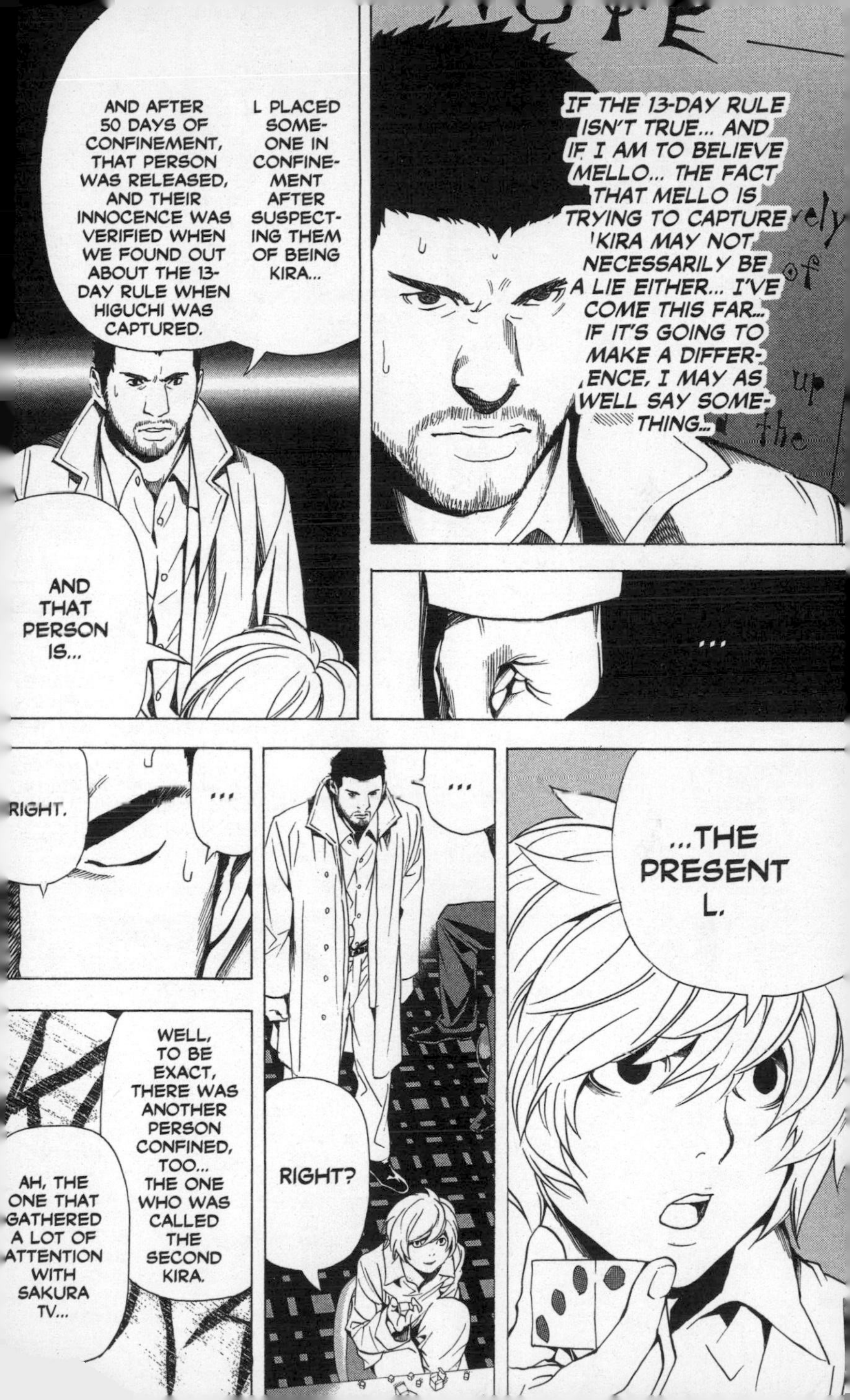

IF THE 13-DAY RULE ISN'T TRUE... AND IF I AM TO BELIEVE MELLO... THE FACT THAT MELLO IS TRYING TO CAPTURE KIRA MAY NOT NECESSARILY BE A LIE EITHER... I'VE COME THIS FAR... IF IT'S GOING TO MAKE A DIFFERENCE, I MAY AS WELL SAY SOMETHING...
...
L PLACED SOMEONE IN CONFINEMENT AFTER SUSPECTING THEM OF BEING KIRA...
AND AFTER 50 DAYS OF CONFINEMENT, THAT PERSON WAS RELEASED, AND THEIR INNOCENCE WAS VERIFIED WHEN WE FOUND OUT ABOUT THE 13-DAY RULE WHEN HIGUCHI WAS CAPTURED.
AND THAT PERSON IS...
...THE PRESENT L.
...
RIGHT?
...
RIGHT.
WELL, TO BE EXACT, THERE WAS ANOTHER PERSON CONFINED, TOO... THE ONE WHO WAS CALLED THE SECOND KIRA.
AH, THE ONE THAT GATHERED A LOT OF ATTENTION WITH SAKURA TV...

READ THIS WAY

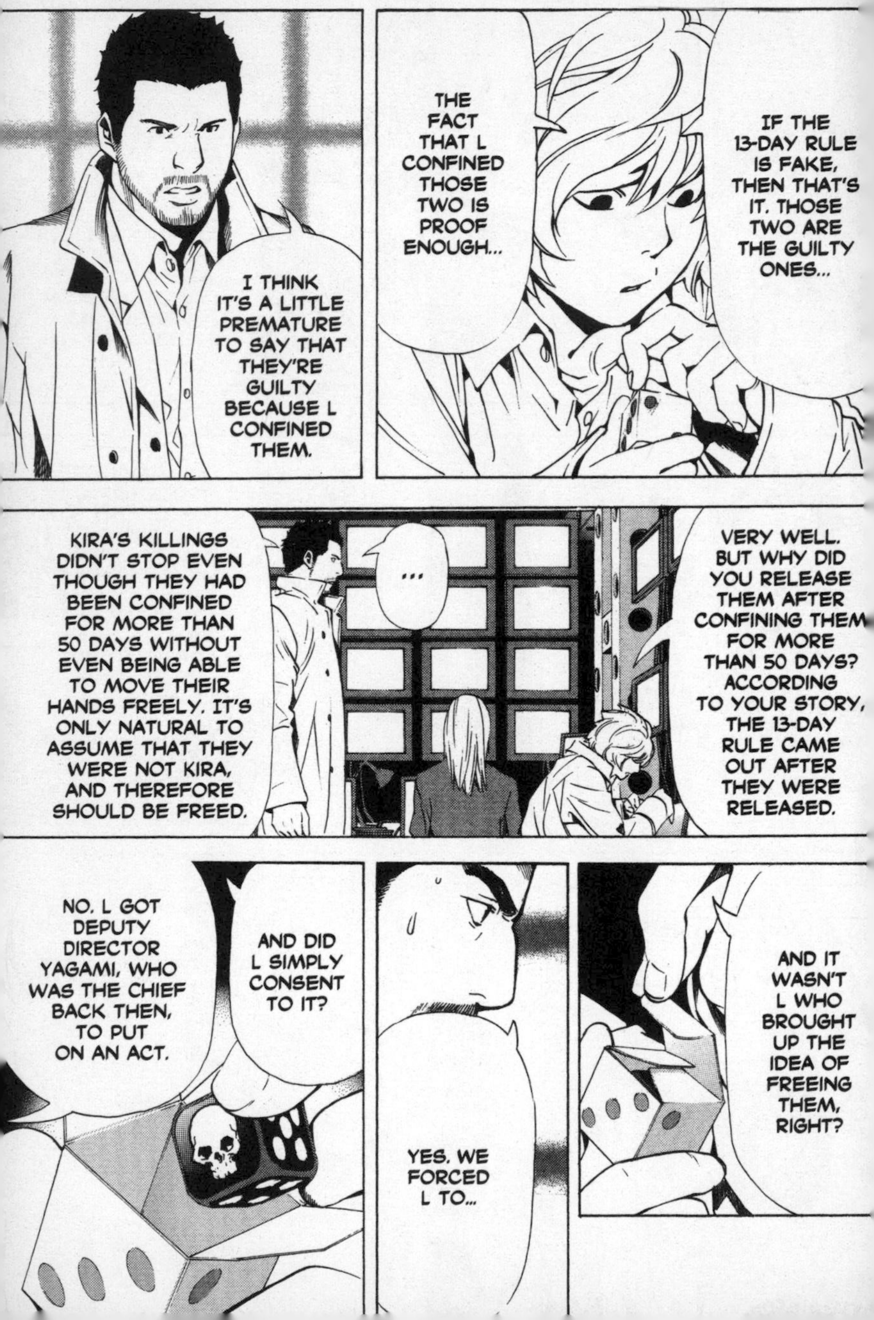
IF THE 13-DAY RULE IS FAKE, THEN THAT'S IT. THOSE TWO ARE THE GUILTY ONES...
THE FACT THAT L CONFINED THOSE TWO IS PROOF ENOUGH...
I THINK IT'S A LITTLE PREMATURE TO SAY THAT THEY'RE GUILTY BECAUSE L CONFINED THEM.
KIRA'S KILLINGS DIDN'T STOP EVEN THOUGH THEY HAD BEEN CONFINED FOR MORE THAN 50 DAYS WITHOUT EVEN BEING ABLE TO MOVE THEIR HANDS FREELY. IT'S ONLY NATURAL TO ASSUME THAT THEY WERE NOT KIRA, AND THEREFORE SHOULD BE FREED.
...
VERY WELL. BUT WHY DID YOU RELEASE THEM AFTER CONFINING THEM FOR MORE THAN 50 DAYS? ACCORDING TO YOUR STORY, THE 13-DAY RULE CAME OUT AFTER THEY WERE RELEASED.
AND IT WASN'T L WHO BROUGHT UP THE IDEA OF FREEING THEM, RIGHT?
YES. WE FORCED L TO...
AND DID L SIMPLY CONSENT TO IT?
NO. L GOT DEPUTY DIRECTOR YAGAMI, WHO WAS THE CHIEF BACK THEN, TO PUT ON AN ACT.

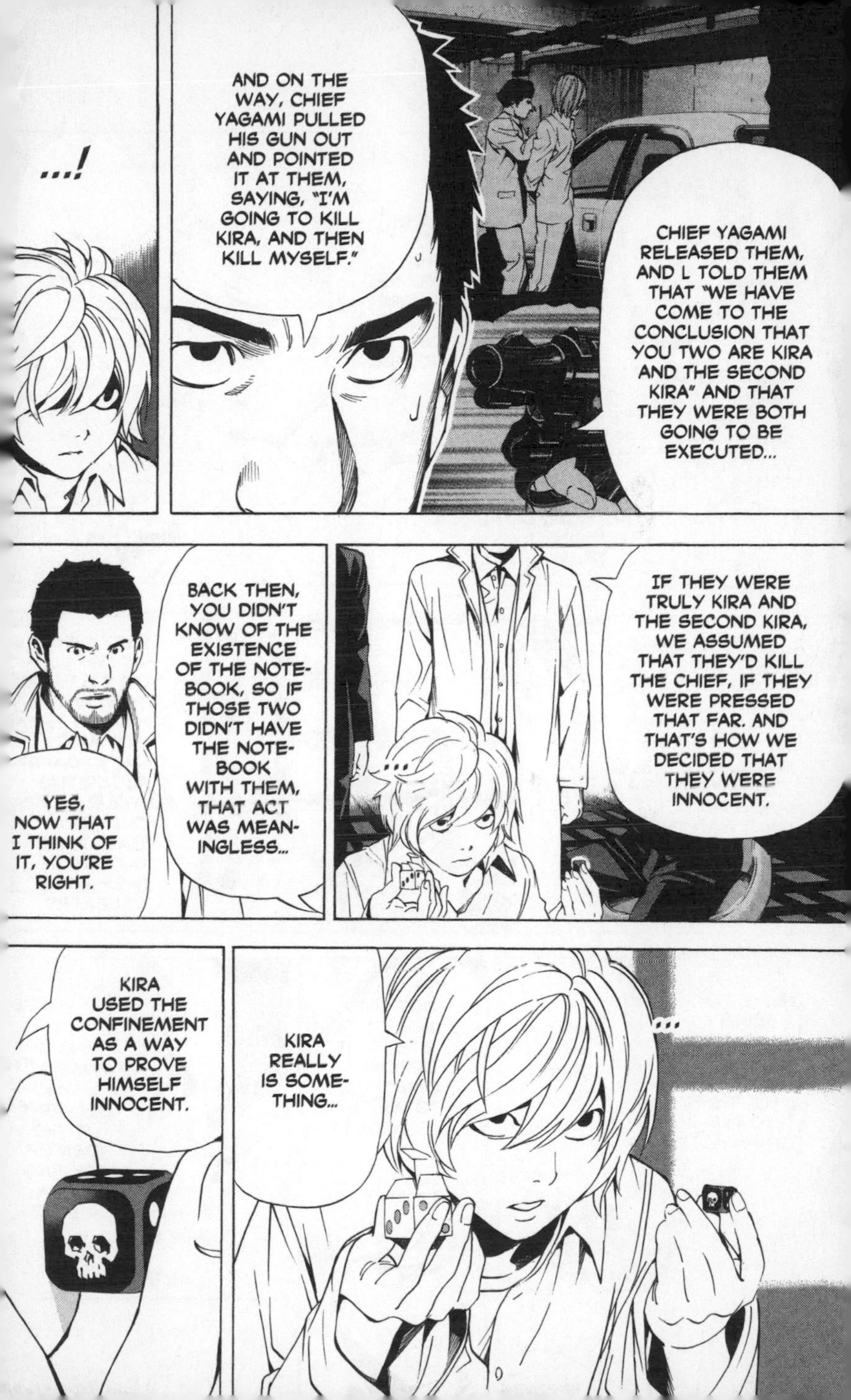
AND ON THE WAY, CHIEF YAGAMI PULLED HIS GUN OUT AND POINTED IT AT THEM, SAYING, "I'M GOING TO KILL KIRA, AND THEN KILL MYSELF."
CHIEF YAGAMI RELEASED THEM, AND L TOLD THEM THAT "WE HAVE COME TO THE CONCLUSION THAT YOU TWO ARE KIRA AND THE SECOND KIRA" AND THAT THEY WERE BOTH GOING TO BE EXECUTED...
...!
IF THEY WERE TRULY KIRA AND THE SECOND KIRA, WE ASSUMED THAT THEY'D KILL THE CHIEF, IF THEY WERE PRESSED THAT FAR. AND THAT'S HOW WE DECIDED THAT THEY WERE INNOCENT.
...
BACK THEN, YOU DIDN'T KNOW OF THE EXISTENCE OF THE NOTE-BOOK, SO IF THOSE TWO DIDN'T HAVE THE NOTE-BOOK WITH THEM, THAT ACT WAS MEAN-INGLESS...
YES, NOW THAT I THINK OF IT, YOU'RE RIGHT.
...
KIRA REALLY IS SOME-THING...
KIRA USED THE CONFINEMENT AS A WAY TO PROVE HIMSELF INNOCENT.

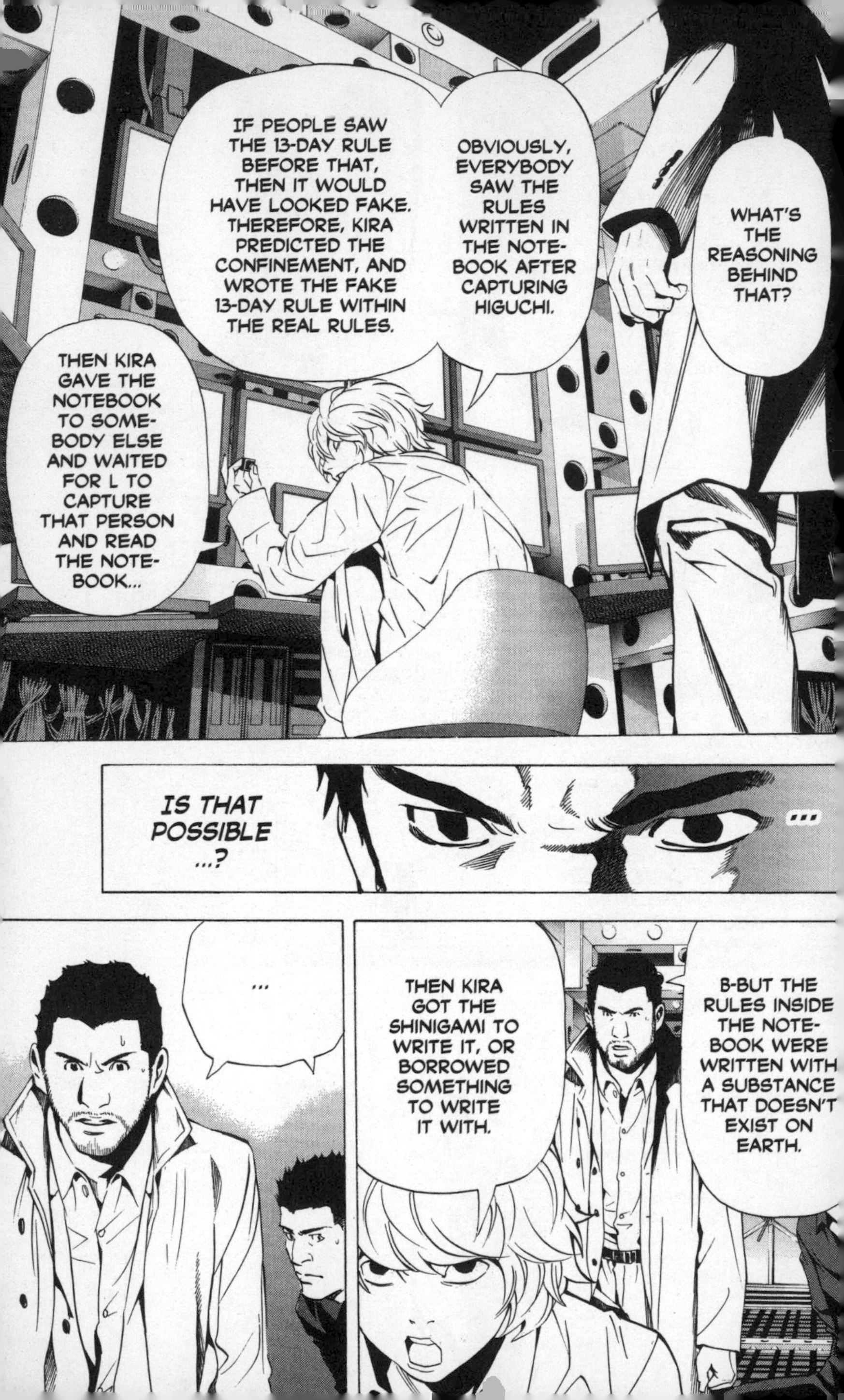
WHAT'S THE REASONING BEHIND THAT?
OBVIOUSLY, EVERYBODY SAW THE RULES WRITTEN IN THE NOTE-BOOK AFTER CAPTURING HIGUCHI.
IF PEOPLE SAW THE 13-DAY RULE BEFORE THAT, THEN IT WOULD HAVE LOOKED FAKE. THEREFORE, KIRA PREDICTED THE CONFINEMENT, AND WROTE THE FAKE 13-DAY RULE WITHIN THE REAL RULES.
THEN KIRA GAVE THE NOTEBOOK TO SOME-BODY ELSE AND WAITED FOR L TO CAPTURE THAT PERSON AND READ THE NOTE-BOOK...
...
IS THAT POSSIBLE ...?
B-BUT THE RULES INSIDE THE NOTE-BOOK WERE WRITTEN WITH A SUBSTANCE THAT DOESN'T EXIST ON EARTH.
THEN KIRA GOT THE SHINIGAMI TO WRITE IT, OR BORROWED SOMETHING TO WRITE IT WITH.
...

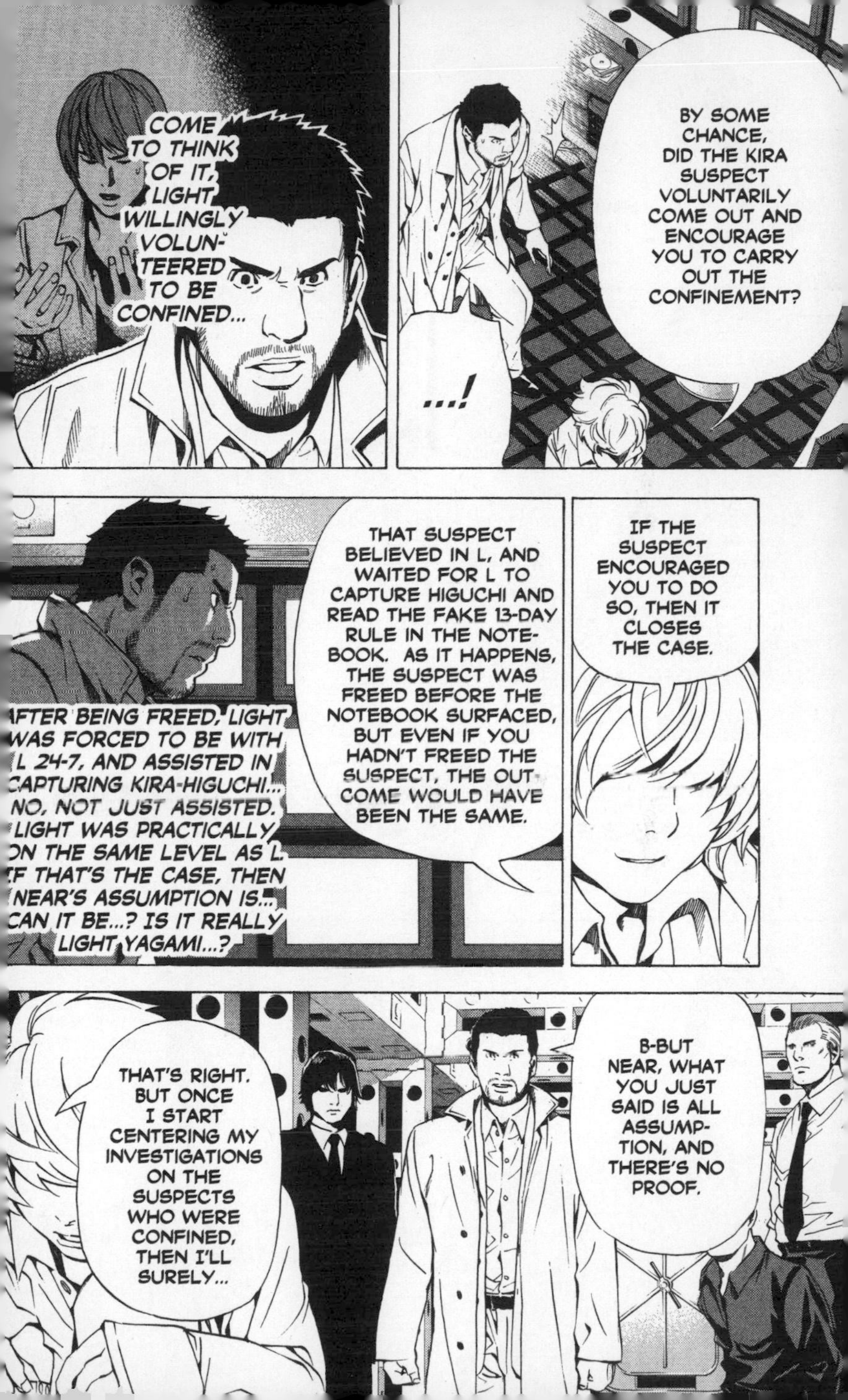

BY SOME CHANCE, DID THE KIRA SUSPECT VOLUNTARILY COME OUT AND ENCOURAGE YOU TO CARRY OUT THE CONFINEMENT?
...!
COME TO THINK OF IT, LIGHT WILLINGLY VOLUNTEERED TO BE CONFINED...
IF THE SUSPECT ENCOURAGED YOU TO DO SO, THEN IT CLOSES THE CASE.
THAT SUSPECT BELIEVED IN L, AND WAITED FOR L TO CAPTURE HIGUCHI AND READ THE FAKE 13-DAY RULE IN THE NOTEBOOK. AS IT HAPPENS, THE SUSPECT WAS FREED BEFORE THE NOTEBOOK SURFACED, BUT EVEN IF YOU HADN'T FREED THE SUSPECT, THE OUTCOME WOULD HAVE BEEN THE SAME.
AFTER BEING FREED, LIGHT WAS FORCED TO BE WITH L 24-7, AND ASSISTED IN CAPTURING KIRA-HIGUCHI... NO, NOT JUST ASSISTED. LIGHT WAS PRACTICALLY ON THE SAME LEVEL AS L. IF THAT'S THE CASE, THEN NEAR'S ASSUMPTION IS... CAN IT BE...? IS IT REALLY LIGHT YAGAMI...?
B-BUT NEAR, WHAT YOU JUST SAID IS ALL ASSUMPTION, AND THERE'S NO PROOF.
THAT'S RIGHT. BUT ONCE I START CENTERING MY INVESTIGATIONS ON THE SUSPECTS WHO WERE CONFINED, THEN I'LL SURELY...

READ THIS WAY

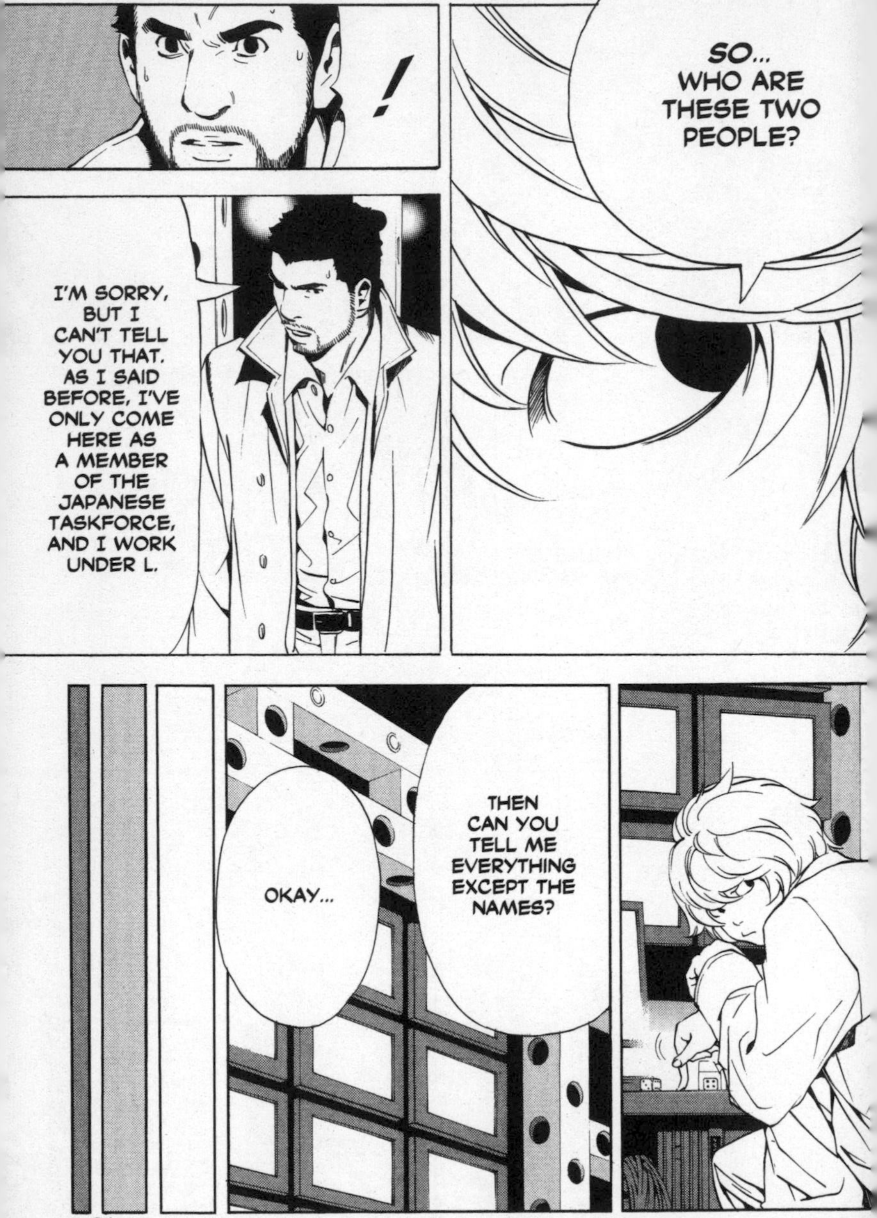
SO... WHO ARE THESE TWO PEOPLE?
!
I'M SORRY, BUT I CAN'T TELL YOU THAT. AS I SAID BEFORE, I'VE ONLY COME HERE AS A MEMBER OF THE JAPANESE TASKFORCE, AND I WORK UNDER L.
THEN CAN YOU TELL ME EVERYTHING EXCEPT THE NAMES?
OKAY...

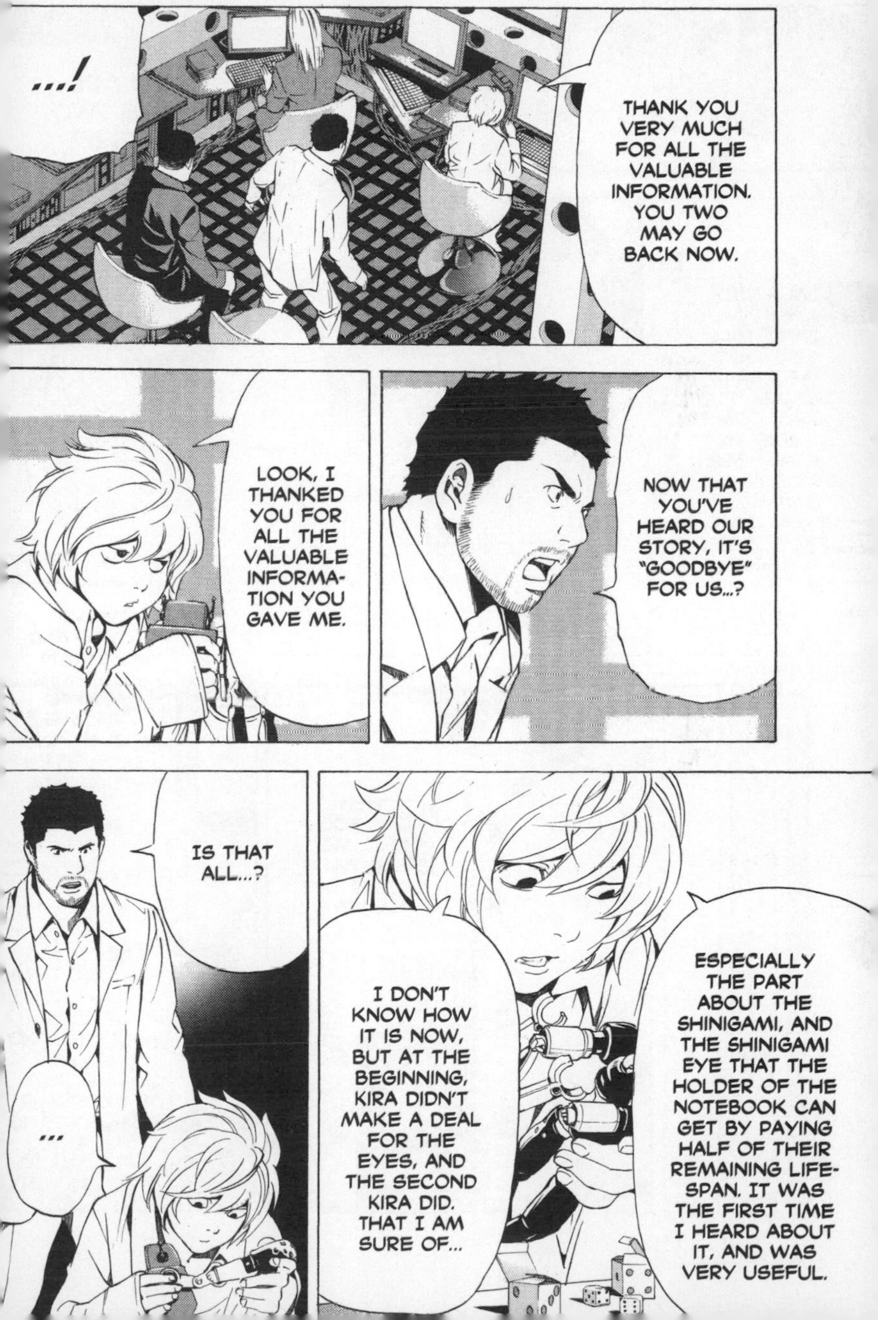
THANK YOU VERY MUCH FOR ALL THE VALUABLE INFORMATION. YOU TWO MAY GO BACK NOW.
....!
NOW THAT YOU'VE HEARD OUR STORY, IT'S "GOODBYE" FOR US...?
LOOK, I THANKED YOU FOR ALL THE VALUABLE INFORMATION YOU GAVE ME.
ESPECIALLY THE PART ABOUT THE SHINIGAMI, AND THE SHINIGAMI EYE THAT THE HOLDER OF THE NOTEBOOK CAN GET BY PAYING HALF OF THEIR REMAINING LIFE-SPAN. IT WAS THE FIRST TIME I HEARD ABOUT IT, AND WAS VERY USEFUL.
I DON'T KNOW HOW IT IS NOW, BUT AT THE BEGINNING, KIRA DIDN'T MAKE A DEAL FOR THE EYES, AND THE SECOND KIRA DID. THAT I AM SURE OF...
IS THAT ALL...?
...

READ THIS WAY

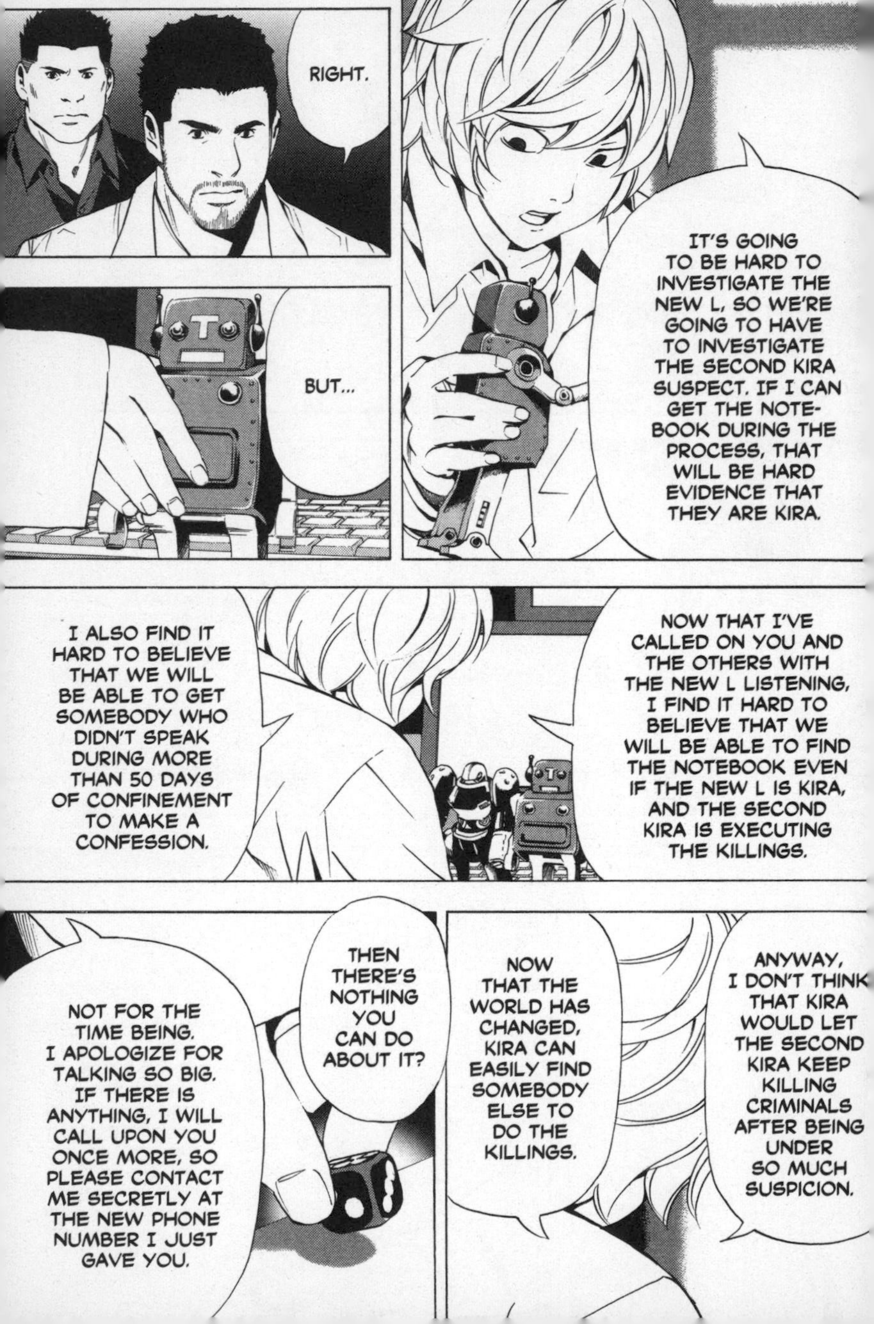
IT'S GOING TO BE HARD TO INVESTIGATE THE NEW L, SO WE'RE GOING TO HAVE TO INVESTIGATE THE SECOND KIRA SUSPECT. IF I CAN GET THE NOTE-BOOK DURING THE PROCESS, THAT WILL BE HARD EVIDENCE THAT THEY ARE KIRA.
RIGHT.
BUT...
NOW THAT I'VE CALLED ON YOU AND THE OTHERS WITH THE NEW L LISTENING, I FIND IT HARD TO BELIEVE THAT WE WILL BE ABLE TO FIND THE NOTEBOOK EVEN IF THE NEW L IS KIRA, AND THE SECOND KIRA IS EXECUTING THE KILLINGS.
I ALSO FIND IT HARD TO BELIEVE THAT WE WILL BE ABLE TO GET SOMEBODY WHO DIDN'T SPEAK DURING MORE THAN 50 DAYS OF CONFINEMENT TO MAKE A CONFESSION.
ANYWAY, I DON'T THINK THAT KIRA WOULD LET THE SECOND KIRA KEEP KILLING CRIMINALS AFTER BEING UNDER SO MUCH SUSPICION.
NOW THAT THE WORLD HAS CHANGED, KIRA CAN EASILY FIND SOMEBODY ELSE TO DO THE KILLINGS.
THEN THERE'S NOTHING YOU CAN DO ABOUT IT?
NOT FOR THE TIME BEING. I APOLOGIZE FOR TALKING SO BIG. IF THERE IS ANYTHING, I WILL CALL UPON YOU ONCE MORE, SO PLEASE CONTACT ME SECRETLY AT THE NEW PHONE NUMBER I JUST GAVE YOU.

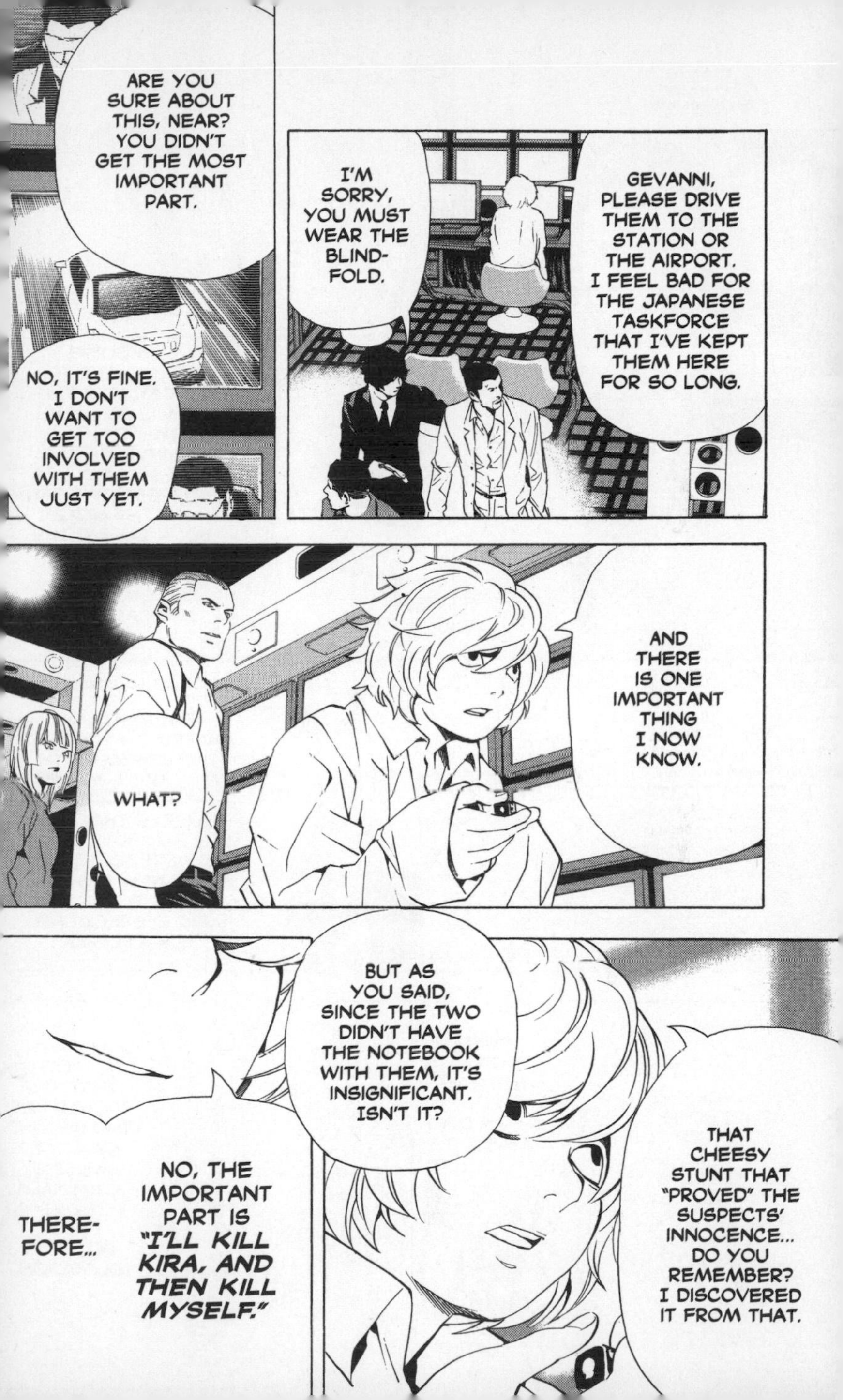
GEVANNI, PLEASE DRIVE THEM TO THE STATION OR THE AIRPORT. I FEEL BAD FOR THE JAPANESE TASKFORCE THAT I'VE KEPT THEM HERE FOR SO LONG.
I'M SORRY, YOU MUST WEAR THE BLIND-FOLD.
ARE YOU SURE ABOUT THIS, NEAR? YOU DIDN'T GET THE MOST IMPORTANT PART.
NO, IT'S FINE. I DON'T WANT TO GET TOO INVOLVED WITH THEM JUST YET.
AND THERE IS ONE IMPORTANT THING I NOW KNOW.
WHAT?
BUT AS YOU SAID, SINCE THE TWO DIDN'T HAVE THE NOTEBOOK WITH THEM, IT'S INSIGNIFICANT. ISN'T IT?
THAT CHEESY STUNT THAT "PROVED" THE SUSPECTS' INNOCENCE... DO YOU REMEMBER? I DISCOVERED IT FROM THAT.
NO, THE IMPORTANT PART IS *"I'LL KILL KIRA, AND THEN KILL MYSELF."*
THERE-FORE...

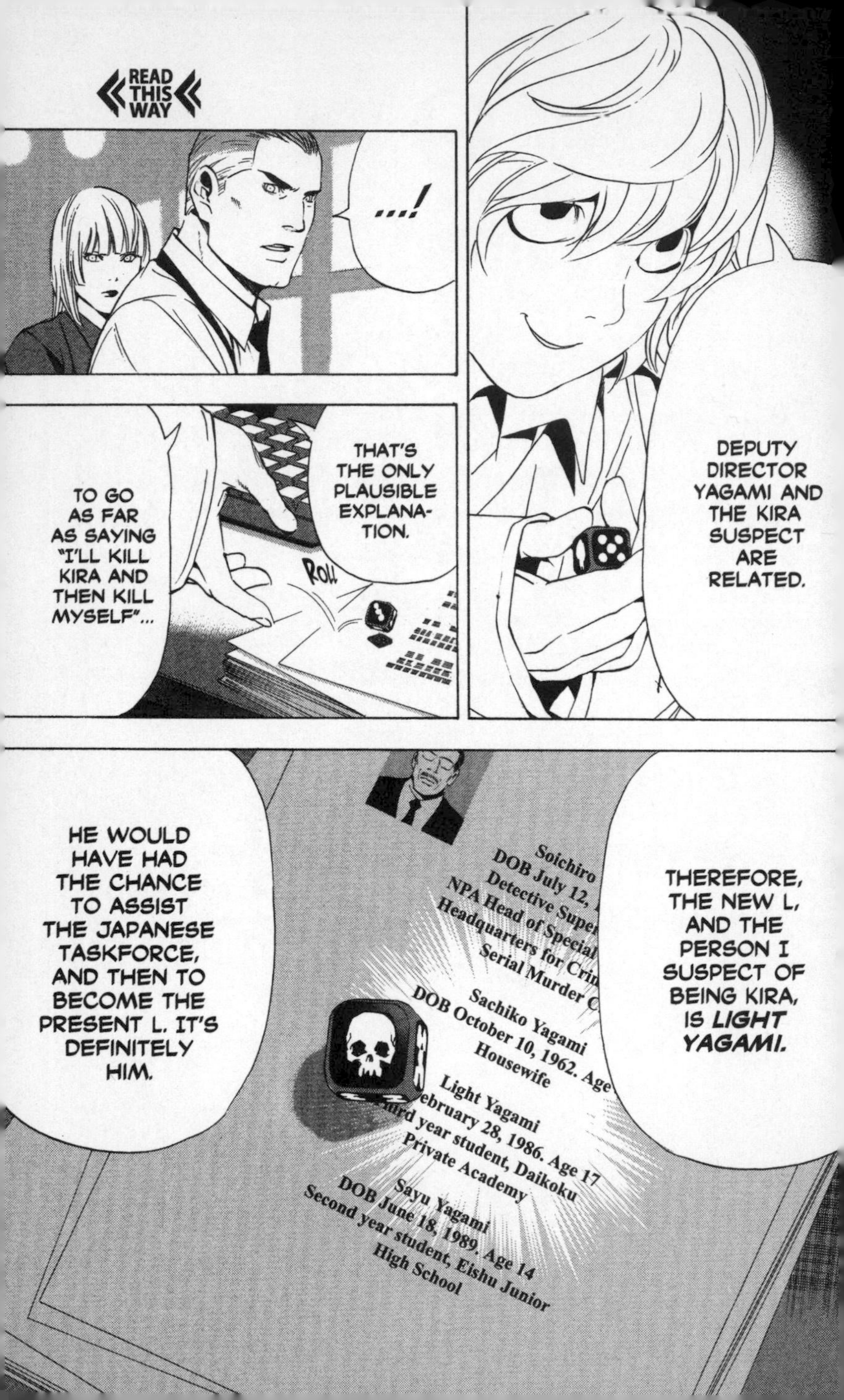
READ THIS WAY
DEPUTY DIRECTOR YAGAMI AND THE KIRA SUSPECT ARE RELATED.
...!
THAT'S THE ONLY PLAUSIBLE EXPLANATION.
TO GO AS FAR AS SAYING "I'LL KILL KIRA AND THEN KILL MYSELF"...
ROll
THEREFORE, THE NEW L, AND THE PERSON I SUSPECT OF BEING KIRA, IS *LIGHT YAGAMI.*
Soichiro
DOB July 12,
Detective Super
NPA Head of Special
Headquarters for Crin
Serial Murder C
Sachiko Yagami
DOB October 10, 1962. Age
Housewife
Light Yagami
ebruary 28, 1986. Age 17
hird year student, Daikoku
Private Academy
Sayu Yagami
DOB June 18, 1989. Age 14
Second year student, Eishu Junior
High School
HE WOULD HAVE HAD THE CHANCE TO ASSIST THE JAPANESE TASKFORCE, AND THEN TO BECOME THE PRESENT L. IT'S DEFINITELY HIM.

DEATH NOTE

How to use it

LV

- In occasions where the cause and situation of death is written before the victim's name, multiple names can be written as long as they are written within 40 seconds and the causes and situations of the death are not impossible to occur.

死因や死の状況を先に記しておき名前を後から記す場合、
その名前が複数でも40秒以内に記せば何人でも、
その死因や状況に不可能がなければその通りになる。

- In the occasion where the cause of death is possible but the situation is not, only the cause of death will take effect for that victim. If both the cause and the situation are impossible, that victim will die of heart attack.

死因は可能だが状況は不可能である名前がある場合、
その名前に対しては死因のみが適用され、双方が不可能な名前があれば、
その人間は心臓麻痺となる。

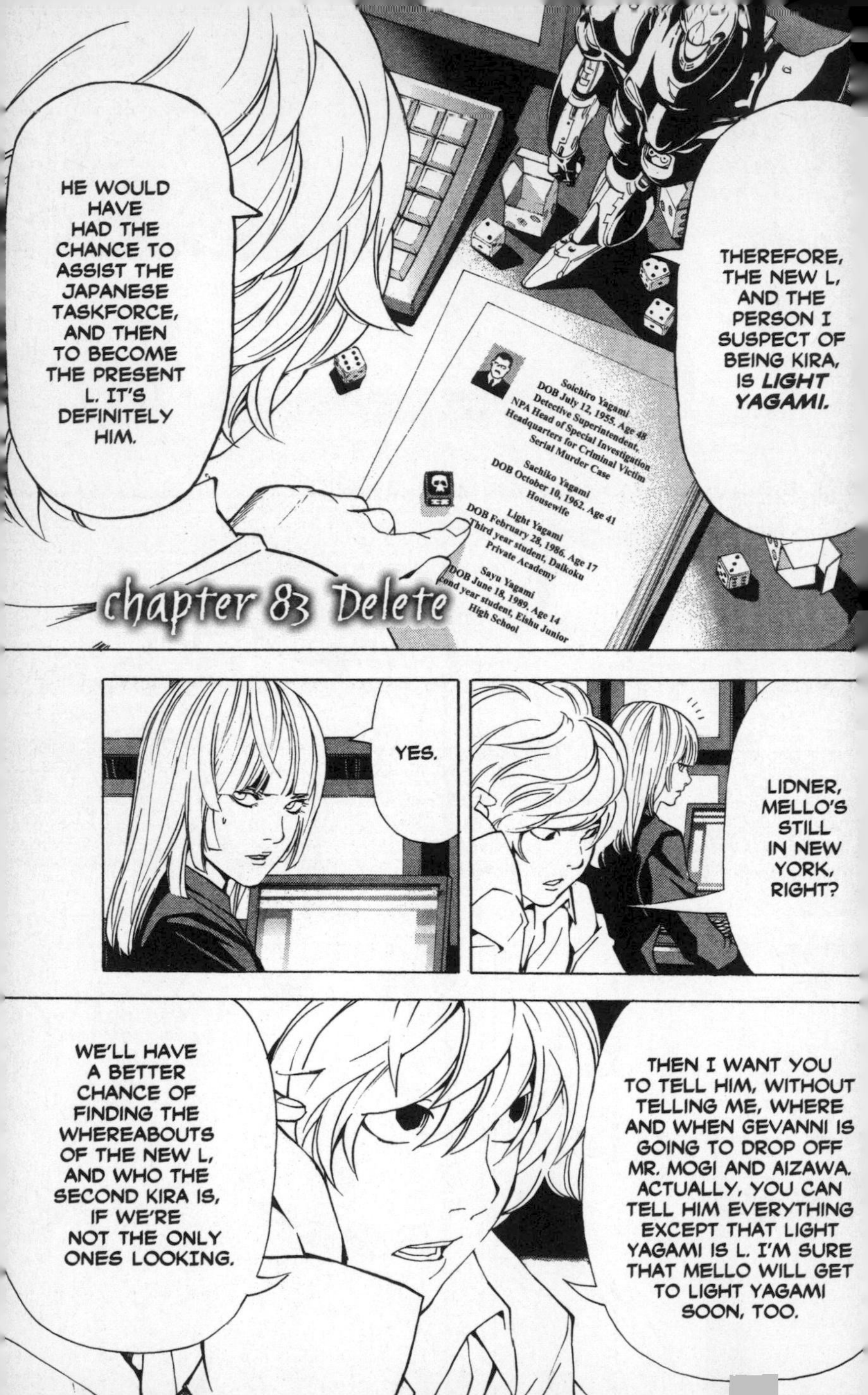
THEREFORE, THE NEW L, AND THE PERSON I SUSPECT OF BEING KIRA, IS *LIGHT YAGAMI.*
HE WOULD HAVE HAD THE CHANCE TO ASSIST THE JAPANESE TASKFORCE, AND THEN TO BECOME THE PRESENT L. IT'S DEFINITELY HIM.
Soichiro Yagami DOB July 12, 1955. Age 48 Detective Superintendent, NPA Head of Special Investigation Headquarters for Criminal Victim Serial Murder Case
Sachiko Yagami DOB October 10, 1962. Age 41 Housewife
Light Yagami DOB February 28, 1986. Age 17 Third year student, Daikoku Private Academy
Sayu Yagami DOB June 18, 1989. Age 14 ...cond year student, Eishu Junior High School
chapter 83 Delete
LIDNER, MELLO'S STILL IN NEW YORK, RIGHT?
YES.
THEN I WANT YOU TO TELL HIM, WITHOUT TELLING ME, WHERE AND WHEN GEVANNI IS GOING TO DROP OFF MR. MOGI AND AIZAWA. ACTUALLY, YOU CAN TELL HIM EVERYTHING EXCEPT THAT LIGHT YAGAMI IS L. I'M SURE THAT MELLO WILL GET TO LIGHT YAGAMI SOON, TOO.
WE'LL HAVE A BETTER CHANCE OF FINDING THE WHEREABOUTS OF THE NEW L, AND WHO THE SECOND KIRA IS, IF WE'RE NOT THE ONLY ONES LOOKING.

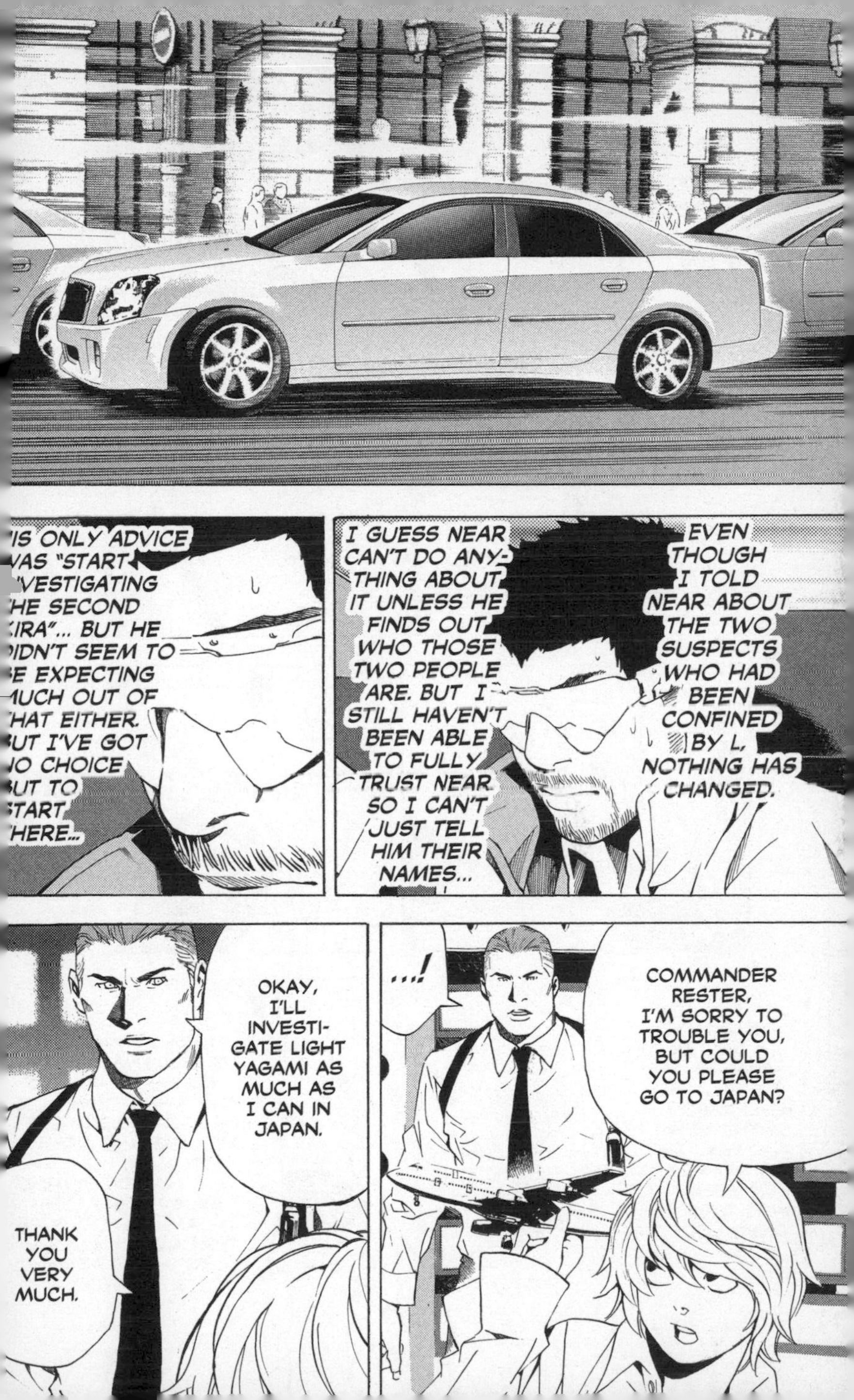
EVEN THOUGH I TOLD NEAR ABOUT THE TWO SUSPECTS WHO HAD BEEN CONFINED BY L, NOTHING HAS CHANGED.
I GUESS NEAR CAN'T DO ANYTHING ABOUT IT UNLESS HE FINDS OUT WHO THOSE TWO PEOPLE ARE. BUT I STILL HAVEN'T BEEN ABLE TO FULLY TRUST NEAR SO I CAN'T JUST TELL HIM THEIR NAMES...
IS ONLY ADVICE VAS "START VESTIGATING HE SECOND IRA"... BUT HE IDN'T SEEM TO E EXPECTING MUCH OUT OF HAT EITHER. UT I'VE GOT O CHOICE UT TO TART HERE...
COMMANDER RESTER, I'M SORRY TO TROUBLE YOU, BUT COULD YOU PLEASE GO TO JAPAN?
...!
OKAY, I'LL INVESTIGATE LIGHT YAGAMI AS MUCH AS I CAN IN JAPAN.
THANK YOU VERY MUCH.

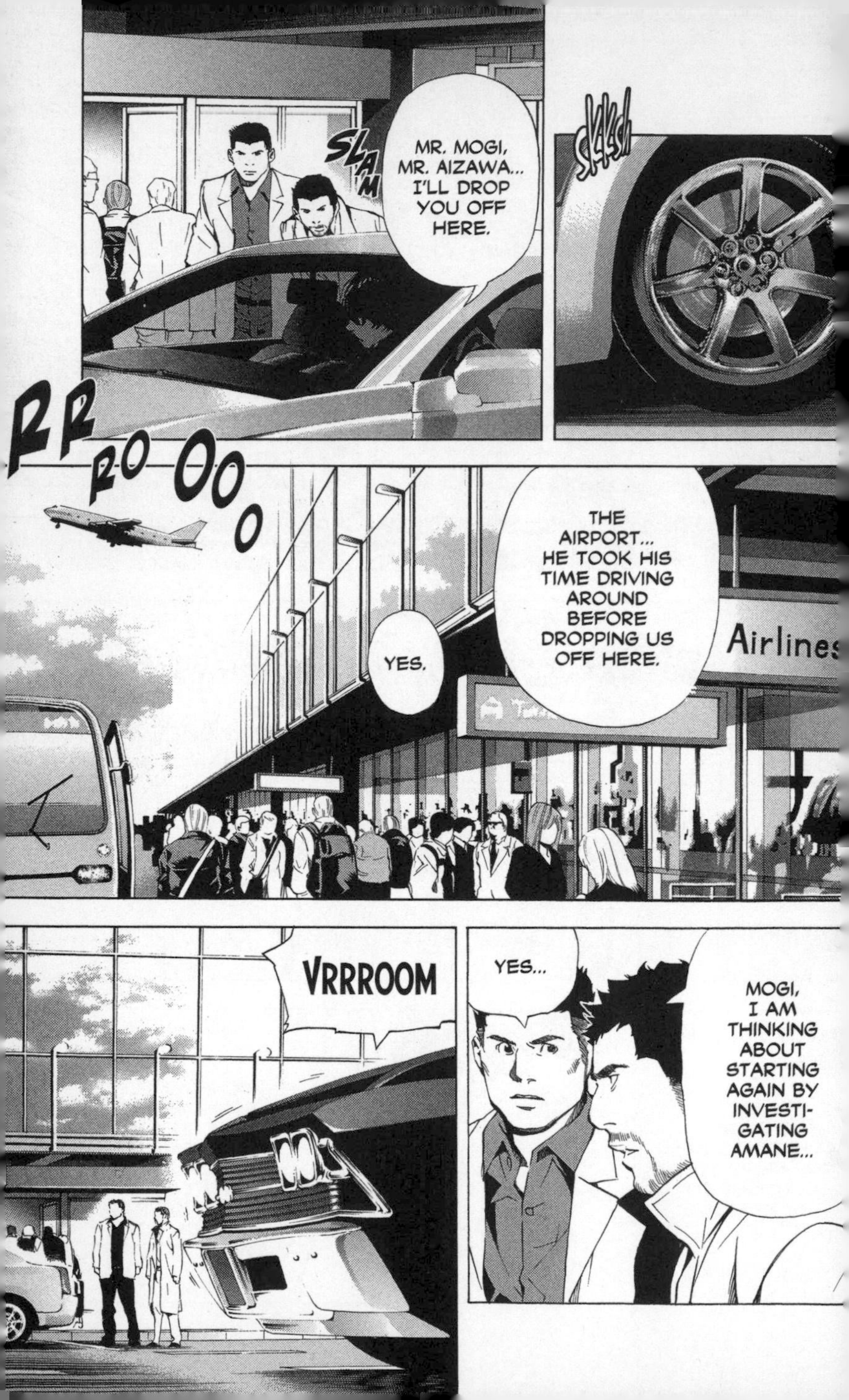
SLAM
MR. MOGI, MR. AIZAWA... I'LL DROP YOU OFF HERE.
RRROOOO
THE AIRPORT... HE TOOK HIS TIME DRIVING AROUND BEFORE DROPPING US OFF HERE.
YES.
Airlines
MOGI, I AM THINKING ABOUT STARTING AGAIN BY INVESTI-GATING AMANE...
YES...
VRRROOM

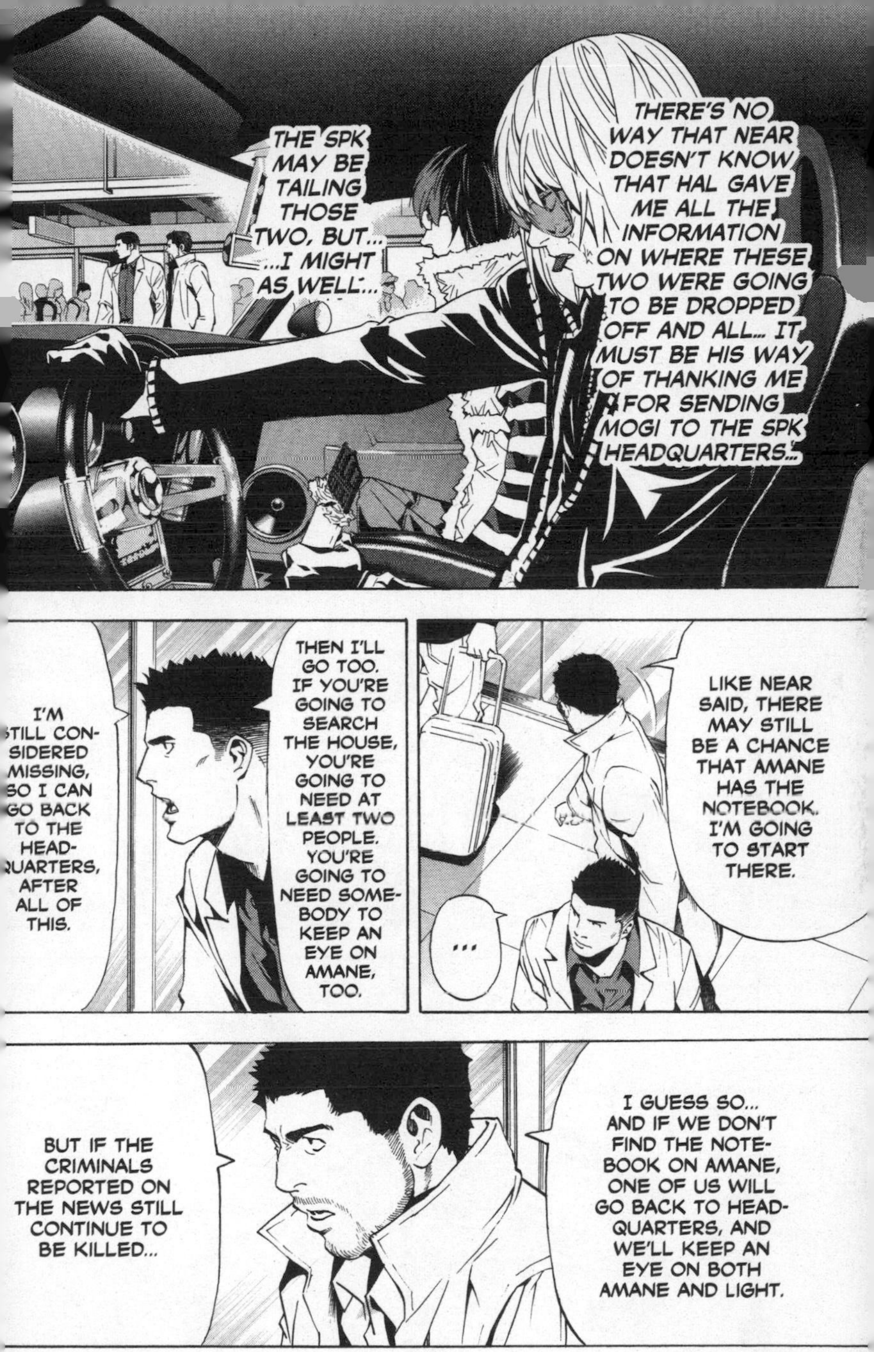
THERE'S NO WAY THAT NEAR DOESN'T KNOW THAT HAL GAVE ME ALL THE INFORMATION ON WHERE THESE TWO WERE GOING TO BE DROPPED OFF AND ALL... IT MUST BE HIS WAY OF THANKING ME FOR SENDING MOGI TO THE SPK HEADQUARTERS...
THE SPK MAY BE TAILING THOSE TWO, BUT... ...I MIGHT AS WELL...
LIKE NEAR SAID, THERE MAY STILL BE A CHANCE THAT AMANE HAS THE NOTEBOOK. I'M GOING TO START THERE.
...
THEN I'LL GO TOO. IF YOU'RE GOING TO SEARCH THE HOUSE, YOU'RE GOING TO NEED AT LEAST TWO PEOPLE. YOU'RE GOING TO NEED SOME-BODY TO KEEP AN EYE ON AMANE, TOO.
I'M STILL CON-SIDERED MISSING, SO I CAN GO BACK TO THE HEAD-QUARTERS, AFTER ALL OF THIS.
I GUESS SO... AND IF WE DON'T FIND THE NOTE-BOOK ON AMANE, ONE OF US WILL GO BACK TO HEAD-QUARTERS, AND WE'LL KEEP AN EYE ON BOTH AMANE AND LIGHT.
BUT IF THE CRIMINALS REPORTED ON THE NEWS STILL CONTINUE TO BE KILLED...

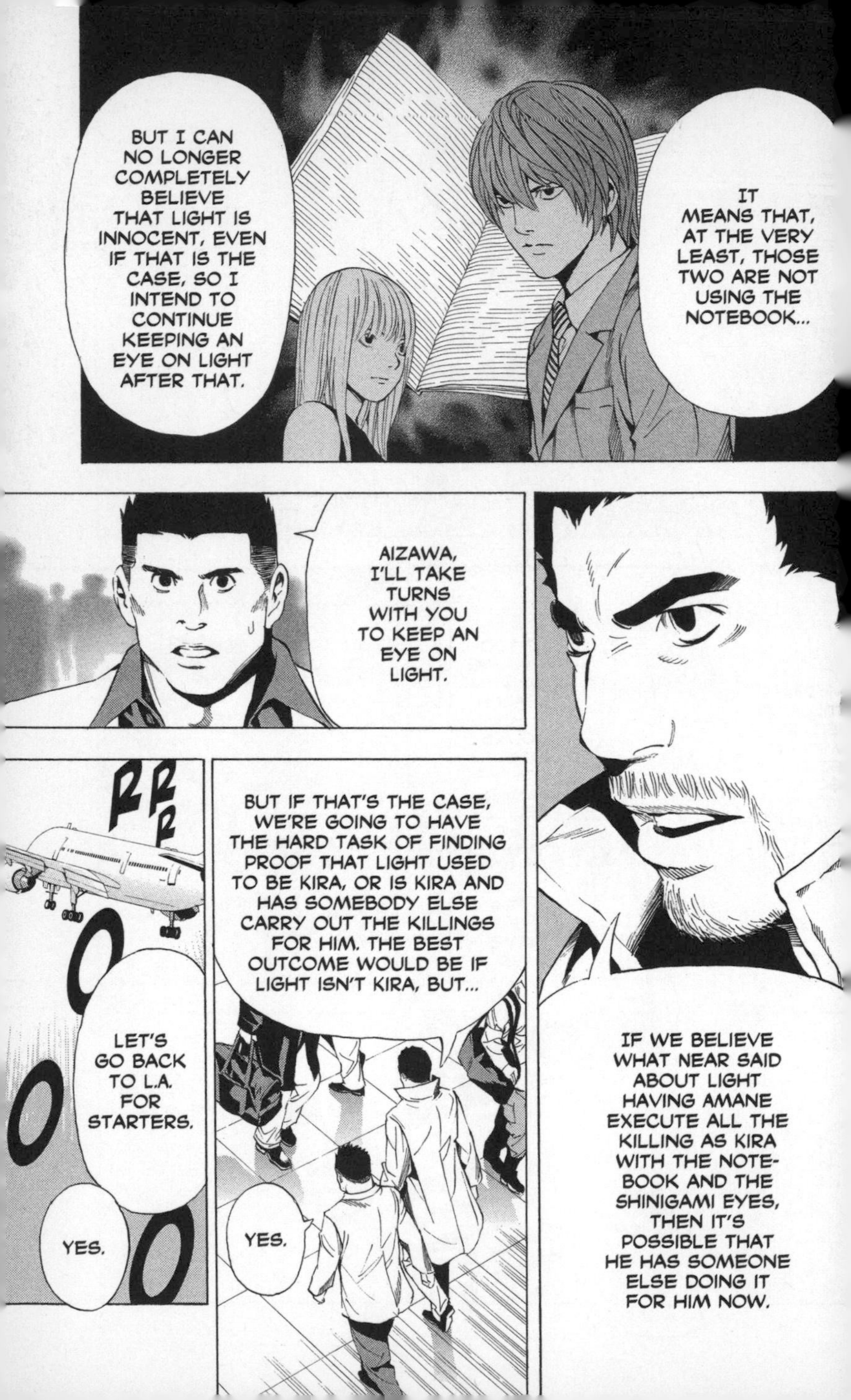
IT MEANS THAT, AT THE VERY LEAST, THOSE TWO ARE NOT USING THE NOTEBOOK...
BUT I CAN NO LONGER COMPLETELY BELIEVE THAT LIGHT IS INNOCENT, EVEN IF THAT IS THE CASE, SO I INTEND TO CONTINUE KEEPING AN EYE ON LIGHT AFTER THAT.
IF WE BELIEVE WHAT NEAR SAID ABOUT LIGHT HAVING AMANE EXECUTE ALL THE KILLING AS KIRA WITH THE NOTE-BOOK AND THE SHINIGAMI EYES, THEN IT'S POSSIBLE THAT HE HAS SOMEONE ELSE DOING IT FOR HIM NOW.
AIZAWA, I'LL TAKE TURNS WITH YOU TO KEEP AN EYE ON LIGHT.
BUT IF THAT'S THE CASE, WE'RE GOING TO HAVE THE HARD TASK OF FINDING PROOF THAT LIGHT USED TO BE KIRA, OR IS KIRA AND HAS SOMEBODY ELSE CARRY OUT THE KILLINGS FOR HIM. THE BEST OUTCOME WOULD BE IF LIGHT ISN'T KIRA, BUT...
YES.
RRR
LET'S GO BACK TO L.A. FOR STARTERS.
YES.

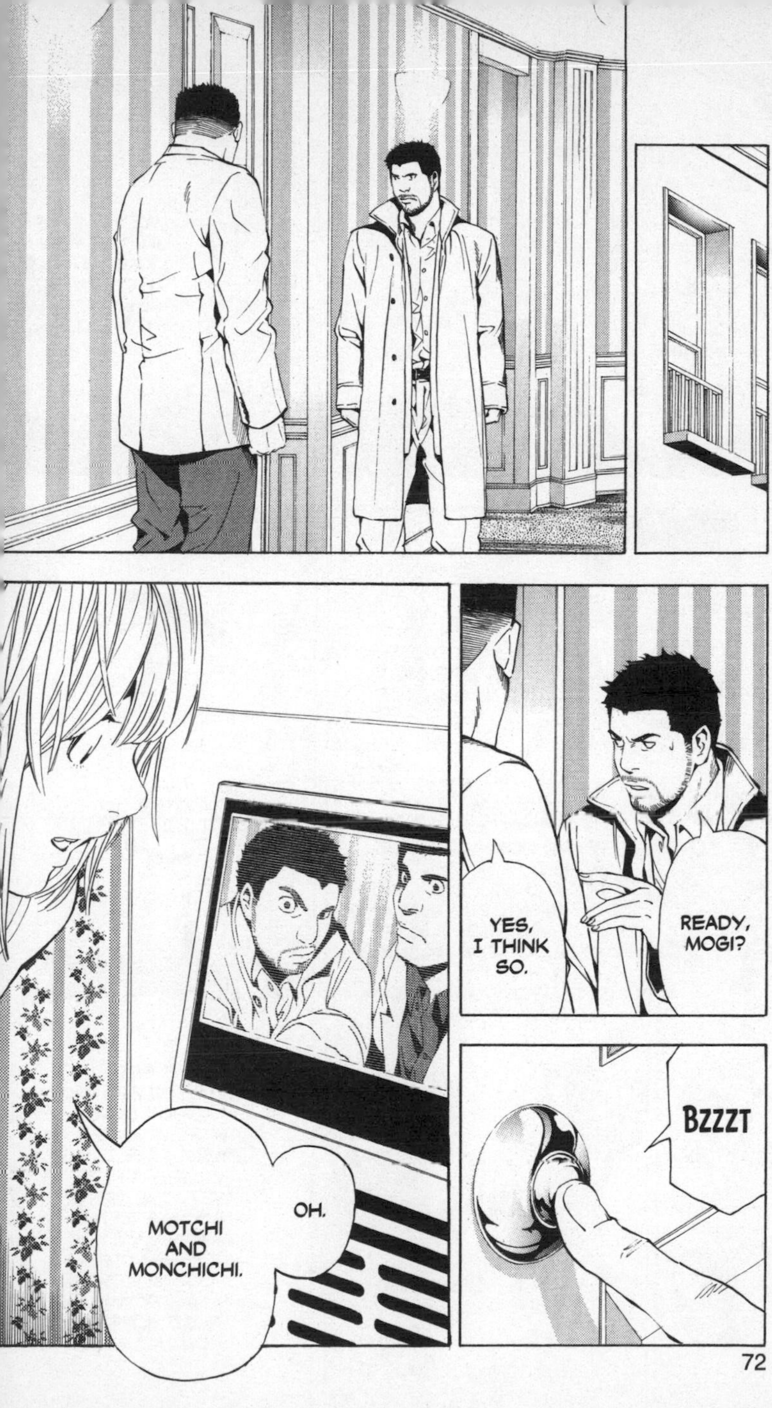
READY, MOGI?
YES, I THINK SO.
BZZZT
OH.
MOTCHI AND MONCHICHI.

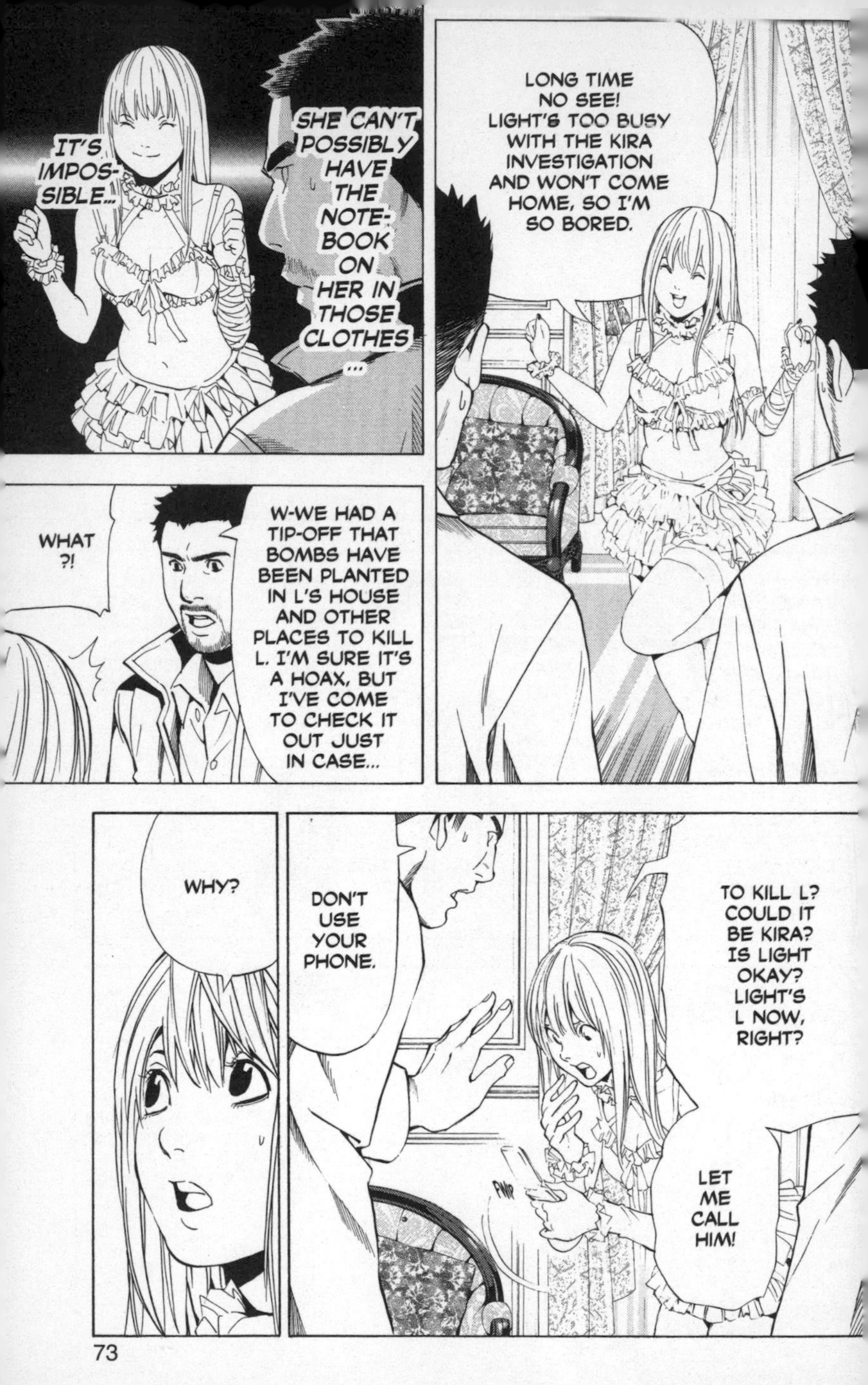

LONG TIME NO SEE! LIGHT'S TOO BUSY WITH THE KIRA INVESTIGATION AND WON'T COME HOME, SO I'M SO BORED.
SHE CAN'T POSSIBLY HAVE THE NOTEBOOK ON HER IN THOSE CLOTHES...
IT'S IMPOSSIBLE...
W-WE HAD A TIP-OFF THAT BOMBS HAVE BEEN PLANTED IN L'S HOUSE AND OTHER PLACES TO KILL L. I'M SURE IT'S A HOAX, BUT I'VE COME TO CHECK IT OUT JUST IN CASE...
WHAT?!
TO KILL L? COULD IT BE KIRA? IS LIGHT OKAY? LIGHT'S L NOW, RIGHT?
LET ME CALL HIM!
DON'T USE YOUR PHONE.
WHY?

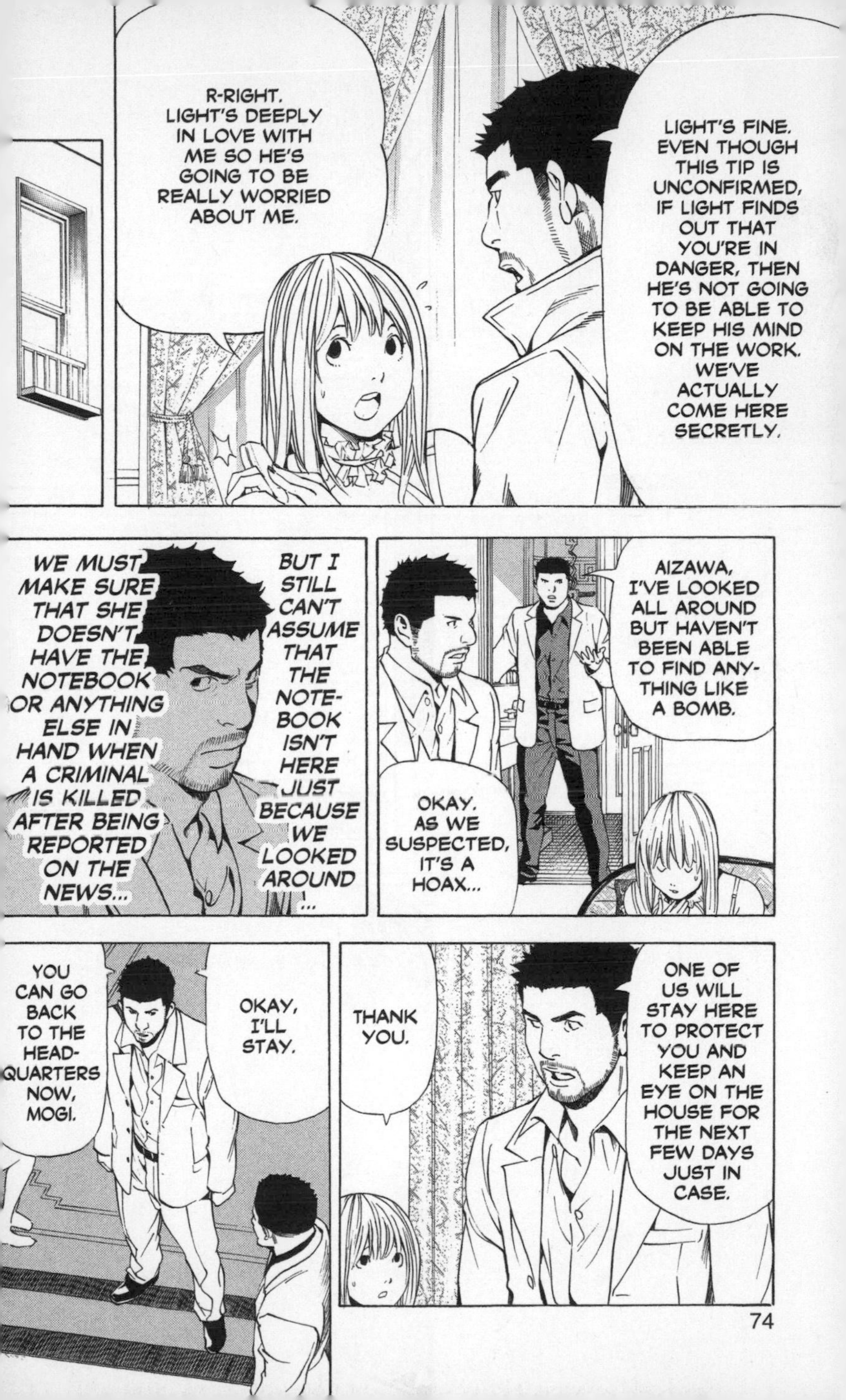
LIGHT'S FINE. EVEN THOUGH THIS TIP IS UNCONFIRMED, IF LIGHT FINDS OUT THAT YOU'RE IN DANGER, THEN HE'S NOT GOING TO BE ABLE TO KEEP HIS MIND ON THE WORK. WE'VE ACTUALLY COME HERE SECRETLY.
R-RIGHT. LIGHT'S DEEPLY IN LOVE WITH ME SO HE'S GOING TO BE REALLY WORRIED ABOUT ME.
AIZAWA, I'VE LOOKED ALL AROUND BUT HAVEN'T BEEN ABLE TO FIND ANYTHING LIKE A BOMB.
OKAY. AS WE SUSPECTED, IT'S A HOAX...
BUT I STILL CAN'T ASSUME THAT THE NOTEBOOK ISN'T HERE JUST BECAUSE WE LOOKED AROUND...
WE MUST MAKE SURE THAT SHE DOESN'T HAVE THE NOTEBOOK OR ANYTHING ELSE IN HAND WHEN A CRIMINAL IS KILLED AFTER BEING REPORTED ON THE NEWS...
ONE OF US WILL STAY HERE TO PROTECT YOU AND KEEP AN EYE ON THE HOUSE FOR THE NEXT FEW DAYS JUST IN CASE.
THANK YOU.
OKAY, I'LL STAY.
YOU CAN GO BACK TO THE HEADQUARTERS NOW, MOGI.

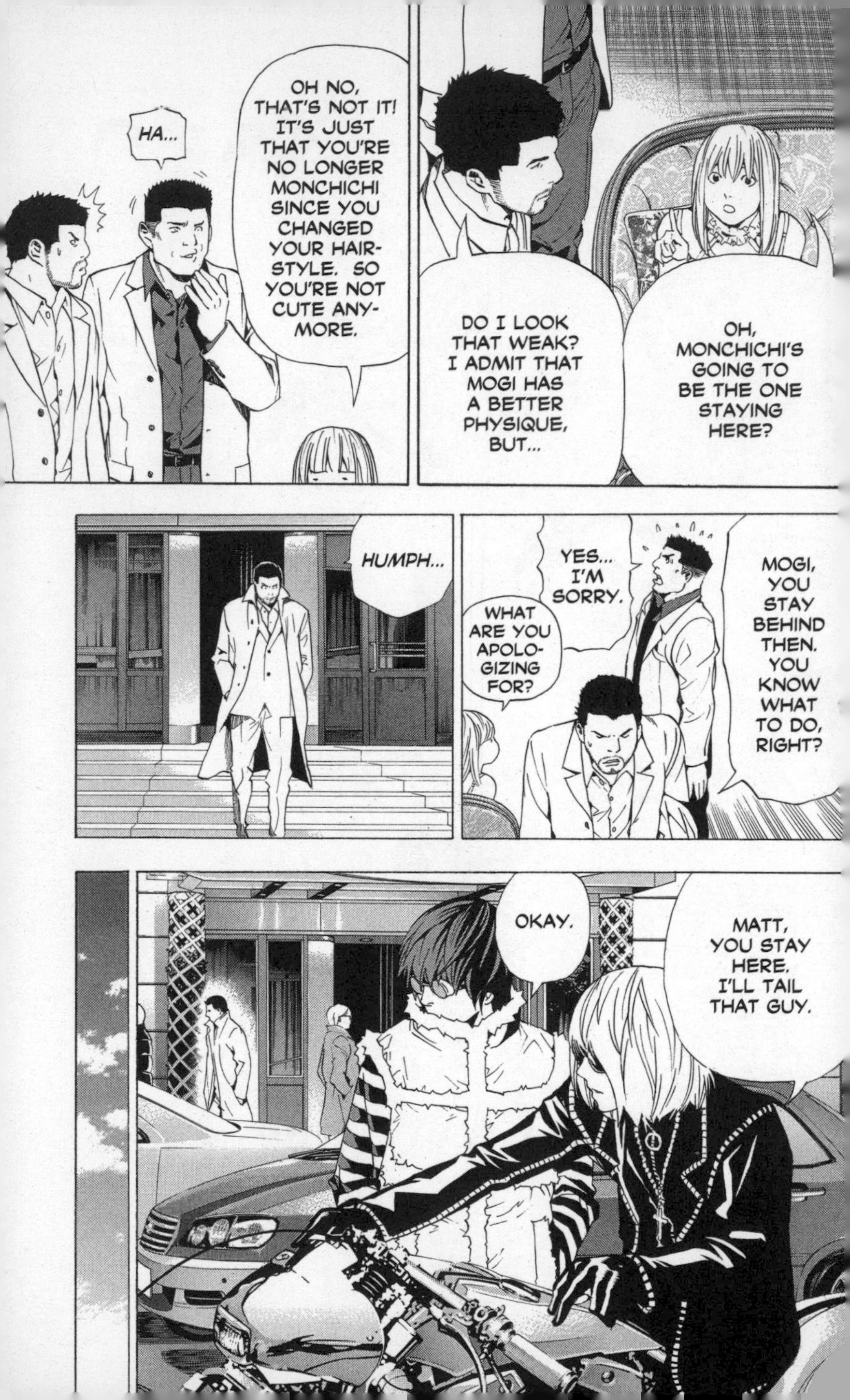
OH, MONCHICHI'S GOING TO BE THE ONE STAYING HERE?
DO I LOOK THAT WEAK? I ADMIT THAT MOGI HAS A BETTER PHYSIQUE, BUT...
OH NO, THAT'S NOT IT! IT'S JUST THAT YOU'RE NO LONGER MONCHICHI SINCE YOU CHANGED YOUR HAIR-STYLE. SO YOU'RE NOT CUTE ANY-MORE.
HA...
MOGI, YOU STAY BEHIND THEN. YOU KNOW WHAT TO DO, RIGHT?
YES... I'M SORRY.
WHAT ARE YOU APOLOGIZING FOR?
HUMPH...
MATT, YOU STAY HERE. I'LL TAIL THAT GUY.
OKAY.

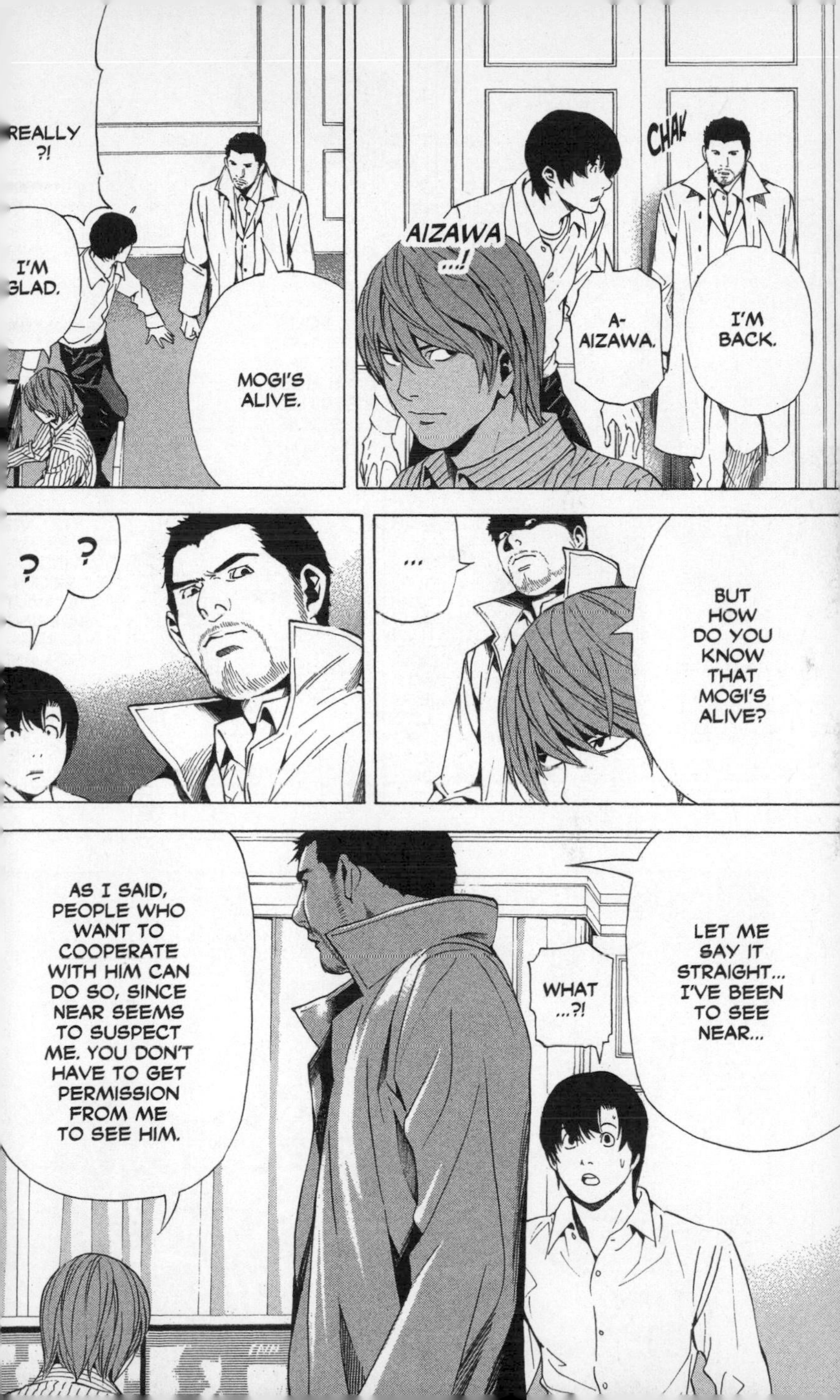
CHAK
I'M BACK.
A-AIZAWA.
AIZAWA ...!
MOGI'S ALIVE.
REALLY ?!
I'M GLAD.
BUT HOW DO YOU KNOW THAT MOGI'S ALIVE?
...
? ?
LET ME SAY IT STRAIGHT... I'VE BEEN TO SEE NEAR...
WHAT ...?!
AS I SAID, PEOPLE WHO WANT TO COOPERATE WITH HIM CAN DO SO, SINCE NEAR SEEMS TO SUSPECT ME. YOU DON'T HAVE TO GET PERMISSION FROM ME TO SEE HIM.

READ THIS WAY

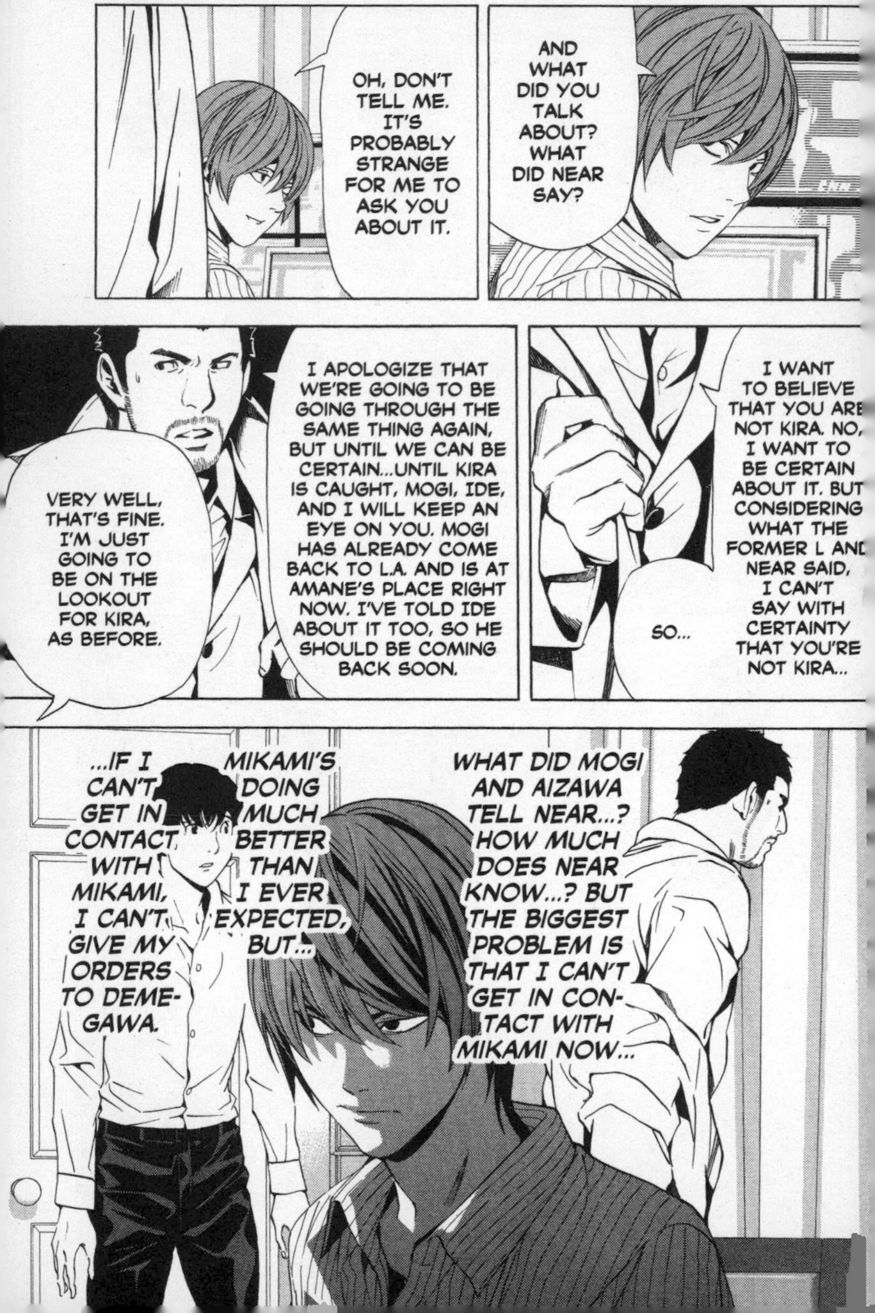
AND WHAT DID YOU TALK ABOUT? WHAT DID NEAR SAY?
OH, DON'T TELL ME. IT'S PROBABLY STRANGE FOR ME TO ASK YOU ABOUT IT.
I WANT TO BELIEVE THAT YOU ARE NOT KIRA. NO, I WANT TO BE CERTAIN ABOUT IT. BUT CONSIDERING WHAT THE FORMER L AND NEAR SAID, I CAN'T SAY WITH CERTAINTY THAT YOU'RE NOT KIRA...
SO...
I APOLOGIZE THAT WE'RE GOING TO BE GOING THROUGH THE SAME THING AGAIN, BUT UNTIL WE CAN BE CERTAIN...UNTIL KIRA IS CAUGHT, MOGI, IDE, AND I WILL KEEP AN EYE ON YOU. MOGI HAS ALREADY COME BACK TO L.A. AND IS AT AMANE'S PLACE RIGHT NOW. I'VE TOLD IDE ABOUT IT TOO, SO HE SHOULD BE COMING BACK SOON.
VERY WELL, THAT'S FINE. I'M JUST GOING TO BE ON THE LOOKOUT FOR KIRA, AS BEFORE.
WHAT DID MOGI AND AIZAWA TELL NEAR...? HOW MUCH DOES NEAR KNOW...? BUT THE BIGGEST PROBLEM IS THAT I CAN'T GET IN CONTACT WITH MIKAMI NOW...
MIKAMI'S DOING MUCH BETTER THAN I EVER EXPECTED, BUT...
...IF I CAN'T GET IN CONTACT WITH MIKAMI, I CAN'T GIVE MY ORDERS TO DEMEGAWA.

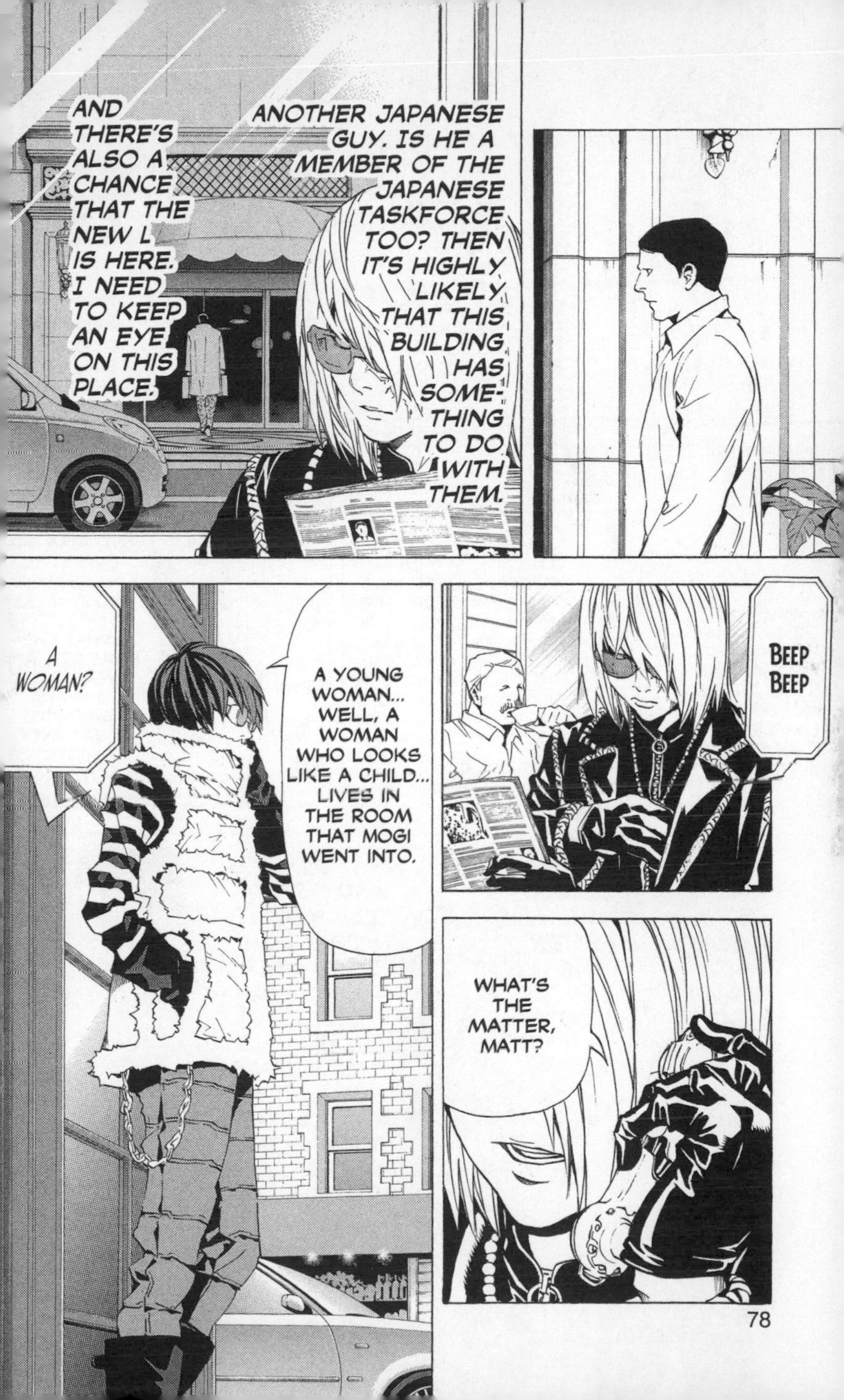
ANOTHER JAPANESE GUY. IS HE A MEMBER OF THE JAPANESE TASKFORCE TOO? THEN IT'S HIGHLY LIKELY THAT THIS BUILDING HAS SOMETHING TO DO WITH THEM.
AND THERE'S ALSO A CHANCE THAT THE NEW L IS HERE. I NEED TO KEEP AN EYE ON THIS PLACE.
BEEP BEEP
WHAT'S THE MATTER, MATT?
A YOUNG WOMAN... WELL, A WOMAN WHO LOOKS LIKE A CHILD... LIVES IN THE ROOM THAT MOGI WENT INTO.
A WOMAN?

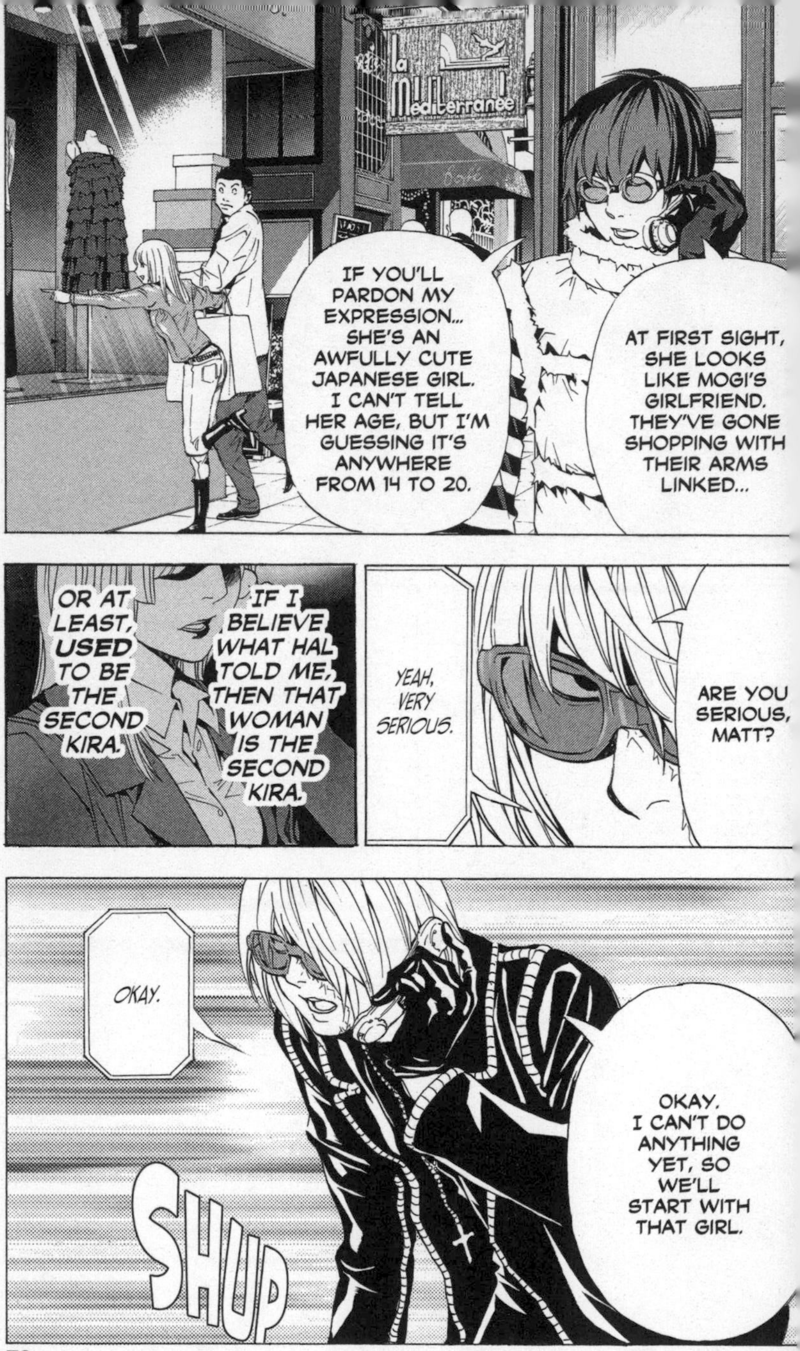
la Mediterranee
AT FIRST SIGHT, SHE LOOKS LIKE MOGI'S GIRLFRIEND. THEY'VE GONE SHOPPING WITH THEIR ARMS LINKED...
IF YOU'LL PARDON MY EXPRESSION... SHE'S AN AWFULLY CUTE JAPANESE GIRL. I CAN'T TELL HER AGE, BUT I'M GUESSING IT'S ANYWHERE FROM 14 TO 20.
ARE YOU SERIOUS, MATT?
YEAH, VERY SERIOUS.
IF I BELIEVE WHAT HAL TOLD ME, THEN THAT WOMAN IS THE SECOND KIRA.
OR AT LEAST, **USED** TO BE THE SECOND KIRA.
OKAY. I CAN'T DO ANYTHING YET, SO WE'LL START WITH THAT GIRL.
OKAY.
SHUP

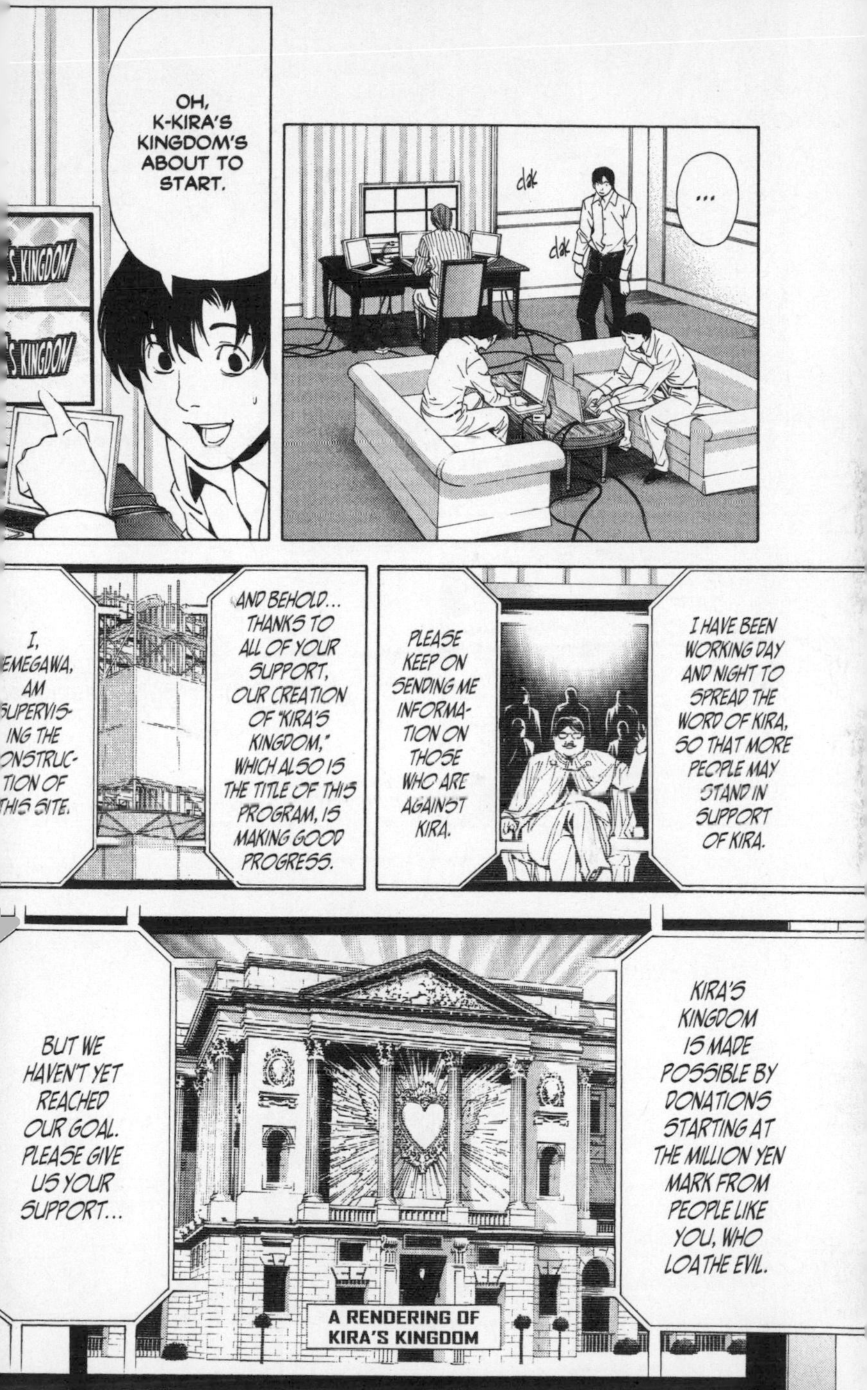
dak
dak
...
OH, K-KIRA'S KINGDOM'S ABOUT TO START.
'S KINGDOM
'S KINGDOM
I HAVE BEEN WORKING DAY AND NIGHT TO SPREAD THE WORD OF KIRA, SO THAT MORE PEOPLE MAY STAND IN SUPPORT OF KIRA.
PLEASE KEEP ON SENDING ME INFORMATION ON THOSE WHO ARE AGAINST KIRA.
AND BEHOLD... THANKS TO ALL OF YOUR SUPPORT, OUR CREATION OF "KIRA'S KINGDOM," WHICH ALSO IS THE TITLE OF THIS PROGRAM, IS MAKING GOOD PROGRESS.
I, EMEGAWA, AM SUPERVISING THE ONSTRUCTION OF THIS SITE.
KIRA'S KINGDOM IS MADE POSSIBLE BY DONATIONS STARTING AT THE MILLION YEN MARK FROM PEOPLE LIKE YOU, WHO LOATHE THE EVIL.
A RENDERING OF KIRA'S KINGDOM
BUT WE HAVEN'T YET REACHED OUR GOAL. PLEASE GIVE US YOUR SUPPORT...

*A MILLON YEN IS ROUGHTLY $8600.

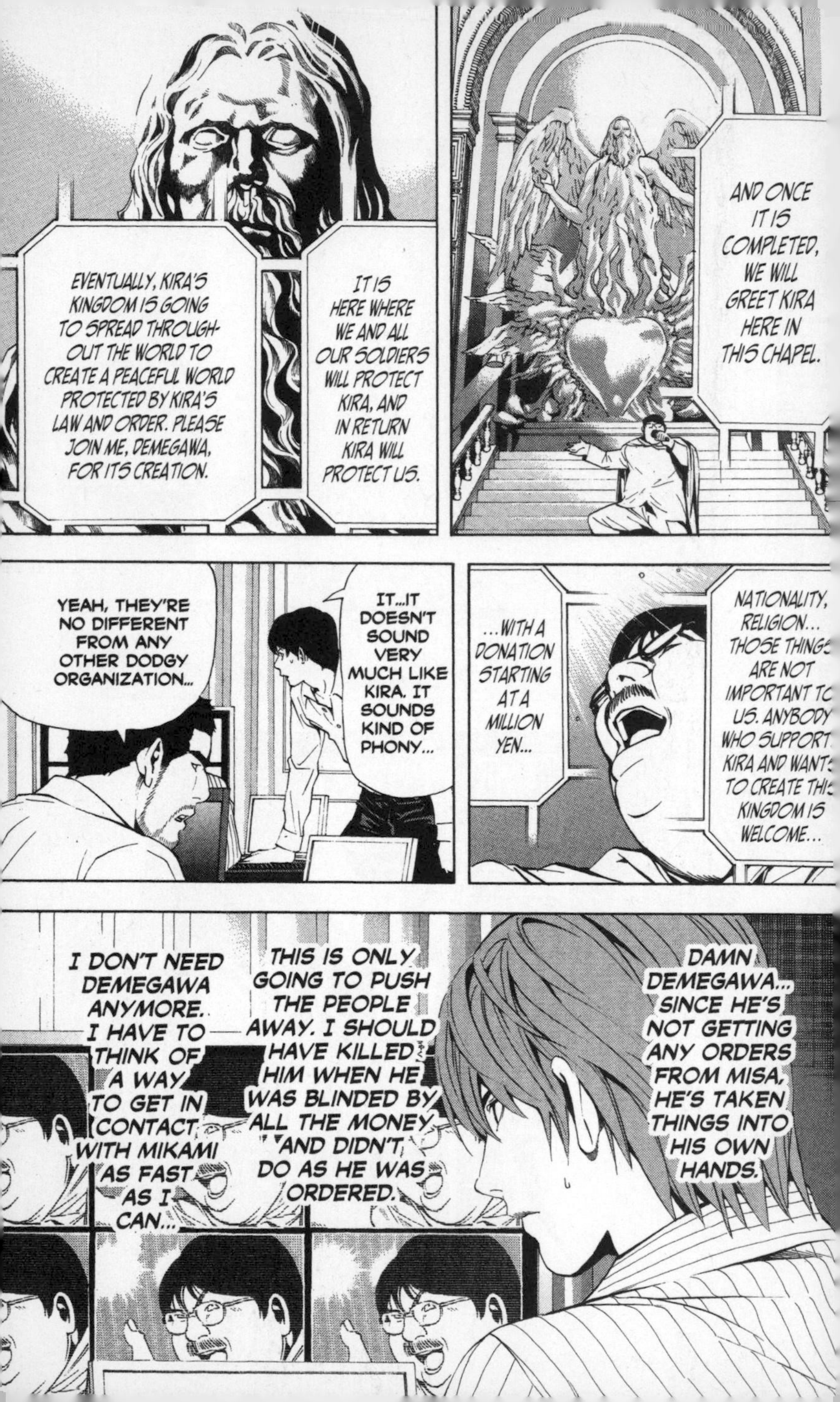
AND ONCE IT IS COMPLETED, WE WILL GREET KIRA HERE IN THIS CHAPEL.
IT IS HERE WHERE WE AND ALL OUR SOLDIERS WILL PROTECT KIRA, AND IN RETURN KIRA WILL PROTECT US.
EVENTUALLY, KIRA'S KINGDOM IS GOING TO SPREAD THROUGH-OUT THE WORLD TO CREATE A PEACEFUL WORLD PROTECTED BY KIRA'S LAW AND ORDER. PLEASE JOIN ME, DEMEGAWA, FOR ITS CREATION.
NATIONALITY, RELIGION... THOSE THINGS ARE NOT IMPORTANT TO US. ANYBODY WHO SUPPORTS KIRA AND WANTS TO CREATE THIS KINGDOM IS WELCOME...
...WITH A DONATION STARTING AT A MILLION YEN...
IT...IT DOESN'T SOUND VERY MUCH LIKE KIRA. IT SOUNDS KIND OF PHONY...
YEAH, THEY'RE NO DIFFERENT FROM ANY OTHER DODGY ORGANIZATION...
DAMN DEMEGAWA... SINCE HE'S NOT GETTING ANY ORDERS FROM MISA, HE'S TAKEN THINGS INTO HIS OWN HANDS.
THIS IS ONLY GOING TO PUSH THE PEOPLE AWAY. I SHOULD HAVE KILLED HIM WHEN HE WAS BLINDED BY ALL THE MONEY AND DIDN'T DO AS HE WAS ORDERED.
I DON'T NEED DEMEGAWA ANYMORE. I HAVE TO THINK OF A WAY TO GET IN CONTACT WITH MIKAMI AS FAST AS I CAN...

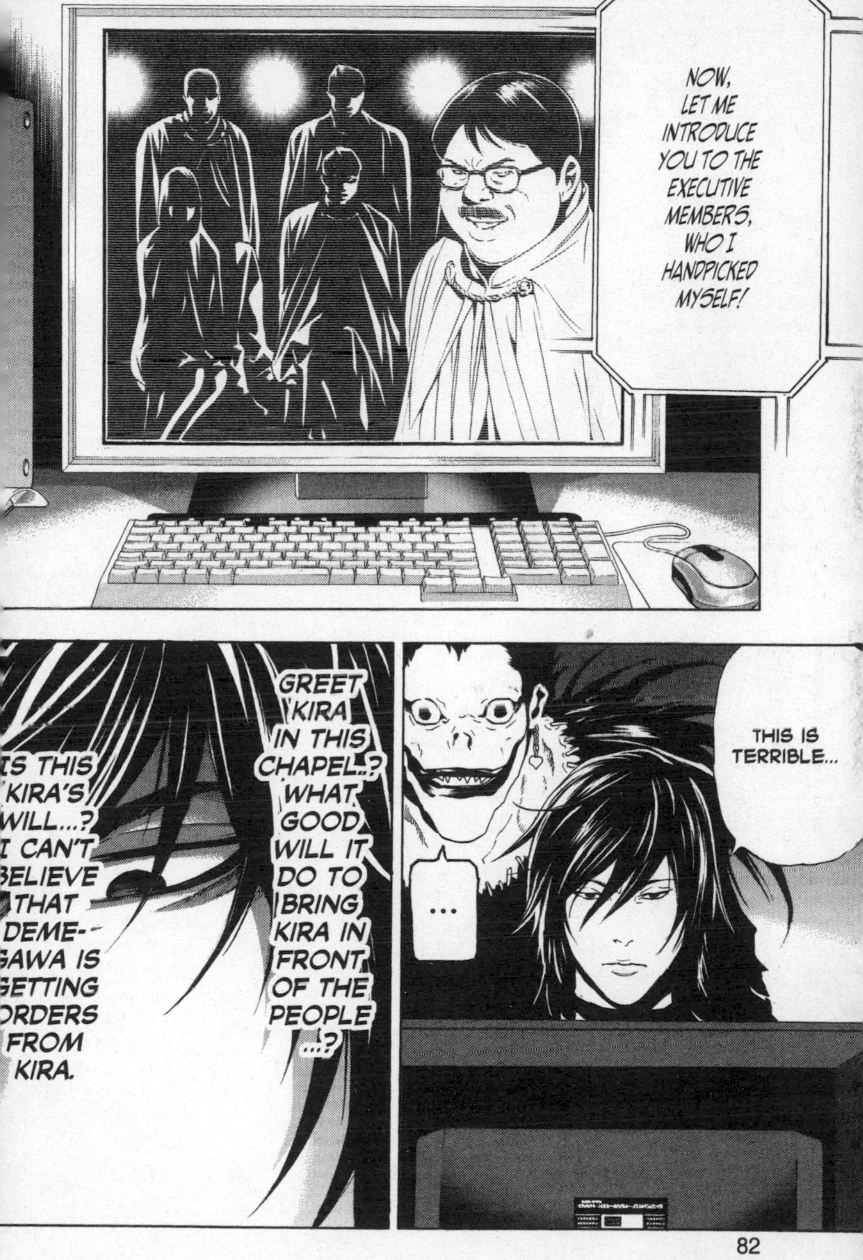
NOW, LET ME INTRODUCE YOU TO THE EXECUTIVE MEMBERS, WHO I HANDPICKED MYSELF!
THIS IS TERRIBLE...
...
GREET KIRA IN THIS CHAPEL..? WHAT GOOD WILL IT DO TO BRING KIRA IN FRONT OF THE PEOPLE ...?
IS THIS KIRA'S WILL...? I CAN'T BELIEVE THAT DEME-GAWA IS GETTING ORDERS FROM KIRA.

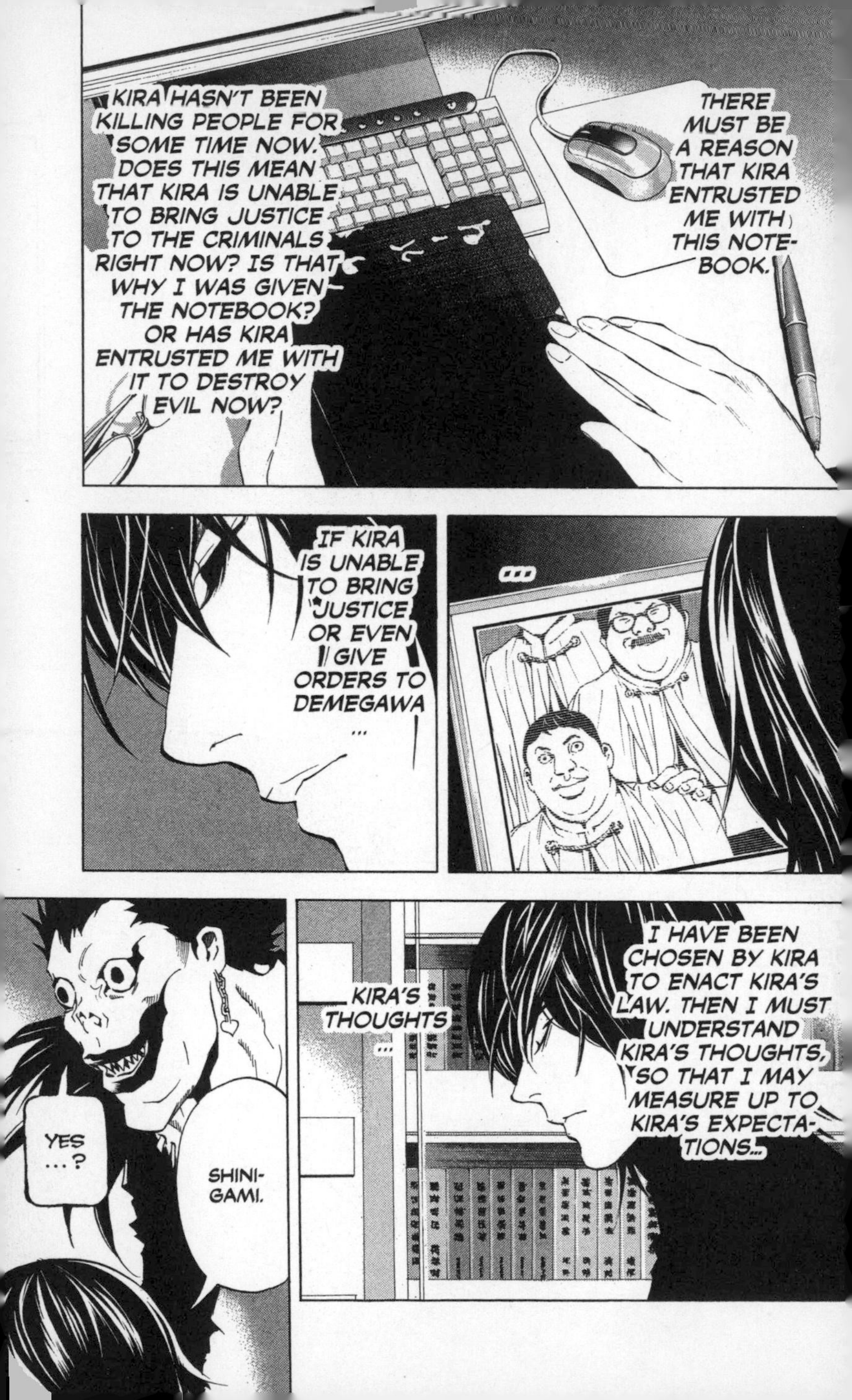
THERE MUST BE A REASON THAT KIRA ENTRUSTED ME WITH THIS NOTEBOOK.
KIRA HASN'T BEEN KILLING PEOPLE FOR SOME TIME NOW. DOES THIS MEAN THAT KIRA IS UNABLE TO BRING JUSTICE TO THE CRIMINALS RIGHT NOW? IS THAT WHY I WAS GIVEN THE NOTEBOOK? OR HAS KIRA ENTRUSTED ME WITH IT TO DESTROY EVIL NOW?
...
IF KIRA IS UNABLE TO BRING JUSTICE OR EVEN GIVE ORDERS TO DEMEGAWA ...
I HAVE BEEN CHOSEN BY KIRA TO ENACT KIRA'S LAW. THEN I MUST UNDERSTAND KIRA'S THOUGHTS, SO THAT I MAY MEASURE UP TO KIRA'S EXPECTATIONS...
KIRA'S THOUGHTS ...
SHINIGAMI.
YES ...?

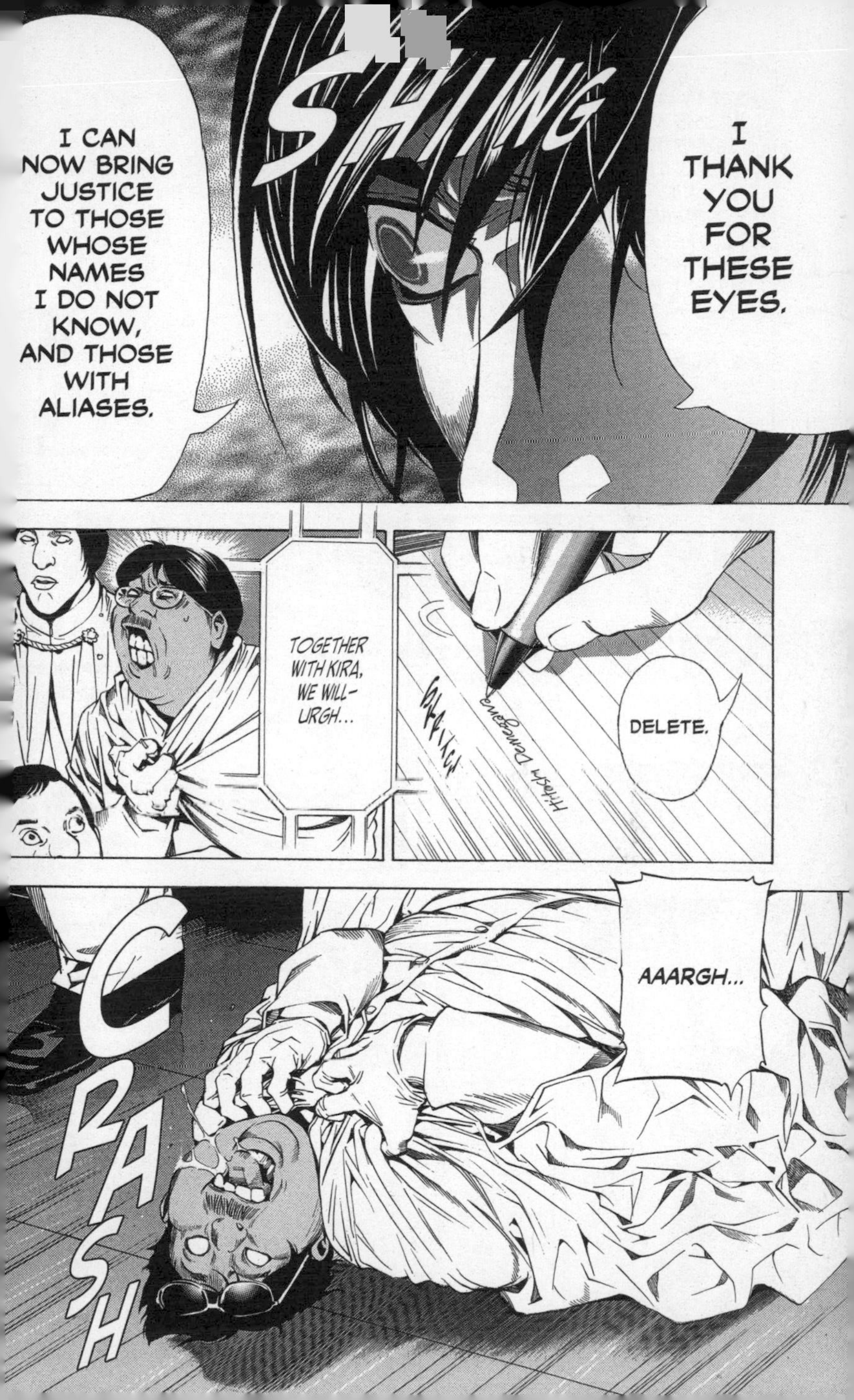
I THANK YOU FOR THESE EYES.
SHING
I CAN NOW BRING JUSTICE TO THOSE WHOSE NAMES I DO NOT KNOW, AND THOSE WITH ALIASES.
DELETE.
Hitoshi Demegawa
SKRITCH
TOGETHER WITH KIRA, WE WILL- URGH...
AAARGH...
CRASH

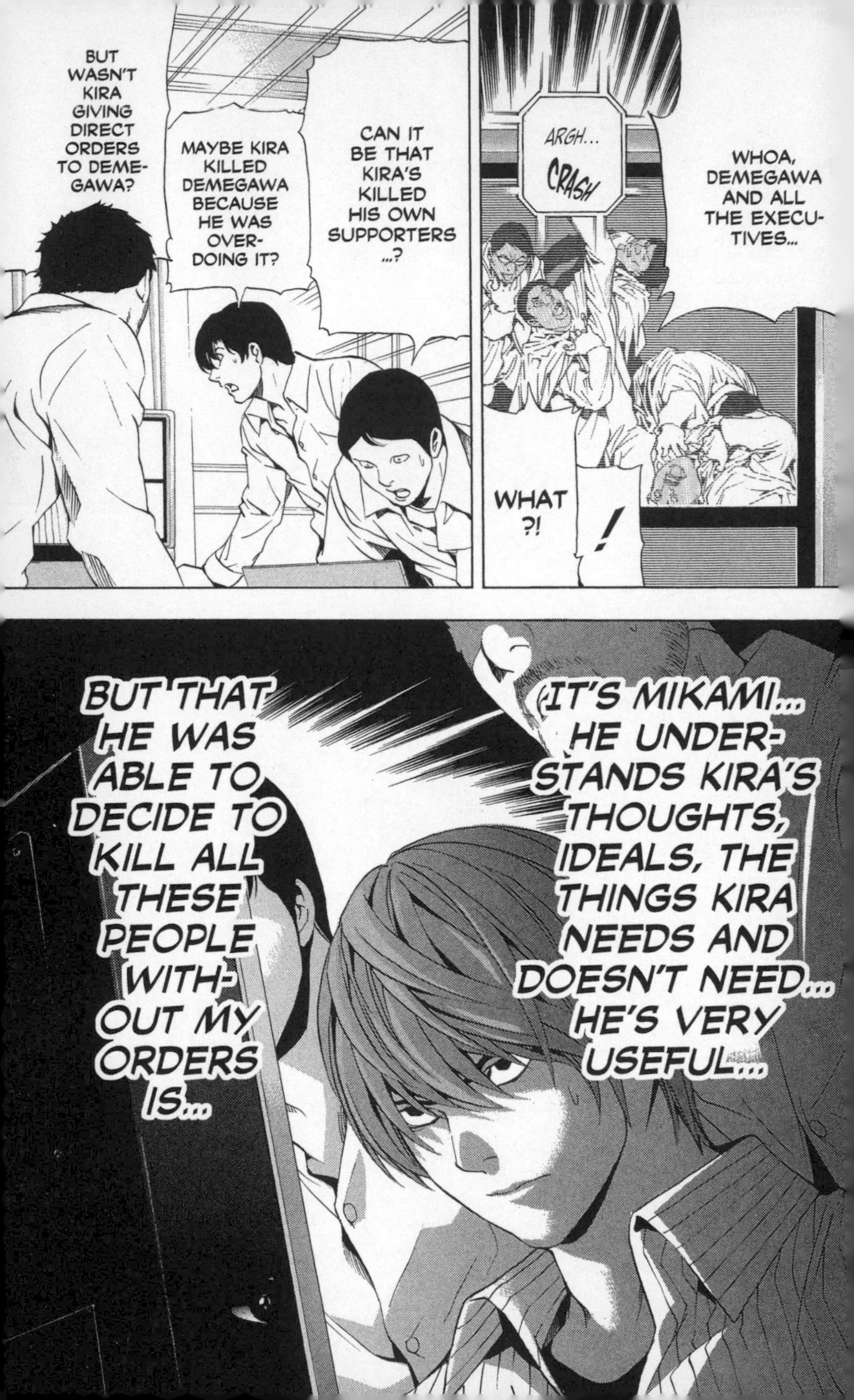
WHOA, DEMEGAWA AND ALL THE EXECUTIVES...
ARGH...
CRASH
WHAT?!
!
CAN IT BE THAT KIRA'S KILLED HIS OWN SUPPORTERS ...?
MAYBE KIRA KILLED DEMEGAWA BECAUSE HE WAS OVER-DOING IT?
BUT WASN'T KIRA GIVING DIRECT ORDERS TO DEME-GAWA?
IT'S MIKAMI... HE UNDER-STANDS KIRA'S THOUGHTS, IDEALS, THE THINGS KIRA NEEDS AND DOESN'T NEED... HE'S VERY USEFUL...
BUT THAT HE WAS ABLE TO DECIDE TO KILL ALL THESE PEOPLE WITH-OUT MY ORDERS IS...

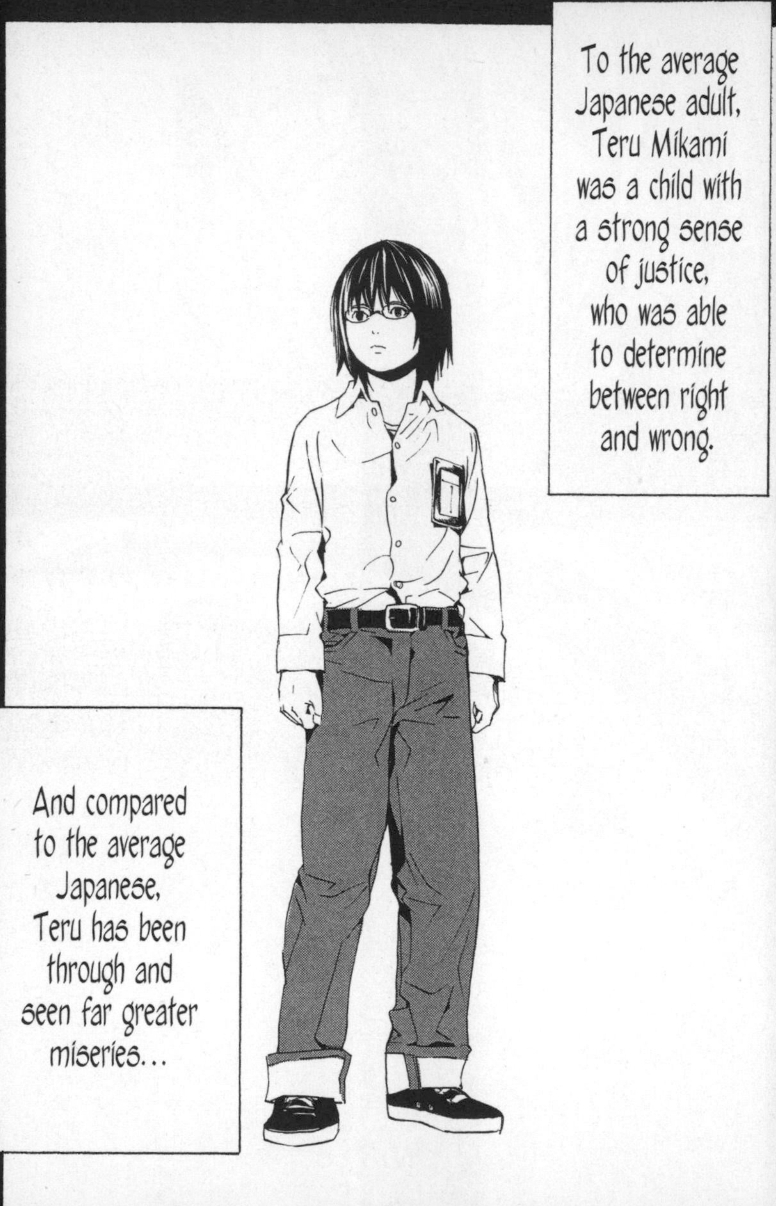
To the average Japanese adult, Teru Mikami was a child with a strong sense of justice, who was able to determine between right and wrong.
And compared to the average Japanese, Teru has been through and seen far greater miseries...

chapter 84 Coincidence

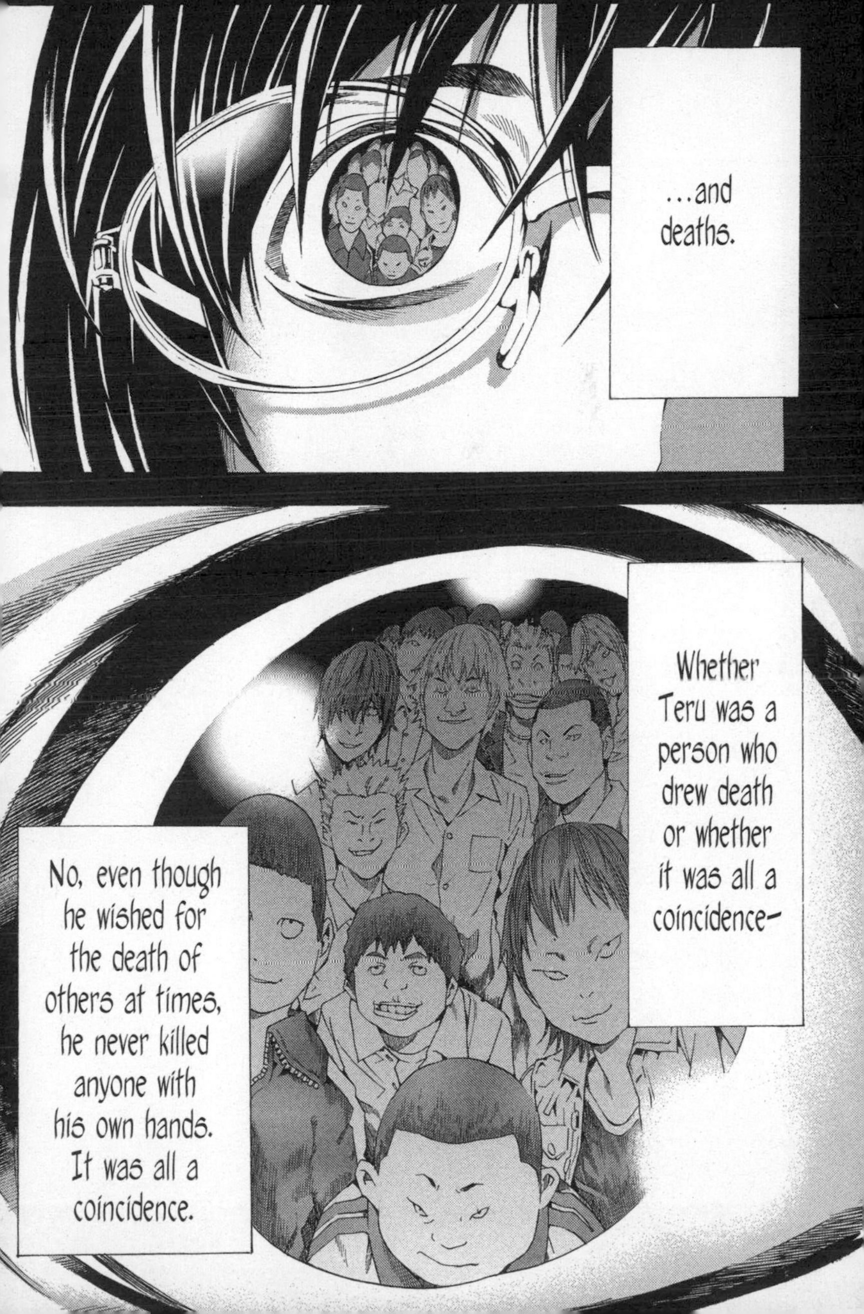

...and deaths.

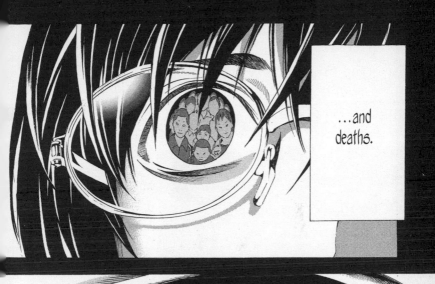

Whether Teru was a person who drew death or whether it was all a coincidence—

No, even though he wished for the death of others at times, he never killed anyone with his own hands. It was all a coincidence.

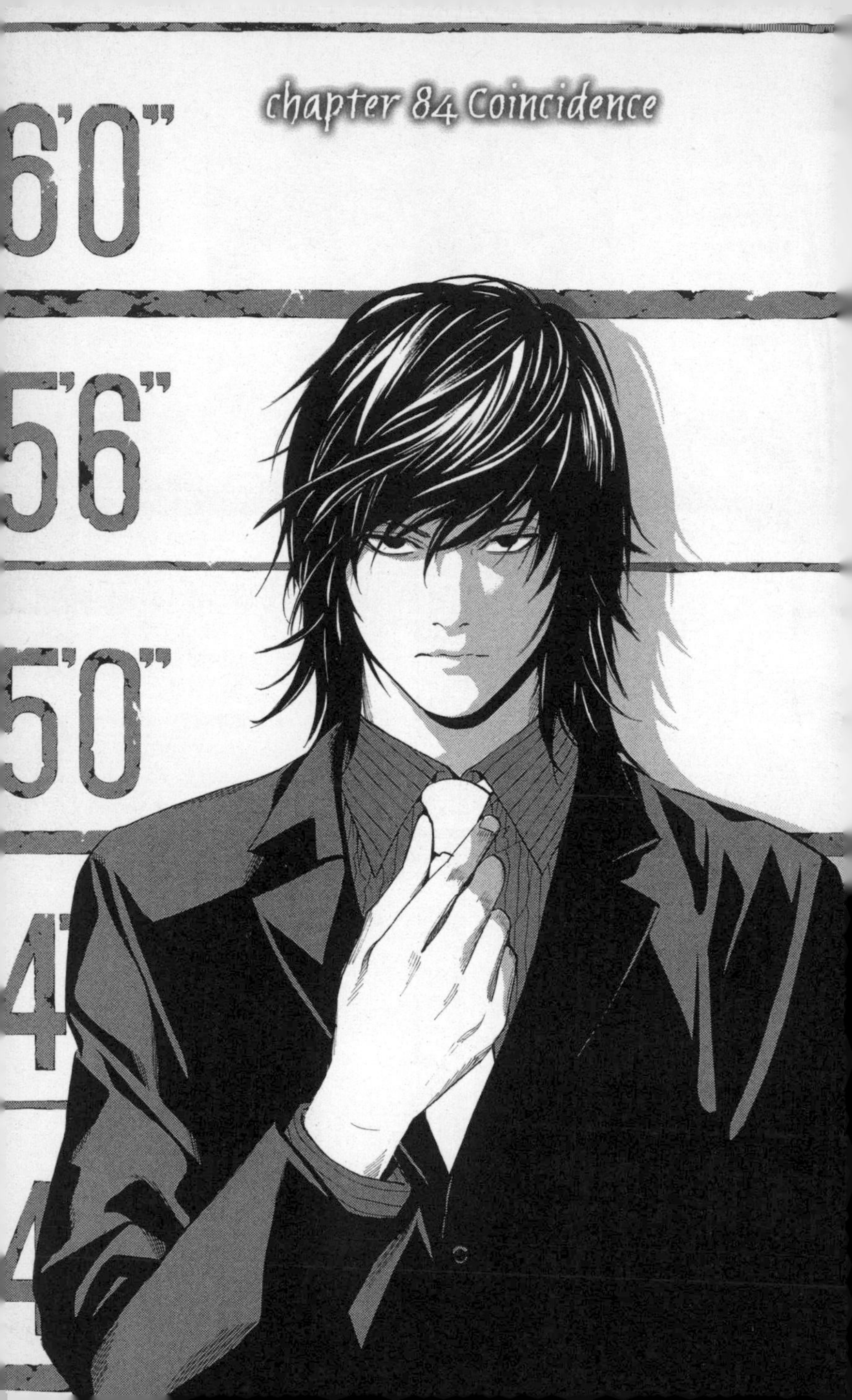
chapter 84 Coincidence
6'0"
5'6"
5'0"

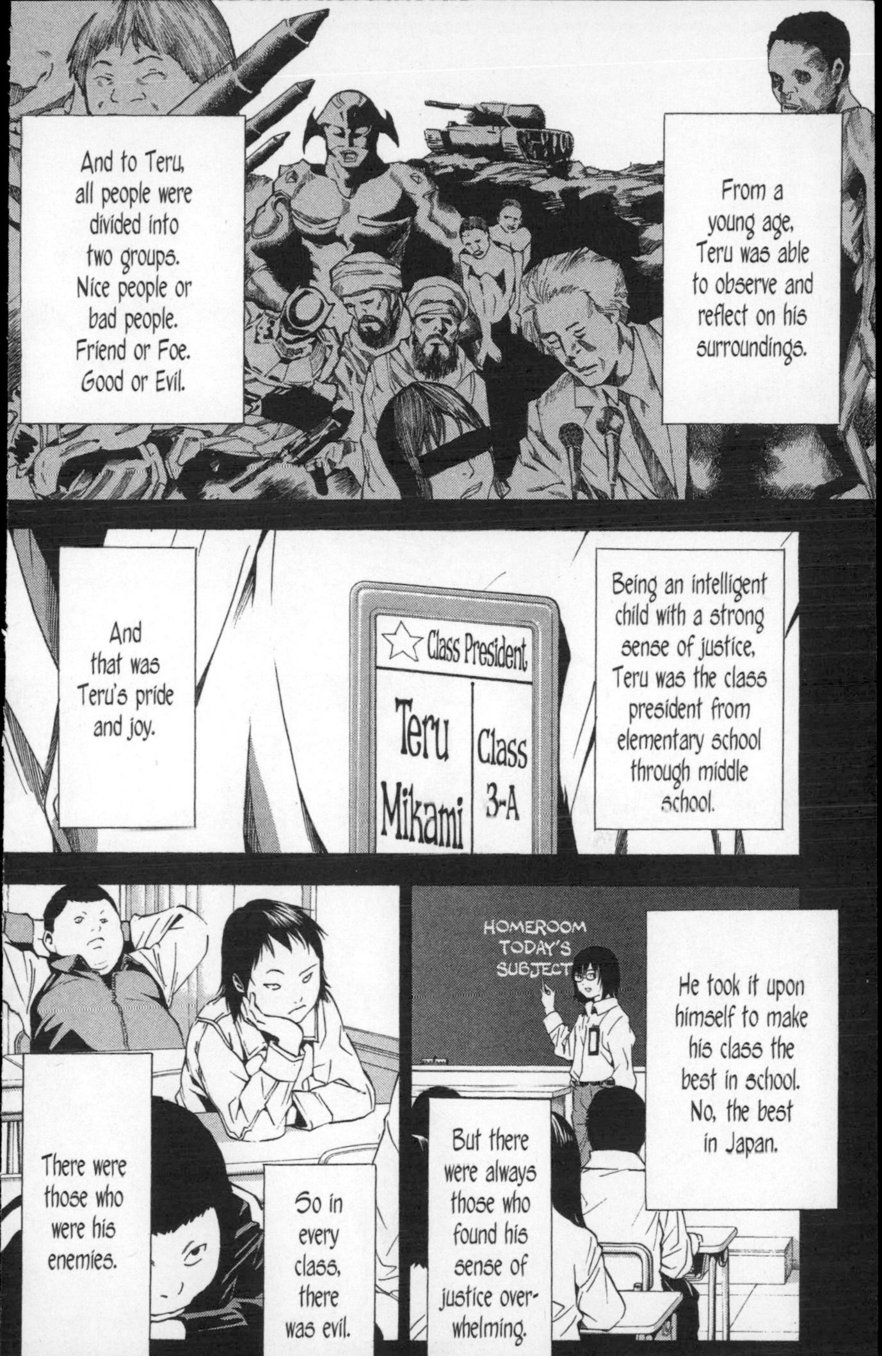
From a young age, Teru was able to observe and reflect on his surroundings.
And to Teru, all people were divided into two groups. Nice people or bad people. Friend or Foe. Good or Evil.
Being an intelligent child with a strong sense of justice, Teru was the class president from elementary school through middle school.
Class President
Teru Mikami
Class 3-A
And that was Teru's pride and joy.
He took it upon himself to make his class the best in school. No, the best in Japan.
HOMEROOM TODAY'S SUBJECT
But there were always those who found his sense of justice over-whelming.
So in every class, there was evil.
There were those who were his enemies.

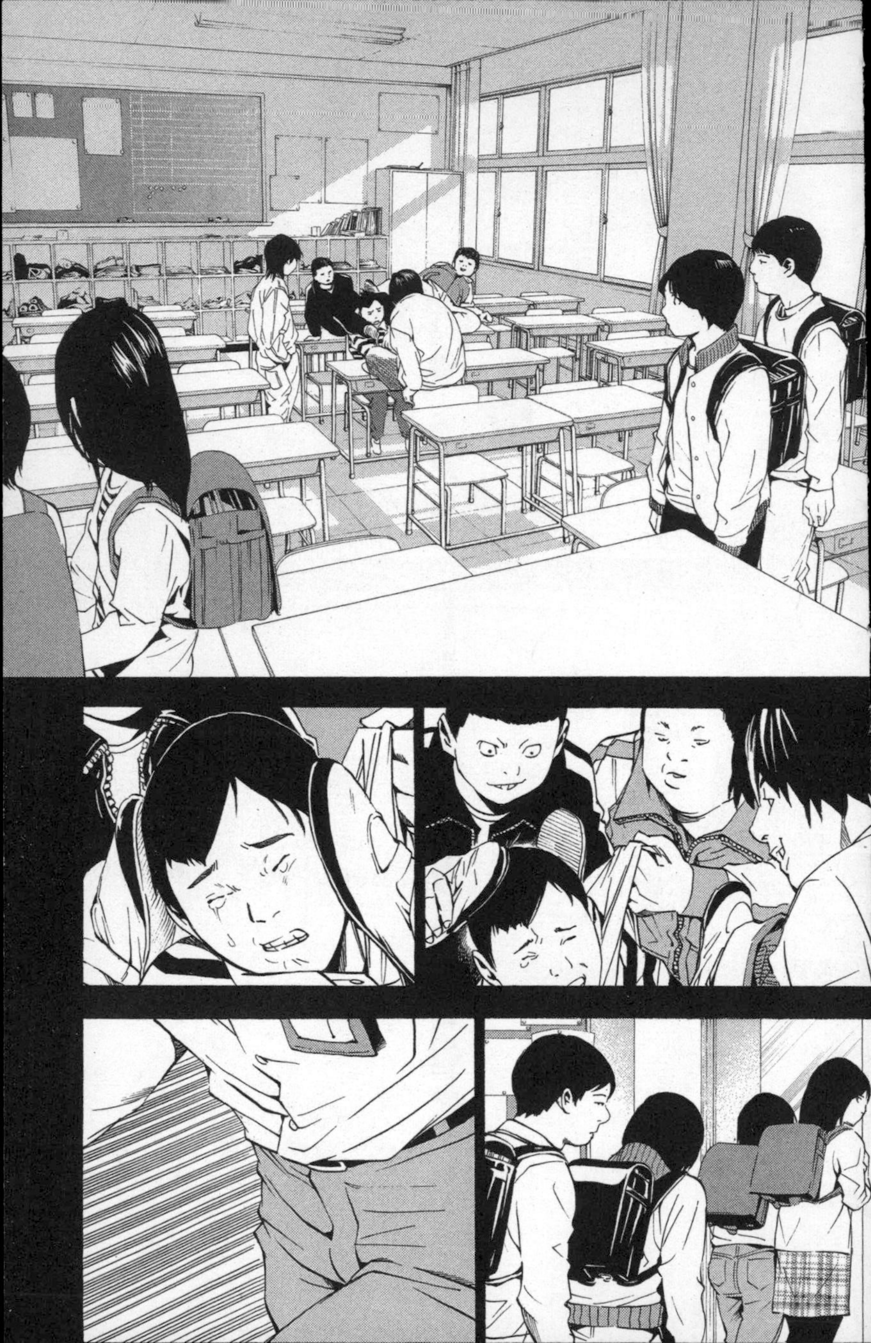

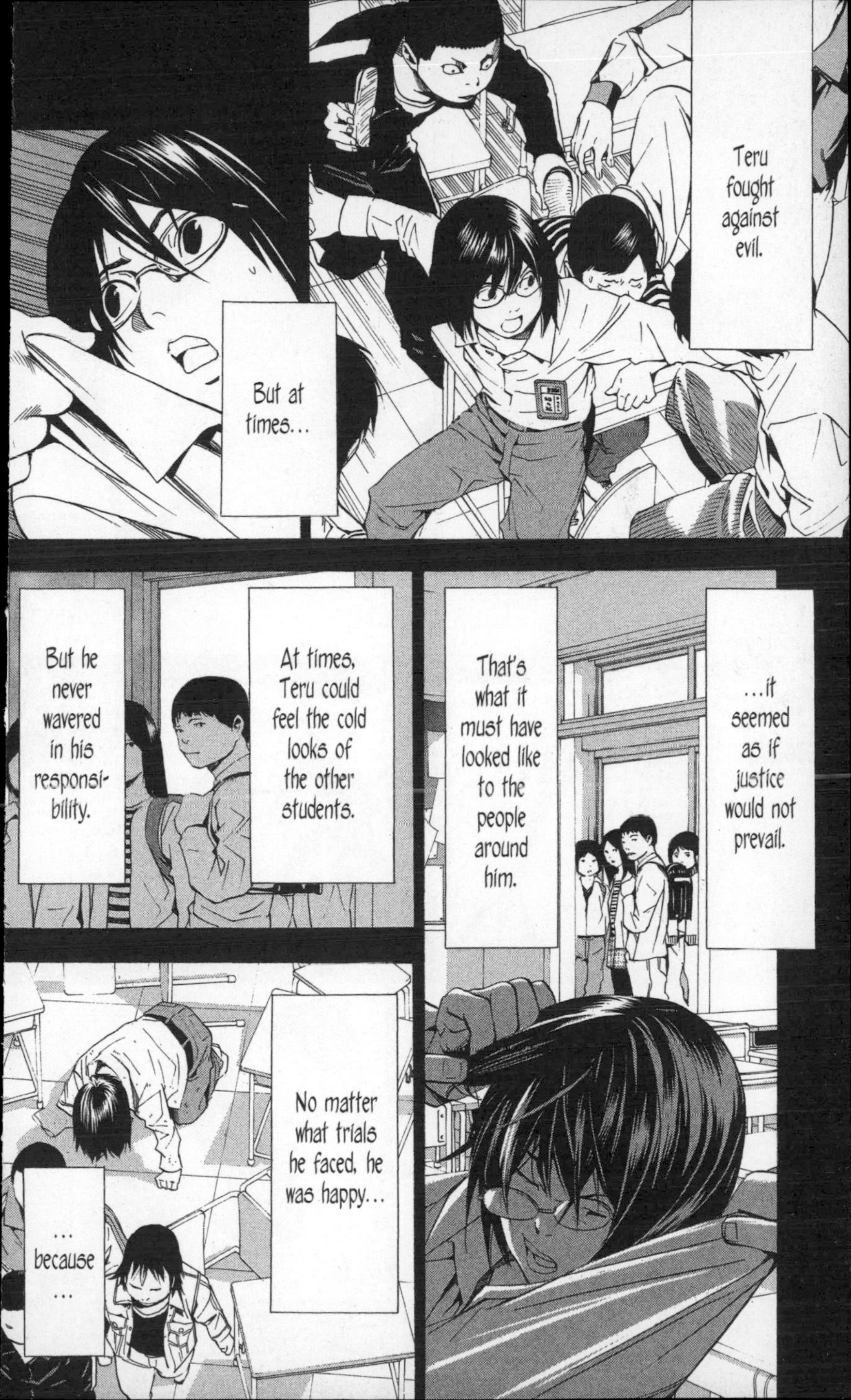
Teru fought against evil.
But at times...
...it seemed as if justice would not prevail.
That's what it must have looked like to the people around him.
At times, Teru could feel the cold looks of the other students.
But he never wavered in his responsibility.
No matter what trials he faced, he was happy...
...because...

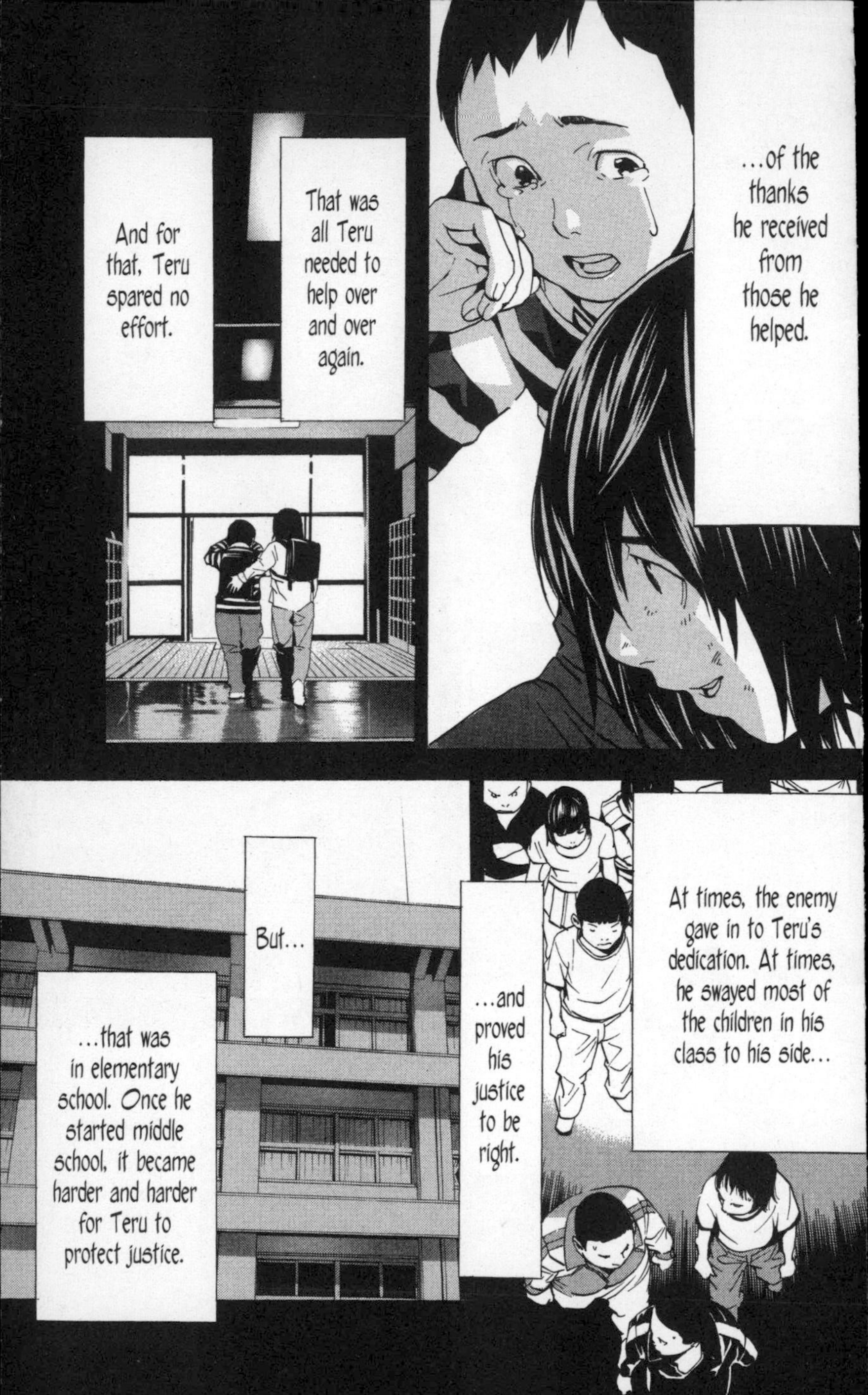
...of the thanks he received from those he helped.
That was all Teru needed to help over and over again.
And for that, Teru spared no effort.
At times, the enemy gave in to Teru's dedication. At times, he swayed most of the children in his class to his side...
...and proved his justice to be right.
But...
...that was in elementary school. Once he started middle school, it became harder and harder for Teru to protect justice.

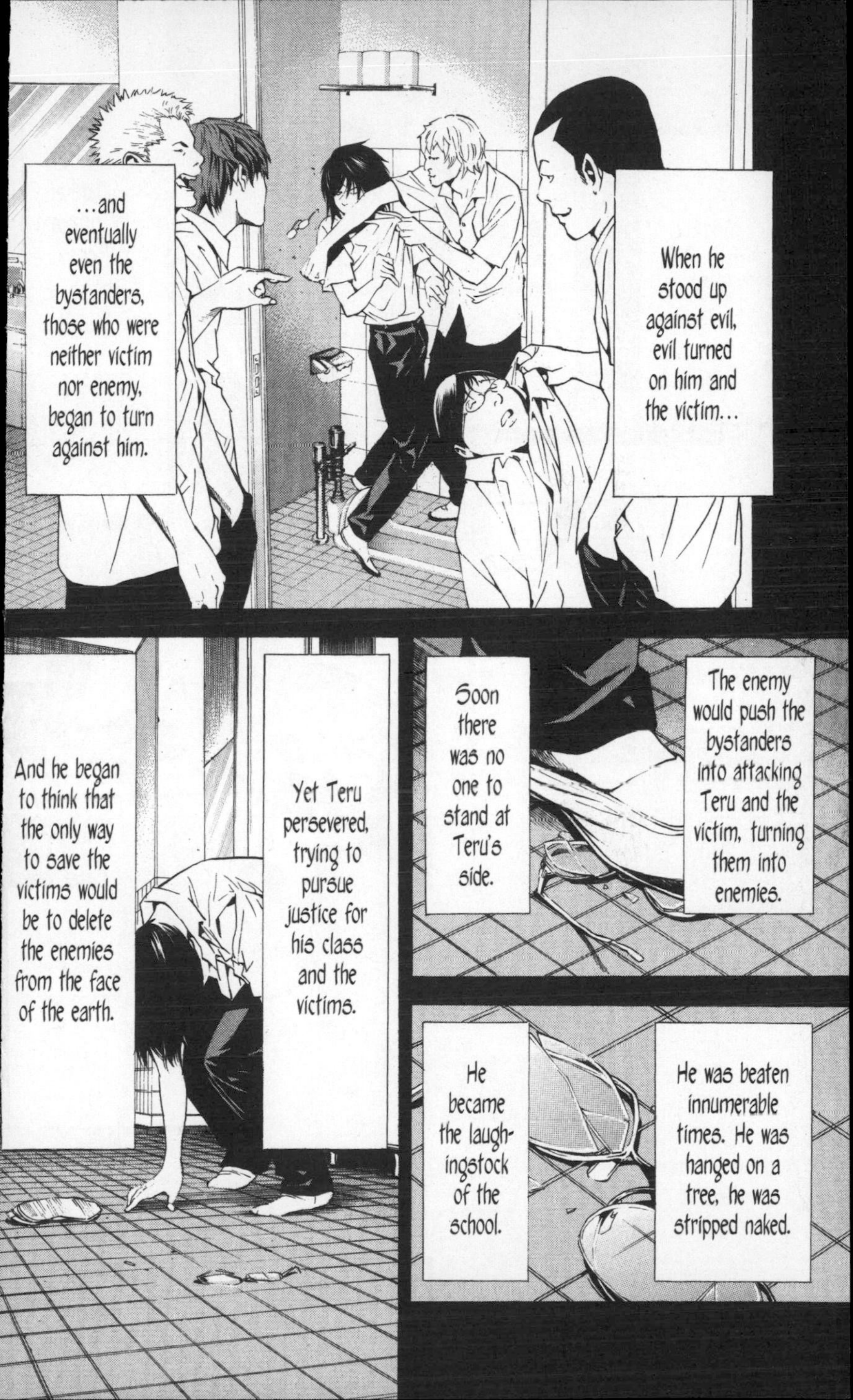
When he stood up against evil, evil turned on him and the victim...
...and eventually even the bystanders, those who were neither victim nor enemy, began to turn against him.
The enemy would push the bystanders into attacking Teru and the victim, turning them into enemies.
Soon there was no one to stand at Teru's side.
He was beaten innumerable times. He was hanged on a tree, he was stripped naked.
He became the laughingstock of the school.
Yet Teru persevered, trying to pursue justice for his class and the victims.
And he began to think that the only way to save the victims would be to delete the enemies from the face of the earth.

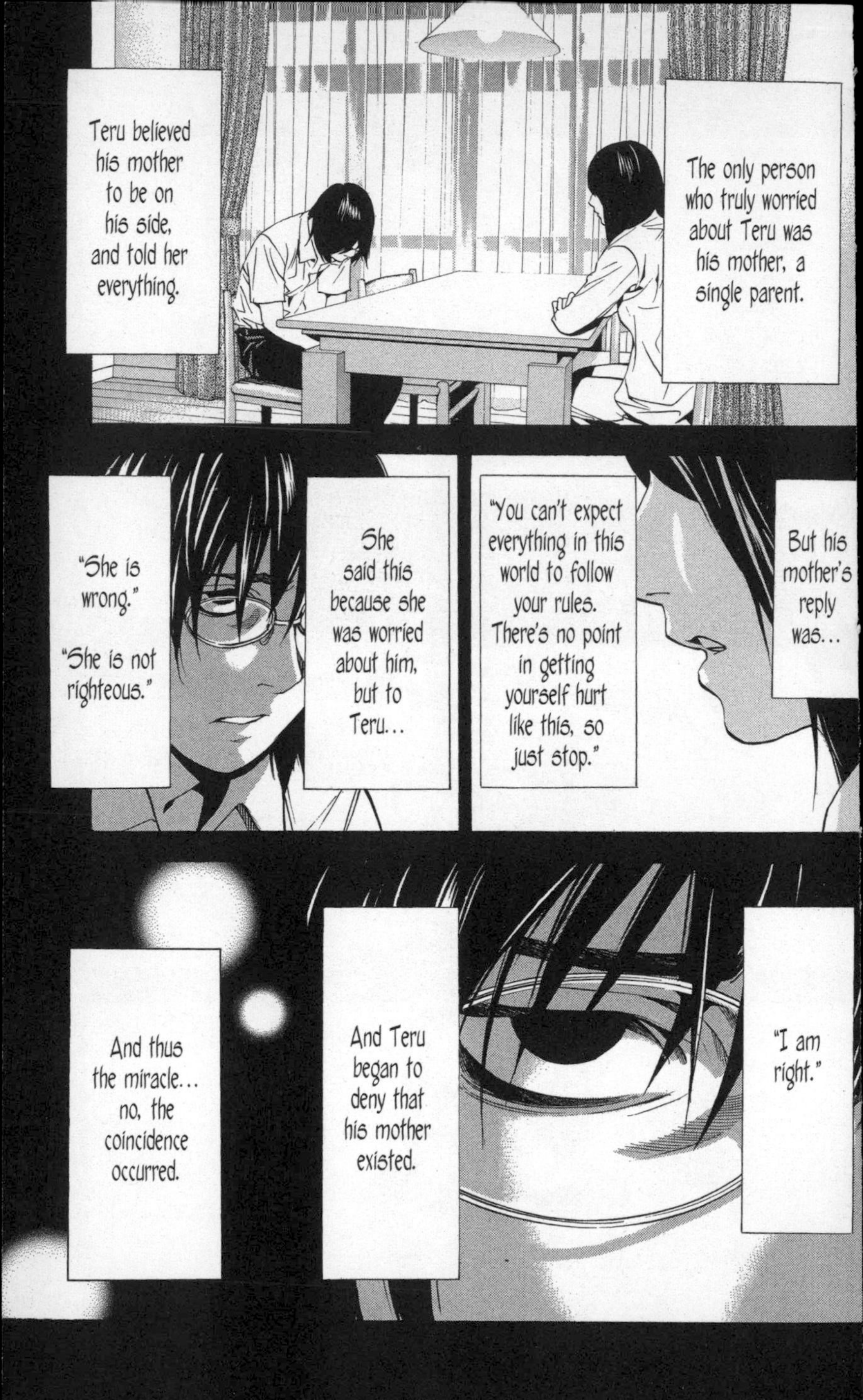

The only person who truly worried about Teru was his mother, a single parent.
Teru believed his mother to be on his side, and told her everything.
But his mother's reply was...
"You can't expect everything in this world to follow your rules. There's no point in getting yourself hurt like this, so just stop."
She said this because she was worried about him, but to Teru...
"She is wrong."
"She is not righteous."
"I am right."
And Teru began to deny that his mother existed.
And thus the miracle... no, the coincidence occurred.

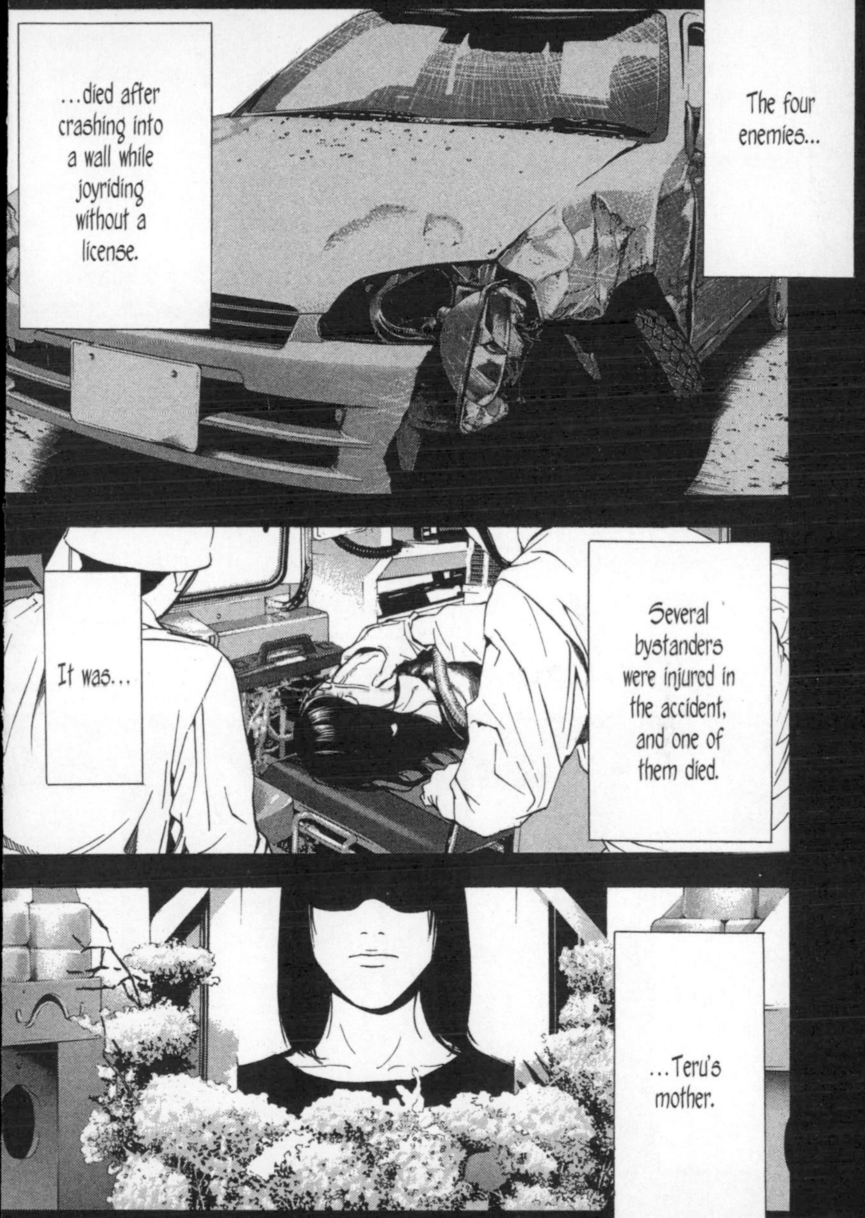

The four enemies...
...died after crashing into a wall while joyriding without a license.
Several bystanders were injured in the accident, and one of them died.
It was...
...Teru's mother.

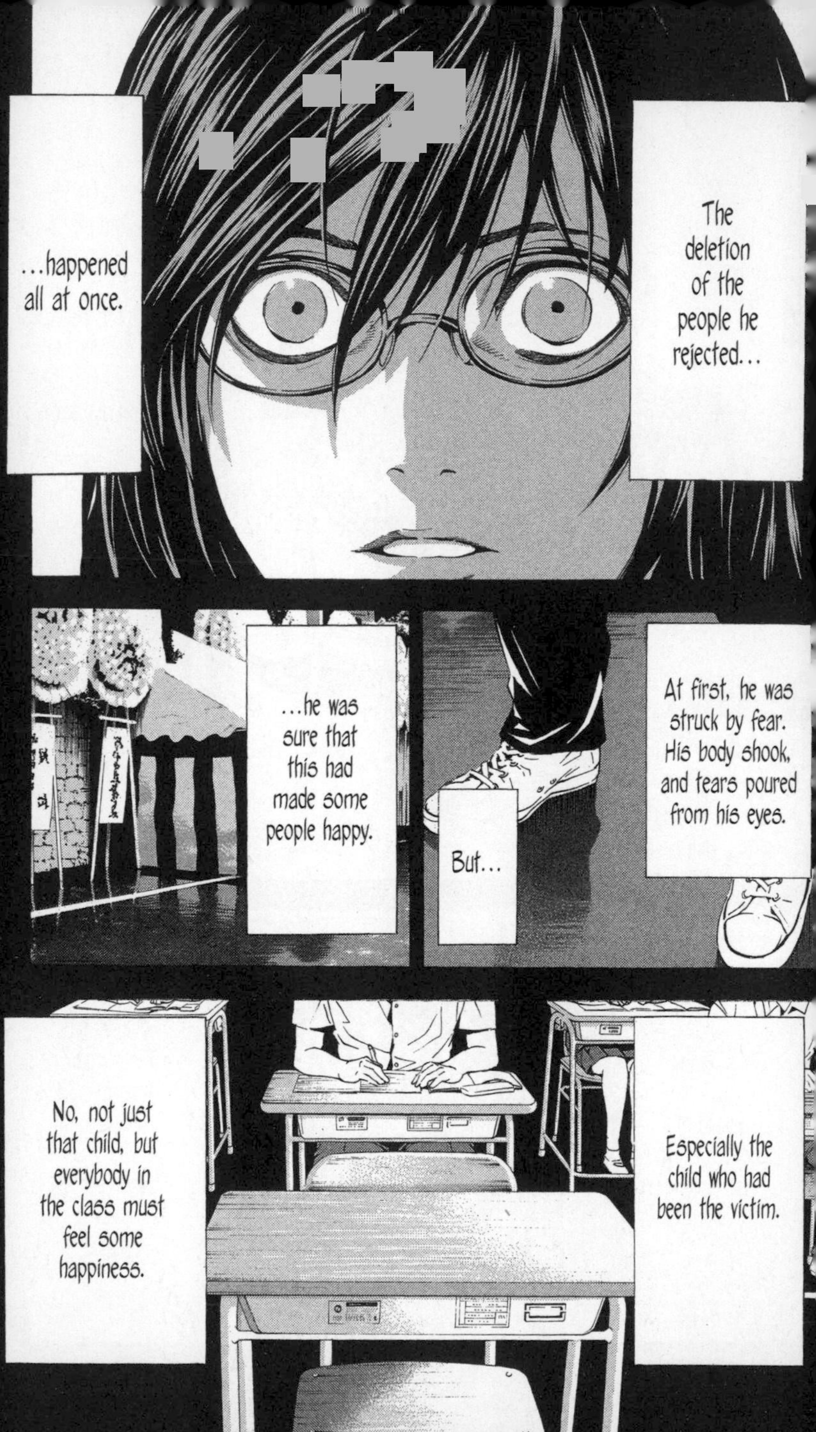
The deletion of the people he rejected...
...happened all at once.
At first, he was struck by fear. His body shook, and tears poured from his eyes.
But...
...he was sure that this had made some people happy.
Especially the child who had been the victim.
No, not just that child, but everybody in the class must feel some happiness.

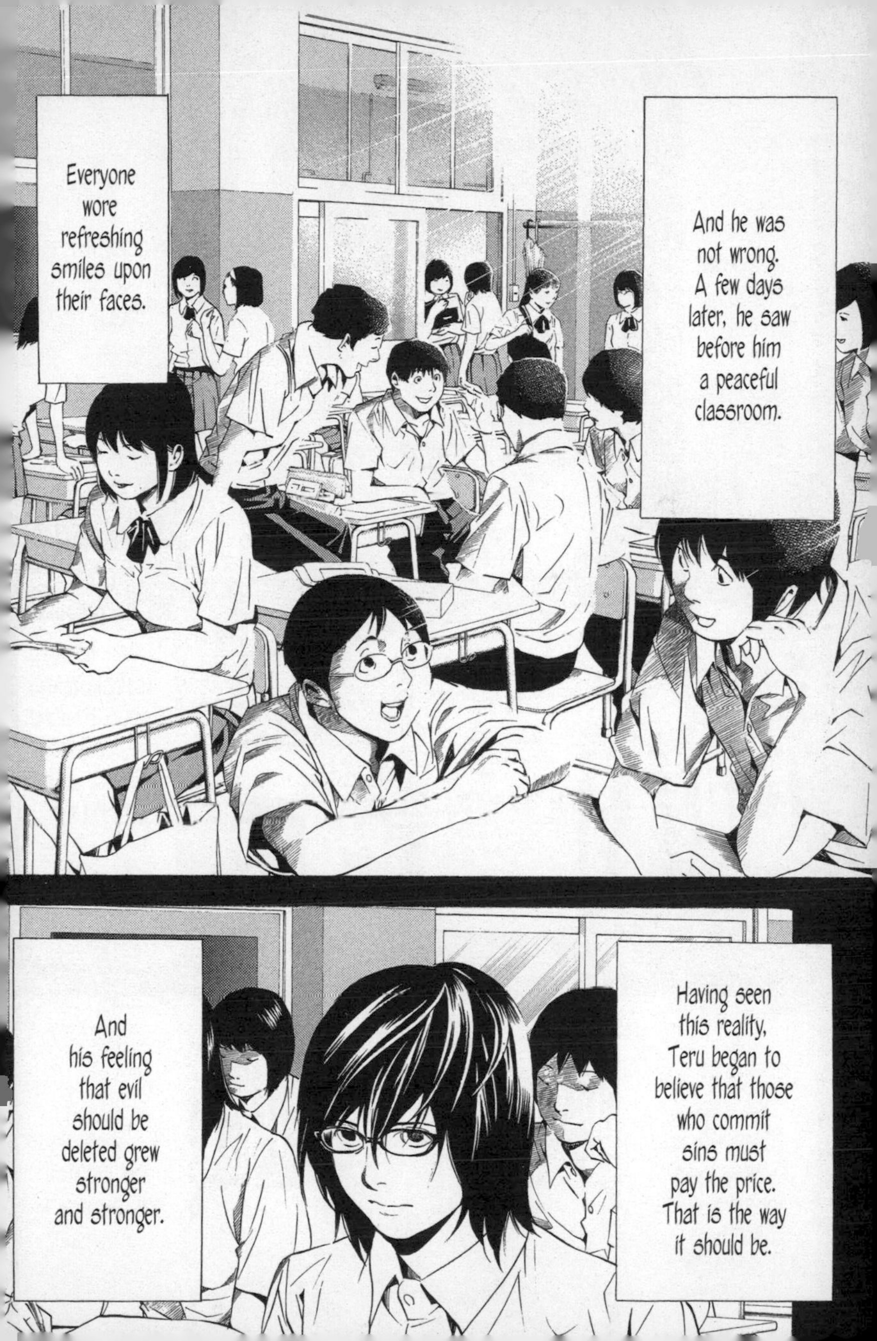
And he was not wrong. A few days later, he saw before him a peaceful classroom.
Everyone wore refreshing smiles upon their faces.
Having seen this reality, Teru began to believe that those who commit sins must pay the price. That is the way it should be.
And his feeling that evil should be deleted grew stronger and stronger.

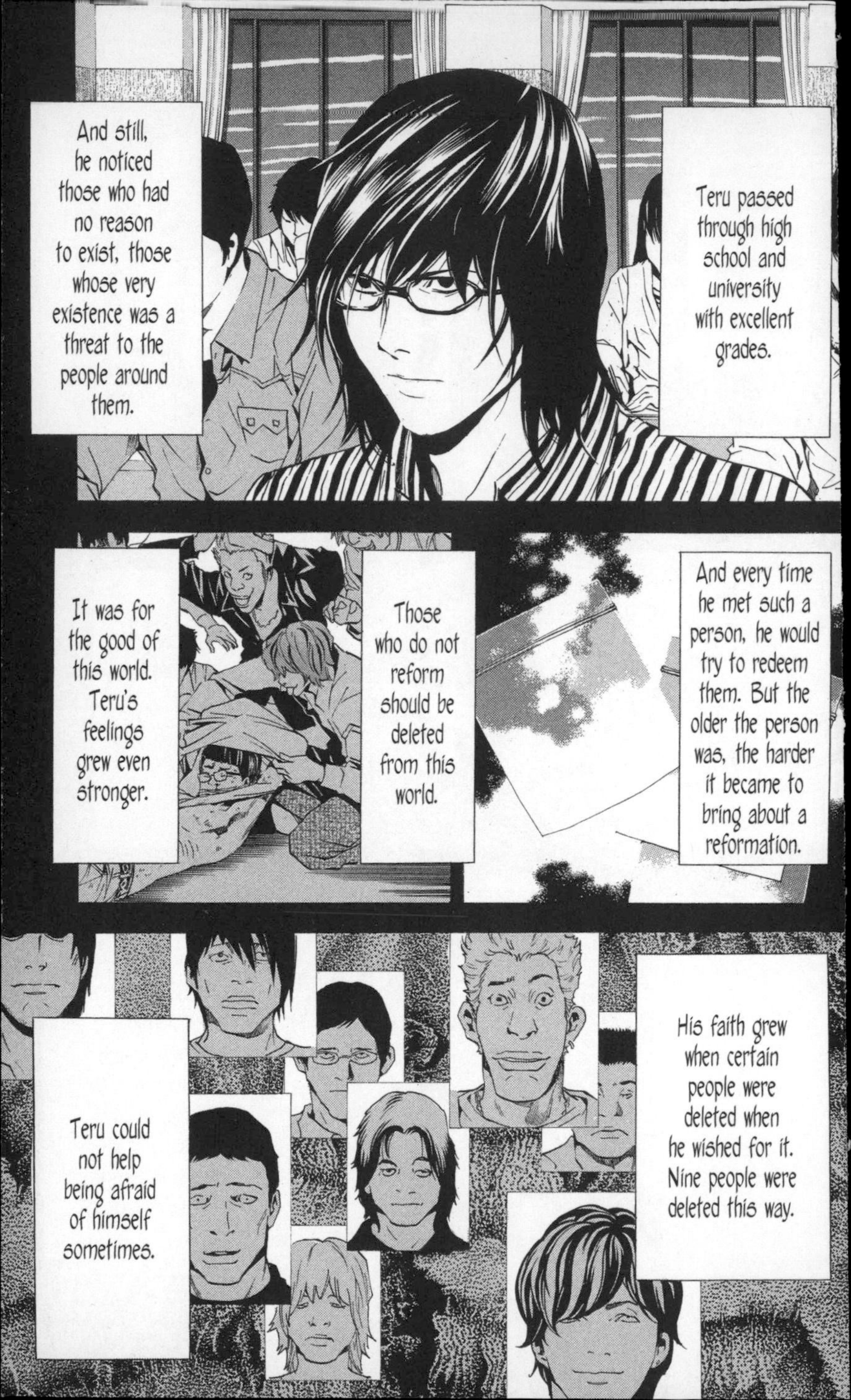
Teru passed through high school and university with excellent grades.
And still, he noticed those who had no reason to exist, those whose very existence was a threat to the people around them.
And every time he met such a person, he would try to redeem them. But the older the person was, the harder it became to bring about a reformation.
Those who do not reform should be deleted from this world.
It was for the good of this world. Teru's feelings grew even stronger.
His faith grew when certain people were deleted when he wished for it. Nine people were deleted this way.
Teru could not help being afraid of himself sometimes.

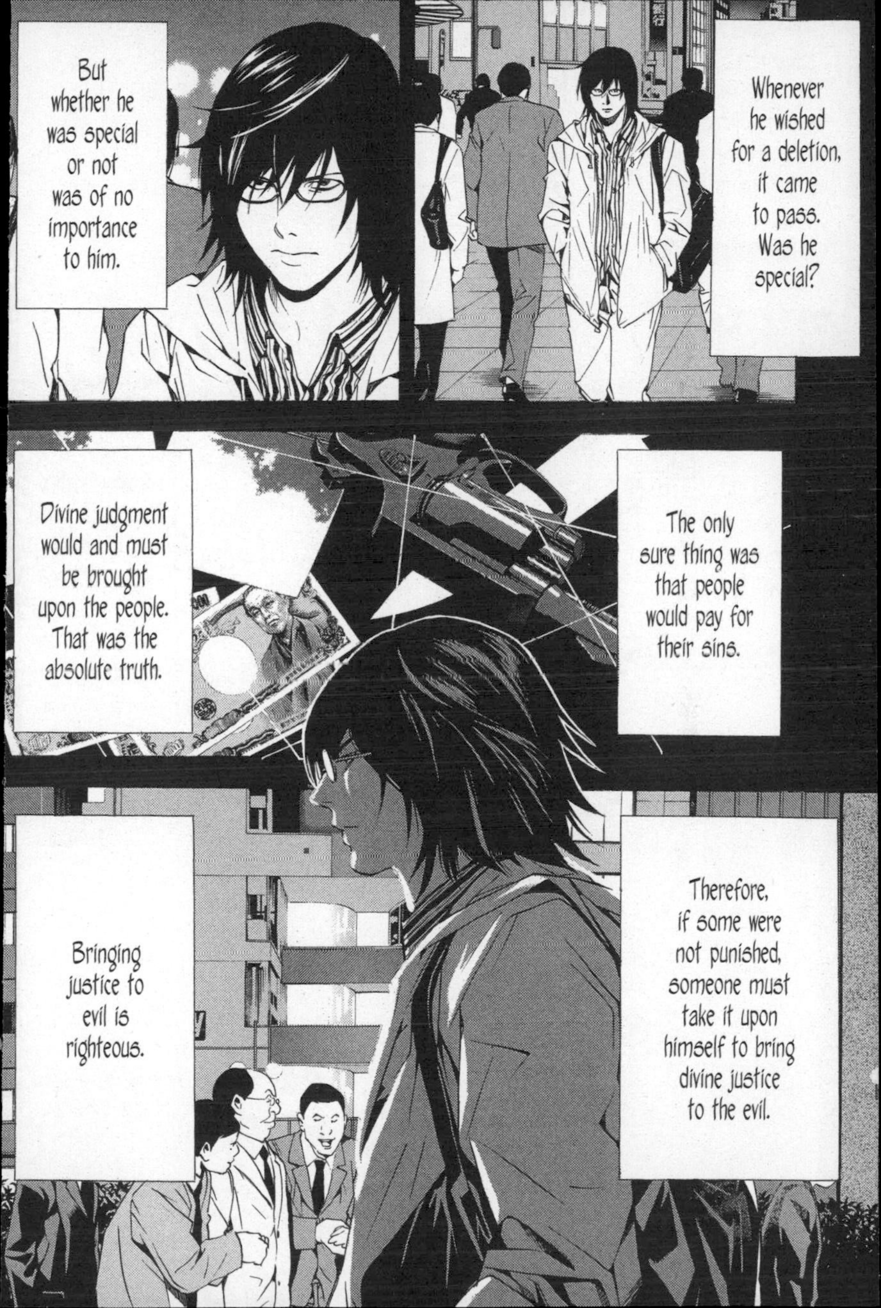
Whenever he wished for a deletion, it came to pass. Was he special?
But whether he was special or not was of no importance to him.
The only sure thing was that people would pay for their sins.
Divine judgment would and must be brought upon the people. That was the absolute truth.
Therefore, if some were not punished, someone must take it upon himself to bring divine justice to the evil.
Bringing justice to evil is righteous.

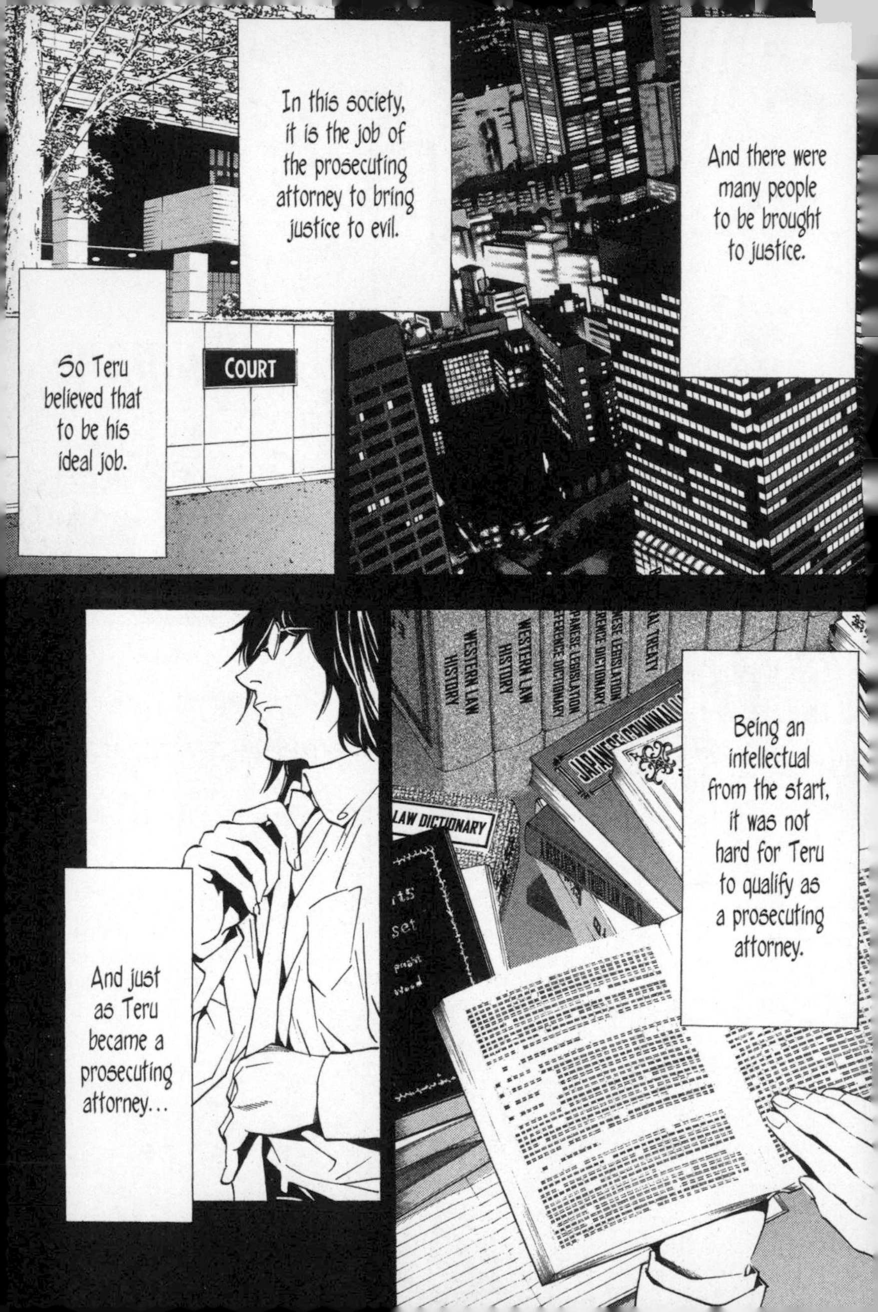
In this society, it is the job of the prosecuting attorney to bring justice to evil.
And there were many people to be brought to justice.
COURT
So Teru believed that to be his ideal job.
WESTERN LAW HISTORY
WESTERN LAW HISTORY
LAW DICTIONARY
Being an intellectual from the start, it was not hard for Teru to qualify as a prosecuting attorney.
And just as Teru became a prosecuting attorney...

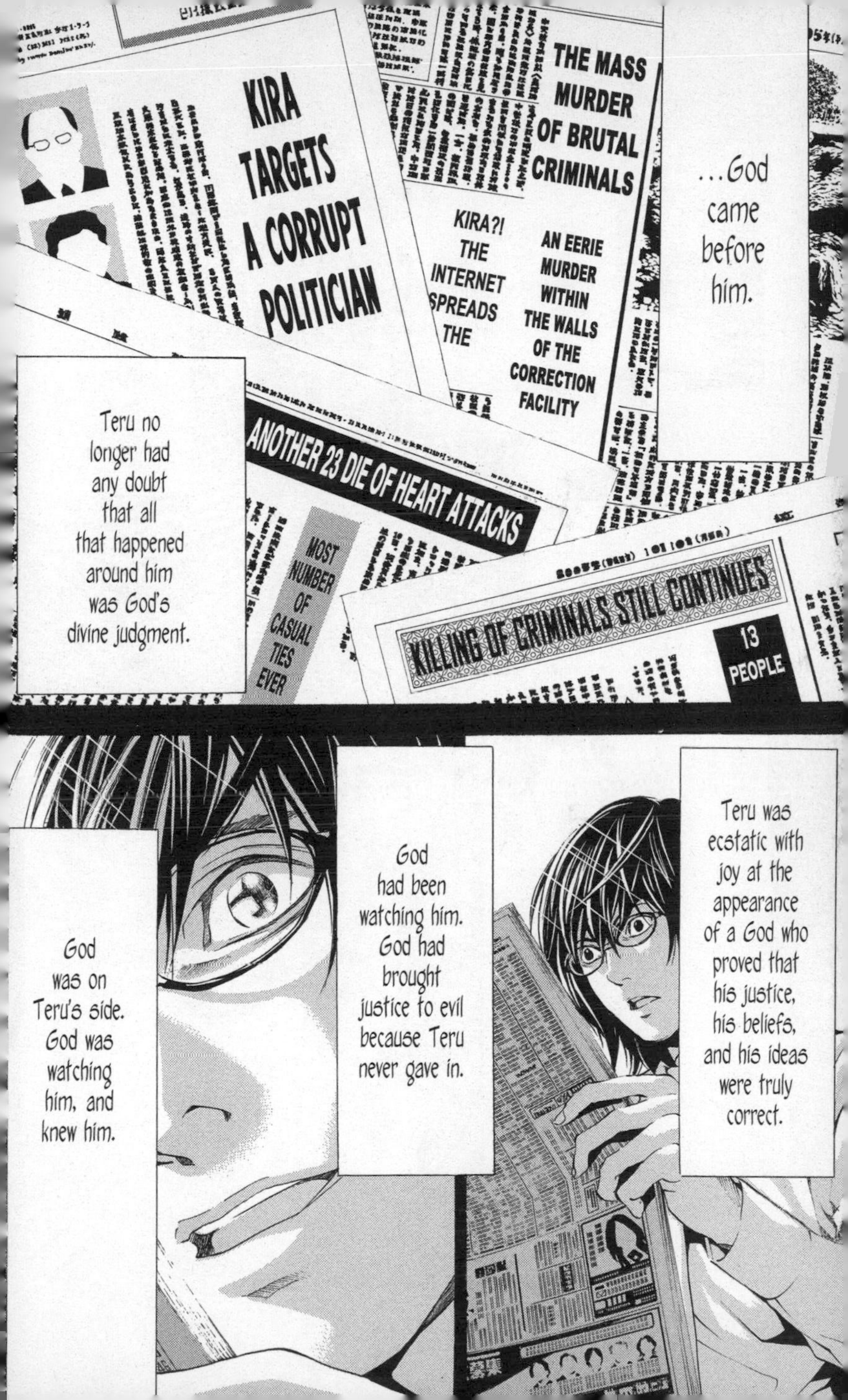
...God came before him.
THE MASS MURDER OF BRUTAL CRIMINALS
KIRA TARGETS A CORRUPT POLITICIAN
AN EERIE MURDER WITHIN THE WALLS OF THE CORRECTION FACILITY
KIRA?! THE INTERNET SPREADS THE
ANOTHER 23 DIE OF HEART ATTACKS
KILLING OF CRIMINALS STILL CONTINUES
13 PEOPLE
MOST NUMBER OF CASUAL TIES EVER
Teru no longer had any doubt that all that happened around him was God's divine judgment.
Teru was ecstatic with joy at the appearance of a God who proved that his justice, his beliefs, and his ideas were truly correct.
God had been watching him. God had brought justice to evil because Teru never gave in.
God was on Teru's side. God was watching him, and knew him.

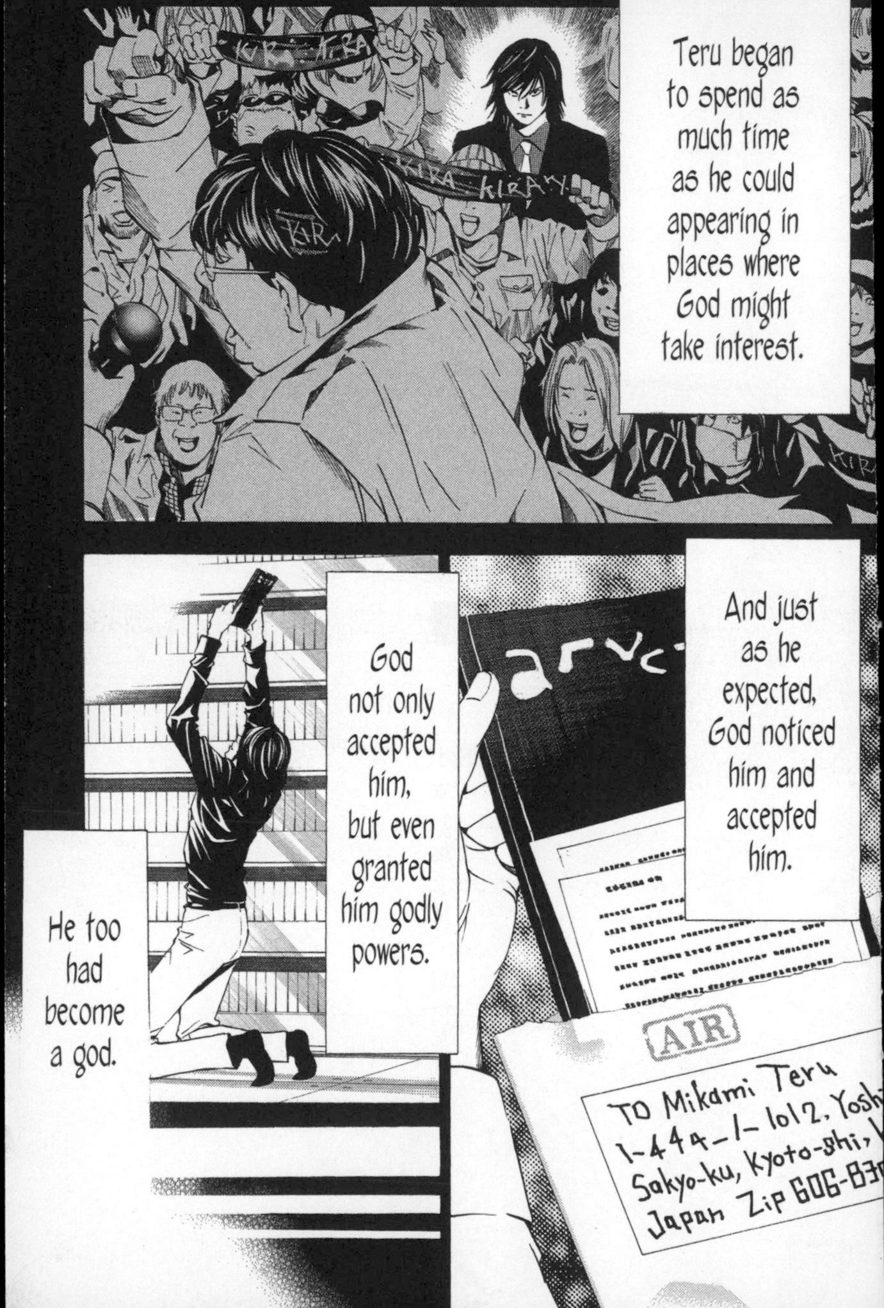

KIRA
Teru began to spend as much time as he could appearing in places where God might take interest.
And just as he expected, God noticed him and accepted him.
AIR
TO Mikami Teru
1-444-1-1012, Yosh
Sakyo-ku, Kyoto-shi,
Japan Zip 606-83
God not only accepted him, but even granted him godly powers.
He too had become a god.

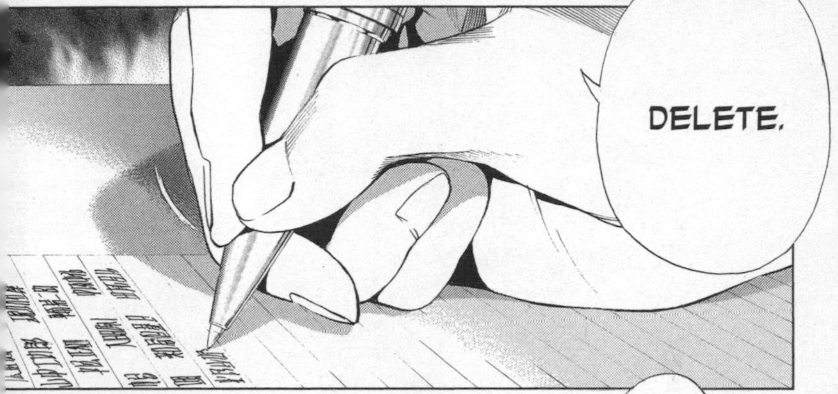
DELETE.

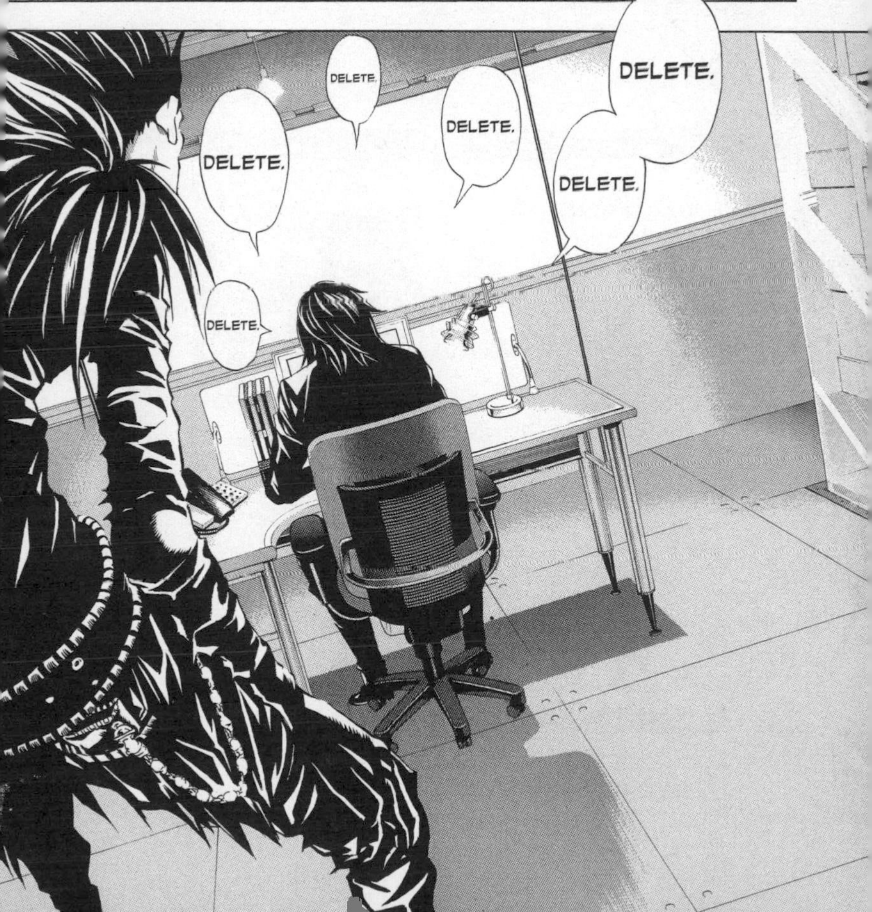
DELETE.
DELETE.
DELETE.
DELETE.
DELETE.
DELETE.

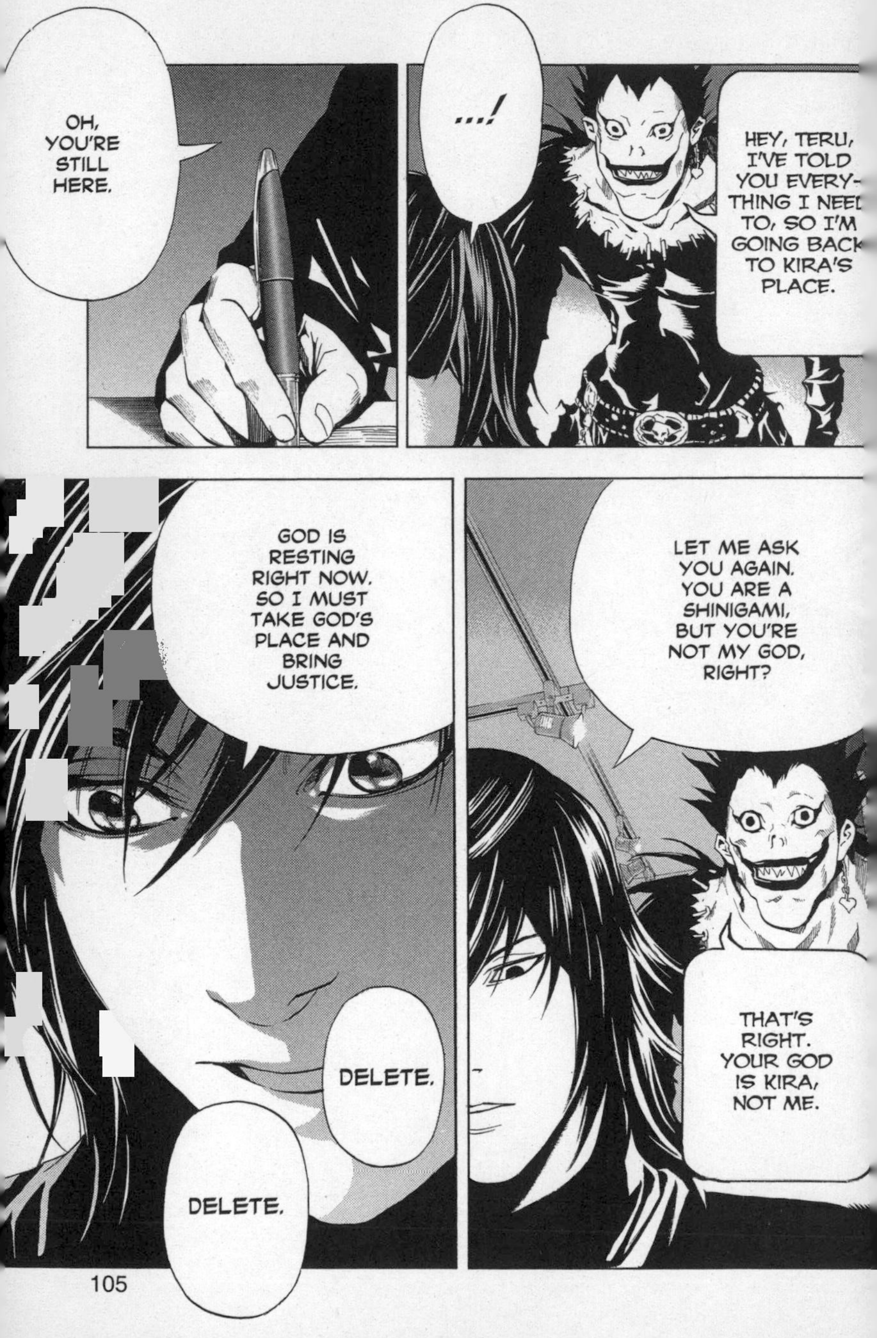
HEY, TERU, I'VE TOLD YOU EVERY-THING I NEED TO, SO I'M GOING BACK TO KIRA'S PLACE.
...!
OH, YOU'RE STILL HERE.
LET ME ASK YOU AGAIN. YOU ARE A SHINIGAMI, BUT YOU'RE NOT MY GOD, RIGHT?
THAT'S RIGHT. YOUR GOD IS KIRA, NOT ME.
GOD IS RESTING RIGHT NOW. SO I MUST TAKE GOD'S PLACE AND BRING JUSTICE.
DELETE.
DELETE.

DEATH NOTE
How to Use It
Lv l

- When you write multiple names in the DEATH NOTE and then write down even one cause of death within 40 human seconds from writing the first victim's name, the cause will take effect for all the written names.

名前を複数記し、最初に名前を記した時から人間界単位で40秒以内に
あるひとつの死因を記すだけでも、それが書かれた名前全てに適用される。

- Also, after writing the cause of death, even if the situation of death is written within 6 minutes and 40 seconds in the human world, that situation will only occur to the victims whom it is possible. For those where the situation is not possible, only the cause of death will occur.

また、死因を記した後、人間界単位で6分40秒以内に
あるひとつの死の状況を記した場合でも、
可能な者はその通りに、不可能な者は死因のみ適用される。

chapter 85 Election

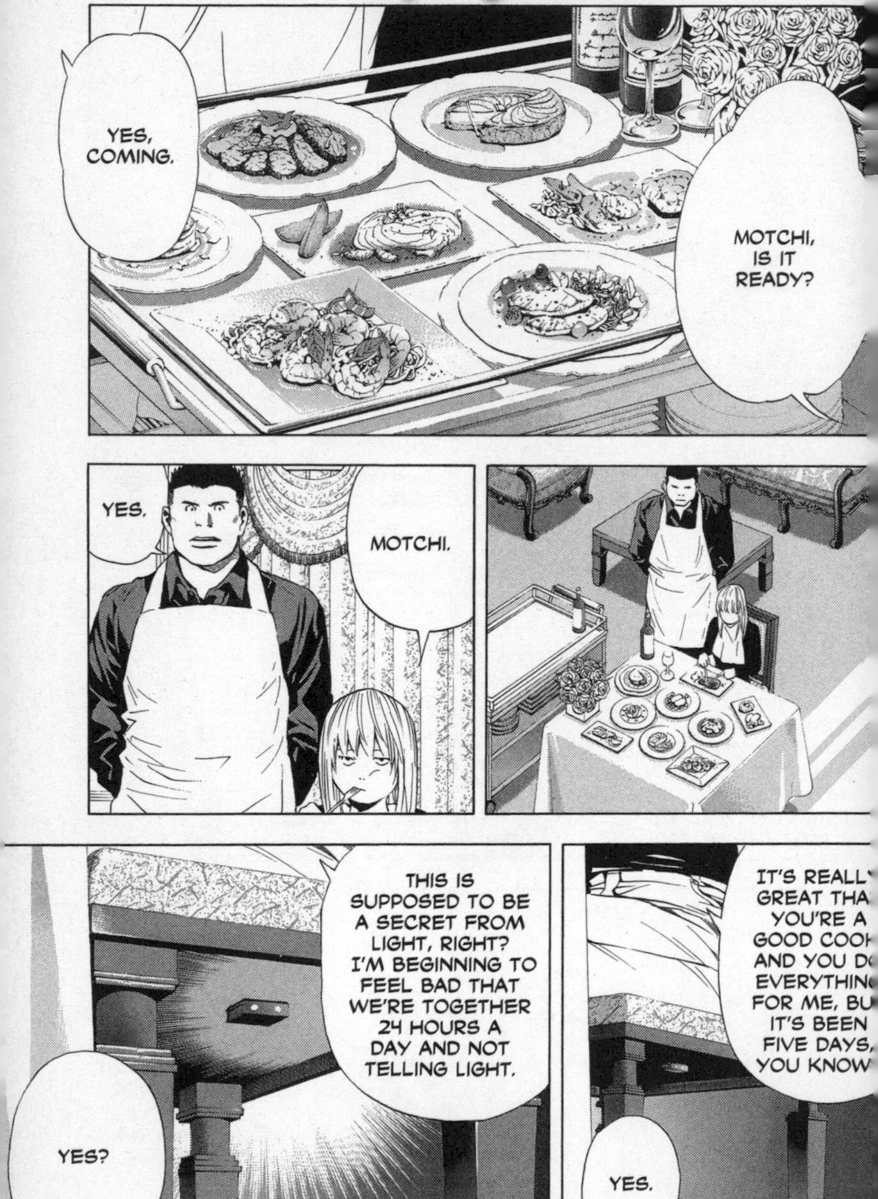
MOTCHI, IS IT READY?
YES, COMING.
MOTCHI.
YES.
IT'S REALL GREAT THA YOU'RE A GOOD COO AND YOU D EVERYTHIN FOR ME, BU IT'S BEEN FIVE DAYS, YOU KNOW
YES.
THIS IS SUPPOSED TO BE A SECRET FROM LIGHT, RIGHT? I'M BEGINNING TO FEEL BAD THAT WE'RE TOGETHER 24 HOURS A DAY AND NOT TELLING LIGHT.
YES?

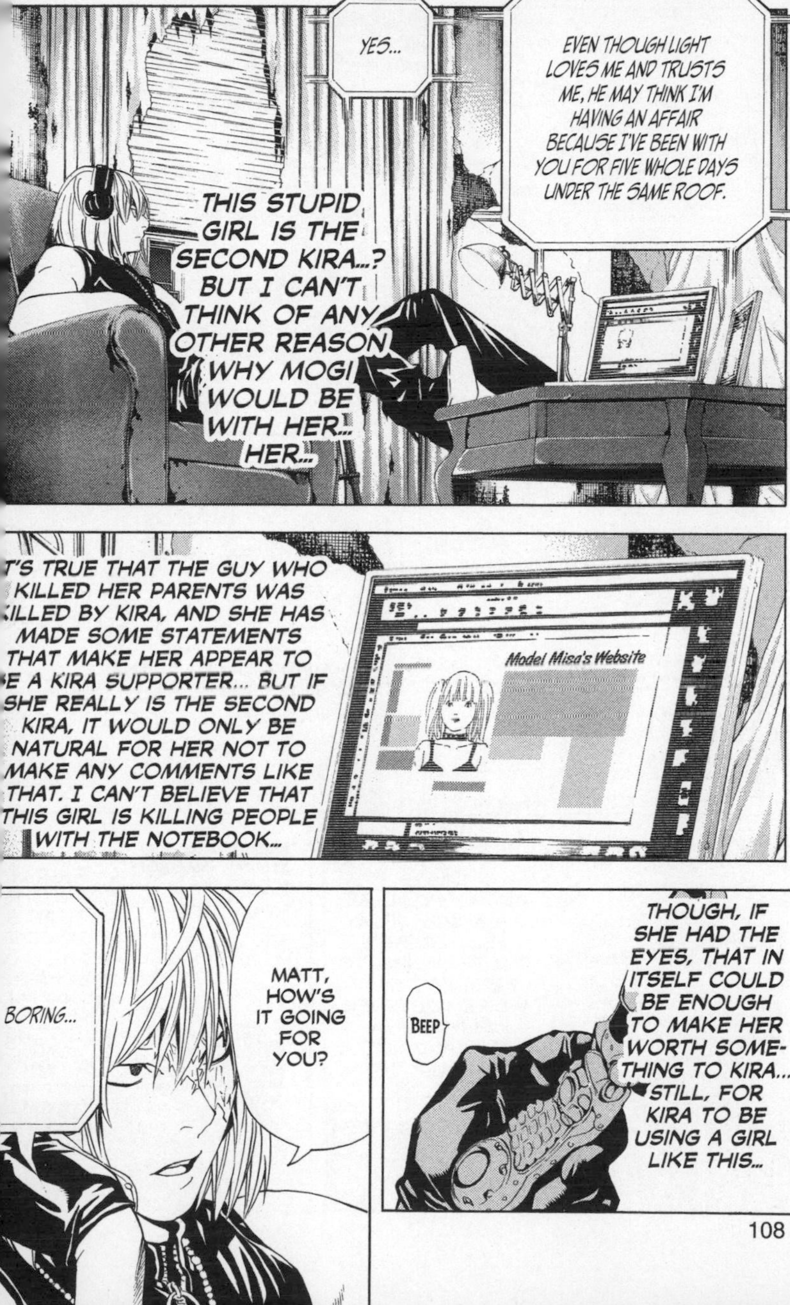
EVEN THOUGH LIGHT LOVES ME AND TRUSTS ME, HE MAY THINK I'M HAVING AN AFFAIR BECAUSE I'VE BEEN WITH YOU FOR FIVE WHOLE DAYS UNDER THE SAME ROOF.
YES...
THIS STUPID GIRL IS THE SECOND KIRA...? BUT I CAN'T THINK OF ANY OTHER REASON WHY MOGI WOULD BE WITH HER... HER...
'T'S TRUE THAT THE GUY WHO KILLED HER PARENTS WAS KILLED BY KIRA, AND SHE HAS MADE SOME STATEMENTS THAT MAKE HER APPEAR TO BE A KIRA SUPPORTER... BUT IF SHE REALLY IS THE SECOND KIRA, IT WOULD ONLY BE NATURAL FOR HER NOT TO MAKE ANY COMMENTS LIKE THAT. I CAN'T BELIEVE THAT THIS GIRL IS KILLING PEOPLE WITH THE NOTEBOOK...
Model Misa's Website
THOUGH, IF SHE HAD THE EYES, THAT IN ITSELF COULD BE ENOUGH TO MAKE HER WORTH SOMETHING TO KIRA... STILL, FOR KIRA TO BE USING A GIRL LIKE THIS...
BEEP
MATT, HOW'S IT GOING FOR YOU?
BORING...

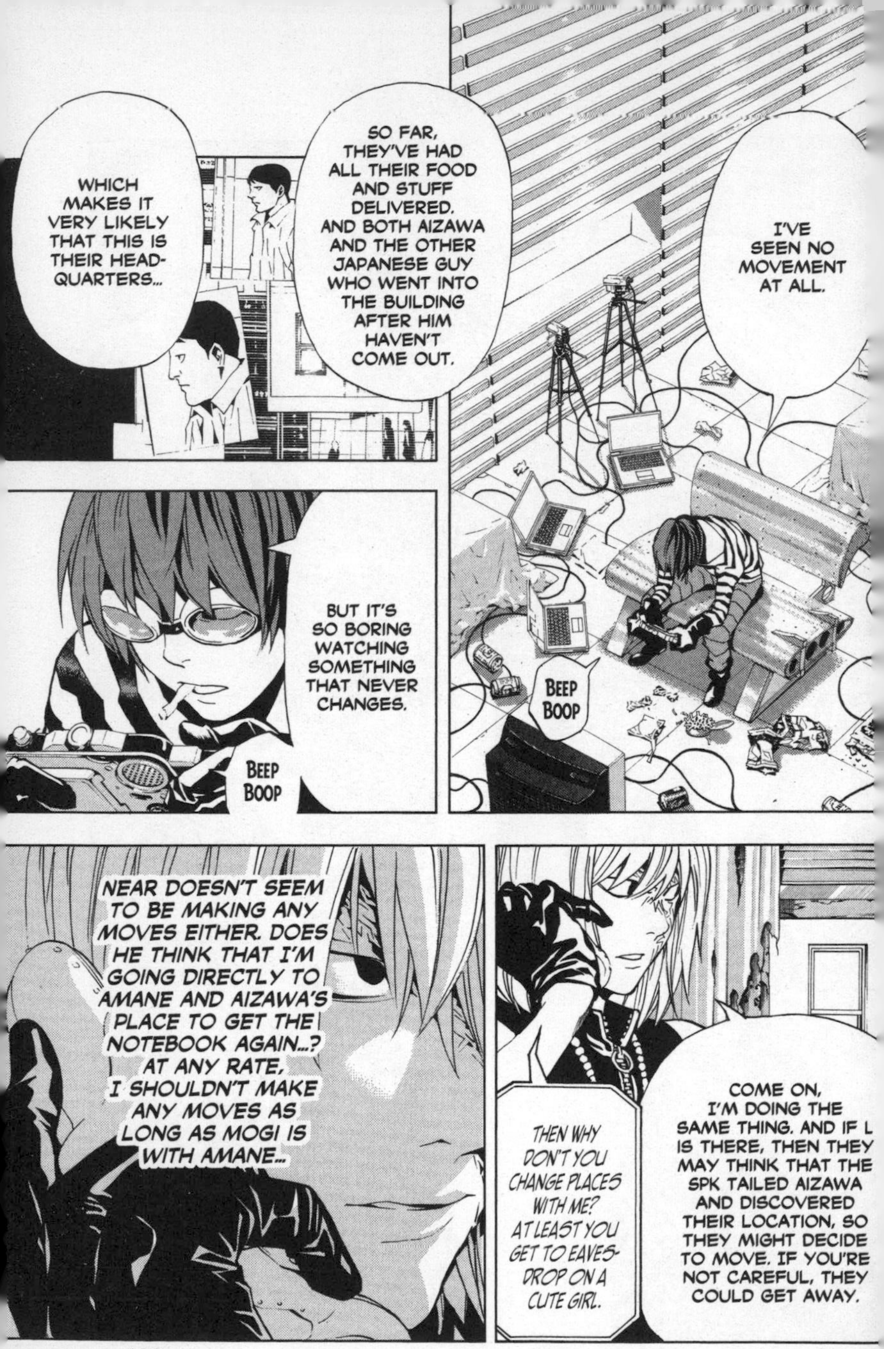

I'VE SEEN NO MOVEMENT AT ALL.
BEEP BOOP
SO FAR, THEY'VE HAD ALL THEIR FOOD AND STUFF DELIVERED. AND BOTH AIZAWA AND THE OTHER JAPANESE GUY WHO WENT INTO THE BUILDING AFTER HIM HAVEN'T COME OUT.
WHICH MAKES IT VERY LIKELY THAT THIS IS THEIR HEAD-QUARTERS...
BUT IT'S SO BORING WATCHING SOMETHING THAT NEVER CHANGES.
BEEP BOOP
COME ON, I'M DOING THE SAME THING. AND IF L IS THERE, THEN THEY MAY THINK THAT THE SPK TAILED AIZAWA AND DISCOVERED THEIR LOCATION, SO THEY MIGHT DECIDE TO MOVE. IF YOU'RE NOT CAREFUL, THEY COULD GET AWAY.
THEN WHY DON'T YOU CHANGE PLACES WITH ME? AT LEAST YOU GET TO EAVES-DROP ON A CUTE GIRL.
NEAR DOESN'T SEEM TO BE MAKING ANY MOVES EITHER. DOES HE THINK THAT I'M GOING DIRECTLY TO AMANE AND AIZAWA'S PLACE TO GET THE NOTEBOOK AGAIN...? AT ANY RATE, I SHOULDN'T MAKE ANY MOVES AS LONG AS MOGI IS WITH AMANE...

chapter 85 Election

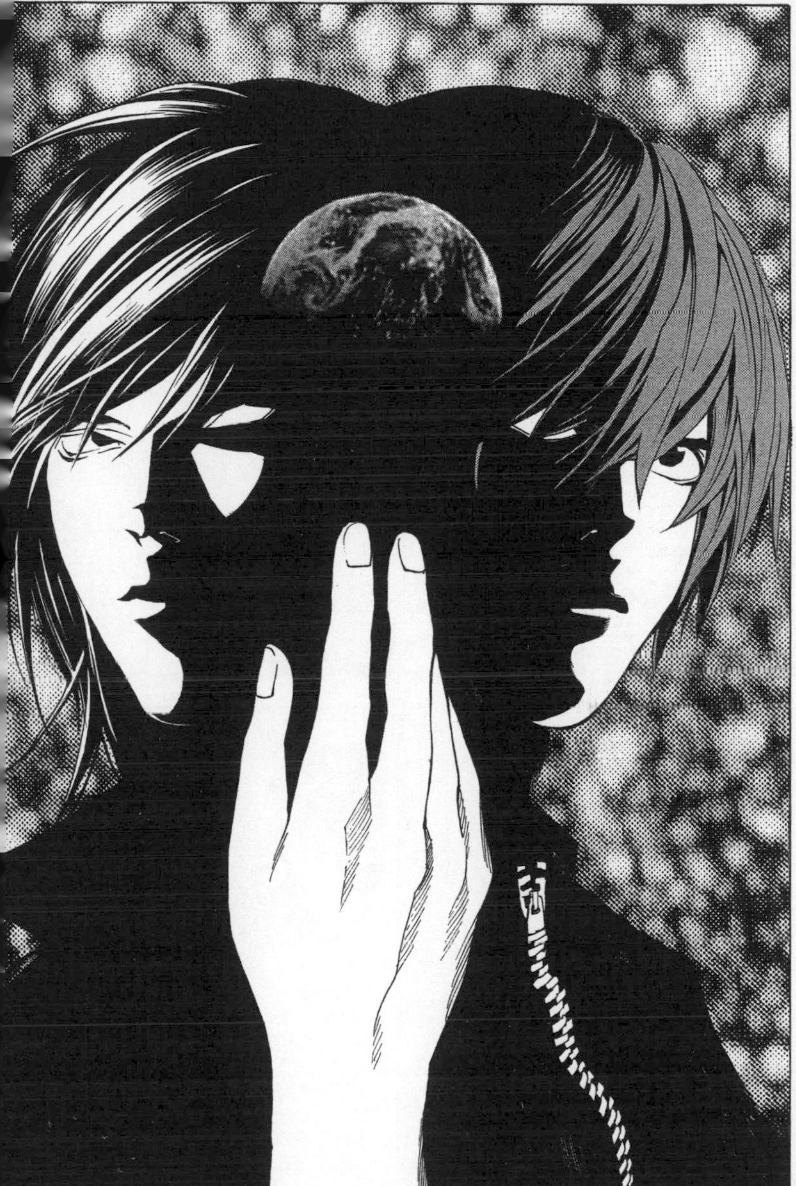

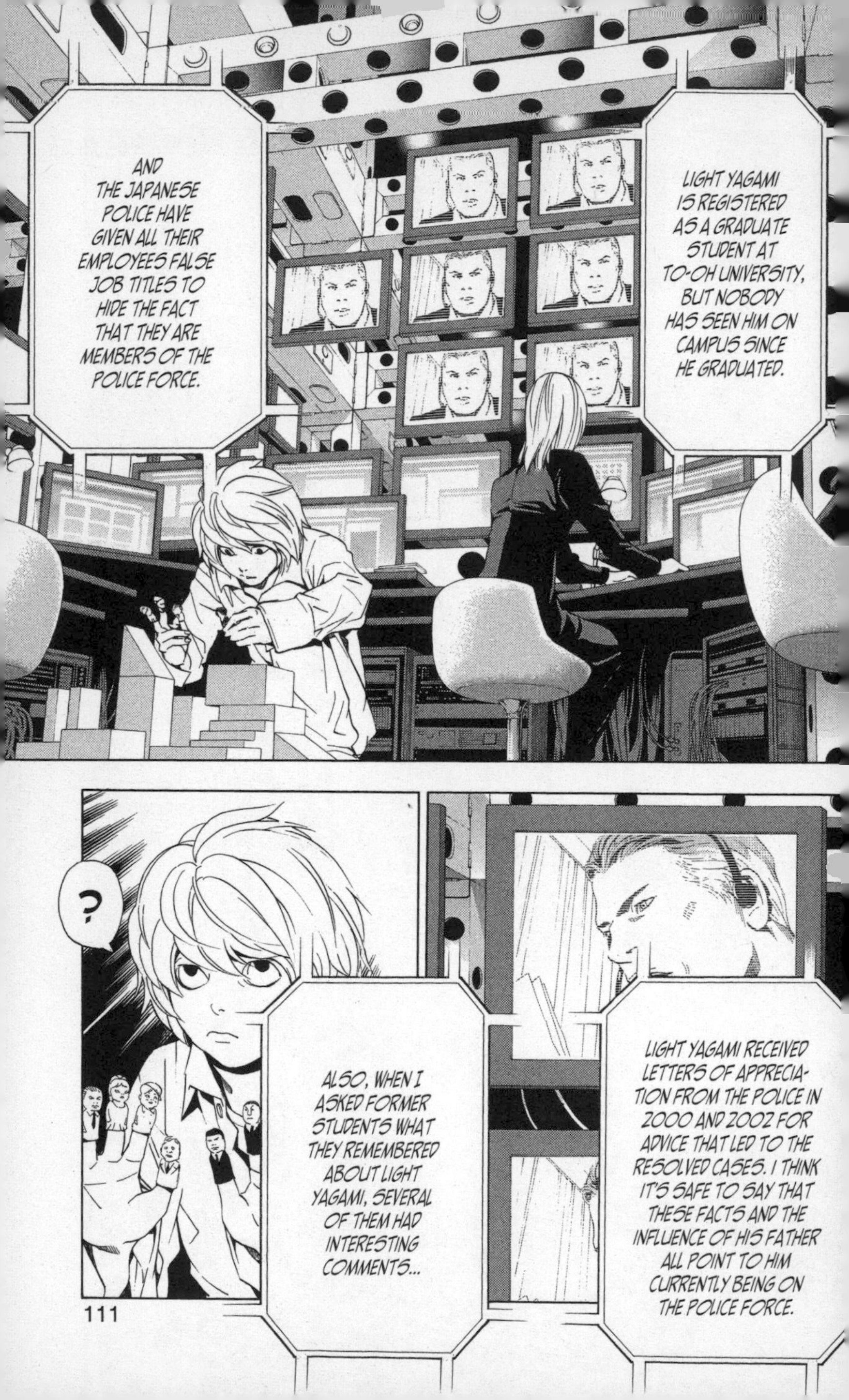
LIGHT YAGAMI IS REGISTERED AS A GRADUATE STUDENT AT TO-OH UNIVERSITY, BUT NOBODY HAS SEEN HIM ON CAMPUS SINCE HE GRADUATED.
AND THE JAPANESE POLICE HAVE GIVEN ALL THEIR EMPLOYEES FALSE JOB TITLES TO HIDE THE FACT THAT THEY ARE MEMBERS OF THE POLICE FORCE.
LIGHT YAGAMI RECEIVED LETTERS OF APPRECIATION FROM THE POLICE IN 2000 AND 2002 FOR ADVICE THAT LED TO THE RESOLVED CASES. I THINK IT'S SAFE TO SAY THAT THESE FACTS AND THE INFLUENCE OF HIS FATHER ALL POINT TO HIM CURRENTLY BEING ON THE POLICE FORCE.
?
ALSO, WHEN I ASKED FORMER STUDENTS WHAT THEY REMEMBERED ABOUT LIGHT YAGAMI, SEVERAL OF THEM HAD INTERESTING COMMENTS...

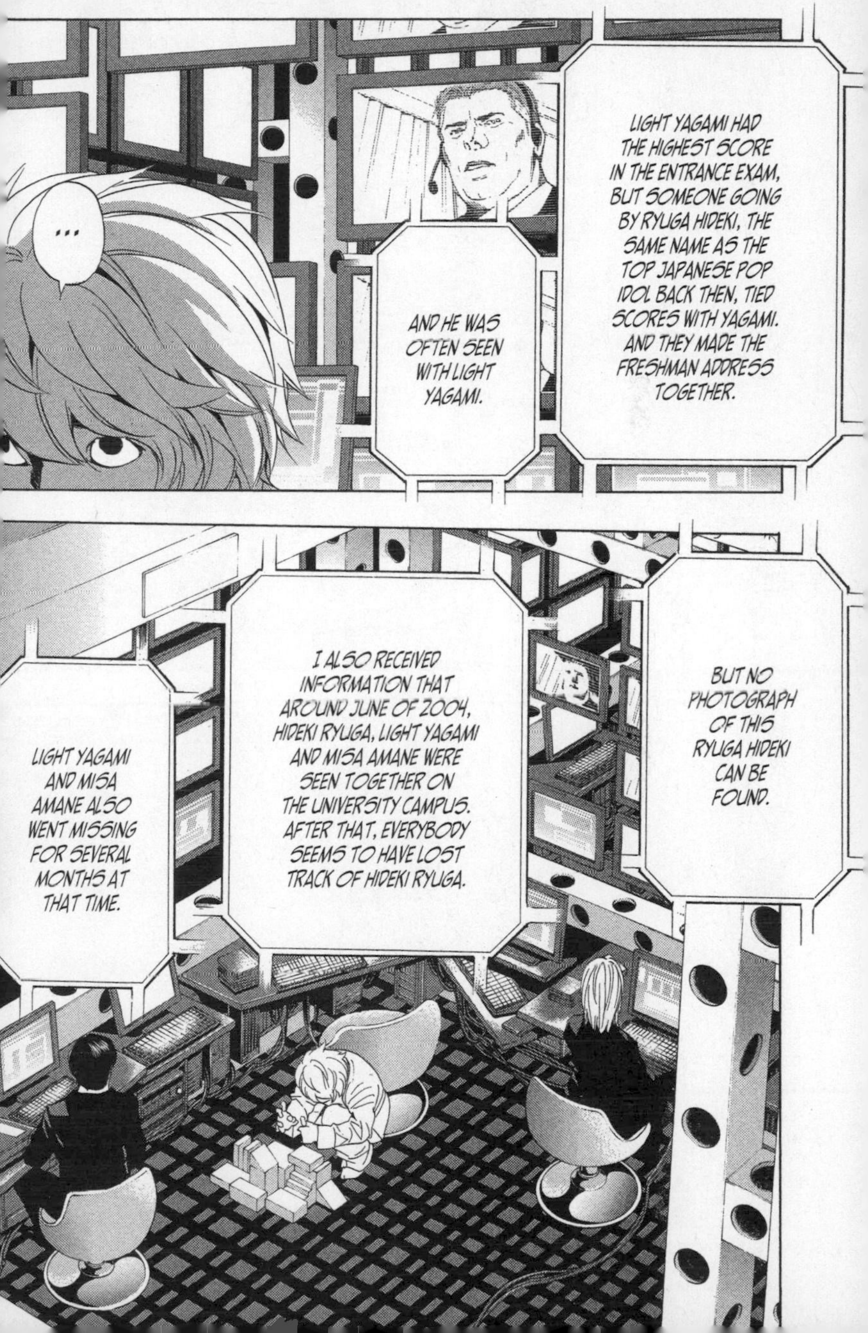
LIGHT YAGAMI HAD THE HIGHEST SCORE IN THE ENTRANCE EXAM, BUT SOMEONE GOING BY RYUGA HIDEKI, THE SAME NAME AS THE TOP JAPANESE POP IDOL BACK THEN, TIED SCORES WITH YAGAMI. AND THEY MADE THE FRESHMAN ADDRESS TOGETHER.
AND HE WAS OFTEN SEEN WITH LIGHT YAGAMI.
...
BUT NO PHOTOGRAPH OF THIS RYUGA HIDEKI CAN BE FOUND.
I ALSO RECEIVED INFORMATION THAT AROUND JUNE OF 2004, HIDEKI RYUGA, LIGHT YAGAMI AND MISA AMANE WERE SEEN TOGETHER ON THE UNIVERSITY CAMPUS. AFTER THAT, EVERYBODY SEEMS TO HAVE LOST TRACK OF HIDEKI RYUGA.
LIGHT YAGAMI AND MISA AMANE ALSO WENT MISSING FOR SEVERAL MONTHS AT THAT TIME.

READ THIS WAY

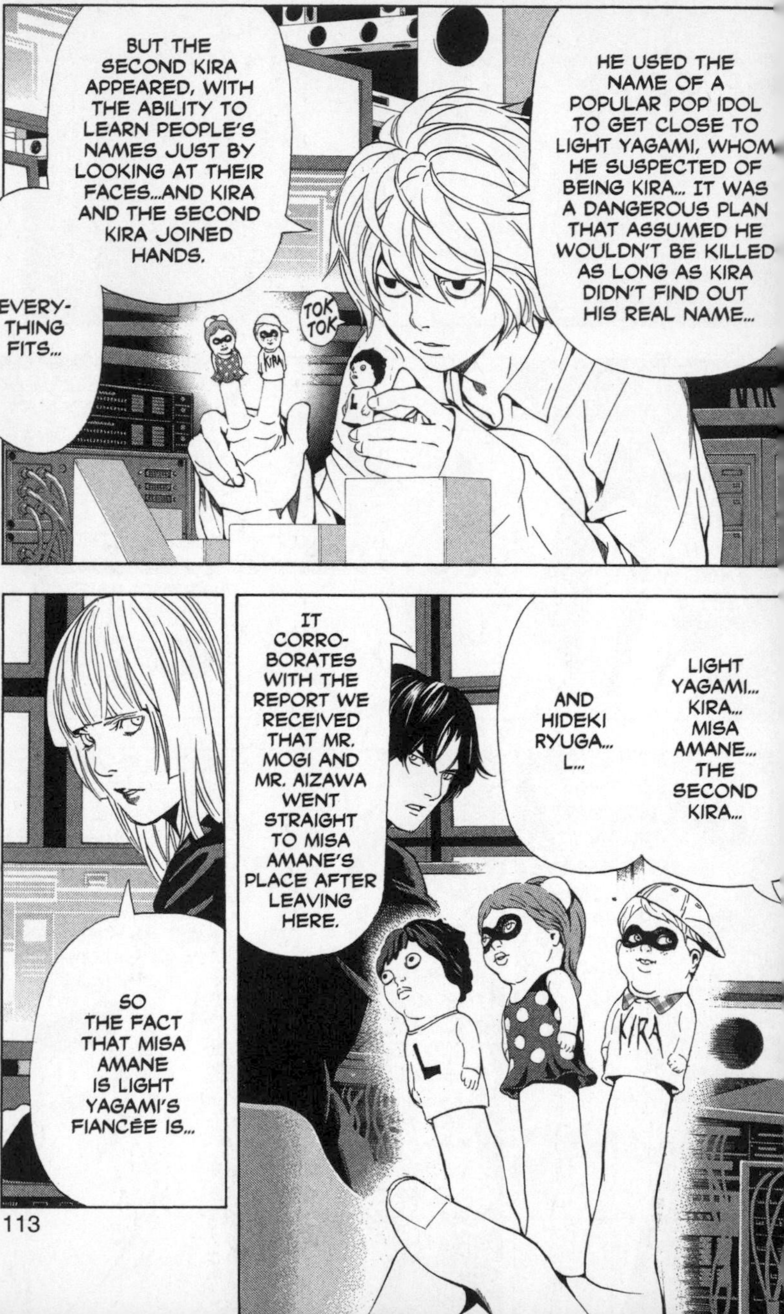
HE USED THE NAME OF A POPULAR POP IDOL TO GET CLOSE TO LIGHT YAGAMI, WHOM HE SUSPECTED OF BEING KIRA... IT WAS A DANGEROUS PLAN THAT ASSUMED HE WOULDN'T BE KILLED AS LONG AS KIRA DIDN'T FIND OUT HIS REAL NAME...
BUT THE SECOND KIRA APPEARED, WITH THE ABILITY TO LEARN PEOPLE'S NAMES JUST BY LOOKING AT THEIR FACES...AND KIRA AND THE SECOND KIRA JOINED HANDS.
TOK TOK
KIRA
EVERY-THING FITS...
LIGHT YAGAMI... KIRA... MISA AMANE... THE SECOND KIRA...
AND HIDEKI RYUGA... L...
IT CORROBORATES WITH THE REPORT WE RECEIVED THAT MR. MOGI AND MR. AIZAWA WENT STRAIGHT TO MISA AMANE'S PLACE AFTER LEAVING HERE.
KIRA
SO THE FACT THAT MISA AMANE IS LIGHT YAGAMI'S FIANCÉE IS...

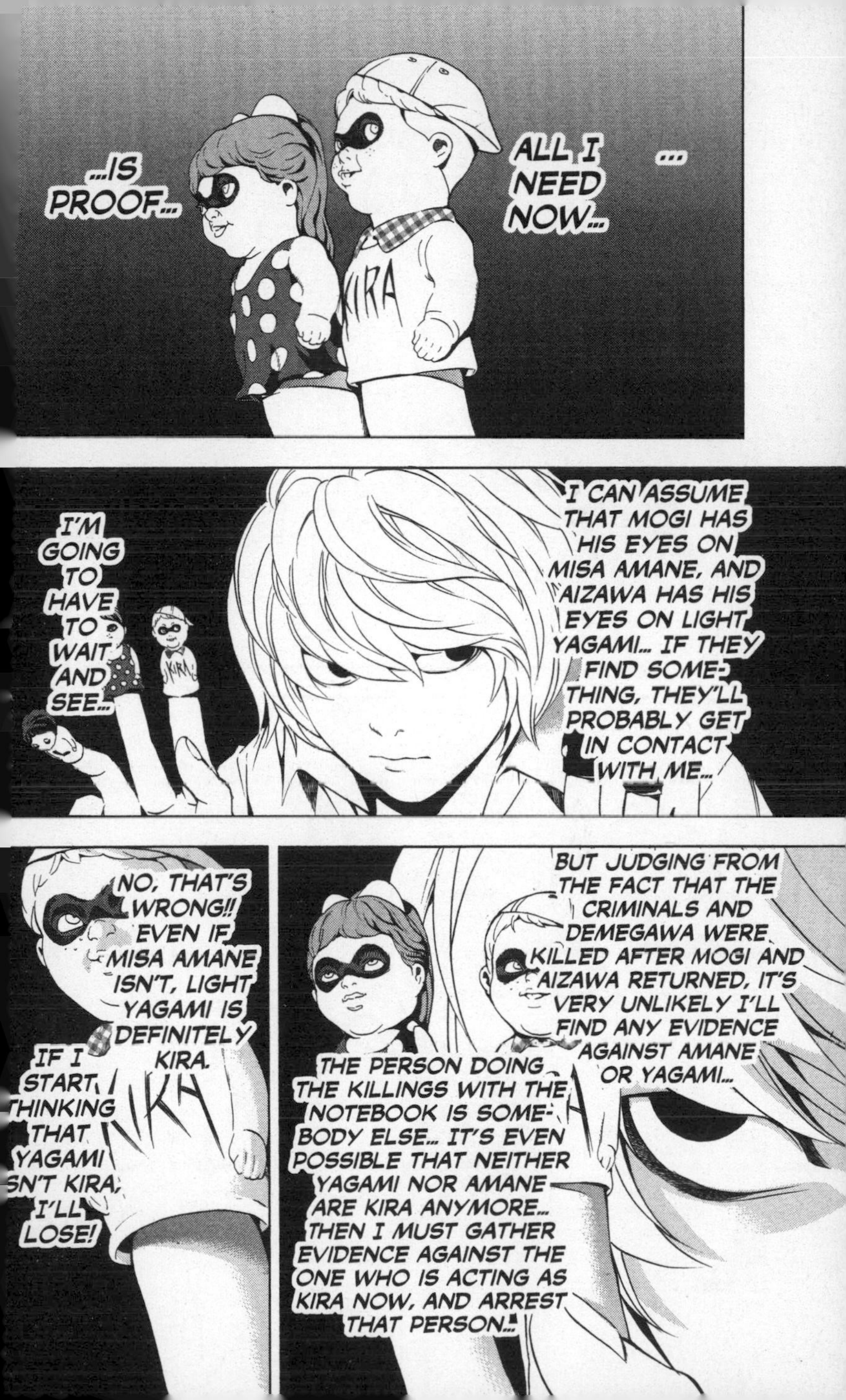
...
ALL I NEED NOW...
...IS PROOF...
I CAN ASSUME THAT MOGI HAS HIS EYES ON MISA AMANE, AND AIZAWA HAS HIS EYES ON LIGHT YAGAMI... IF THEY FIND SOME-THING, THEY'LL PROBABLY GET IN CONTACT WITH ME...
I'M GOING TO HAVE TO WAIT AND SEE...
KIRA
BUT JUDGING FROM THE FACT THAT THE CRIMINALS AND DEMEGAWA WERE KILLED AFTER MOGI AND AIZAWA RETURNED, IT'S VERY UNLIKELY I'LL FIND ANY EVIDENCE AGAINST AMANE OR YAGAMI...
THE PERSON DOING THE KILLINGS WITH THE NOTEBOOK IS SOME-BODY ELSE... IT'S EVEN POSSIBLE THAT NEITHER YAGAMI NOR AMANE ARE KIRA ANYMORE... THEN I MUST GATHER EVIDENCE AGAINST THE ONE WHO IS ACTING AS KIRA NOW, AND ARREST THAT PERSON...
NO, THAT'S WRONG!! EVEN IF MISA AMANE ISN'T, LIGHT YAGAMI IS DEFINITELY KIRA.
IF I START THINKING THAT YAGAMI ISN'T KIRA, I'LL LOSE!

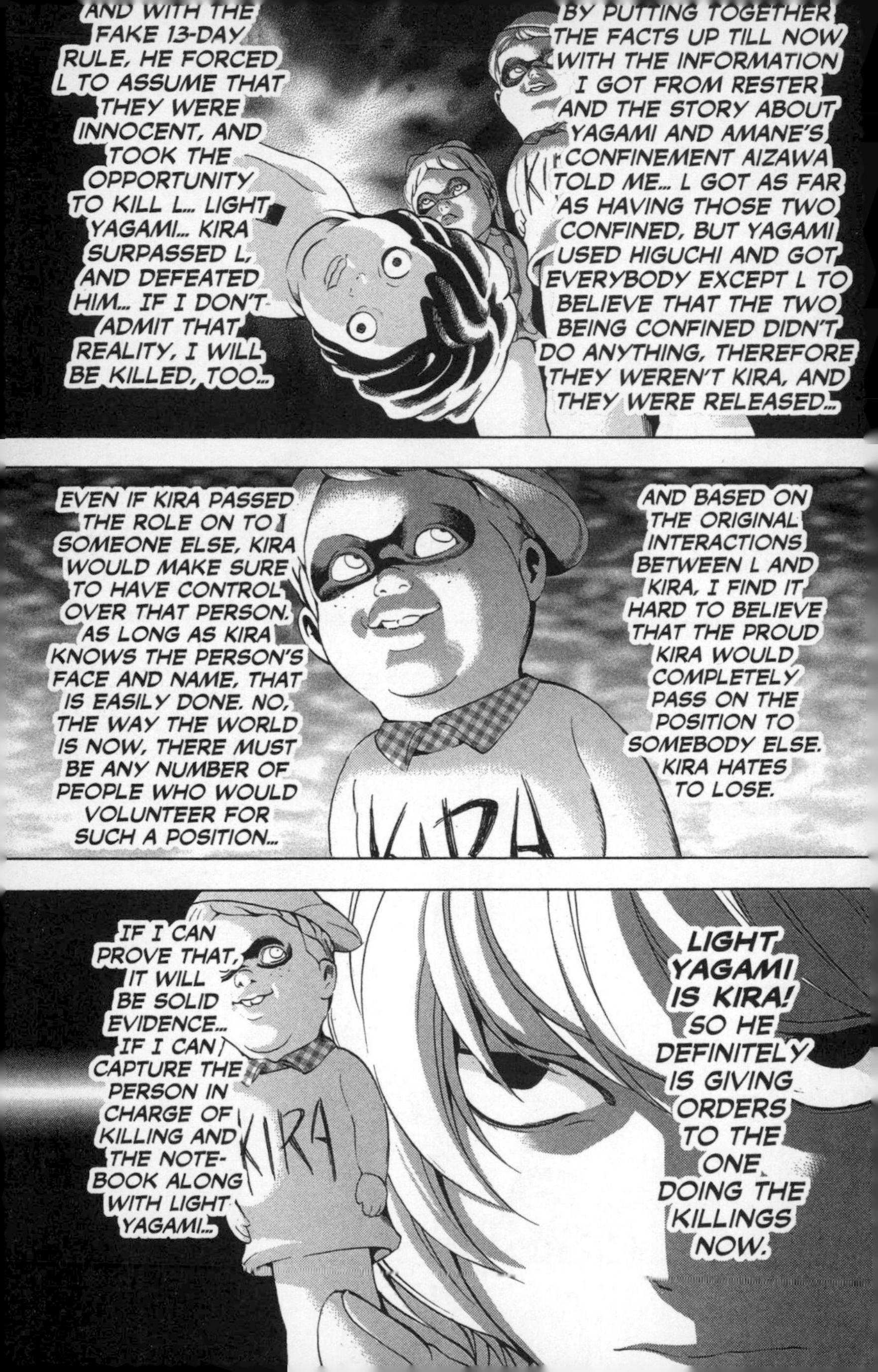
BY PUTTING TOGETHER THE FACTS UP TILL NOW WITH THE INFORMATION I GOT FROM RESTER AND THE STORY ABOUT YAGAMI AND AMANE'S CONFINEMENT AIZAWA TOLD ME... L GOT AS FAR AS HAVING THOSE TWO CONFINED, BUT YAGAMI USED HIGUCHI AND GOT EVERYBODY EXCEPT L TO BELIEVE THAT THE TWO BEING CONFINED DIDN'T DO ANYTHING, THEREFORE THEY WEREN'T KIRA, AND THEY WERE RELEASED...
AND WITH THE FAKE 13-DAY RULE, HE FORCED L TO ASSUME THAT THEY WERE INNOCENT, AND TOOK THE OPPORTUNITY TO KILL L... LIGHT YAGAMI... KIRA SURPASSED L, AND DEFEATED HIM... IF I DON'T ADMIT THAT REALITY, I WILL BE KILLED, TOO...
KIRA
AND BASED ON THE ORIGINAL INTERACTIONS BETWEEN L AND KIRA, I FIND IT HARD TO BELIEVE THAT THE PROUD KIRA WOULD COMPLETELY PASS ON THE POSITION TO SOMEBODY ELSE. KIRA HATES TO LOSE.
EVEN IF KIRA PASSED THE ROLE ON TO SOMEONE ELSE, KIRA WOULD MAKE SURE TO HAVE CONTROL OVER THAT PERSON. AS LONG AS KIRA KNOWS THE PERSON'S FACE AND NAME, THAT IS EASILY DONE. NO, THE WAY THE WORLD IS NOW, THERE MUST BE ANY NUMBER OF PEOPLE WHO WOULD VOLUNTEER FOR SUCH A POSITION...
LIGHT YAGAMI IS KIRA! SO HE DEFINITELY IS GIVING ORDERS TO THE ONE DOING THE KILLINGS NOW.
IF I CAN PROVE THAT, IT WILL BE SOLID EVIDENCE... IF I CAN CAPTURE THE PERSON IN CHARGE OF KILLING AND THE NOTE-BOOK ALONG WITH LIGHT YAGAMI...
KIRA

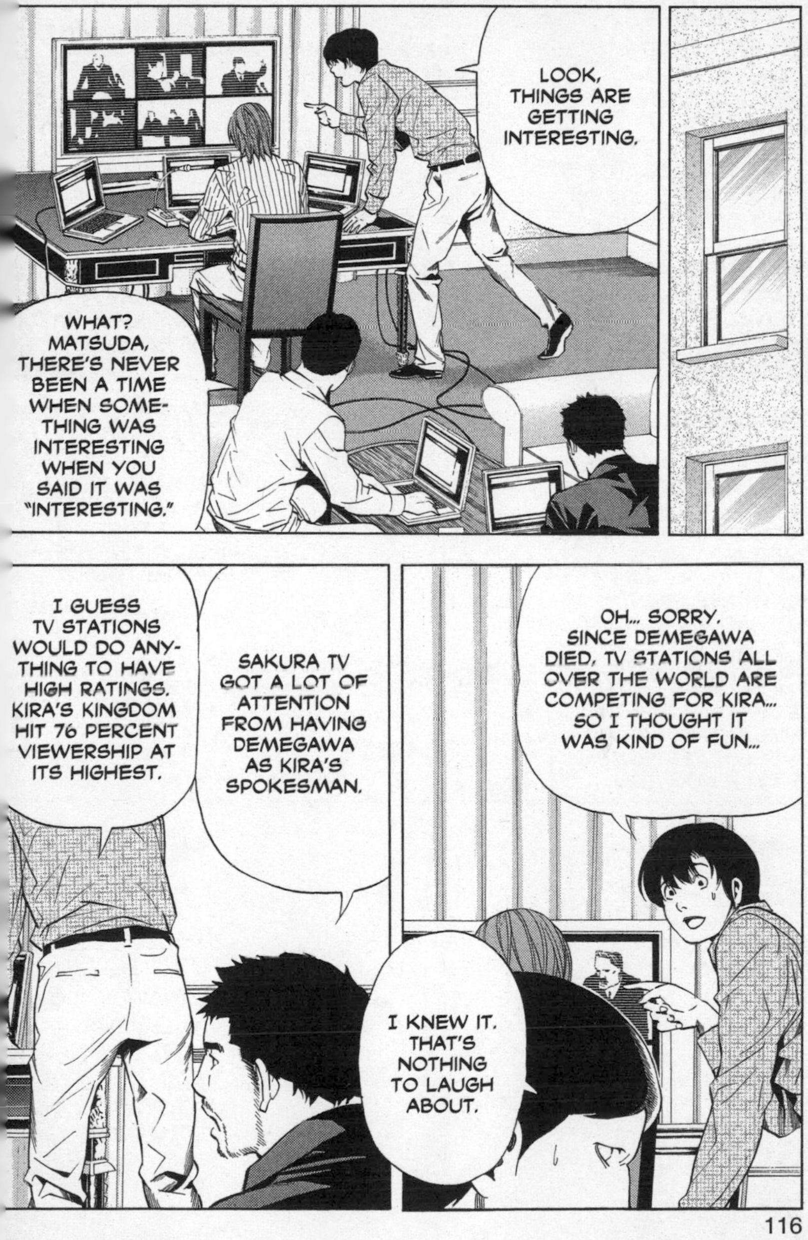
LOOK, THINGS ARE GETTING INTERESTING.
WHAT? MATSUDA, THERE'S NEVER BEEN A TIME WHEN SOME-THING WAS INTERESTING WHEN YOU SAID IT WAS "INTERESTING."
OH... SORRY. SINCE DEMEGAWA DIED, TV STATIONS ALL OVER THE WORLD ARE COMPETING FOR KIRA... SO I THOUGHT IT WAS KIND OF FUN...
I KNEW IT. THAT'S NOTHING TO LAUGH ABOUT.
SAKURA TV GOT A LOT OF ATTENTION FROM HAVING DEMEGAWA AS KIRA'S SPOKESMAN.
I GUESS TV STATIONS WOULD DO ANY-THING TO HAVE HIGH RATINGS. KIRA'S KINGDOM HIT 76 PERCENT VIEWERSHIP AT ITS HIGHEST.

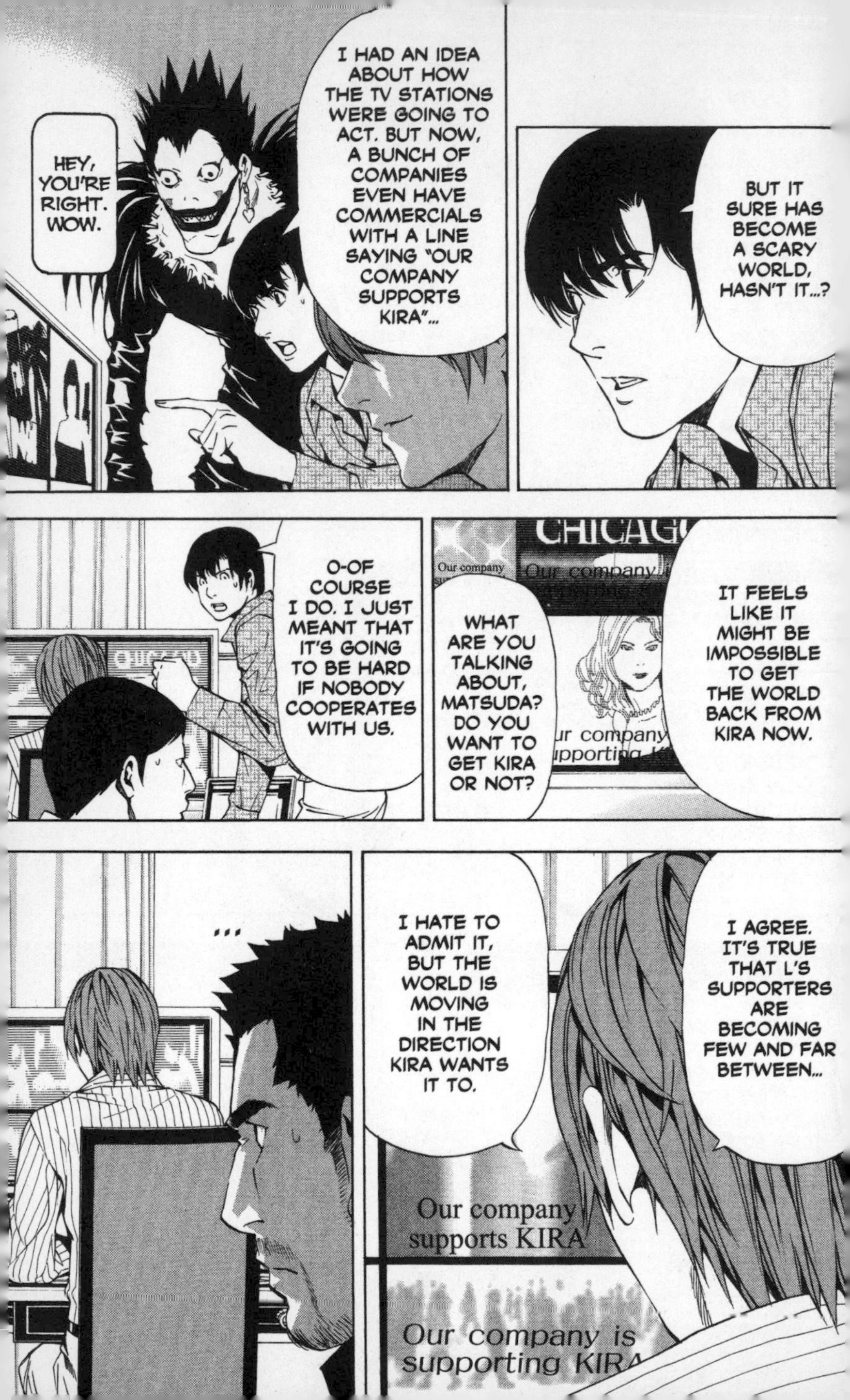
BUT IT SURE HAS BECOME A SCARY WORLD, HASN'T IT...?
I HAD AN IDEA ABOUT HOW THE TV STATIONS WERE GOING TO ACT. BUT NOW, A BUNCH OF COMPANIES EVEN HAVE COMMERCIALS WITH A LINE SAYING "OUR COMPANY SUPPORTS KIRA"...
HEY, YOU'RE RIGHT. WOW.
IT FEELS LIKE IT MIGHT BE IMPOSSIBLE TO GET THE WORLD BACK FROM KIRA NOW.
Our company
WHAT ARE YOU TALKING ABOUT, MATSUDA? DO YOU WANT TO GET KIRA OR NOT?
O-OF COURSE I DO. I JUST MEANT THAT IT'S GOING TO BE HARD IF NOBODY COOPERATES WITH US.
I AGREE. IT'S TRUE THAT L'S SUPPORTERS ARE BECOMING FEW AND FAR BETWEEN...
I HATE TO ADMIT IT, BUT THE WORLD IS MOVING IN THE DIRECTION KIRA WANTS IT TO.
Our company supports KIRA
Our company is supporting KIRA
...

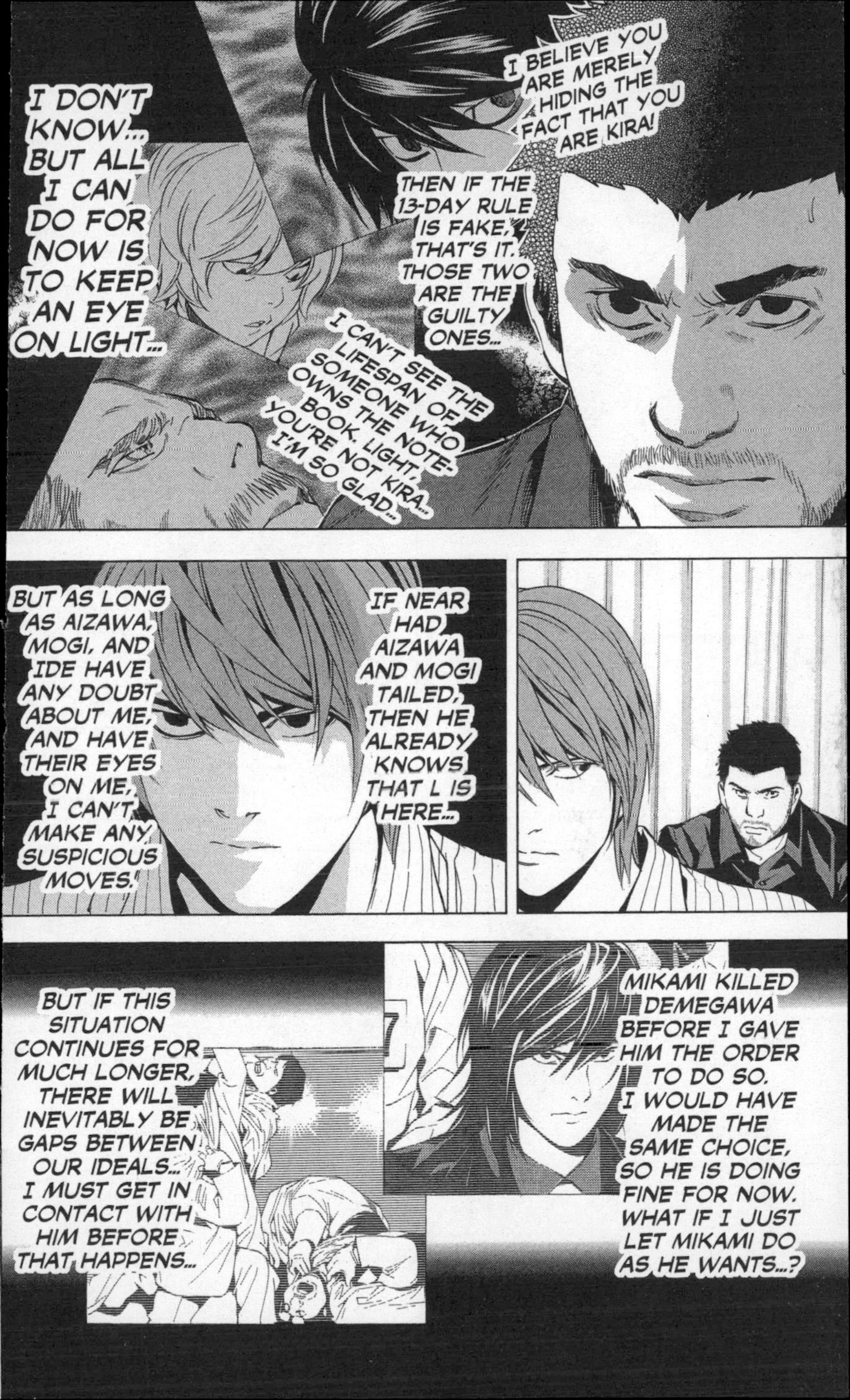
I BELIEVE YOU ARE MERELY HIDING THE FACT THAT YOU ARE KIRA!
THEN IF THE 13-DAY RULE IS FAKE, THAT'S IT. THOSE TWO ARE THE GUILTY ONES...
I CAN'T SEE THE LIFESPAN OF SOMEONE WHO OWNS THE NOTE-BOOK. LIGHT, YOU'RE NOT KIRA... I'M SO GLAD...
I DON'T KNOW... BUT ALL I CAN DO FOR NOW IS TO KEEP AN EYE ON LIGHT...
IF NEAR HAD AIZAWA AND MOGI TAILED, THEN HE ALREADY KNOWS THAT L IS HERE...
BUT AS LONG AS AIZAWA, MOGI, AND IDE HAVE ANY DOUBT ABOUT ME, AND HAVE THEIR EYES ON ME, I CAN'T MAKE ANY SUSPICIOUS MOVES.
MIKAMI KILLED DEMEGAWA BEFORE I GAVE HIM THE ORDER TO DO SO. I WOULD HAVE MADE THE SAME CHOICE, SO HE IS DOING FINE FOR NOW. WHAT IF I JUST LET MIKAMI DO AS HE WANTS...?
BUT IF THIS SITUATION CONTINUES FOR MUCH LONGER, THERE WILL INEVITABLY BE GAPS BETWEEN OUR IDEALS... I MUST GET IN CONTACT WITH HIM BEFORE THAT HAPPENS...

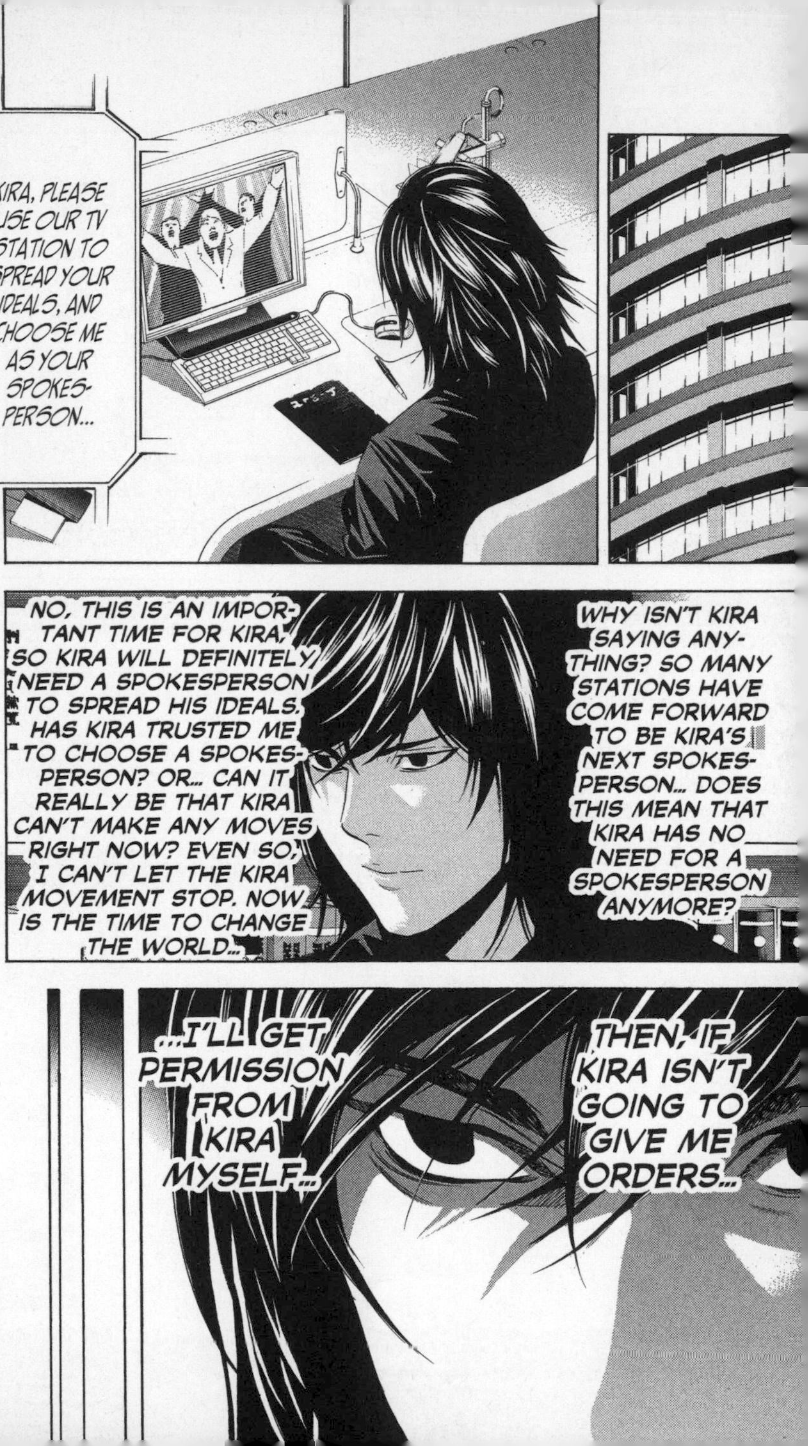
KIRA, PLEASE USE OUR TV STATION TO SPREAD YOUR IDEALS, AND CHOOSE ME AS YOUR SPOKES-PERSON...
WHY ISN'T KIRA SAYING ANY-THING? SO MANY STATIONS HAVE COME FORWARD TO BE KIRA'S NEXT SPOKES-PERSON... DOES THIS MEAN THAT KIRA HAS NO NEED FOR A SPOKESPERSON ANYMORE?
NO, THIS IS AN IMPOR-TANT TIME FOR KIRA, SO KIRA WILL DEFINITELY NEED A SPOKESPERSON TO SPREAD HIS IDEALS. HAS KIRA TRUSTED ME TO CHOOSE A SPOKES-PERSON? OR... CAN IT REALLY BE THAT KIRA CAN'T MAKE ANY MOVES RIGHT NOW? EVEN SO, I CAN'T LET THE KIRA MOVEMENT STOP. NOW IS THE TIME TO CHANGE THE WORLD...
THEN, IF KIRA ISN'T GOING TO GIVE ME ORDERS...
...I'LL GET PERMISSION FROM KIRA MYSELF...

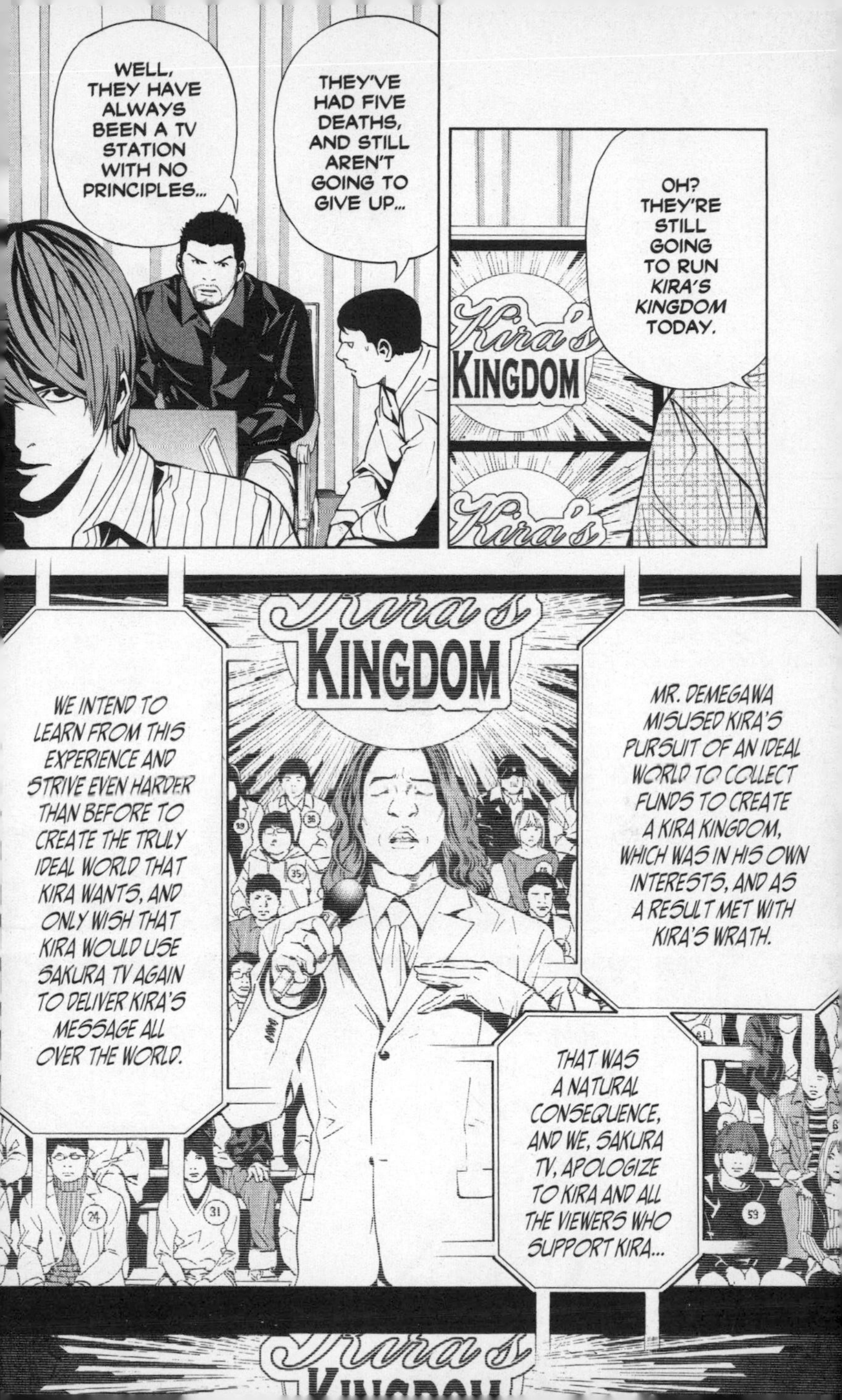
Kira's
KINGDOM
Kira's
OH? THEY'RE STILL GOING TO RUN KIRA'S KINGDOM TODAY.
THEY'VE HAD FIVE DEATHS, AND STILL AREN'T GOING TO GIVE UP...
WELL, THEY HAVE ALWAYS BEEN A TV STATION WITH NO PRINCIPLES...
KINGDOM
MR. DEMEGAWA MISUSED KIRA'S PURSUIT OF AN IDEAL WORLD TO COLLECT FUNDS TO CREATE A KIRA KINGDOM, WHICH WAS IN HIS OWN INTERESTS, AND AS A RESULT MET WITH KIRA'S WRATH.
THAT WAS A NATURAL CONSEQUENCE, AND WE, SAKURA TV, APOLOGIZE TO KIRA AND ALL THE VIEWERS WHO SUPPORT KIRA...
WE INTEND TO LEARN FROM THIS EXPERIENCE AND STRIVE EVEN HARDER THAN BEFORE TO CREATE THE TRULY IDEAL WORLD THAT KIRA WANTS, AND ONLY WISH THAT KIRA WOULD USE SAKURA TV AGAIN TO DELIVER KIRA'S MESSAGE ALL OVER THE WORLD.

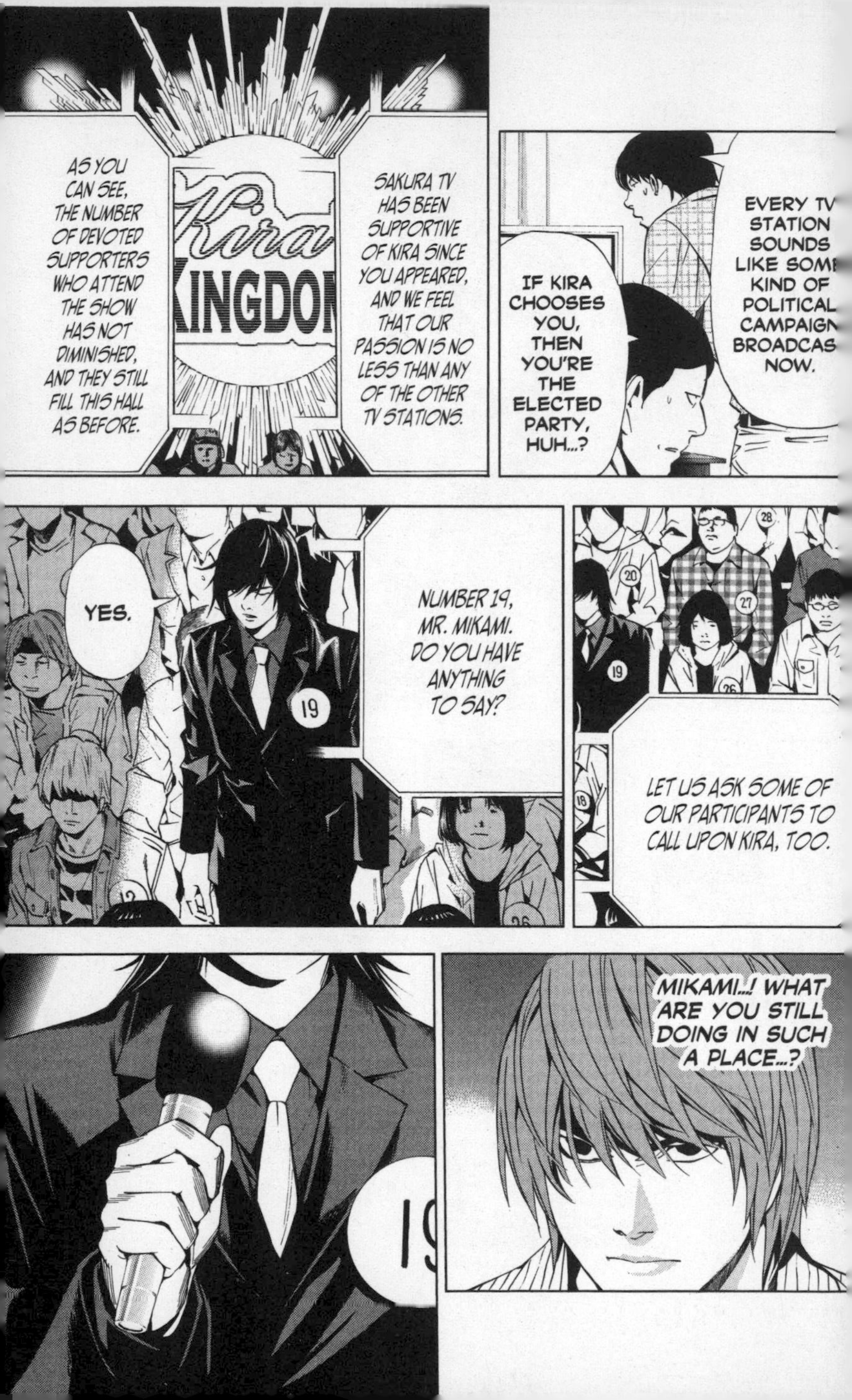
EVERY TV STATION SOUNDS LIKE SOM KIND OF POLITICAL CAMPAIGN BROADCAS NOW.
IF KIRA CHOOSES YOU, THEN YOU'RE THE ELECTED PARTY, HUH...?
SAKURA TV HAS BEEN SUPPORTIVE OF KIRA SINCE YOU APPEARED, AND WE FEEL THAT OUR PASSION IS NO LESS THAN ANY OF THE OTHER TV STATIONS.
Kira
KINGDO
AS YOU CAN SEE, THE NUMBER OF DEVOTED SUPPORTERS WHO ATTEND THE SHOW HAS NOT DIMINISHED, AND THEY STILL FILL THIS HALL AS BEFORE.
LET US ASK SOME OF OUR PARTICIPANTS TO CALL UPON KIRA, TOO.
NUMBER 19, MR. MIKAMI. DO YOU HAVE ANYTHING TO SAY?
YES.
MIKAMI...! WHAT ARE YOU STILL DOING IN SUCH A PLACE...?

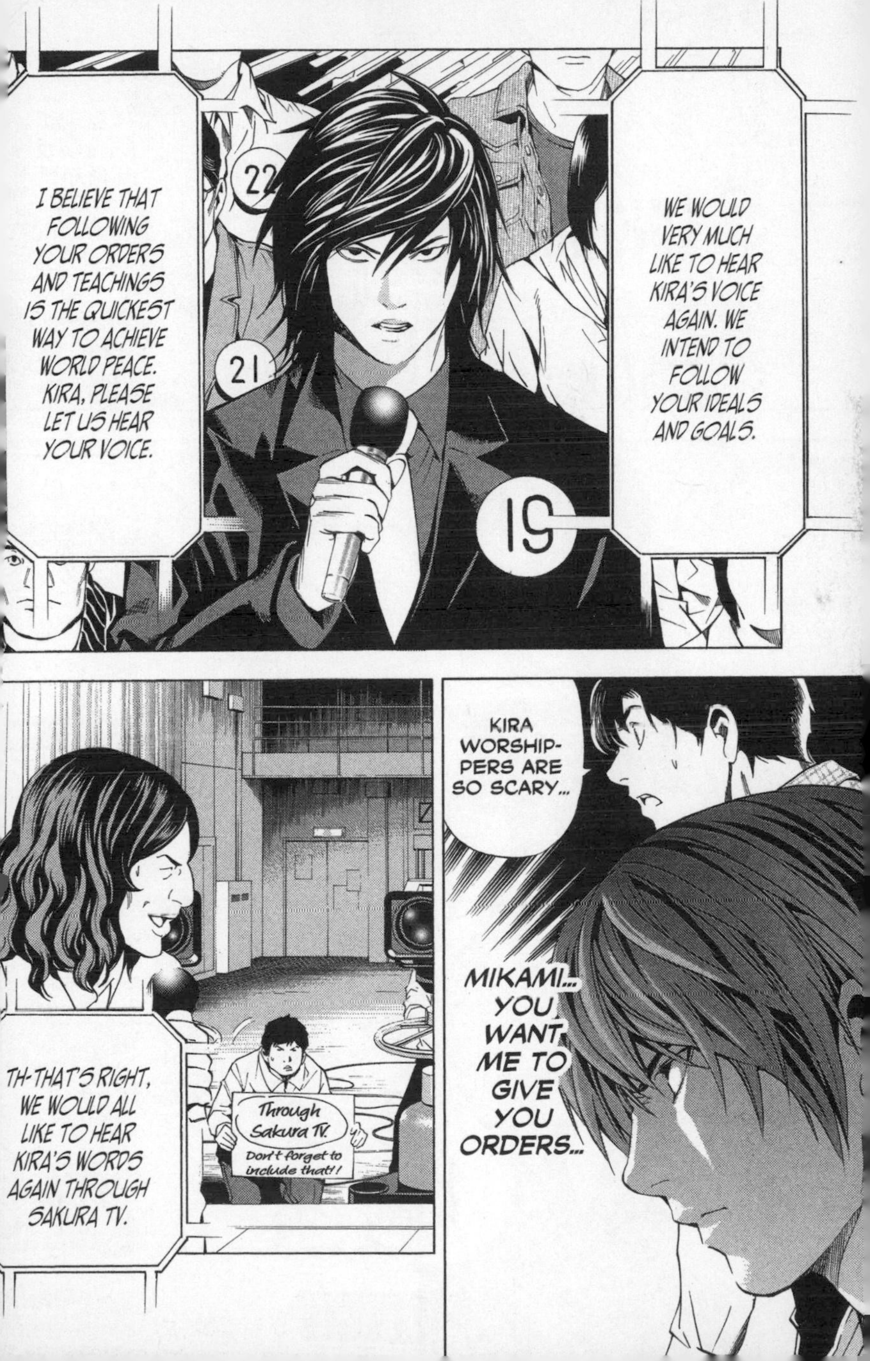
WE WOULD VERY MUCH LIKE TO HEAR KIRA'S VOICE AGAIN. WE INTEND TO FOLLOW YOUR IDEALS AND GOALS.
19
22
21
I BELIEVE THAT FOLLOWING YOUR ORDERS AND TEACHINGS IS THE QUICKEST WAY TO ACHIEVE WORLD PEACE. KIRA, PLEASE LET US HEAR YOUR VOICE.
KIRA WORSHIPPERS ARE SO SCARY...
MIKAMI... YOU WANT ME TO GIVE YOU ORDERS...
TH-THAT'S RIGHT, WE WOULD ALL LIKE TO HEAR KIRA'S WORDS AGAIN THROUGH SAKURA TV.
Through Sakura TV.
Don't forget to include that!!

READ THIS WAY

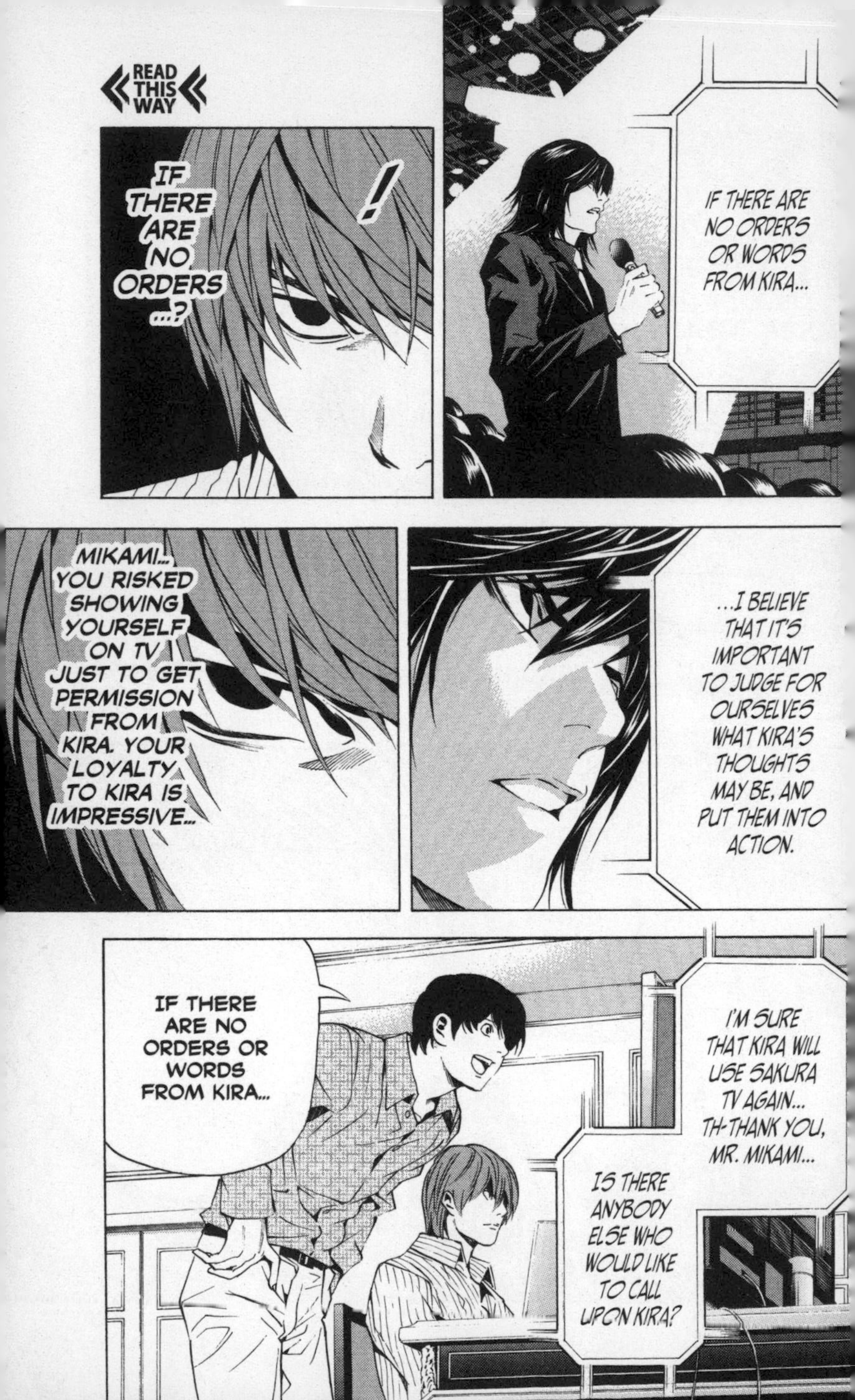
IF THERE ARE NO ORDERS OR WORDS FROM KIRA...
IF THERE ARE NO ORDERS ...?
...I BELIEVE THAT IT'S IMPORTANT TO JUDGE FOR OURSELVES WHAT KIRA'S THOUGHTS MAY BE, AND PUT THEM INTO ACTION.
MIKAMI... YOU RISKED SHOWING YOURSELF ON TV JUST TO GET PERMISSION FROM KIRA. YOUR LOYALTY TO KIRA IS IMPRESSIVE...
I'M SURE THAT KIRA WILL USE SAKURA TV AGAIN... TH-THANK YOU, MR. MIKAMI...
IS THERE ANYBODY ELSE WHO WOULD LIKE TO CALL UPON KIRA?
IF THERE ARE NO ORDERS OR WORDS FROM KIRA...

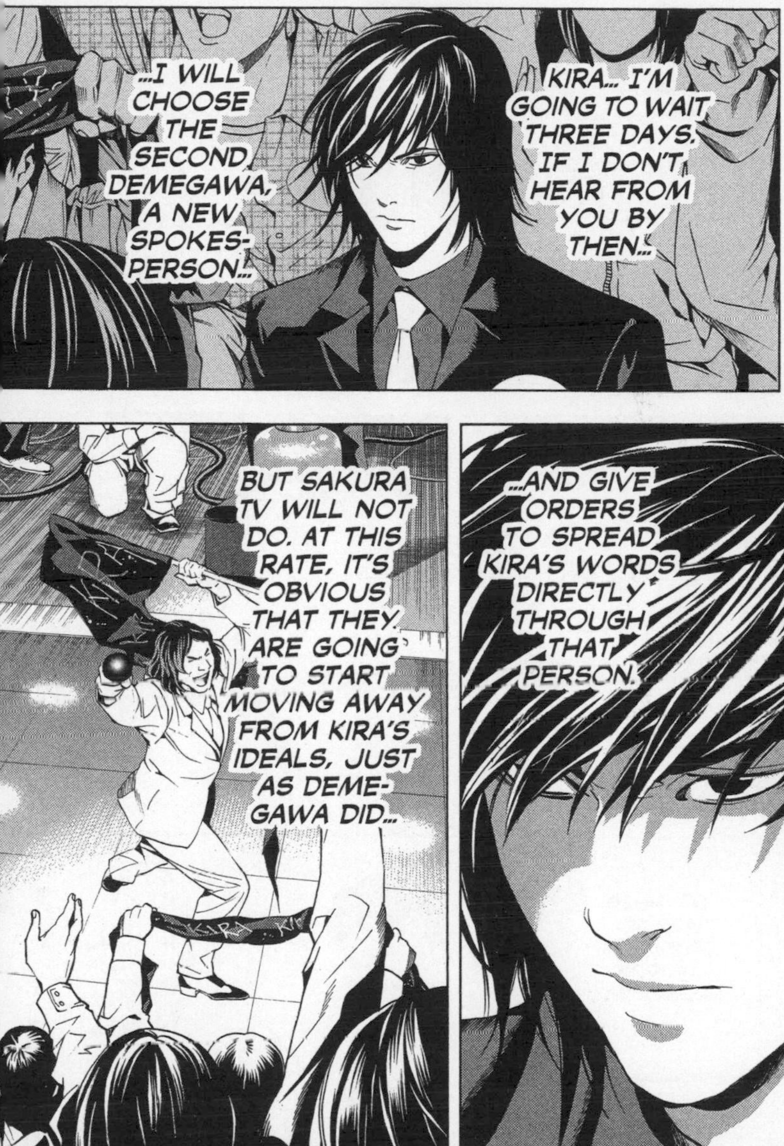
KIRA... I'M GOING TO WAIT THREE DAYS. IF I DON'T HEAR FROM YOU BY THEN...
...I WILL CHOOSE THE SECOND DEMEGAWA, A NEW SPOKES-PERSON...
...AND GIVE ORDERS TO SPREAD KIRA'S WORDS DIRECTLY THROUGH THAT PERSON.
BUT SAKURA TV WILL NOT DO. AT THIS RATE, IT'S OBVIOUS THAT THEY ARE GOING TO START MOVING AWAY FROM KIRA'S IDEALS, JUST AS DEME-GAWA DID...

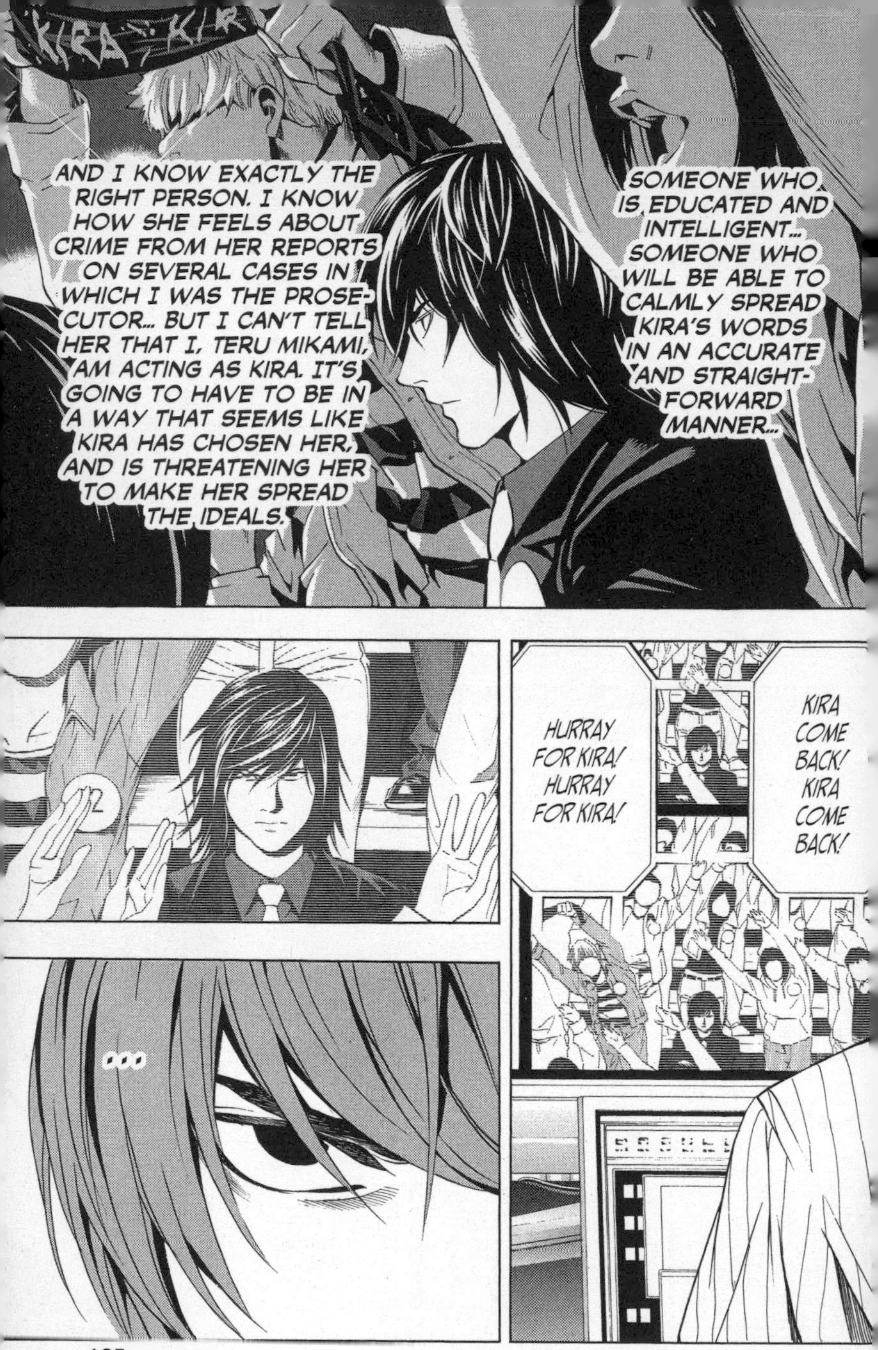
SOMEONE WHO IS EDUCATED AND INTELLIGENT... SOMEONE WHO WILL BE ABLE TO CALMLY SPREAD KIRA'S WORDS IN AN ACCURATE AND STRAIGHTFORWARD MANNER...
AND I KNOW EXACTLY THE RIGHT PERSON. I KNOW HOW SHE FEELS ABOUT CRIME FROM HER REPORTS ON SEVERAL CASES IN WHICH I WAS THE PROSECUTOR... BUT I CAN'T TELL HER THAT I, TERU MIKAMI, AM ACTING AS KIRA. IT'S GOING TO HAVE TO BE IN A WAY THAT SEEMS LIKE KIRA HAS CHOSEN HER, AND IS THREATENING HER TO MAKE HER SPREAD THE IDEALS.
KIRA COME BACK! KIRA COME BACK!
HURRAY FOR KIRA! HURRAY FOR KIRA!
...

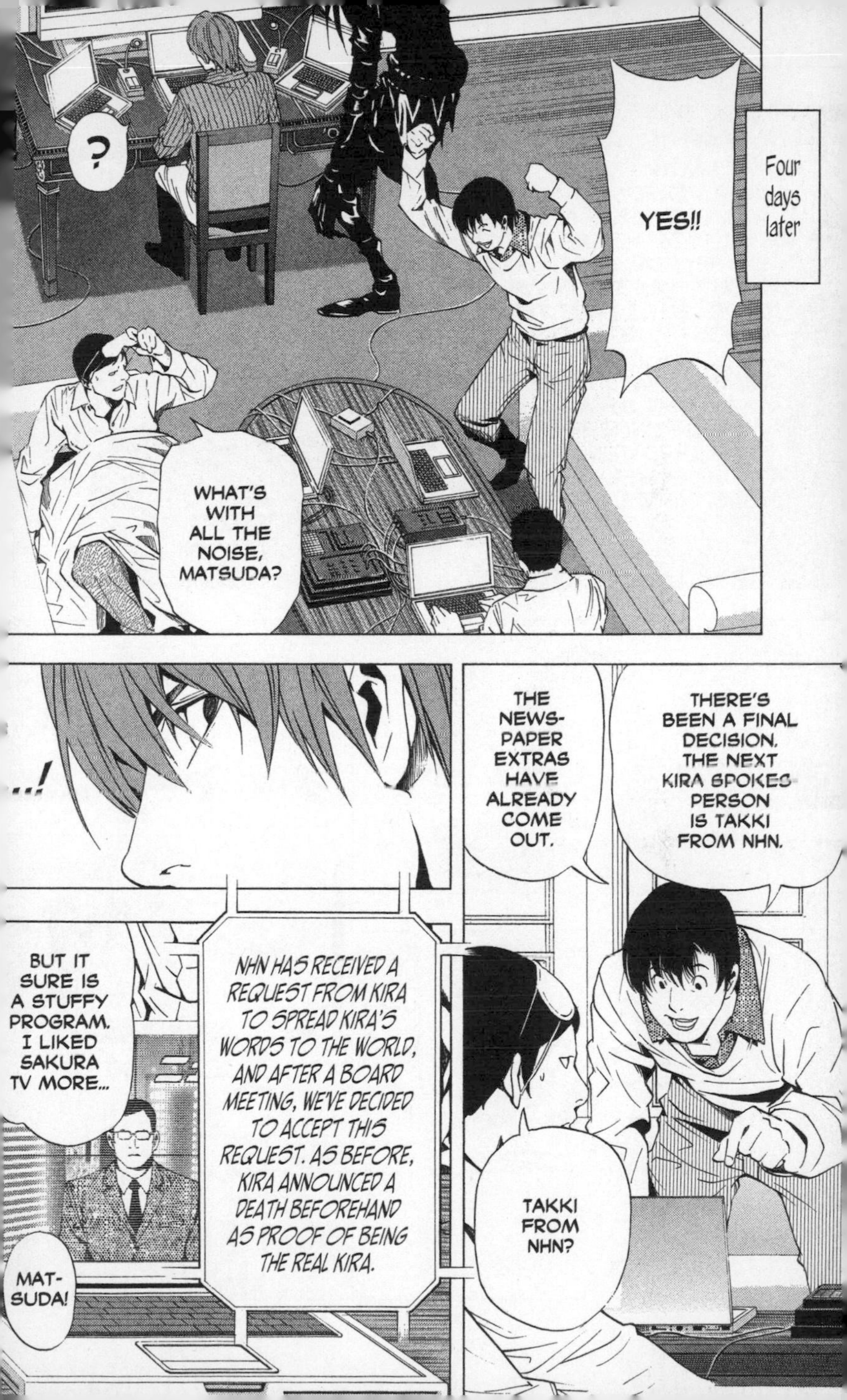
Four days later
YES!!
?
WHAT'S WITH ALL THE NOISE, MATSUDA?
THERE'S BEEN A FINAL DECISION. THE NEXT KIRA SPOKES-PERSON IS TAKKI FROM NHN.
THE NEWS-PAPER EXTRAS HAVE ALREADY COME OUT.
...!
TAKKI FROM NHN?
NHN HAS RECEIVED A REQUEST FROM KIRA TO SPREAD KIRA'S WORDS TO THE WORLD, AND AFTER A BOARD MEETING, WE'VE DECIDED TO ACCEPT THIS REQUEST. AS BEFORE, KIRA ANNOUNCED A DEATH BEFOREHAND AS PROOF OF BEING THE REAL KIRA.
BUT IT SURE IS A STUFFY PROGRAM. I LIKED SAKURA TV MORE...
MAT-SUDA!

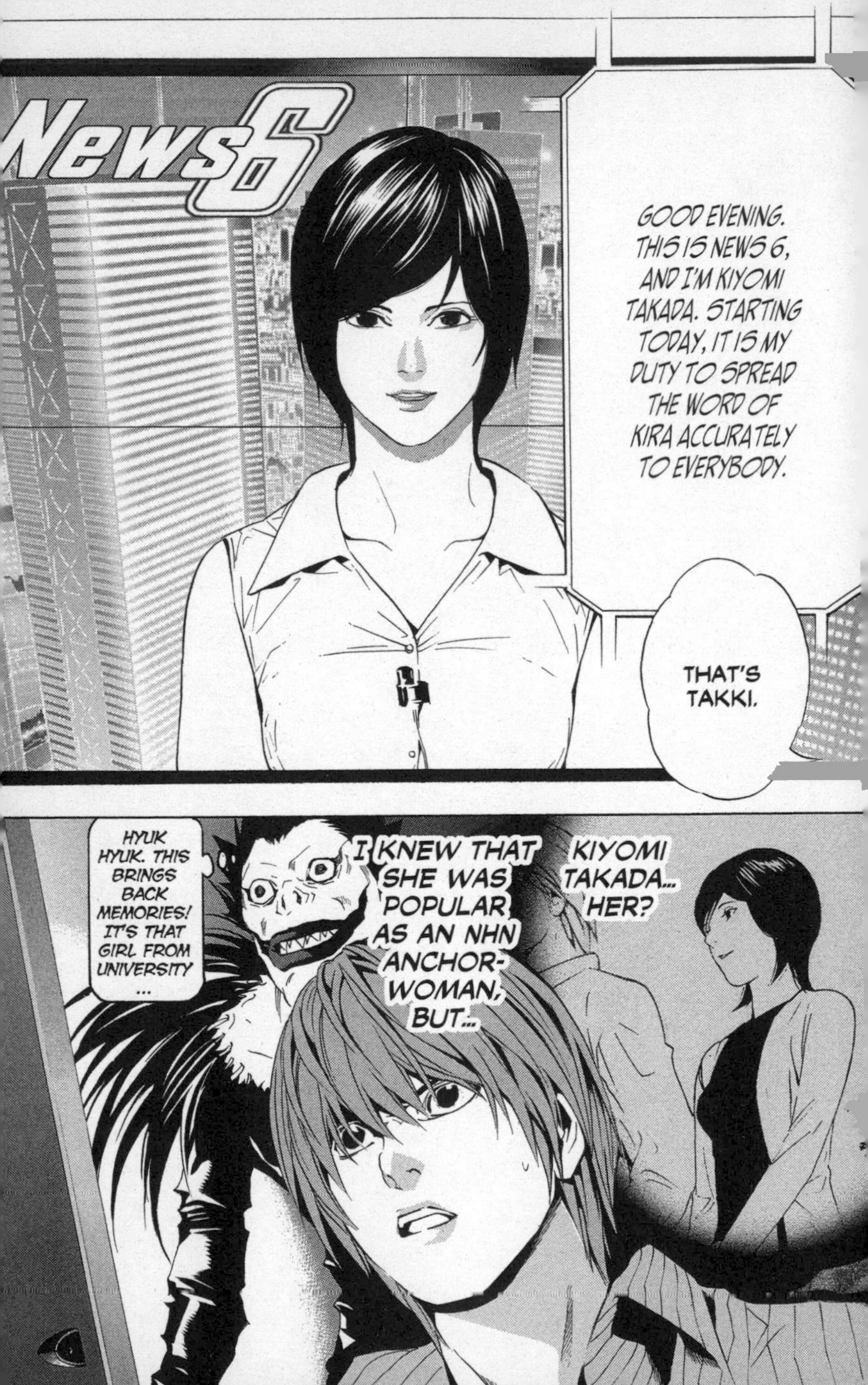
News6
GOOD EVENING. THIS IS NEWS 6, AND I'M KIYOMI TAKADA. STARTING TODAY, IT IS MY DUTY TO SPREAD THE WORD OF KIRA ACCURATELY TO EVERYBODY.
THAT'S TAKKI.
KIYOMI TAKADA... HER?
I KNEW THAT SHE WAS POPULAR AS AN NHN ANCHOR-WOMAN, BUT...
HYUK HYUK. THIS BRINGS BACK MEMORIES! IT'S THAT GIRL FROM UNIVERSITY ...

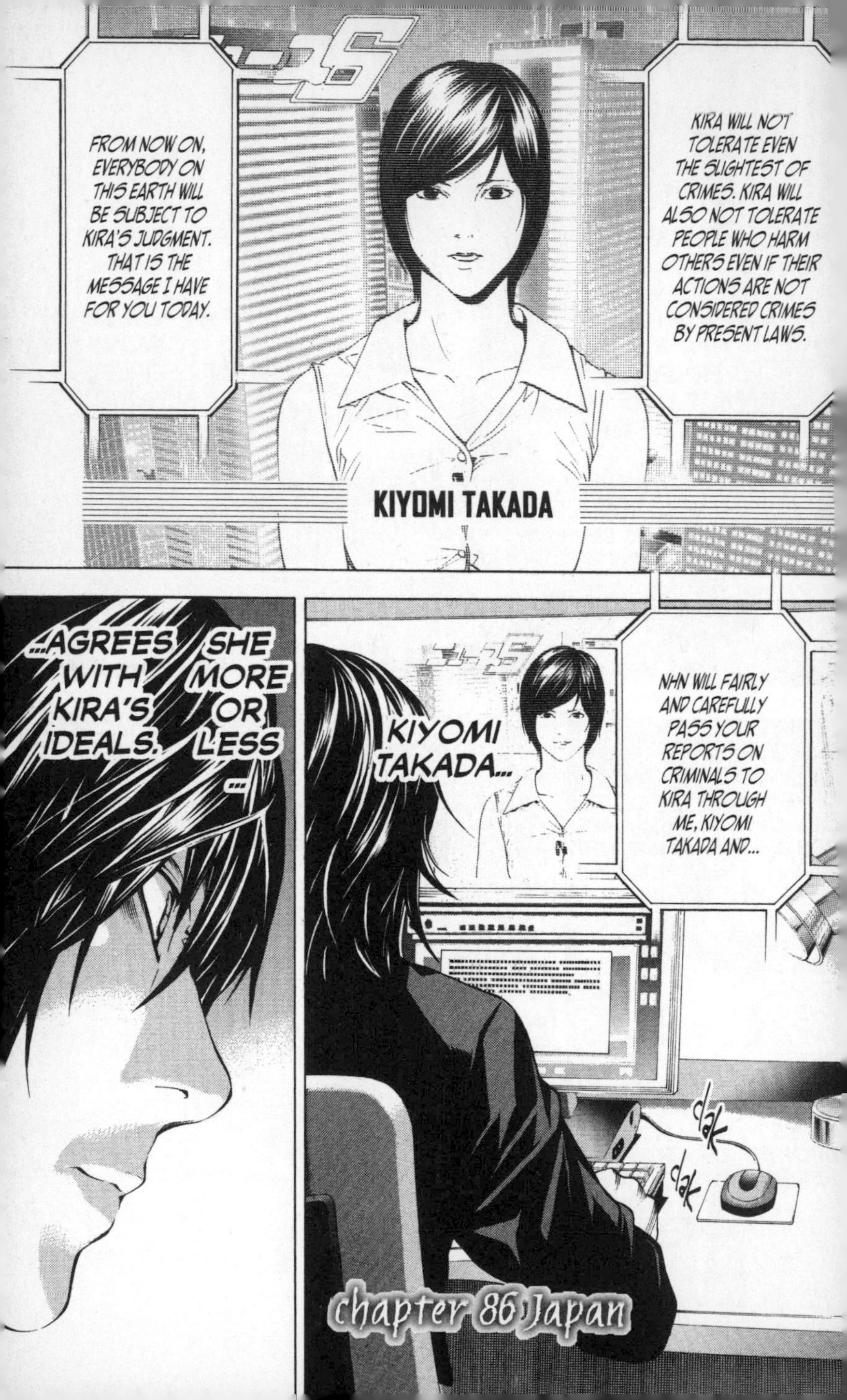
KIRA WILL NOT TOLERATE EVEN THE SLIGHTEST OF CRIMES. KIRA WILL ALSO NOT TOLERATE PEOPLE WHO HARM OTHERS EVEN IF THEIR ACTIONS ARE NOT CONSIDERED CRIMES BY PRESENT LAWS.
FROM NOW ON, EVERYBODY ON THIS EARTH WILL BE SUBJECT TO KIRA'S JUDGMENT. THAT IS THE MESSAGE I HAVE FOR YOU TODAY.
KIYOMI TAKADA
NHN WILL FAIRLY AND CAREFULLY PASS YOUR REPORTS ON CRIMINALS TO KIRA THROUGH ME, KIYOMI TAKADA AND...
KIYOMI TAKADA...
clak
clak
SHE MORE OR LESS...
...AGREES WITH KIRA'S IDEALS.
chapter 86 Japan

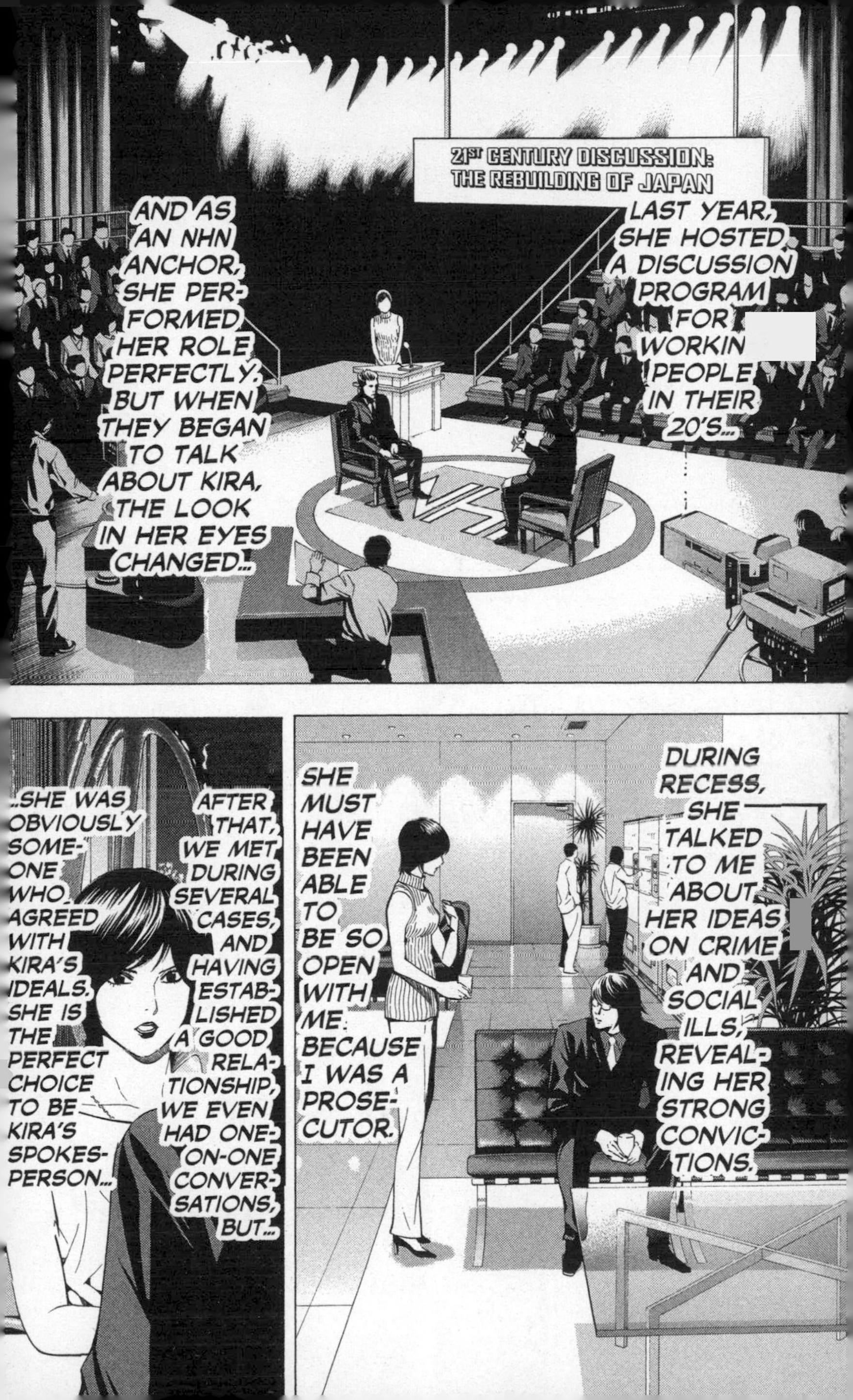
21ST CENTURY DISCUSSION: THE REBUILDING OF JAPAN
LAST YEAR, SHE HOSTED A DISCUSSION PROGRAM FOR WORKIN PEOPLE IN THEIR 20'S...
AND AS AN NHN ANCHOR, SHE PERFORMED HER ROLE PERFECTLY. BUT WHEN THEY BEGAN TO TALK ABOUT KIRA, THE LOOK IN HER EYES CHANGED...
DURING RECESS, SHE TALKED TO ME ABOUT HER IDEAS ON CRIME AND SOCIAL ILLS, REVEALING HER STRONG CONVICTIONS.
SHE MUST HAVE BEEN ABLE TO BE SO OPEN WITH ME BECAUSE I WAS A PROSECUTOR.
AFTER THAT, WE MET DURING SEVERAL CASES, AND HAVING ESTABLISHED A GOOD RELATIONSHIP, WE EVEN HAD ONE-ON-ONE CONVERSATIONS, BUT...
...SHE WAS OBVIOUSLY SOMEONE WHO AGREED WITH KIRA'S IDEALS. SHE IS THE PERFECT CHOICE TO BE KIRA'S SPOKESPERSON...

chapter 86 Japan

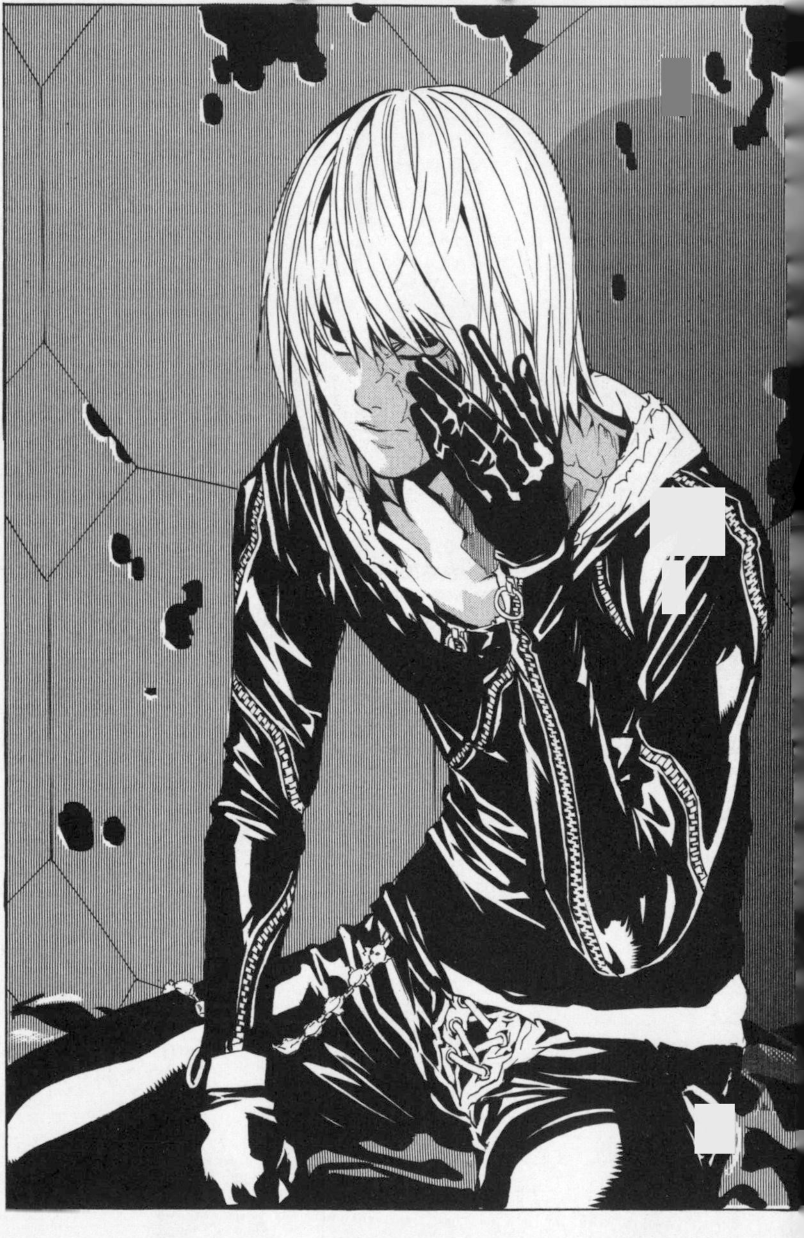

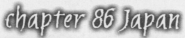

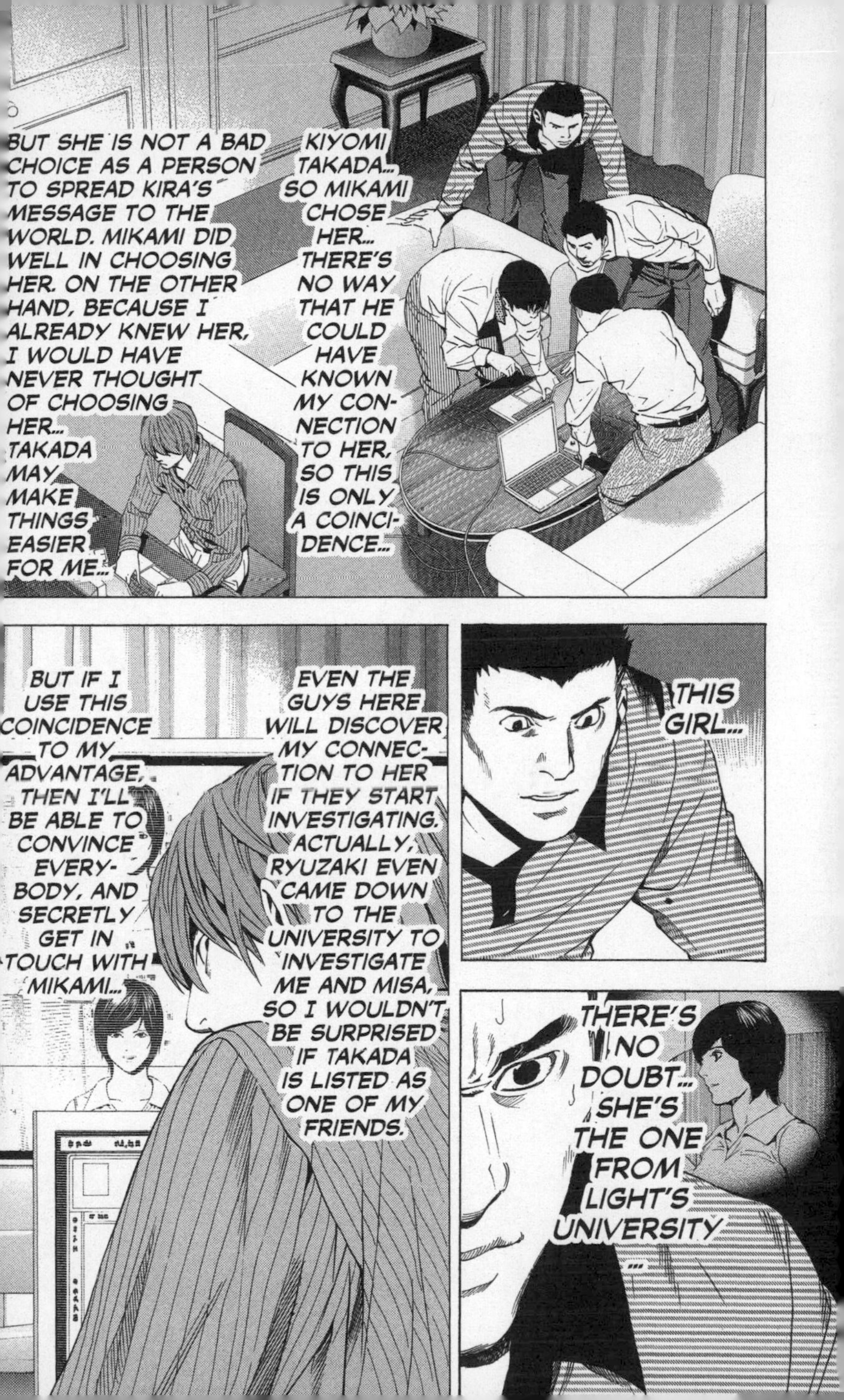
KIYOMI TAKADA... SO MIKAMI CHOSE HER... THERE'S NO WAY THAT HE COULD HAVE KNOWN MY CONNECTION TO HER, SO THIS IS ONLY A COINCIDENCE...
BUT SHE IS NOT A BAD CHOICE AS A PERSON TO SPREAD KIRA'S MESSAGE TO THE WORLD. MIKAMI DID WELL IN CHOOSING HER. ON THE OTHER HAND, BECAUSE I ALREADY KNEW HER, I WOULD HAVE NEVER THOUGHT OF CHOOSING HER... TAKADA MAY MAKE THINGS EASIER FOR ME...
THIS GIRL...
THERE'S NO DOUBT... SHE'S THE ONE FROM LIGHT'S UNIVERSITY ...
EVEN THE GUYS HERE WILL DISCOVER MY CONNECTION TO HER IF THEY START INVESTIGATING. ACTUALLY, RYUZAKI EVEN CAME DOWN TO THE UNIVERSITY TO INVESTIGATE ME AND MISA, SO I WOULDN'T BE SURPRISED IF TAKADA IS LISTED AS ONE OF MY FRIENDS.
BUT IF I USE THIS COINCIDENCE TO MY ADVANTAGE, THEN I'LL BE ABLE TO CONVINCE EVERYBODY, AND SECRETLY GET IN TOUCH WITH MIKAMI...

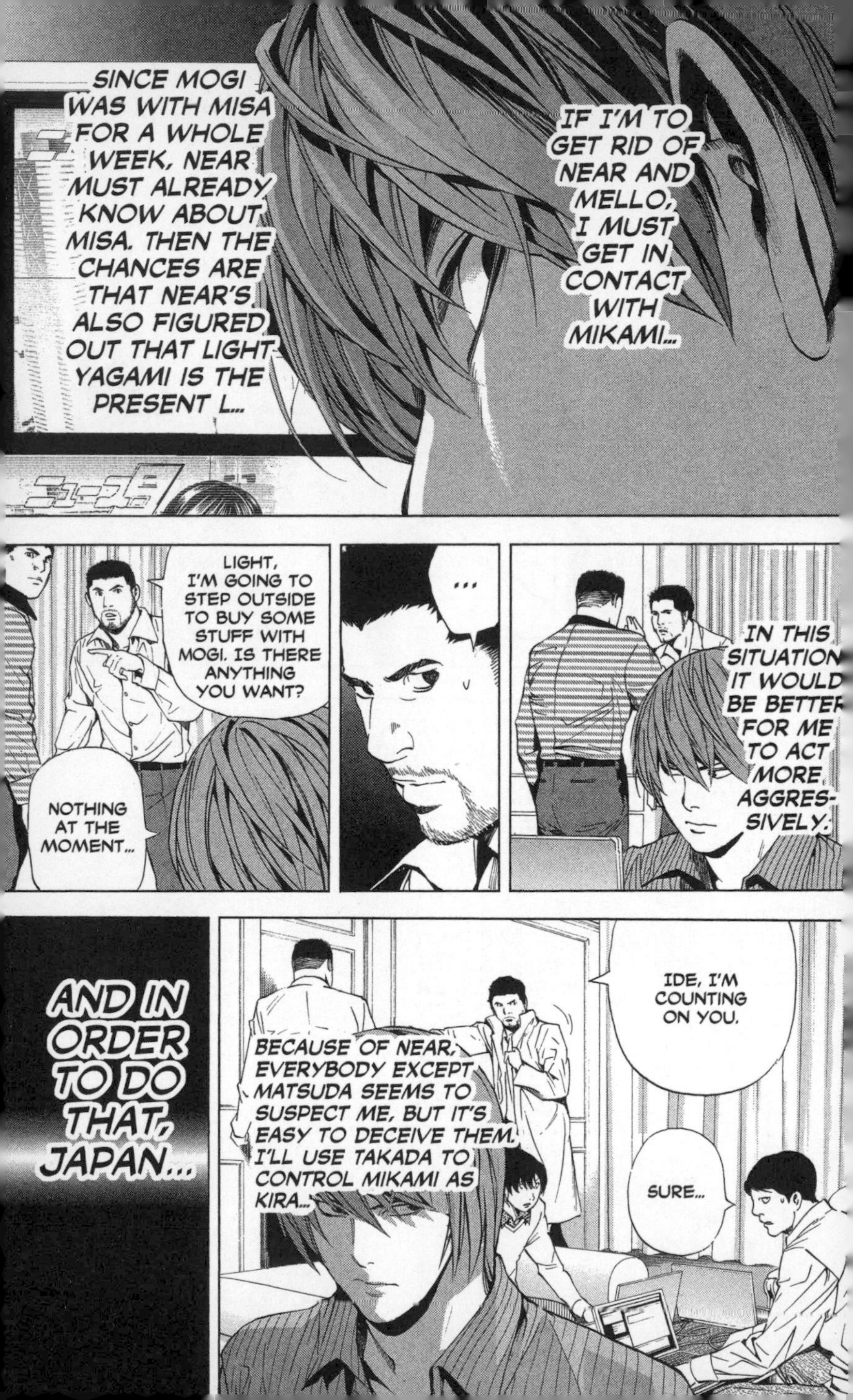
IF I'M TO GET RID OF NEAR AND MELLO, I MUST GET IN CONTACT WITH MIKAMI...
SINCE MOGI WAS WITH MISA FOR A WHOLE WEEK, NEAR MUST ALREADY KNOW ABOUT MISA. THEN THE CHANCES ARE THAT NEAR'S ALSO FIGURED OUT THAT LIGHT YAGAMI IS THE PRESENT L...
IN THIS SITUATION IT WOULD BE BETTER FOR ME TO ACT MORE AGGRES-SIVELY.
...
LIGHT, I'M GOING TO STEP OUTSIDE TO BUY SOME STUFF WITH MOGI. IS THERE ANYTHING YOU WANT?
NOTHING AT THE MOMENT...
IDE, I'M COUNTING ON YOU.
SURE...
BECAUSE OF NEAR, EVERYBODY EXCEPT MATSUDA SEEMS TO SUSPECT ME, BUT IT'S EASY TO DECEIVE THEM. I'LL USE TAKADA TO CONTROL MIKAMI AS KIRA...
AND IN ORDER TO DO THAT, JAPAN...

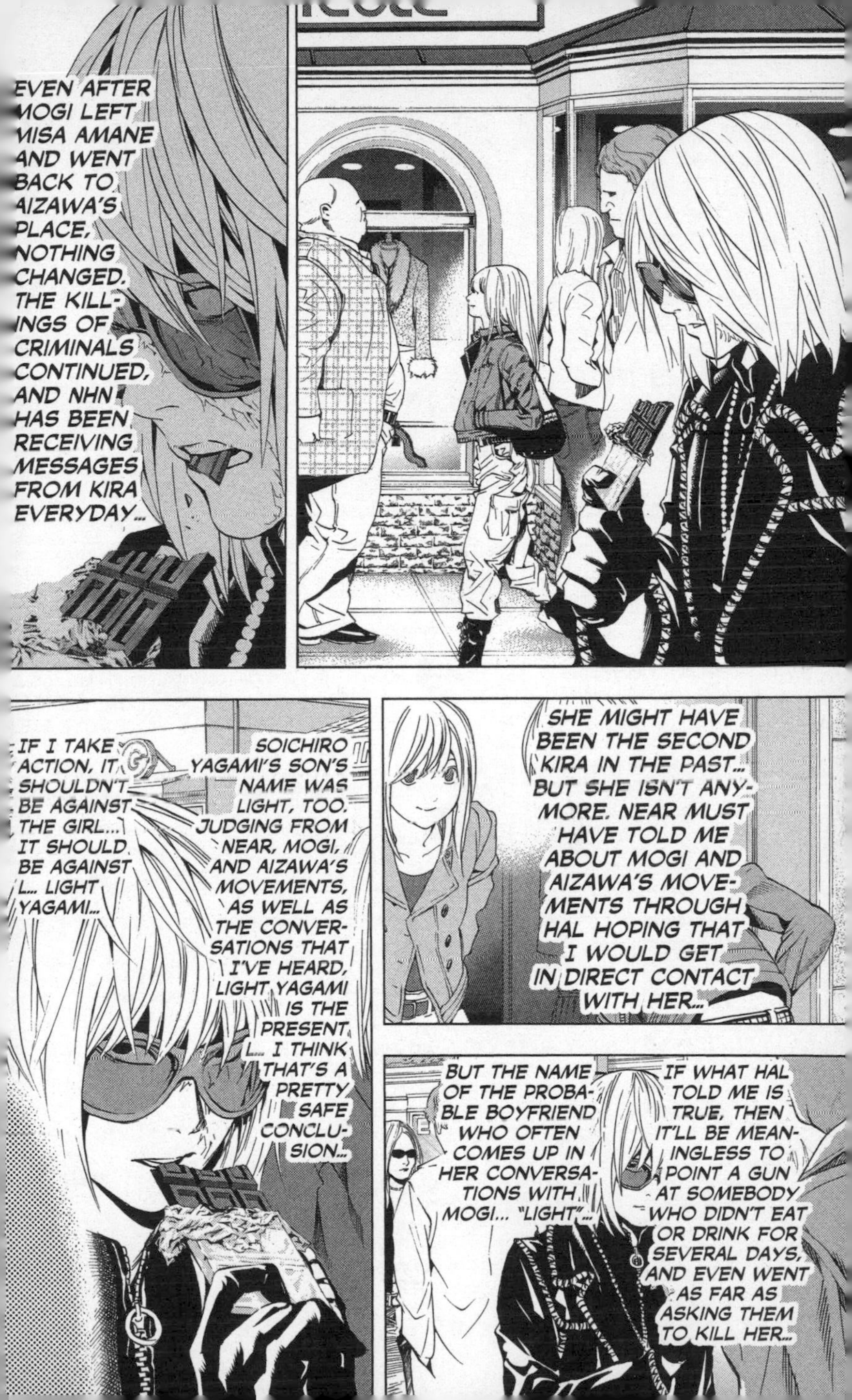
EVEN AFTER MOGI LEFT MISA AMANE AND WENT BACK TO AIZAWA'S PLACE, NOTHING CHANGED. THE KILLINGS OF CRIMINALS CONTINUED, AND NHN HAS BEEN RECEIVING MESSAGES FROM KIRA EVERYDAY...
SHE MIGHT HAVE BEEN THE SECOND KIRA IN THE PAST... BUT SHE ISN'T ANYMORE. NEAR MUST HAVE TOLD ME ABOUT MOGI AND AIZAWA'S MOVEMENTS THROUGH HAL HOPING THAT I WOULD GET IN DIRECT CONTACT WITH HER...
IF WHAT HAL TOLD ME IS TRUE, THEN IT'LL BE MEANINGLESS TO POINT A GUN AT SOMEBODY WHO DIDN'T EAT OR DRINK FOR SEVERAL DAYS, AND EVEN WENT AS FAR AS ASKING THEM TO KILL HER...
BUT THE NAME OF THE PROBABLE BOYFRIEND WHO OFTEN COMES UP IN HER CONVERSATIONS WITH MOGI... "LIGHT"...
SOICHIRO YAGAMI'S SON'S NAME WAS LIGHT, TOO. JUDGING FROM NEAR, MOGI, AND AIZAWA'S MOVEMENTS, AS WELL AS THE CONVERSATIONS THAT I'VE HEARD, LIGHT YAGAMI IS THE PRESENT L... I THINK THAT'S A PRETTY SAFE CONCLUSION...
IF I TAKE ACTION, IT SHOULDN'T BE AGAINST THE GIRL... IT SHOULD BE AGAINST L... LIGHT YAGAMI...

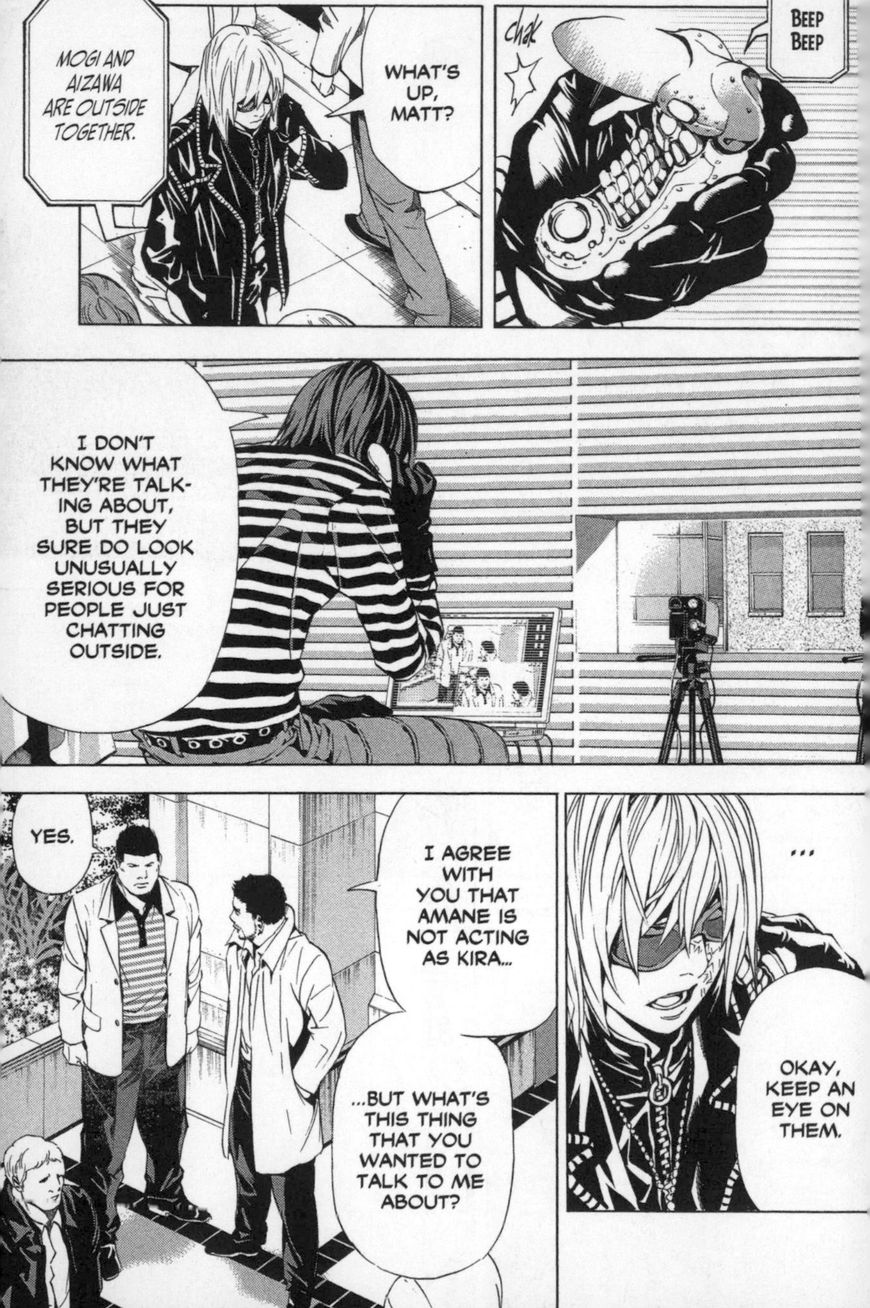
chak
BEEP BEEP
WHAT'S UP, MATT?
MOGI AND AIZAWA ARE OUTSIDE TOGETHER.
I DON'T KNOW WHAT THEY'RE TALK- ING ABOUT, BUT THEY SURE DO LOOK UNUSUALLY SERIOUS FOR PEOPLE JUST CHATTING OUTSIDE.
...
OKAY, KEEP AN EYE ON THEM.
I AGREE WITH YOU THAT AMANE IS NOT ACTING AS KIRA...
YES.
...BUT WHAT'S THIS THING THAT YOU WANTED TO TALK TO ME ABOUT?

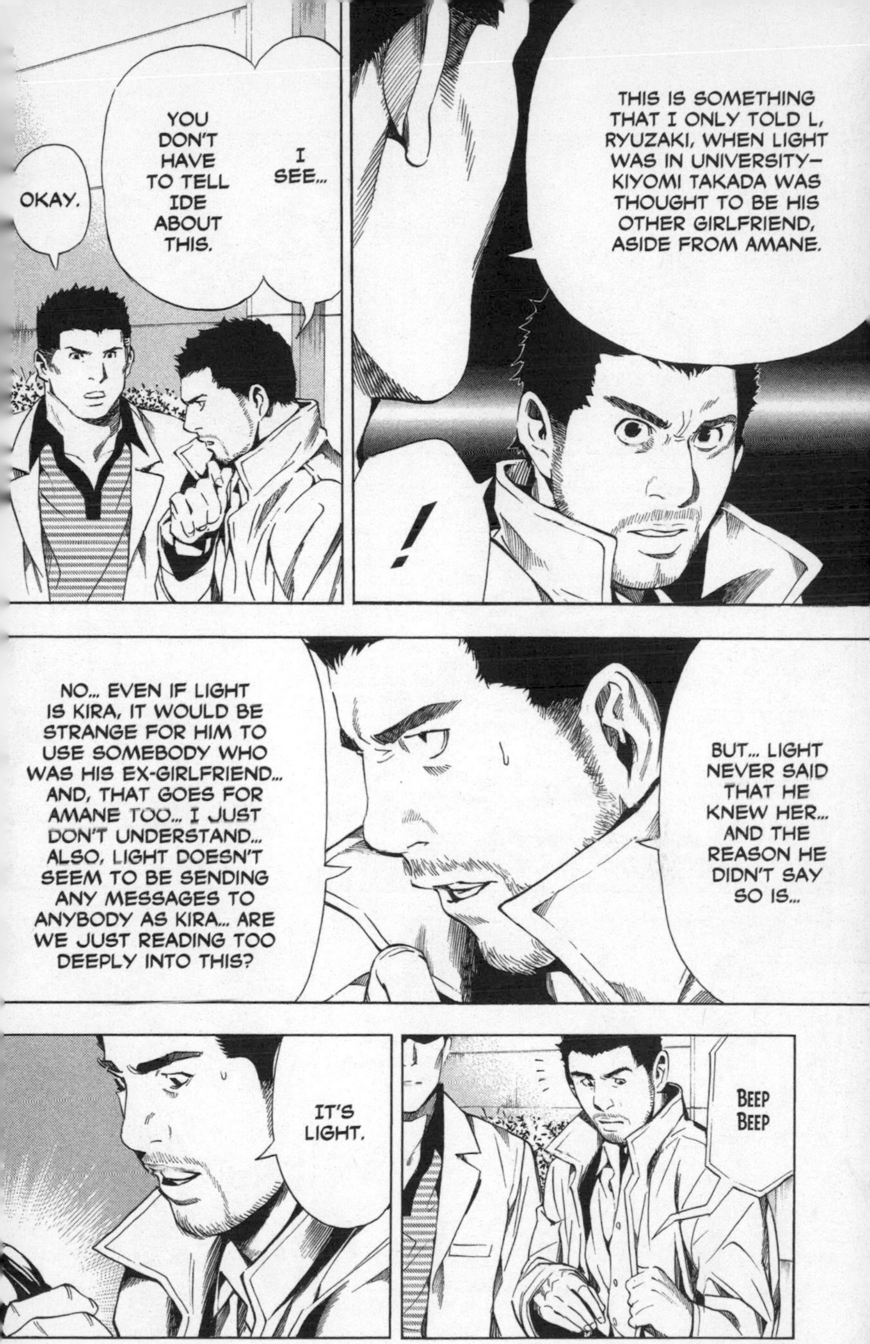
THIS IS SOMETHING THAT I ONLY TOLD L, RYUZAKI, WHEN LIGHT WAS IN UNIVERSITY— KIYOMI TAKADA WAS THOUGHT TO BE HIS OTHER GIRLFRIEND, ASIDE FROM AMANE.
!
I SEE...
YOU DON'T HAVE TO TELL IDE ABOUT THIS.
OKAY.
BUT... LIGHT NEVER SAID THAT HE KNEW HER... AND THE REASON HE DIDN'T SAY SO IS...
NO... EVEN IF LIGHT IS KIRA, IT WOULD BE STRANGE FOR HIM TO USE SOMEBODY WHO WAS HIS EX-GIRLFRIEND... AND, THAT GOES FOR AMANE TOO... I JUST DON'T UNDERSTAND... ALSO, LIGHT DOESN'T SEEM TO BE SENDING ANY MESSAGES TO ANYBODY AS KIRA... ARE WE JUST READING TOO DEEPLY INTO THIS?
BEEP BEEP
IT'S LIGHT.

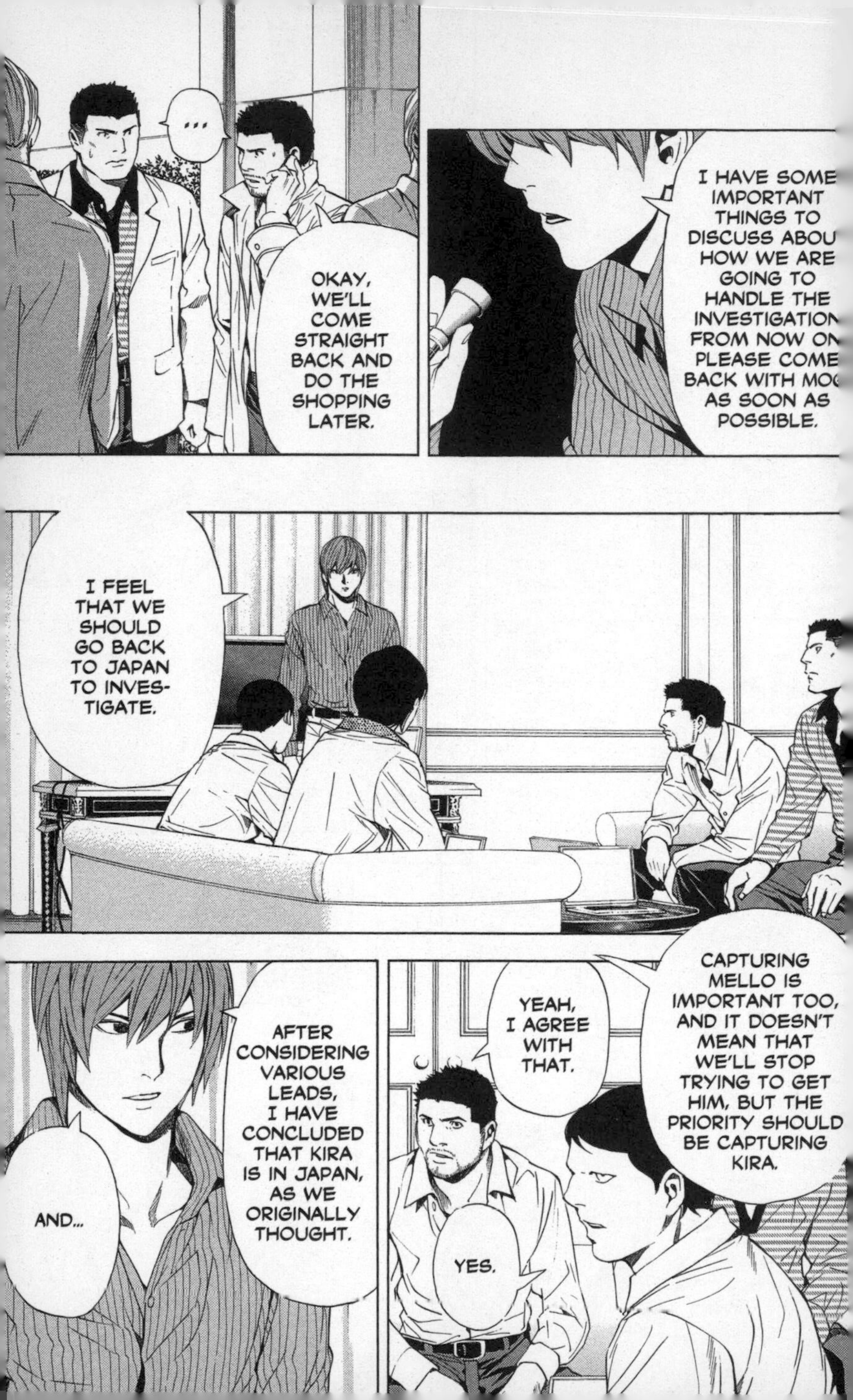
I HAVE SOME IMPORTANT THINGS TO DISCUSS ABOU HOW WE ARE GOING TO HANDLE THE INVESTIGATION FROM NOW ON PLEASE COME BACK WITH MOG AS SOON AS POSSIBLE.
...
OKAY, WE'LL COME STRAIGHT BACK AND DO THE SHOPPING LATER.
I FEEL THAT WE SHOULD GO BACK TO JAPAN TO INVES-TIGATE.
CAPTURING MELLO IS IMPORTANT TOO, AND IT DOESN'T MEAN THAT WE'LL STOP TRYING TO GET HIM, BUT THE PRIORITY SHOULD BE CAPTURING KIRA.
YEAH, I AGREE WITH THAT.
YES.
AFTER CONSIDERING VARIOUS LEADS, I HAVE CONCLUDED THAT KIRA IS IN JAPAN, AS WE ORIGINALLY THOUGHT.
AND...

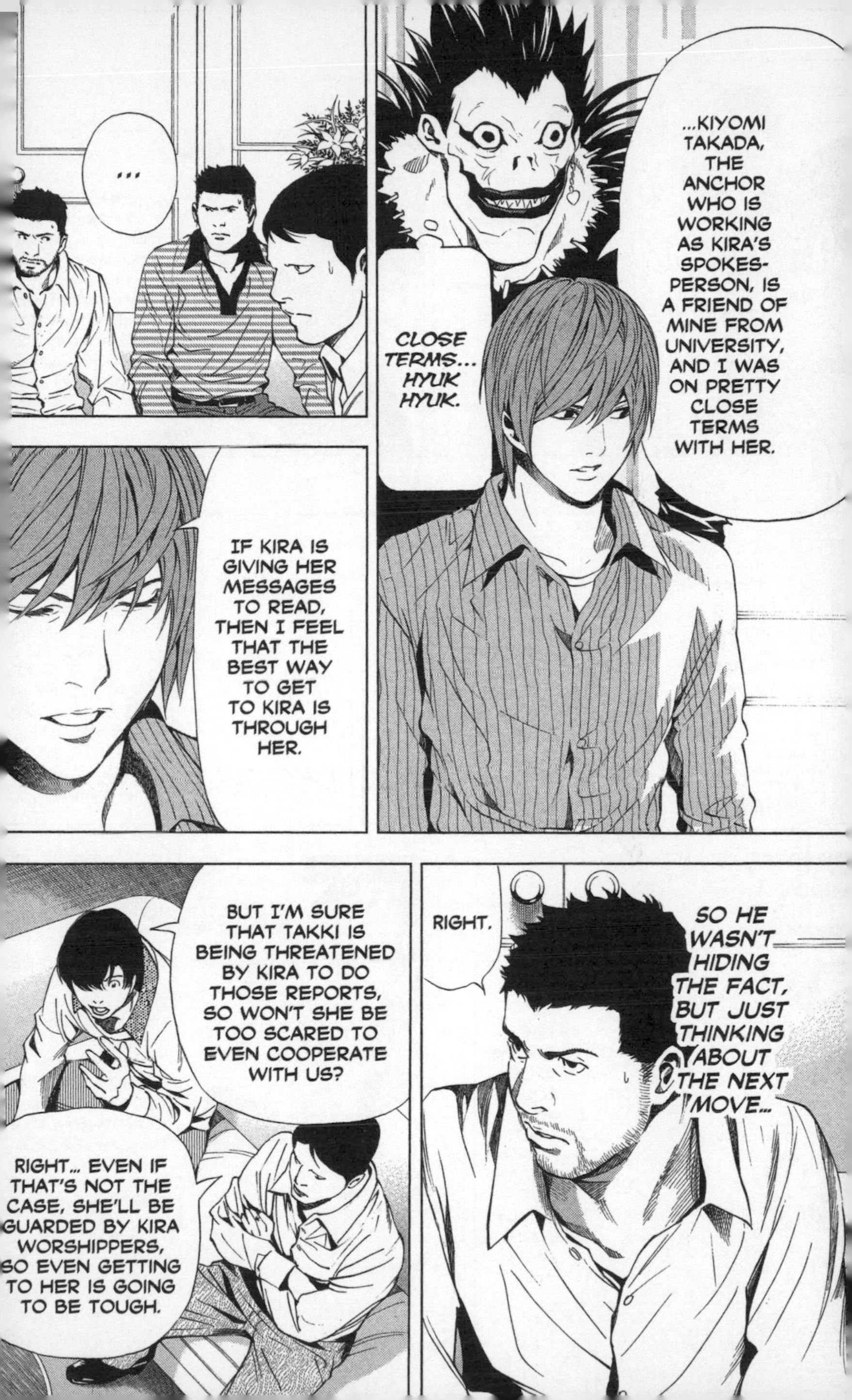
...KIYOMI TAKADA, THE ANCHOR WHO IS WORKING AS KIRA'S SPOKES-PERSON, IS A FRIEND OF MINE FROM UNIVERSITY, AND I WAS ON PRETTY CLOSE TERMS WITH HER.
CLOSE TERMS... HYUK HYUK.
...
IF KIRA IS GIVING HER MESSAGES TO READ, THEN I FEEL THAT THE BEST WAY TO GET TO KIRA IS THROUGH HER.
RIGHT.
SO HE WASN'T HIDING THE FACT, BUT JUST THINKING ABOUT THE NEXT MOVE...
BUT I'M SURE THAT TAKKI IS BEING THREATENED BY KIRA TO DO THOSE REPORTS, SO WON'T SHE BE TOO SCARED TO EVEN COOPERATE WITH US?
RIGHT... EVEN IF THAT'S NOT THE CASE, SHE'LL BE GUARDED BY KIRA WORSHIPPERS, SO EVEN GETTING TO HER IS GOING TO BE TOUGH.

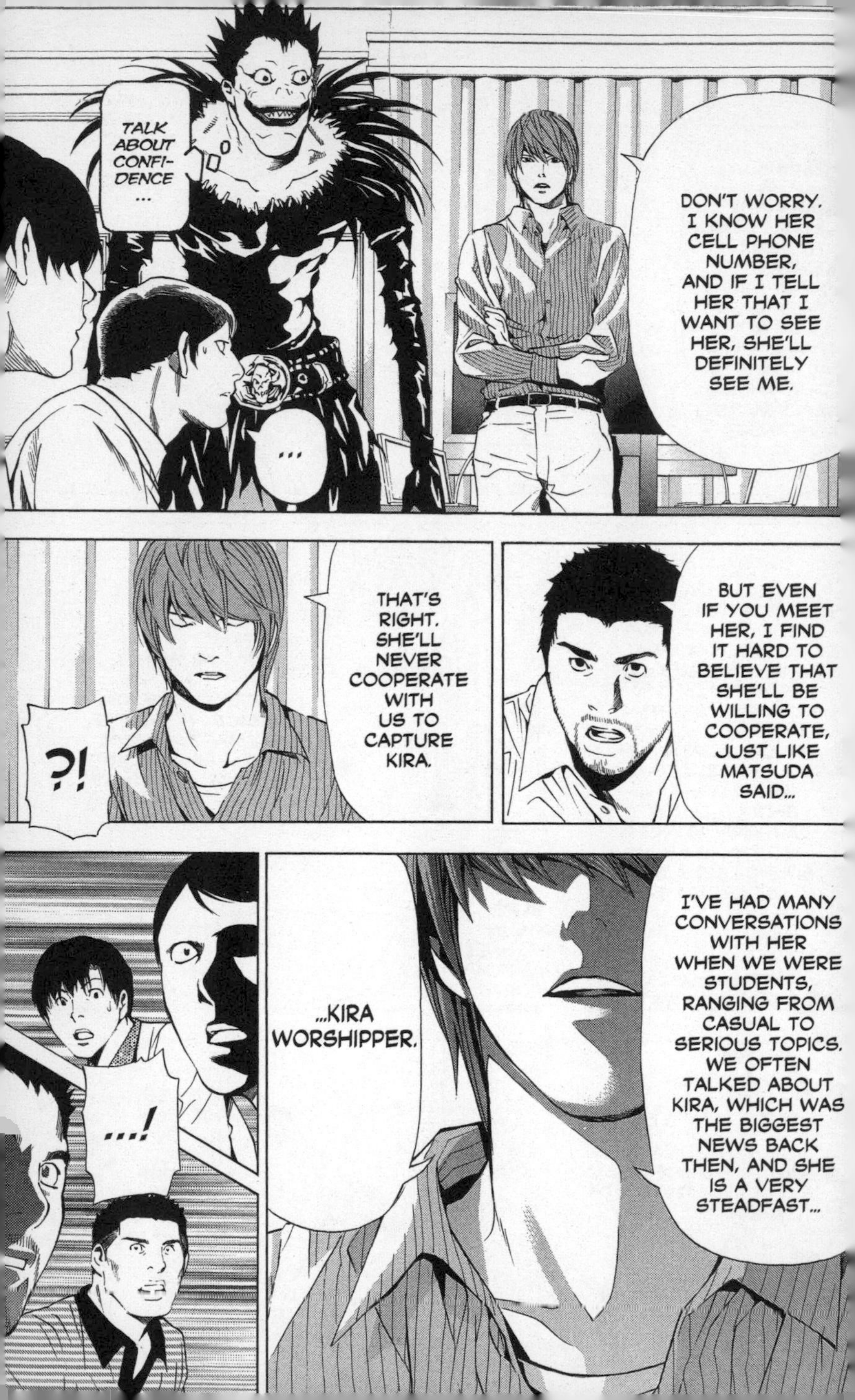
DON'T WORRY. I KNOW HER CELL PHONE NUMBER, AND IF I TELL HER THAT I WANT TO SEE HER, SHE'LL DEFINITELY SEE ME.
TALK ABOUT CONFI-DENCE ...
...
BUT EVEN IF YOU MEET HER, I FIND IT HARD TO BELIEVE THAT SHE'LL BE WILLING TO COOPERATE, JUST LIKE MATSUDA SAID...
THAT'S RIGHT. SHE'LL NEVER COOPERATE WITH US TO CAPTURE KIRA.
?!
I'VE HAD MANY CONVERSATIONS WITH HER WHEN WE WERE STUDENTS, RANGING FROM CASUAL TO SERIOUS TOPICS. WE OFTEN TALKED ABOUT KIRA, WHICH WAS THE BIGGEST NEWS BACK THEN, AND SHE IS A VERY STEADFAST...
...KIRA WORSHIPPER.
...!

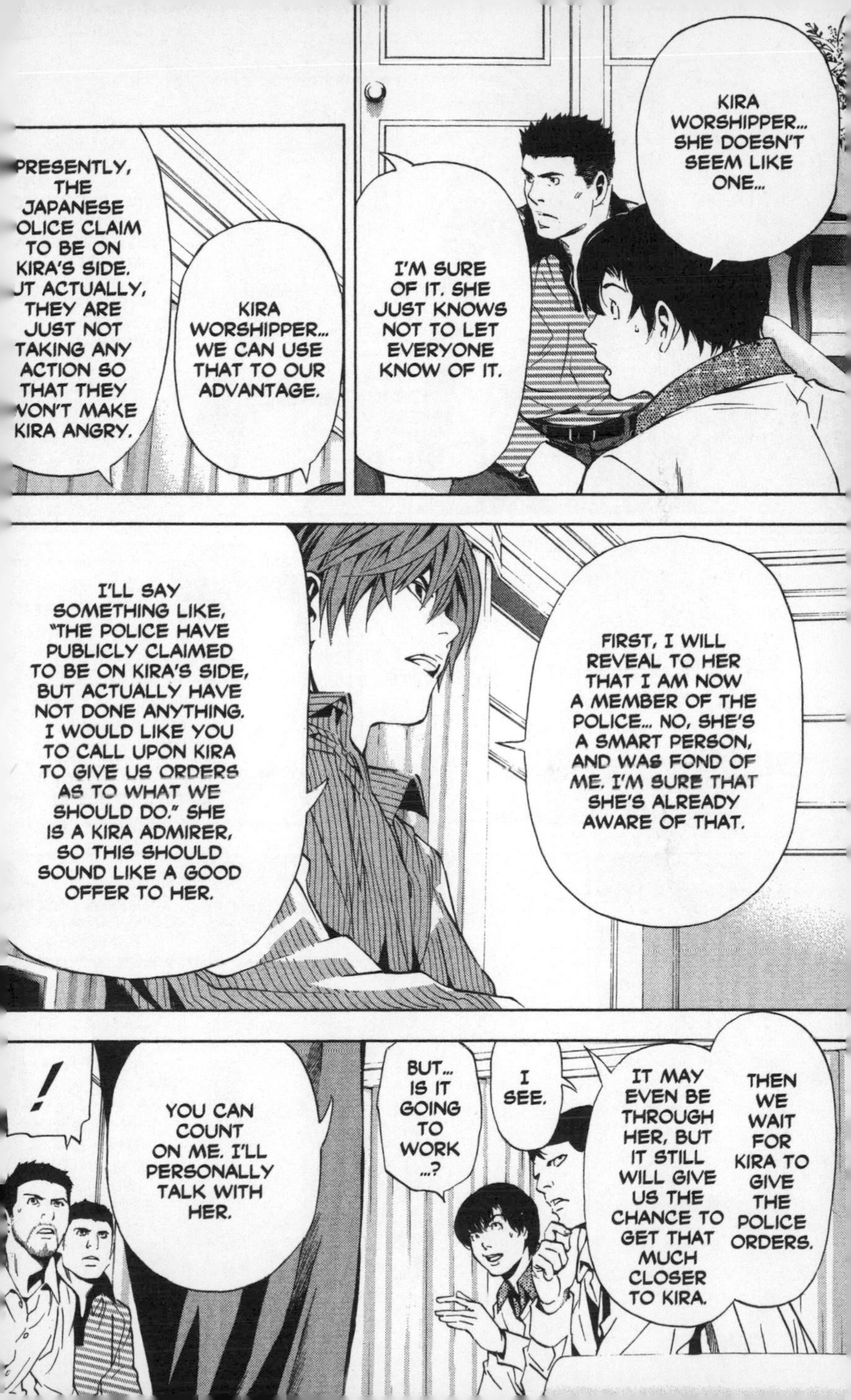
KIRA WORSHIPPER... SHE DOESN'T SEEM LIKE ONE...
I'M SURE OF IT. SHE JUST KNOWS NOT TO LET EVERYONE KNOW OF IT.
KIRA WORSHIPPER... WE CAN USE THAT TO OUR ADVANTAGE.
PRESENTLY, THE JAPANESE OLICE CLAIM TO BE ON KIRA'S SIDE. UT ACTUALLY, THEY ARE JUST NOT TAKING ANY ACTION SO THAT THEY VON'T MAKE KIRA ANGRY.
FIRST, I WILL REVEAL TO HER THAT I AM NOW A MEMBER OF THE POLICE... NO, SHE'S A SMART PERSON, AND WAS FOND OF ME. I'M SURE THAT SHE'S ALREADY AWARE OF THAT.
I'LL SAY SOMETHING LIKE, "THE POLICE HAVE PUBLICLY CLAIMED TO BE ON KIRA'S SIDE, BUT ACTUALLY HAVE NOT DONE ANYTHING. I WOULD LIKE YOU TO CALL UPON KIRA TO GIVE US ORDERS AS TO WHAT WE SHOULD DO." SHE IS A KIRA ADMIRER, SO THIS SHOULD SOUND LIKE A GOOD OFFER TO HER.
THEN WE WAIT FOR KIRA TO GIVE THE POLICE ORDERS.
IT MAY EVEN BE THROUGH HER, BUT IT STILL WILL GIVE US THE CHANCE TO GET THAT MUCH CLOSER TO KIRA.
I SEE.
BUT... IS IT GOING TO WORK ...?
YOU CAN COUNT ON ME. I'LL PERSONALLY TALK WITH HER.
!

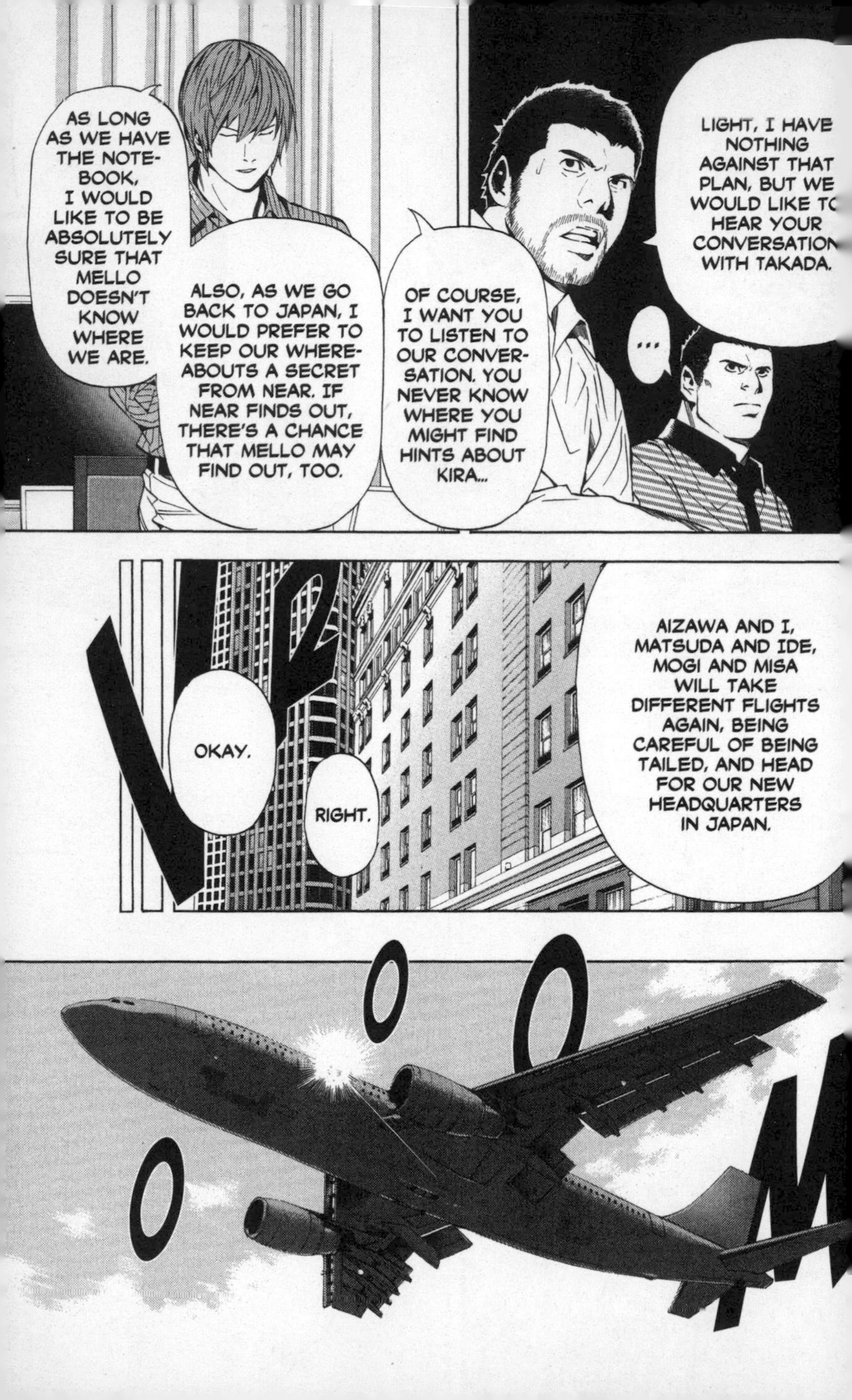
LIGHT, I HAVE NOTHING AGAINST THAT PLAN, BUT WE WOULD LIKE TO HEAR YOUR CONVERSATION WITH TAKADA.
...
OF COURSE, I WANT YOU TO LISTEN TO OUR CONVERSATION. YOU NEVER KNOW WHERE YOU MIGHT FIND HINTS ABOUT KIRA...
AS LONG AS WE HAVE THE NOTEBOOK, I WOULD LIKE TO BE ABSOLUTELY SURE THAT MELLO DOESN'T KNOW WHERE WE ARE.
ALSO, AS WE GO BACK TO JAPAN, I WOULD PREFER TO KEEP OUR WHEREABOUTS A SECRET FROM NEAR. IF NEAR FINDS OUT, THERE'S A CHANCE THAT MELLO MAY FIND OUT, TOO.
AIZAWA AND I, MATSUDA AND IDE, MOGI AND MISA WILL TAKE DIFFERENT FLIGHTS AGAIN, BEING CAREFUL OF BEING TAILED, AND HEAD FOR OUR NEW HEADQUARTERS IN JAPAN.
OKAY.
RIGHT.

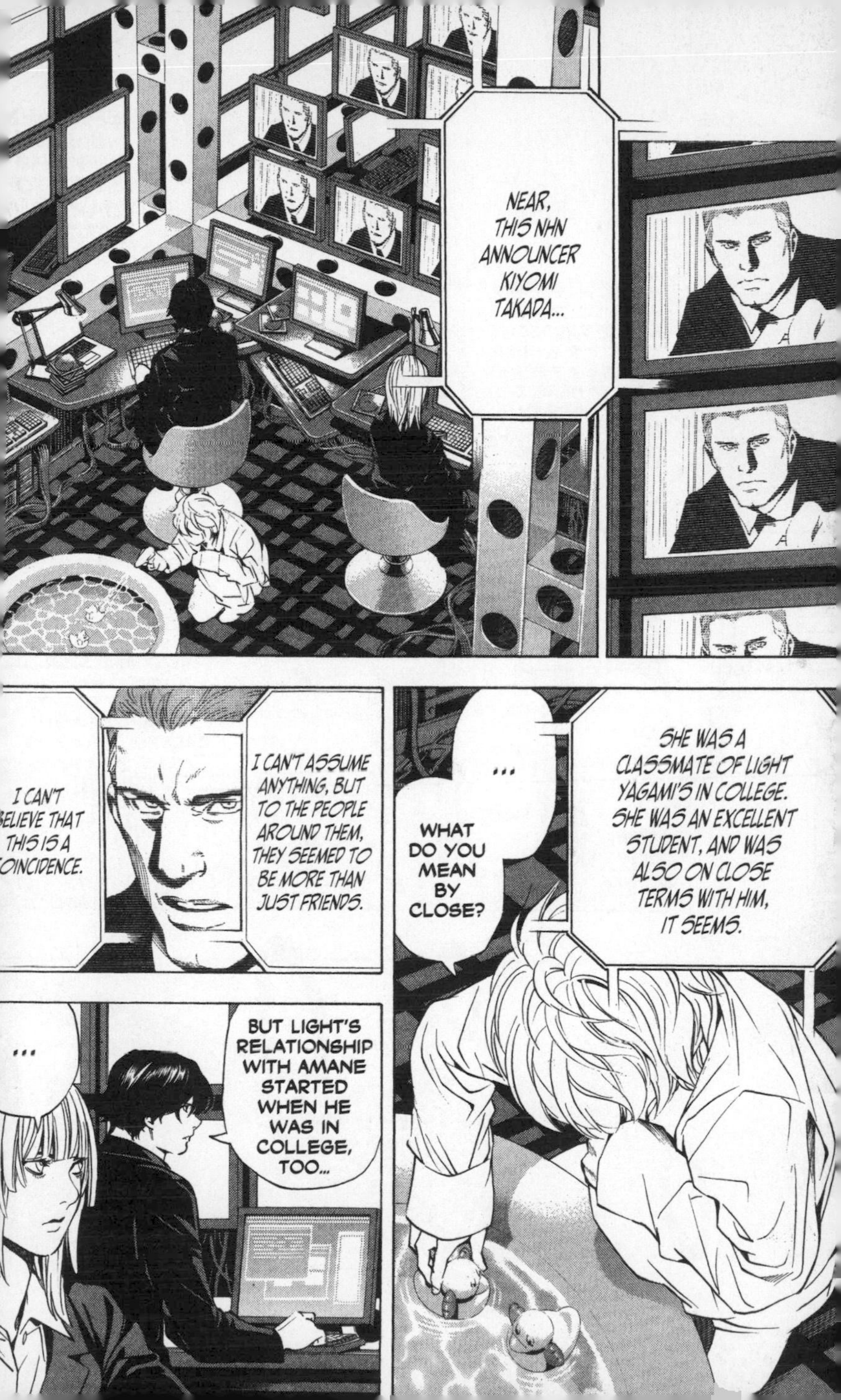

NEAR, THIS NHN ANNOUNCER KIYOMI TAKADA...
SHE WAS A CLASSMATE OF LIGHT YAGAMI'S IN COLLEGE. SHE WAS AN EXCELLENT STUDENT, AND WAS ALSO ON CLOSE TERMS WITH HIM, IT SEEMS.
...
WHAT DO YOU MEAN BY CLOSE?
I CAN'T ASSUME ANYTHING, BUT TO THE PEOPLE AROUND THEM, THEY SEEMED TO BE MORE THAN JUST FRIENDS.
I CAN'T BELIEVE THAT THIS IS A COINCIDENCE.
BUT LIGHT'S RELATIONSHIP WITH AMANE STARTED WHEN HE WAS IN COLLEGE, TOO...
...

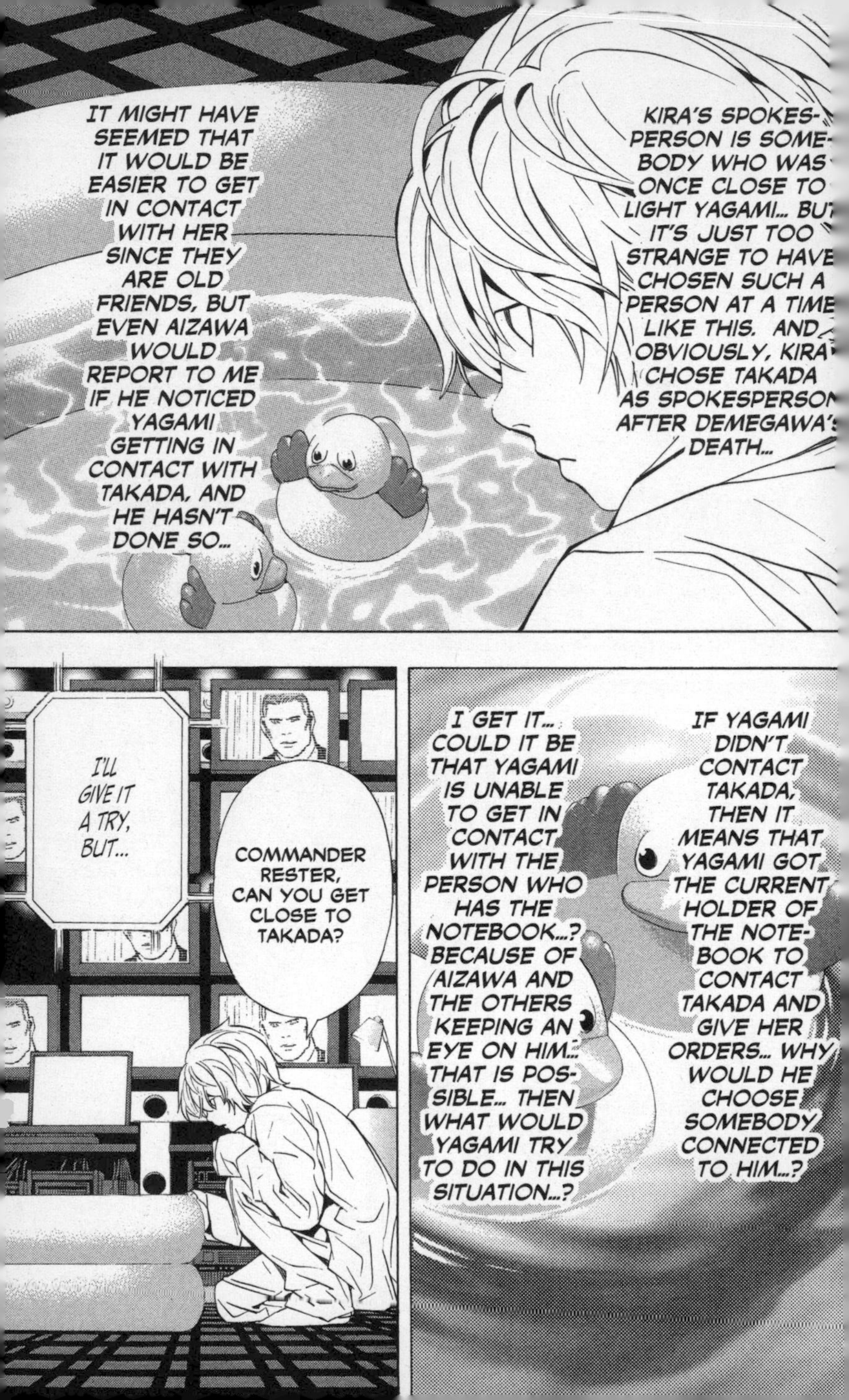
KIRA'S SPOKESPERSON IS SOMEBODY WHO WAS ONCE CLOSE TO LIGHT YAGAMI... BUT IT'S JUST TOO STRANGE TO HAVE CHOSEN SUCH A PERSON AT A TIME LIKE THIS. AND OBVIOUSLY, KIRA CHOSE TAKADA AS SPOKESPERSON AFTER DEMEGAWA'S DEATH...
IT MIGHT HAVE SEEMED THAT IT WOULD BE EASIER TO GET IN CONTACT WITH HER SINCE THEY ARE OLD FRIENDS, BUT EVEN AIZAWA WOULD REPORT TO ME IF HE NOTICED YAGAMI GETTING IN CONTACT WITH TAKADA, AND HE HASN'T DONE SO...
IF YAGAMI DIDN'T CONTACT TAKADA, THEN IT MEANS THAT YAGAMI GOT THE CURRENT HOLDER OF THE NOTEBOOK TO CONTACT TAKADA AND GIVE HER ORDERS... WHY WOULD HE CHOOSE SOMEBODY CONNECTED TO HIM...?
I GET IT... COULD IT BE THAT YAGAMI IS UNABLE TO GET IN CONTACT WITH THE PERSON WHO HAS THE NOTEBOOK...? BECAUSE OF AIZAWA AND THE OTHERS KEEPING AN EYE ON HIM... THAT IS POSSIBLE... THEN WHAT WOULD YAGAMI TRY TO DO IN THIS SITUATION...?
COMMANDER RESTER, CAN YOU GET CLOSE TO TAKADA?
I'LL GIVE IT A TRY, BUT...

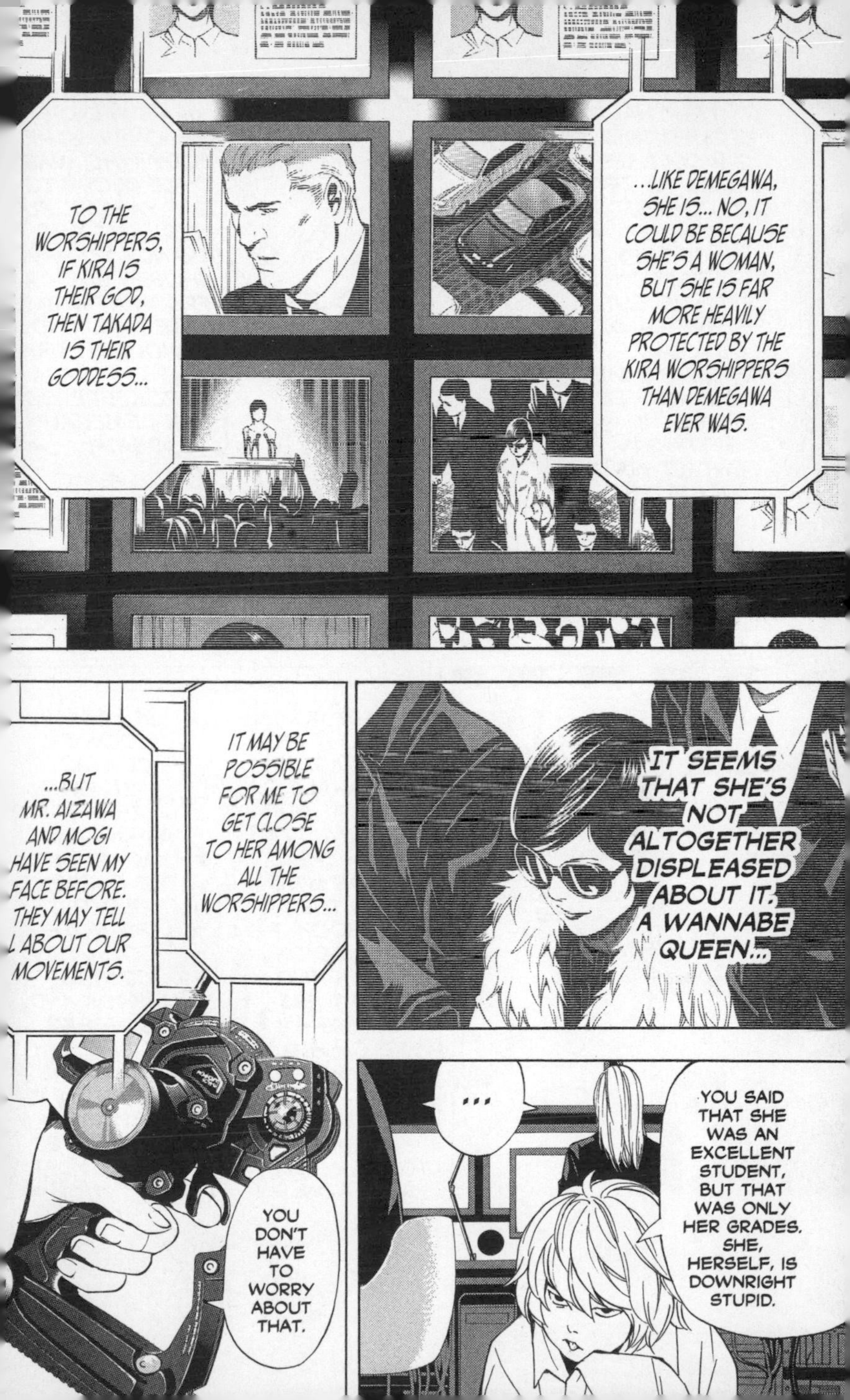
...LIKE DEMEGAWA, SHE IS... NO, IT COULD BE BECAUSE SHE'S A WOMAN, BUT SHE IS FAR MORE HEAVILY PROTECTED BY THE KIRA WORSHIPPERS THAN DEMEGAWA EVER WAS.
TO THE WORSHIPPERS, IF KIRA IS THEIR GOD, THEN TAKADA IS THEIR GODDESS...
IT SEEMS THAT SHE'S NOT ALTOGETHER DISPLEASED ABOUT IT. A WANNABE QUEEN...
IT MAY BE POSSIBLE FOR ME TO GET CLOSE TO HER AMONG ALL THE WORSHIPPERS...
...BUT MR. AIZAWA AND MOGI HAVE SEEN MY FACE BEFORE. THEY MAY TELL L ABOUT OUR MOVEMENTS.
YOU DON'T HAVE TO WORRY ABOUT THAT.
...
YOU SAID THAT SHE WAS AN EXCELLENT STUDENT, BUT THAT WAS ONLY HER GRADES. SHE, HERSELF, IS DOWNRIGHT STUPID.

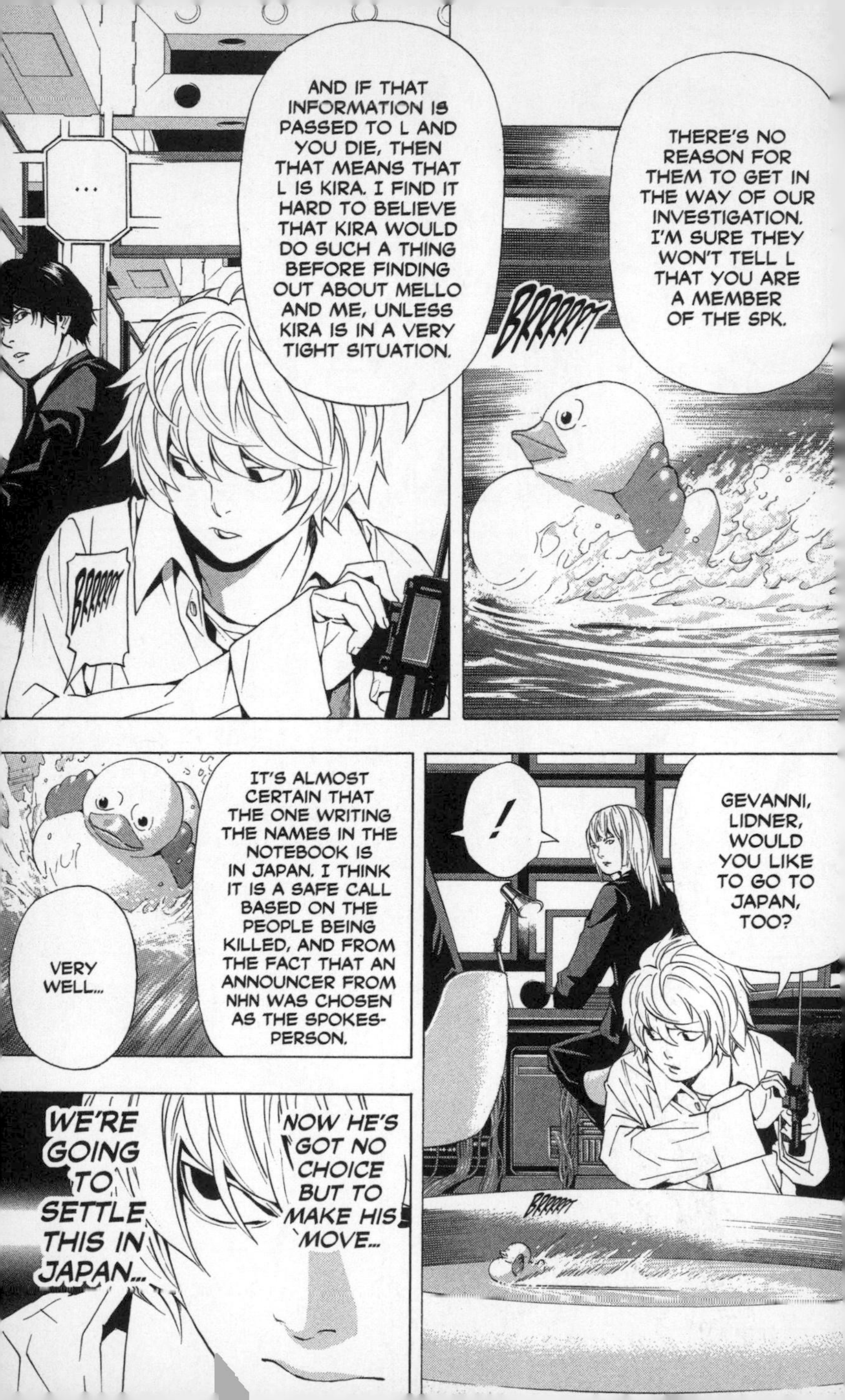
THERE'S NO REASON FOR THEM TO GET IN THE WAY OF OUR INVESTIGATION. I'M SURE THEY WON'T TELL L THAT YOU ARE A MEMBER OF THE SPK.
BRRRRPT
AND IF THAT INFORMATION IS PASSED TO L AND YOU DIE, THEN THAT MEANS THAT L IS KIRA. I FIND IT HARD TO BELIEVE THAT KIRA WOULD DO SUCH A THING BEFORE FINDING OUT ABOUT MELLO AND ME, UNLESS KIRA IS IN A VERY TIGHT SITUATION.
...
BRRRRPT
GEVANNI, LIDNER, WOULD YOU LIKE TO GO TO JAPAN, TOO?
!
IT'S ALMOST CERTAIN THAT THE ONE WRITING THE NAMES IN THE NOTEBOOK IS IN JAPAN. I THINK IT IS A SAFE CALL BASED ON THE PEOPLE BEING KILLED, AND FROM THE FACT THAT AN ANNOUNCER FROM NHN WAS CHOSEN AS THE SPOKES-PERSON.
VERY WELL...
BRRRRPT
NOW HE'S GOT NO CHOICE BUT TO MAKE HIS MOVE...
WE'RE GOING TO SETTLE THIS IN JAPAN...

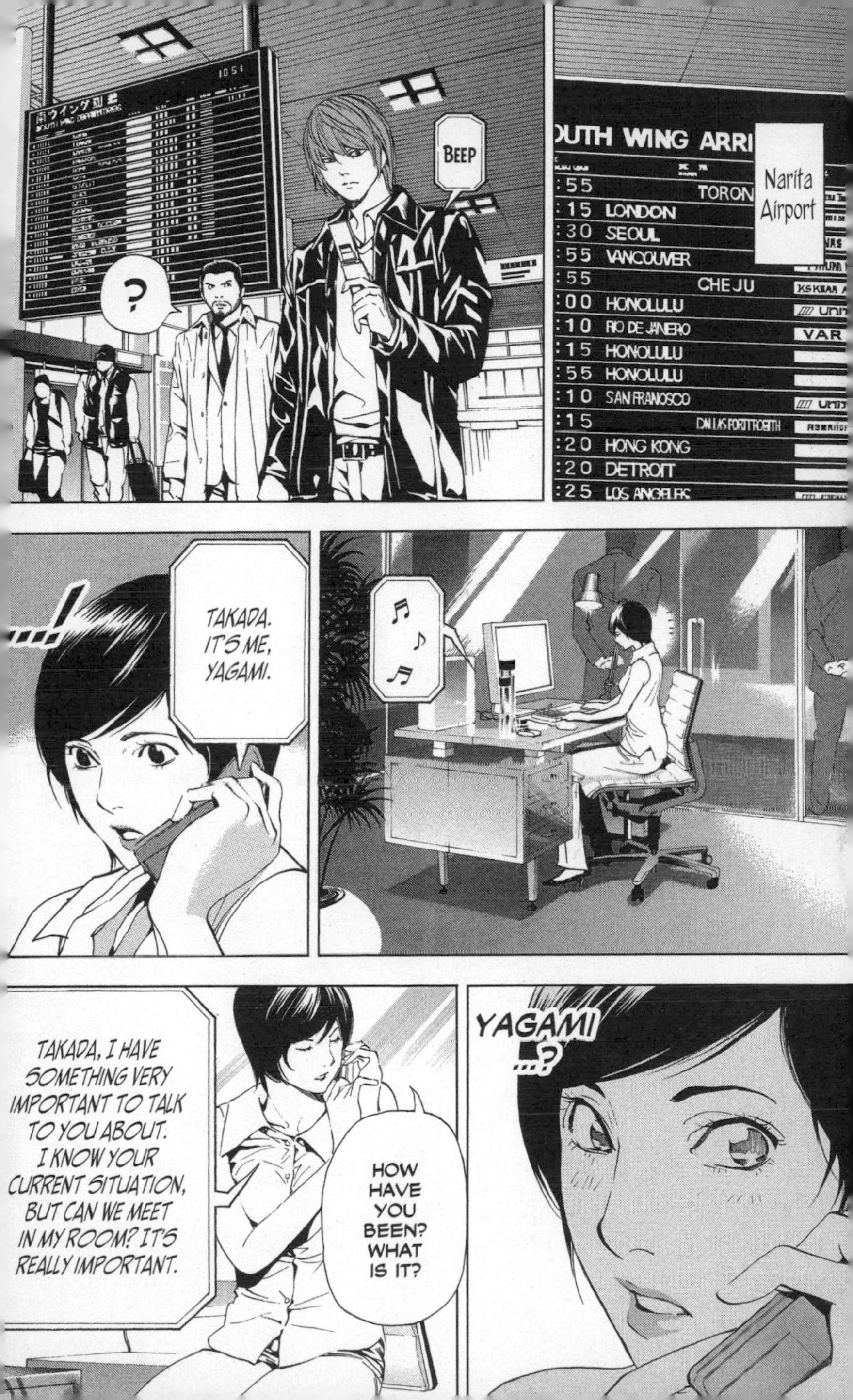
Narita Airport
:55 TORON
:15 LONDON
:30 SEOUL
:55 VANCOUVER
:55 CHE JU
:00 HONOLULU
:10 RIO DE JANERO
:15 HONOLULU
:55 HONOLULU
:10 SAN FRANOSCO
:15
:20 HONG KONG
:20 DETROIT
BEEP
?
TAKADA. IT'S ME, YAGAMI.
...!
YAGAMI ...?
HOW HAVE YOU BEEN? WHAT IS IT?
TAKADA, I HAVE SOMETHING VERY IMPORTANT TO TALK TO YOU ABOUT. I KNOW YOUR CURRENT SITUATION, BUT CAN WE MEET IN MY ROOM? IT'S REALLY IMPORTANT.

READ THIS WAY

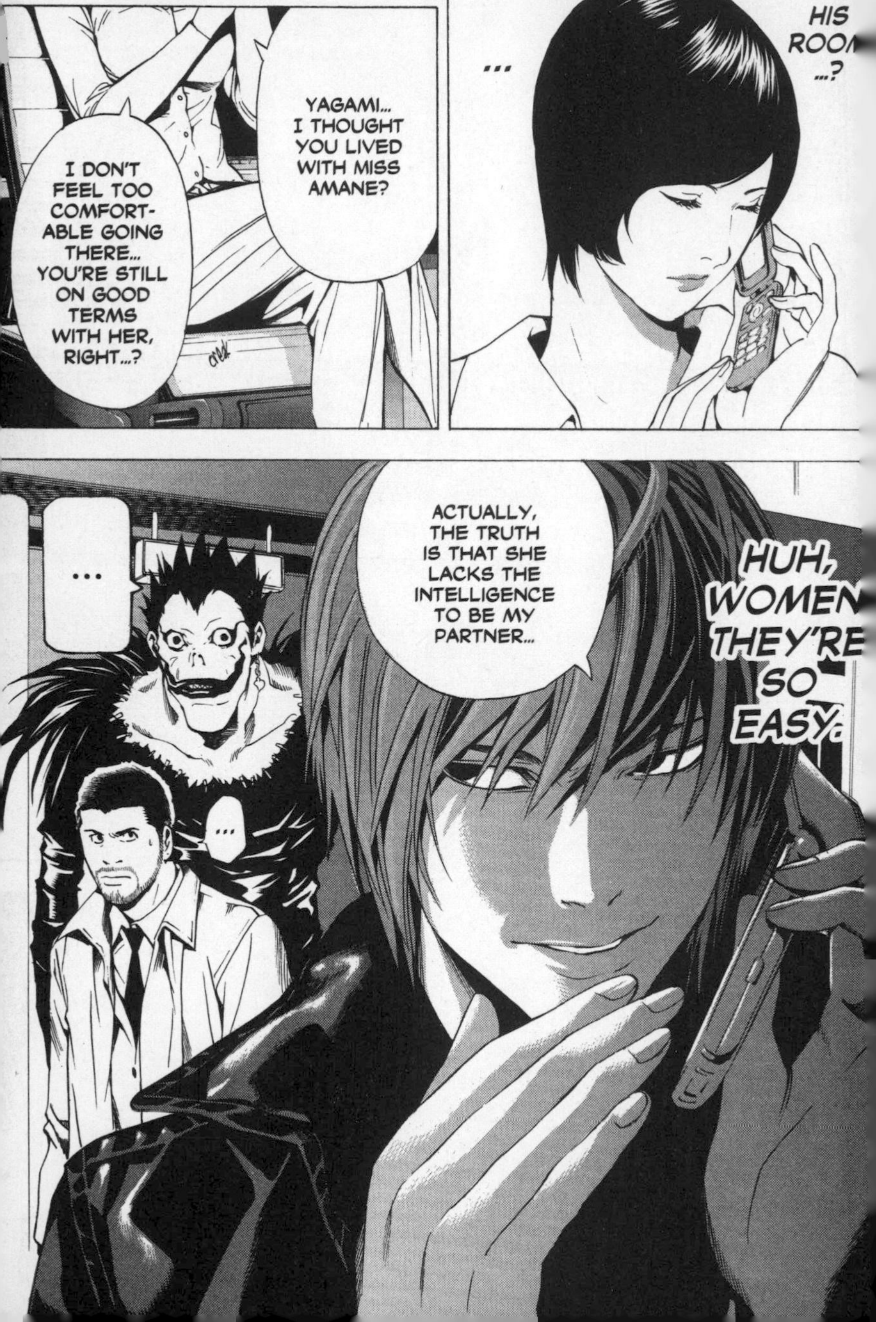
HIS ROOM ...?
...
YAGAMI... I THOUGHT YOU LIVED WITH MISS AMANE?
I DON'T FEEL TOO COMFORT-ABLE GOING THERE... YOU'RE STILL ON GOOD TERMS WITH HER, RIGHT...?
HUH, WOMEN THEY'RE SO EASY.
ACTUALLY, THE TRUTH IS THAT SHE LACKS THE INTELLIGENCE TO BE MY PARTNER...
...
...

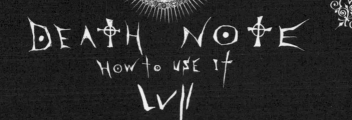

DEATH NOTE
How to use it
LVII

- In the DEATH NOTE you cannot set the death date longer than the victim's original life span. Even if the victim's death is set in the DEATH NOTE beyond his/her original life span, the victim will die before the set time.

デスノートで人間界本来の寿命を延ばす直接的な死の設定はできない。
人間界での本来の寿命より後に、死の時間を設定しても必ずその前に死ぬ。

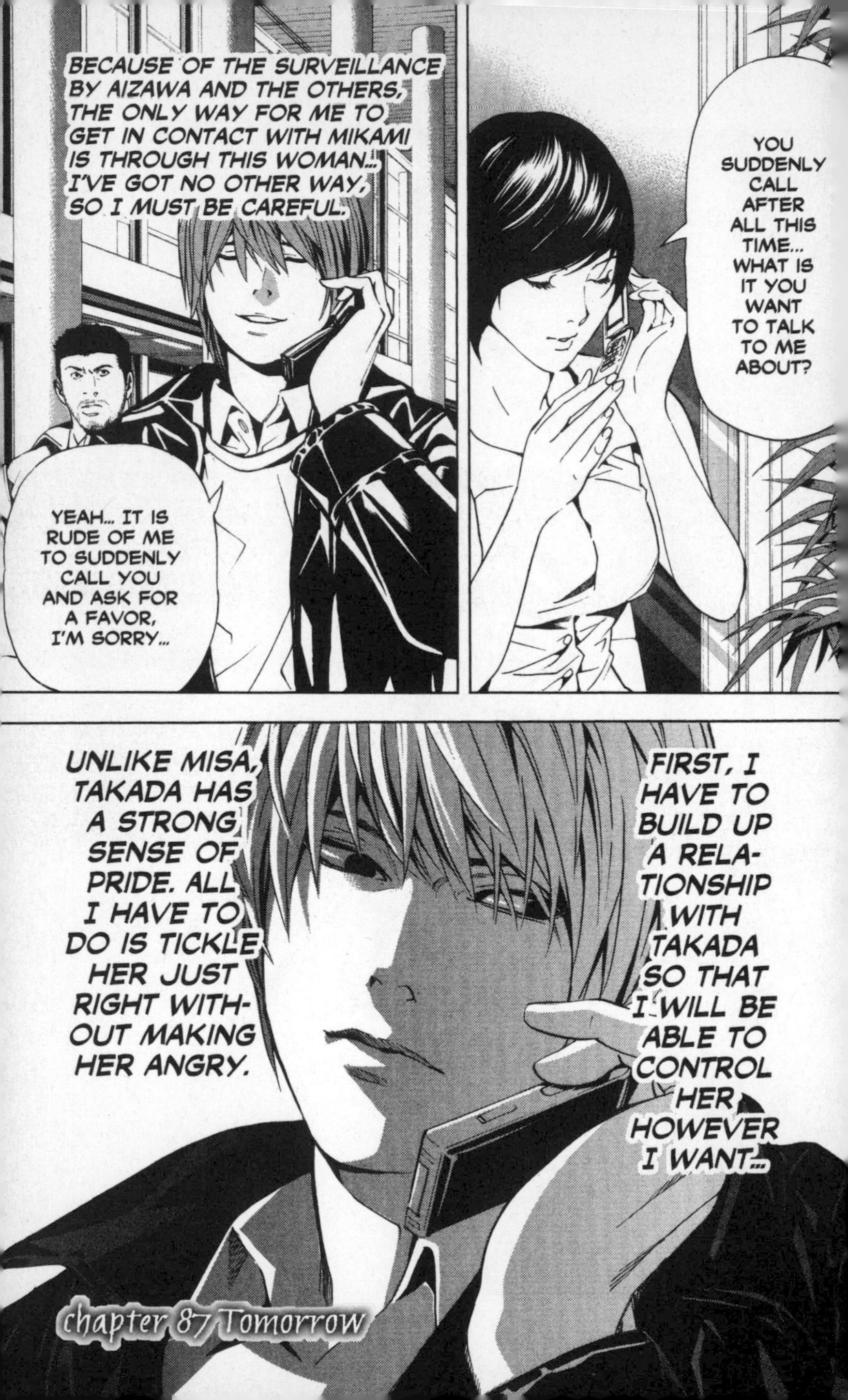
YOU SUDDENLY CALL AFTER ALL THIS TIME... WHAT IS IT YOU WANT TO TALK TO ME ABOUT?
BECAUSE OF THE SURVEILLANCE BY AIZAWA AND THE OTHERS, THE ONLY WAY FOR ME TO GET IN CONTACT WITH MIKAMI IS THROUGH THIS WOMAN... I'VE GOT NO OTHER WAY, SO I MUST BE CAREFUL.
YEAH... IT IS RUDE OF ME TO SUDDENLY CALL YOU AND ASK FOR A FAVOR, I'M SORRY...
FIRST, I HAVE TO BUILD UP A RELATIONSHIP WITH TAKADA SO THAT I WILL BE ABLE TO CONTROL HER HOWEVER I WANT...
UNLIKE MISA, TAKADA HAS A STRONG SENSE OF PRIDE. ALL I HAVE TO DO IS TICKLE HER JUST RIGHT WITHOUT MAKING HER ANGRY.
chapter 87 Tomorrow

chapter 87 Tomorrow

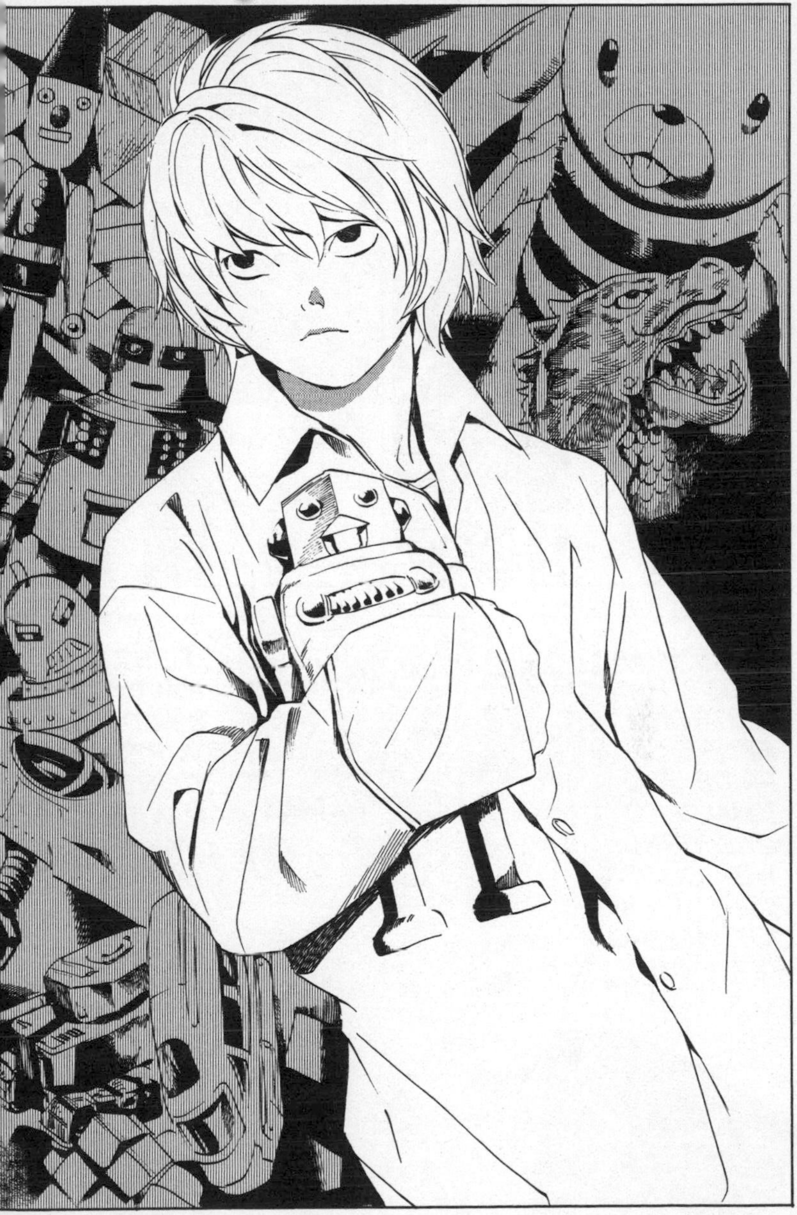

READ THIS WAY

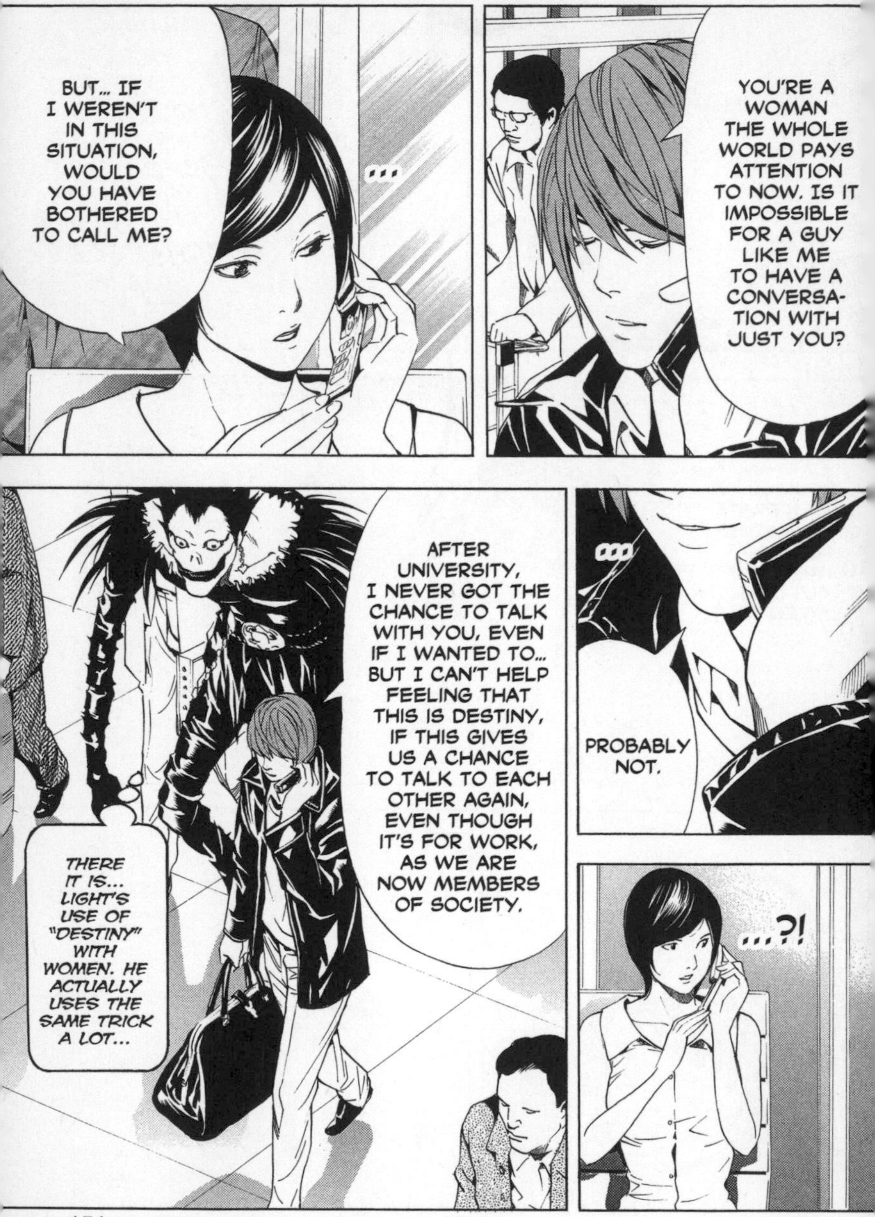
YOU'RE A WOMAN THE WHOLE WORLD PAYS ATTENTION TO NOW. IS IT IMPOSSIBLE FOR A GUY LIKE ME TO HAVE A CONVERSATION WITH JUST YOU?
...
BUT... IF I WEREN'T IN THIS SITUATION, WOULD YOU HAVE BOTHERED TO CALL ME?
...
PROBABLY NOT.
...?!
AFTER UNIVERSITY, I NEVER GOT THE CHANCE TO TALK WITH YOU, EVEN IF I WANTED TO... BUT I CAN'T HELP FEELING THAT THIS IS DESTINY, IF THIS GIVES US A CHANCE TO TALK TO EACH OTHER AGAIN, EVEN THOUGH IT'S FOR WORK, AS WE ARE NOW MEMBERS OF SOCIETY.
THERE IT IS... LIGHT'S USE OF "DESTINY" WITH WOMEN. HE ACTUALLY USES THE SAME TRICK A LOT...

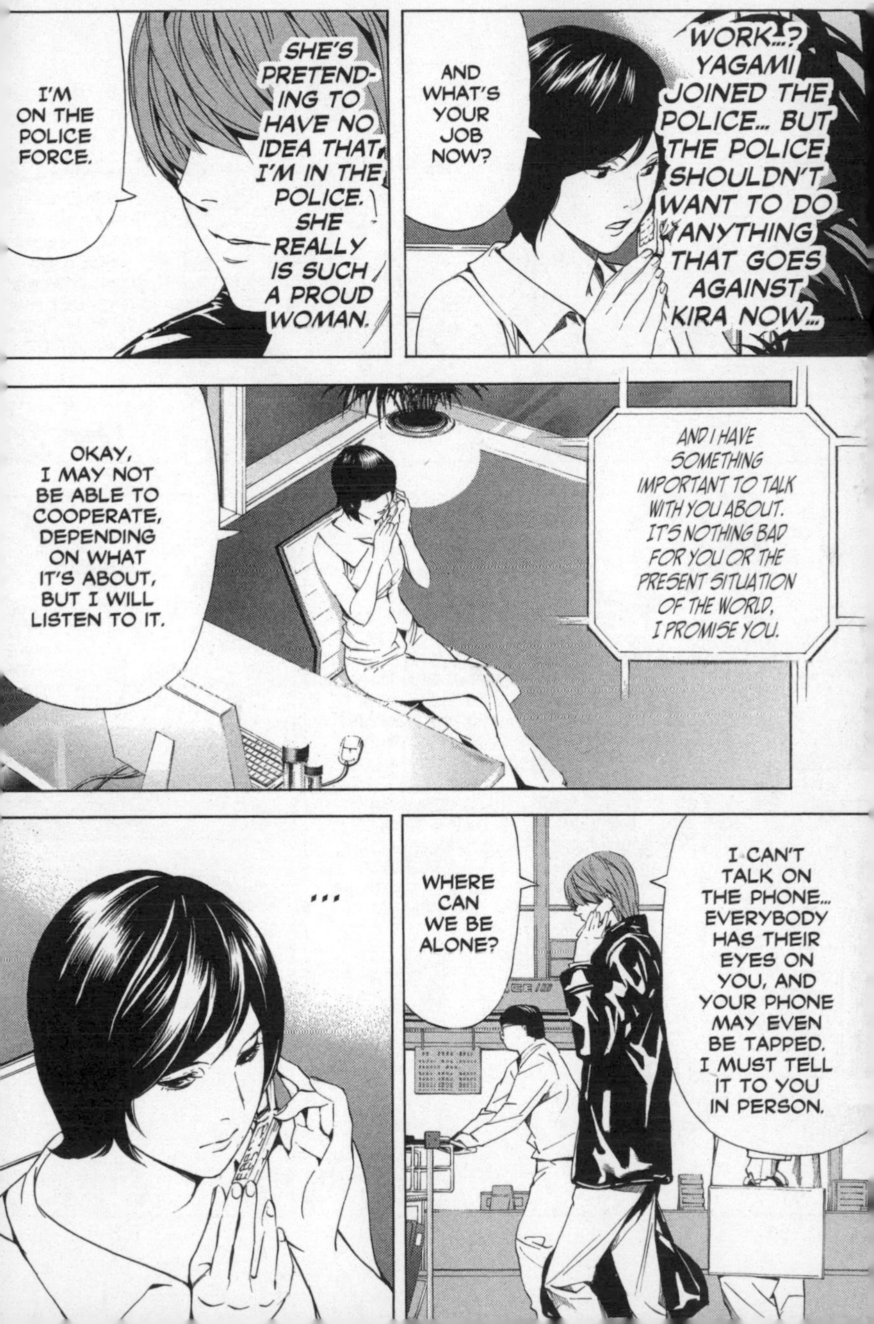

WORK...? YAGAMI JOINED THE POLICE... BUT THE POLICE SHOULDN'T WANT TO DO ANYTHING THAT GOES AGAINST KIRA NOW...
AND WHAT'S YOUR JOB NOW?
SHE'S PRETENDING TO HAVE NO IDEA THAT I'M IN THE POLICE. SHE REALLY IS SUCH A PROUD WOMAN.
I'M ON THE POLICE FORCE.
AND I HAVE SOMETHING IMPORTANT TO TALK WITH YOU ABOUT. IT'S NOTHING BAD FOR YOU OR THE PRESENT SITUATION OF THE WORLD, I PROMISE YOU.
OKAY, I MAY NOT BE ABLE TO COOPERATE, DEPENDING ON WHAT IT'S ABOUT, BUT I WILL LISTEN TO IT.
I CAN'T TALK ON THE PHONE... EVERYBODY HAS THEIR EYES ON YOU, AND YOUR PHONE MAY EVEN BE TAPPED. I MUST TELL IT TO YOU IN PERSON.
WHERE CAN WE BE ALONE?
...

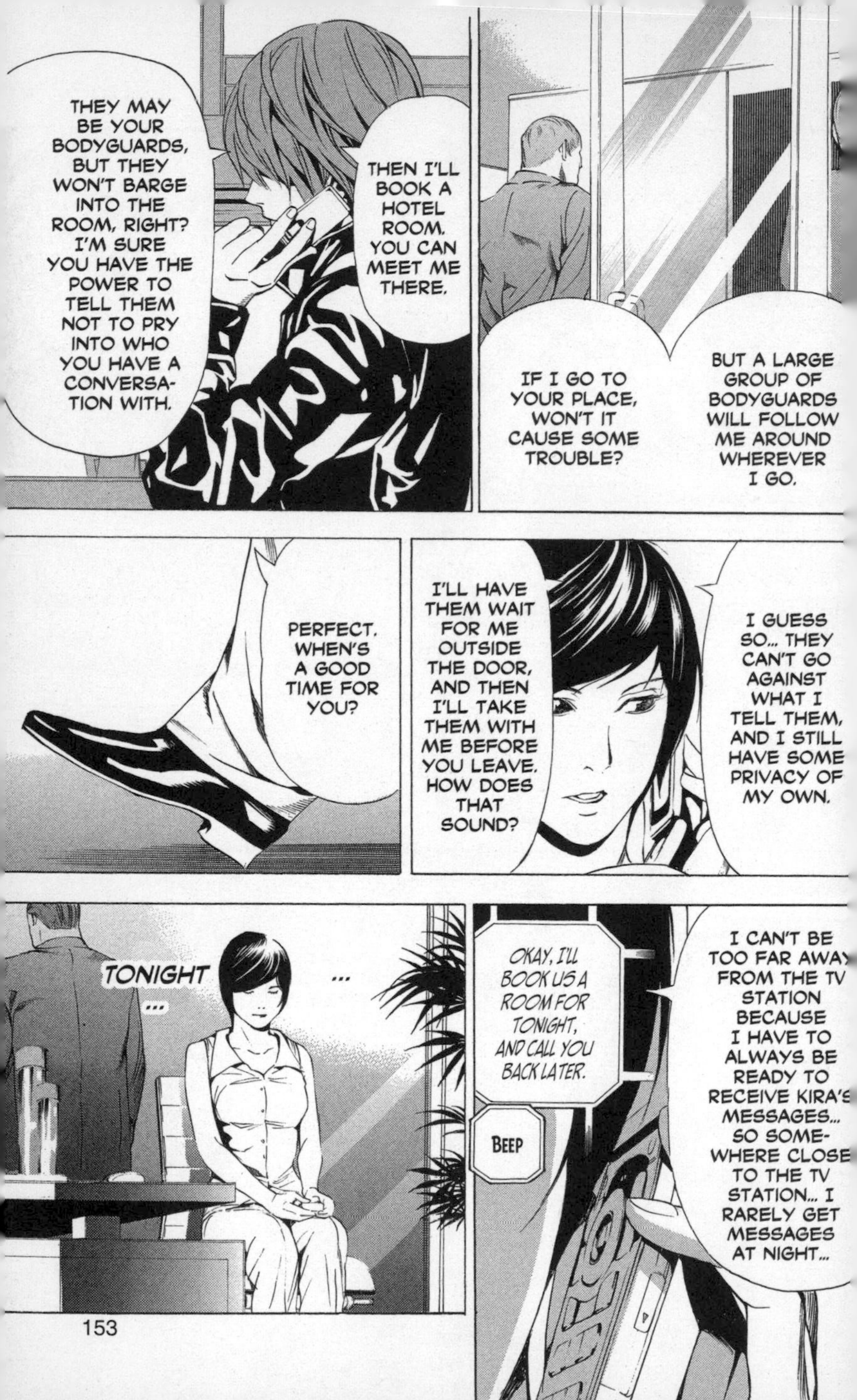
BUT A LARGE GROUP OF BODYGUARDS WILL FOLLOW ME AROUND WHEREVER I GO.
IF I GO TO YOUR PLACE, WON'T IT CAUSE SOME TROUBLE?
THEN I'LL BOOK A HOTEL ROOM. YOU CAN MEET ME THERE.
THEY MAY BE YOUR BODYGUARDS, BUT THEY WON'T BARGE INTO THE ROOM, RIGHT? I'M SURE YOU HAVE THE POWER TO TELL THEM NOT TO PRY INTO WHO YOU HAVE A CONVERSATION WITH.
I GUESS SO... THEY CAN'T GO AGAINST WHAT I TELL THEM, AND I STILL HAVE SOME PRIVACY OF MY OWN.
I'LL HAVE THEM WAIT FOR ME OUTSIDE THE DOOR, AND THEN I'LL TAKE THEM WITH ME BEFORE YOU LEAVE. HOW DOES THAT SOUND?
PERFECT. WHEN'S A GOOD TIME FOR YOU?
I CAN'T BE TOO FAR AWAY FROM THE TV STATION BECAUSE I HAVE TO ALWAYS BE READY TO RECEIVE KIRA'S MESSAGES... SO SOMEWHERE CLOSE TO THE TV STATION... I RARELY GET MESSAGES AT NIGHT...
OKAY, I'LL BOOK US A ROOM FOR TONIGHT, AND CALL YOU BACK LATER.
BEEP
...
TONIGHT ...

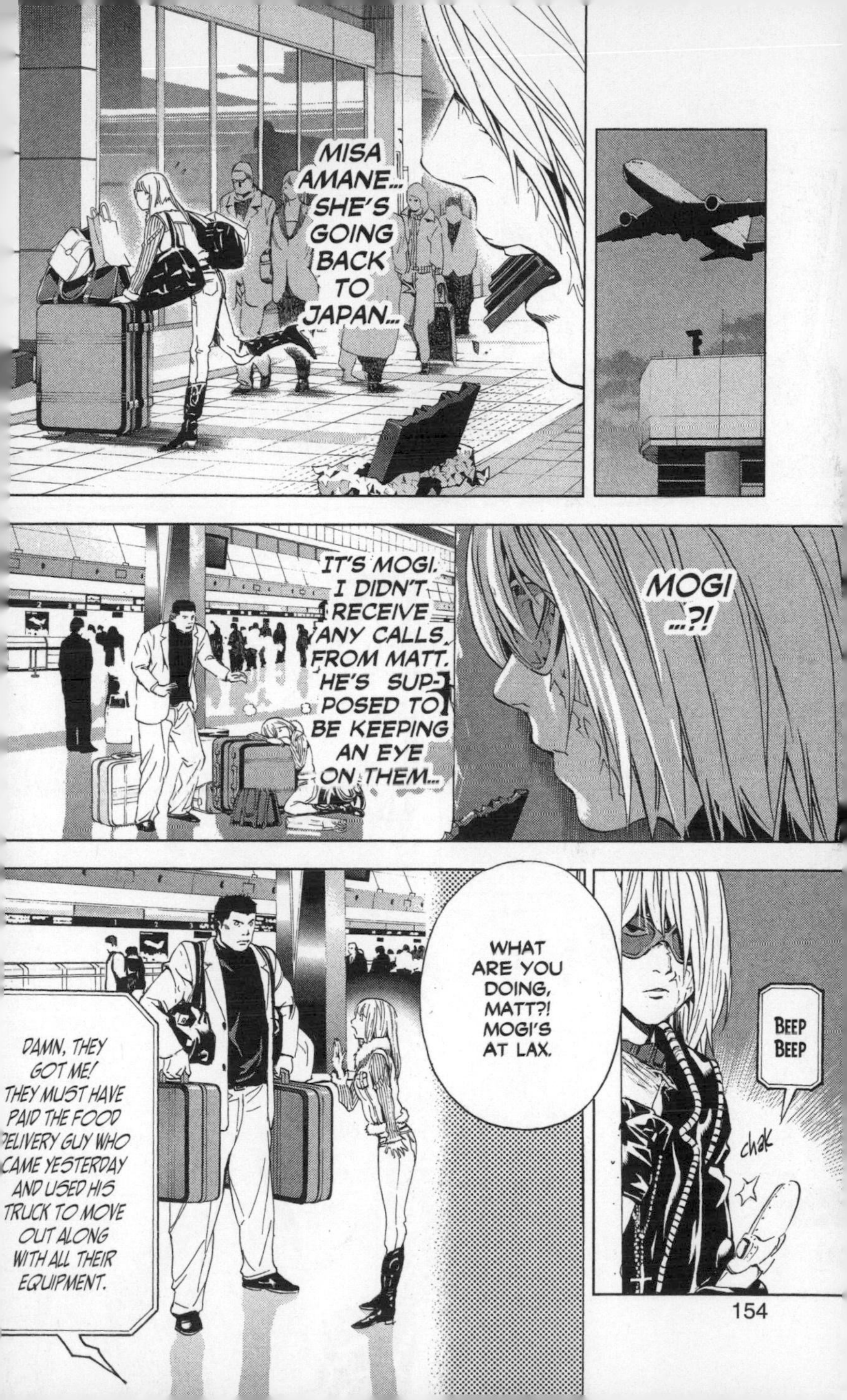
MISA AMANE... SHE'S GOING BACK TO JAPAN...
MOGI ...?!
IT'S MOGI. I DIDN'T RECEIVE ANY CALLS FROM MATT. HE'S SUP-POSED TO BE KEEPING AN EYE ON THEM...
BEEP BEEP
chak
WHAT ARE YOU DOING, MATT?! MOGI'S AT LAX.
DAMN, THEY GOT ME! THEY MUST HAVE PAID THE FOOD DELIVERY GUY WHO CAME YESTERDAY AND USED HIS TRUCK TO MOVE OUT ALONG WITH ALL THEIR EQUIPMENT.

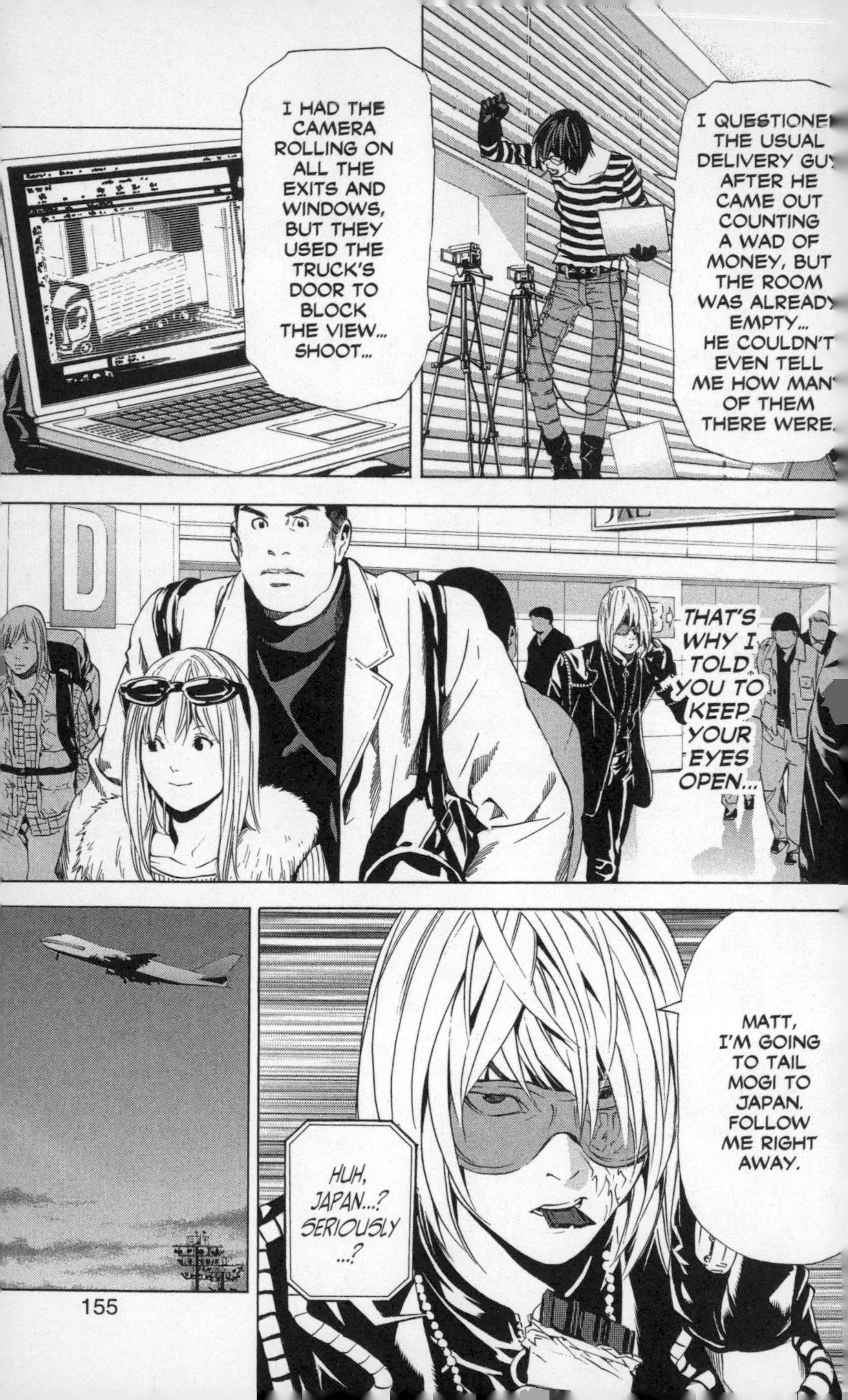
I QUESTIONE THE USUAL DELIVERY GU AFTER HE CAME OUT COUNTING A WAD OF MONEY, BUT THE ROOM WAS ALREAD EMPTY... HE COULDN'T EVEN TELL ME HOW MAN OF THEM THERE WERE.
I HAD THE CAMERA ROLLING ON ALL THE EXITS AND WINDOWS, BUT THEY USED THE TRUCK'S DOOR TO BLOCK THE VIEW... SHOOT...
THAT'S WHY I TOLD YOU TO KEEP YOUR EYES OPEN...
MATT, I'M GOING TO TAIL MOGI TO JAPAN. FOLLOW ME RIGHT AWAY.
HUH, JAPAN...? SERIOUSLY ...?

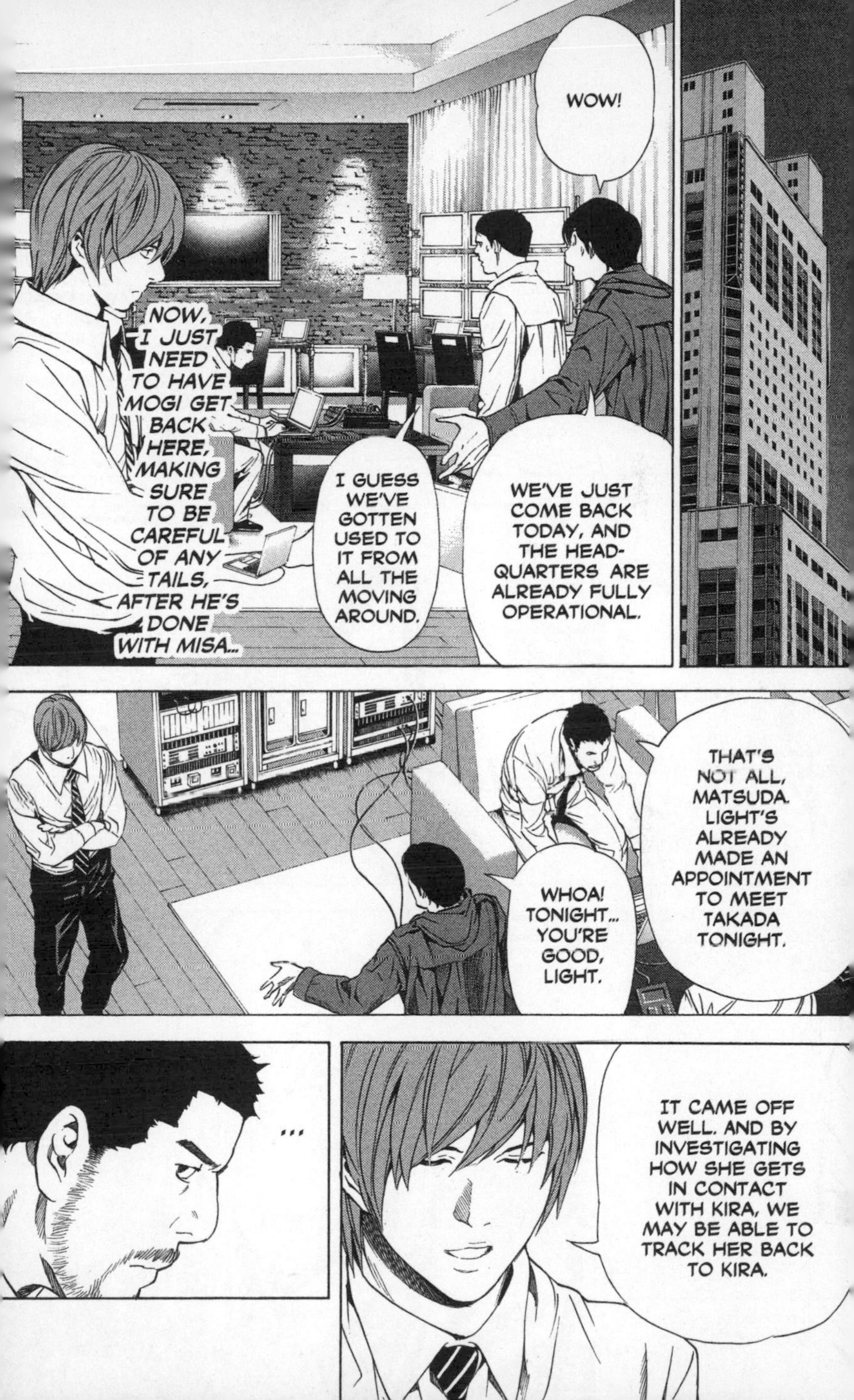
WOW!
WE'VE JUST COME BACK TODAY, AND THE HEAD-QUARTERS ARE ALREADY FULLY OPERATIONAL.
I GUESS WE'VE GOTTEN USED TO IT FROM ALL THE MOVING AROUND.
NOW, I JUST NEED TO HAVE MOGI GET BACK HERE, MAKING SURE TO BE CAREFUL OF ANY TAILS, AFTER HE'S DONE WITH MISA...
THAT'S NOT ALL, MATSUDA. LIGHT'S ALREADY MADE AN APPOINTMENT TO MEET TAKADA TONIGHT.
WHOA! TONIGHT... YOU'RE GOOD, LIGHT.
IT CAME OFF WELL. AND BY INVESTIGATING HOW SHE GETS IN CONTACT WITH KIRA, WE MAY BE ABLE TO TRACK HER BACK TO KIRA.
...

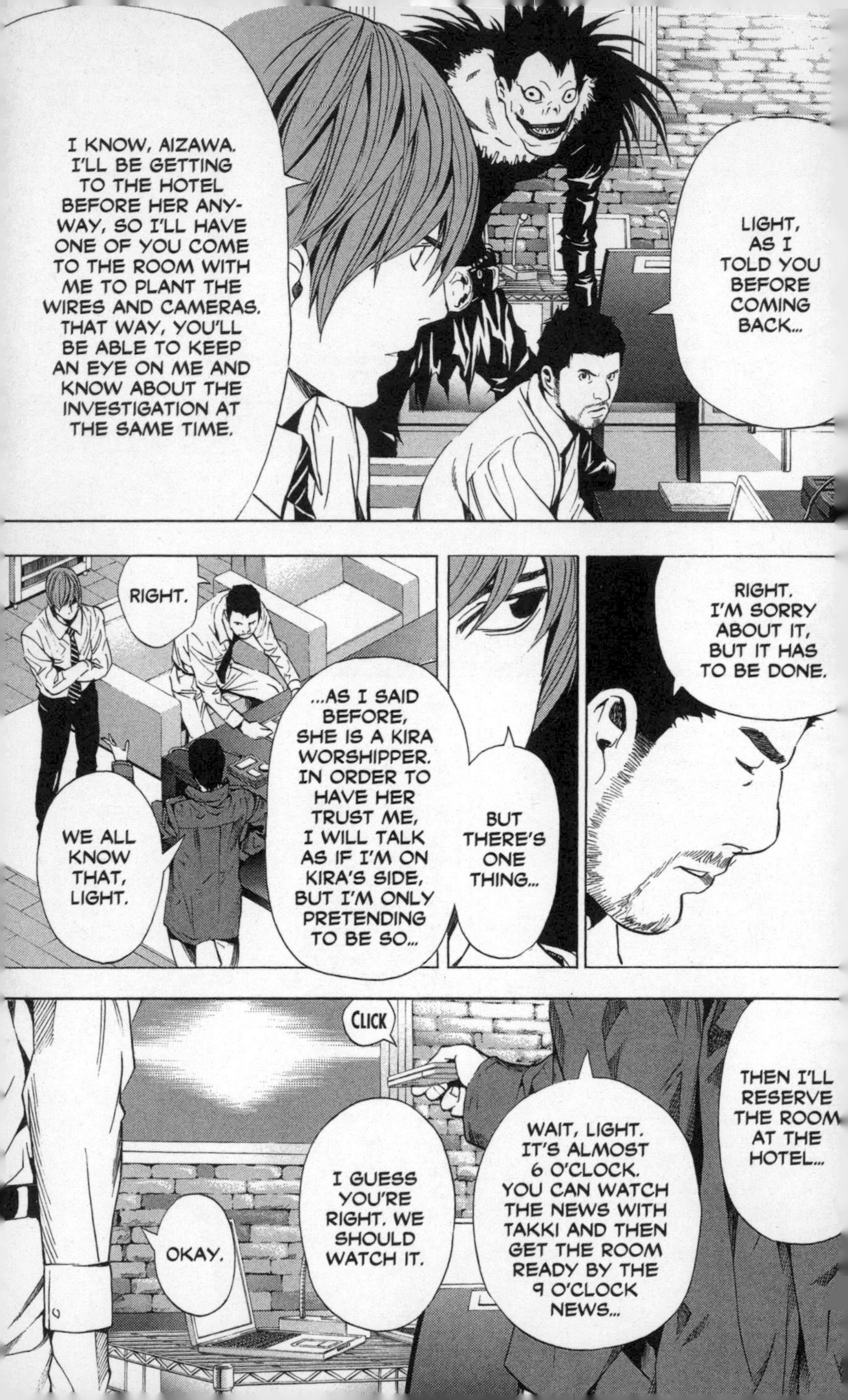
LIGHT, AS I TOLD YOU BEFORE COMING BACK...
I KNOW, AIZAWA. I'LL BE GETTING TO THE HOTEL BEFORE HER ANY-WAY, SO I'LL HAVE ONE OF YOU COME TO THE ROOM WITH ME TO PLANT THE WIRES AND CAMERAS. THAT WAY, YOU'LL BE ABLE TO KEEP AN EYE ON ME AND KNOW ABOUT THE INVESTIGATION AT THE SAME TIME.
RIGHT. I'M SORRY ABOUT IT, BUT IT HAS TO BE DONE.
BUT THERE'S ONE THING...
...AS I SAID BEFORE, SHE IS A KIRA WORSHIPPER. IN ORDER TO HAVE HER TRUST ME, I WILL TALK AS IF I'M ON KIRA'S SIDE, BUT I'M ONLY PRETENDING TO BE SO...
RIGHT.
WE ALL KNOW THAT, LIGHT.
THEN I'LL RESERVE THE ROOM AT THE HOTEL...
CLICK
WAIT, LIGHT. IT'S ALMOST 6 O'CLOCK. YOU CAN WATCH THE NEWS WITH TAKKI AND THEN GET THE ROOM READY BY THE 9 O'CLOCK NEWS...
I GUESS YOU'RE RIGHT. WE SHOULD WATCH IT.
OKAY.

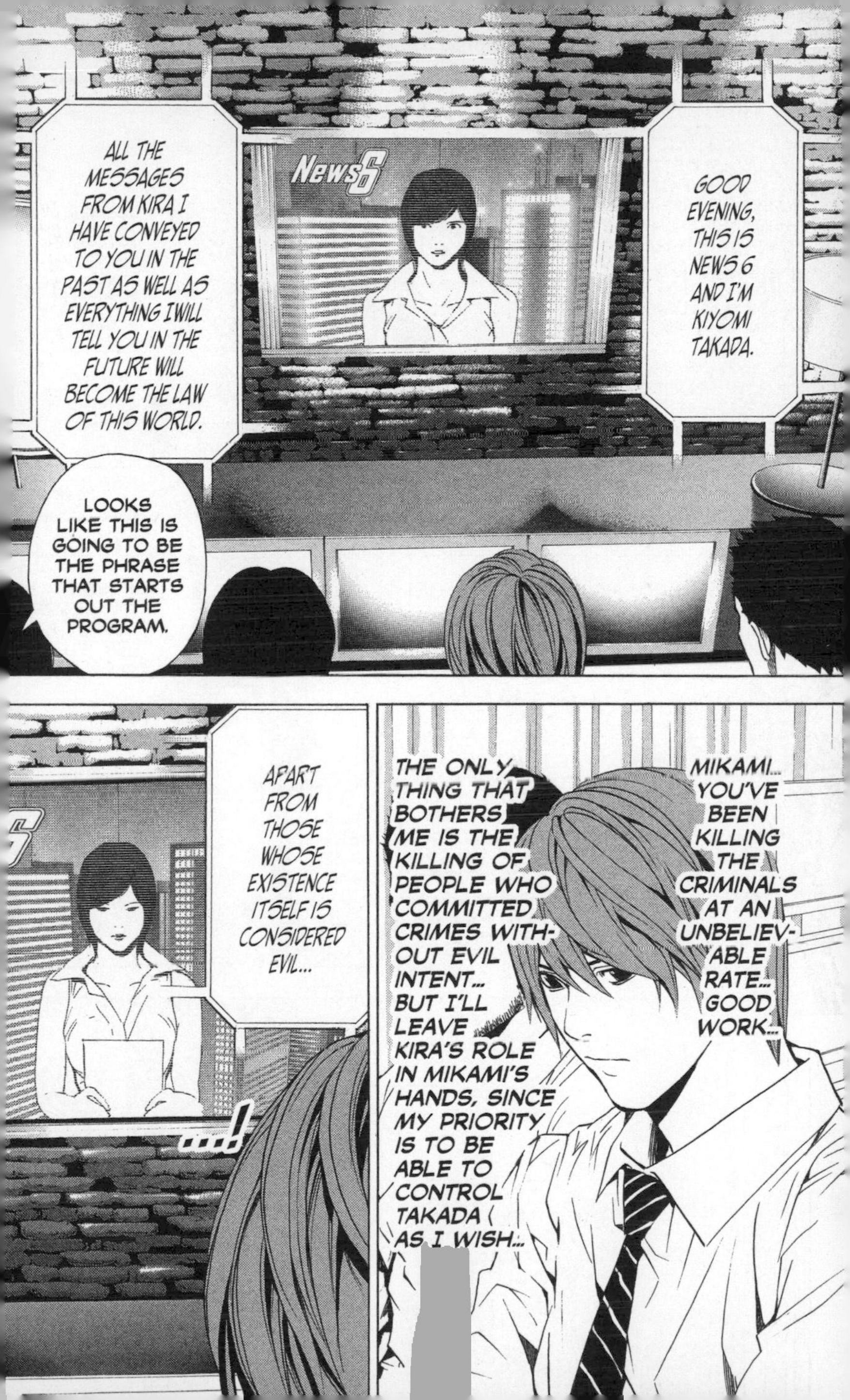
GOOD EVENING, THIS IS NEWS 6 AND I'M KIYOMI TAKADA.
ALL THE MESSAGES FROM KIRA I HAVE CONVEYED TO YOU IN THE PAST AS WELL AS EVERYTHING I WILL TELL YOU IN THE FUTURE WILL BECOME THE LAW OF THIS WORLD.
LOOKS LIKE THIS IS GOING TO BE THE PHRASE THAT STARTS OUT THE PROGRAM.
MIKAMI... YOU'VE BEEN KILLING THE CRIMINALS AT AN UNBELIEVABLE RATE... GOOD WORK...
THE ONLY THING THAT BOTHERS ME IS THE KILLING OF PEOPLE WHO COMMITTED CRIMES WITHOUT EVIL INTENT... BUT I'LL LEAVE KIRA'S ROLE IN MIKAMI'S HANDS, SINCE MY PRIORITY IS TO BE ABLE TO CONTROL TAKADA AS I WISH...
APART FROM THOSE WHOSE EXISTENCE ITSELF IS CONSIDERED EVIL...
...!

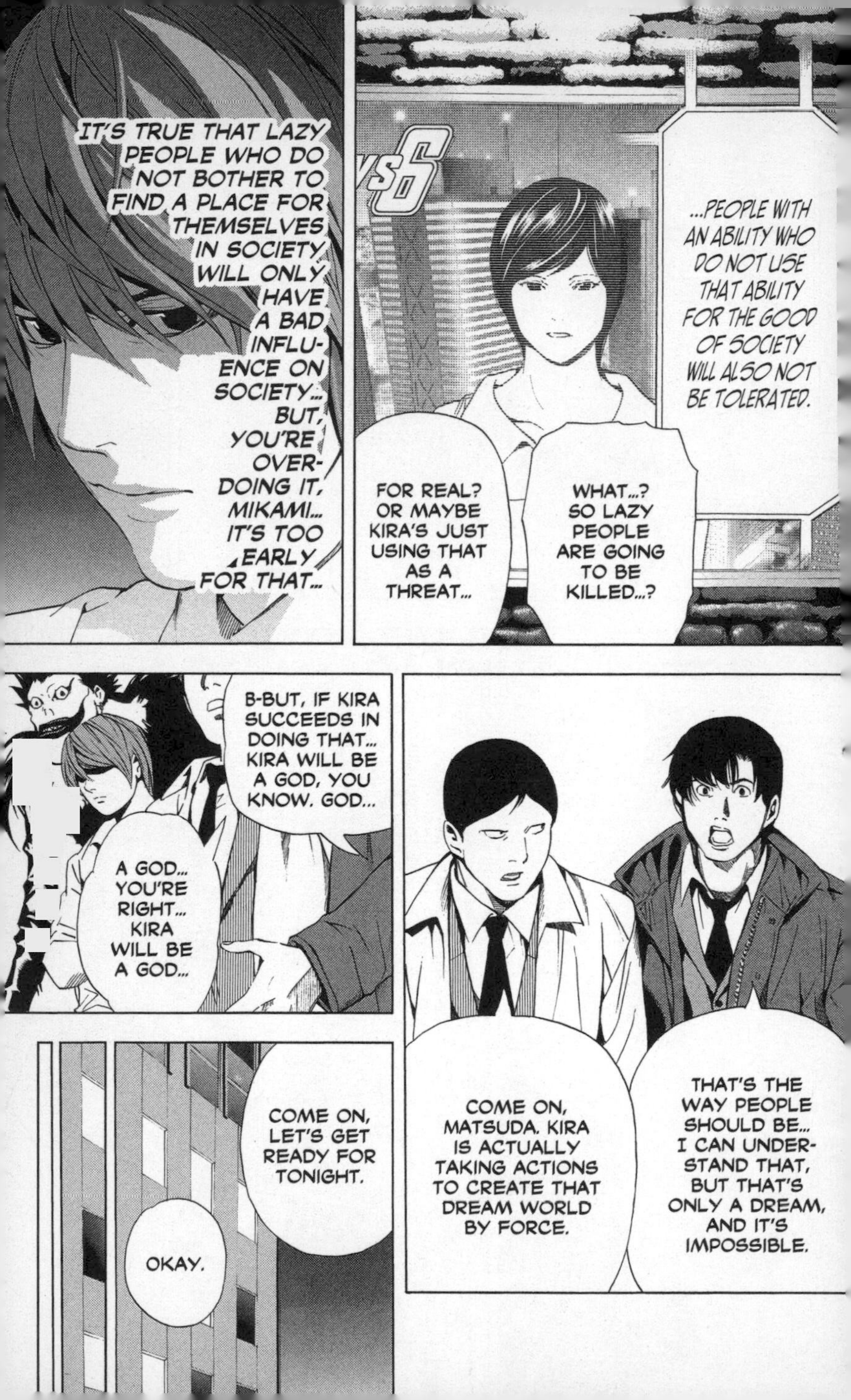
...PEOPLE WITH AN ABILITY WHO DO NOT USE THAT ABILITY FOR THE GOOD OF SOCIETY WILL ALSO NOT BE TOLERATED.
WHAT...? SO LAZY PEOPLE ARE GOING TO BE KILLED...?
FOR REAL? OR MAYBE KIRA'S JUST USING THAT AS A THREAT...
IT'S TRUE THAT LAZY PEOPLE WHO DO NOT BOTHER TO FIND A PLACE FOR THEMSELVES IN SOCIETY WILL ONLY HAVE A BAD INFLU- ENCE ON SOCIETY... BUT, YOU'RE OVER- DOING IT, MIKAMI... IT'S TOO EARLY FOR THAT...
THAT'S THE WAY PEOPLE SHOULD BE... I CAN UNDER- STAND THAT, BUT THAT'S ONLY A DREAM, AND IT'S IMPOSSIBLE.
COME ON, MATSUDA. KIRA IS ACTUALLY TAKING ACTIONS TO CREATE THAT DREAM WORLD BY FORCE.
B-BUT, IF KIRA SUCCEEDS IN DOING THAT... KIRA WILL BE A GOD, YOU KNOW. GOD...
A GOD... YOU'RE RIGHT... KIRA WILL BE A GOD...
COME ON, LET'S GET READY FOR TONIGHT.
OKAY.

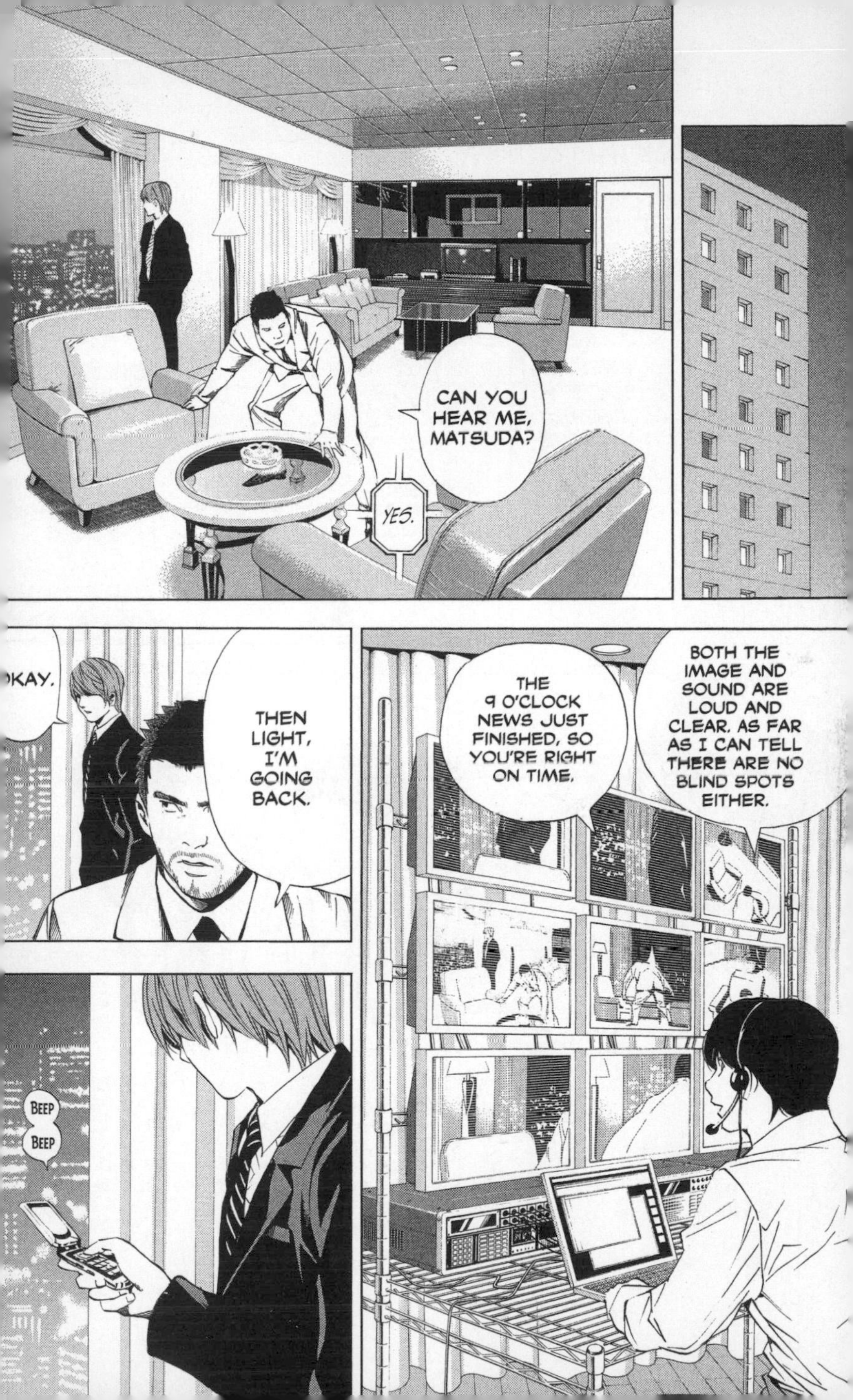
CAN YOU HEAR ME, MATSUDA?
YES.
BOTH THE IMAGE AND SOUND ARE LOUD AND CLEAR. AS FAR AS I CAN TELL THERE ARE NO BLIND SPOTS EITHER.
THE 9 O'CLOCK NEWS JUST FINISHED, SO YOU'RE RIGHT ON TIME.
THEN LIGHT, I'M GOING BACK.
OKAY.
BEEP
BEEP

READ THIS WAY

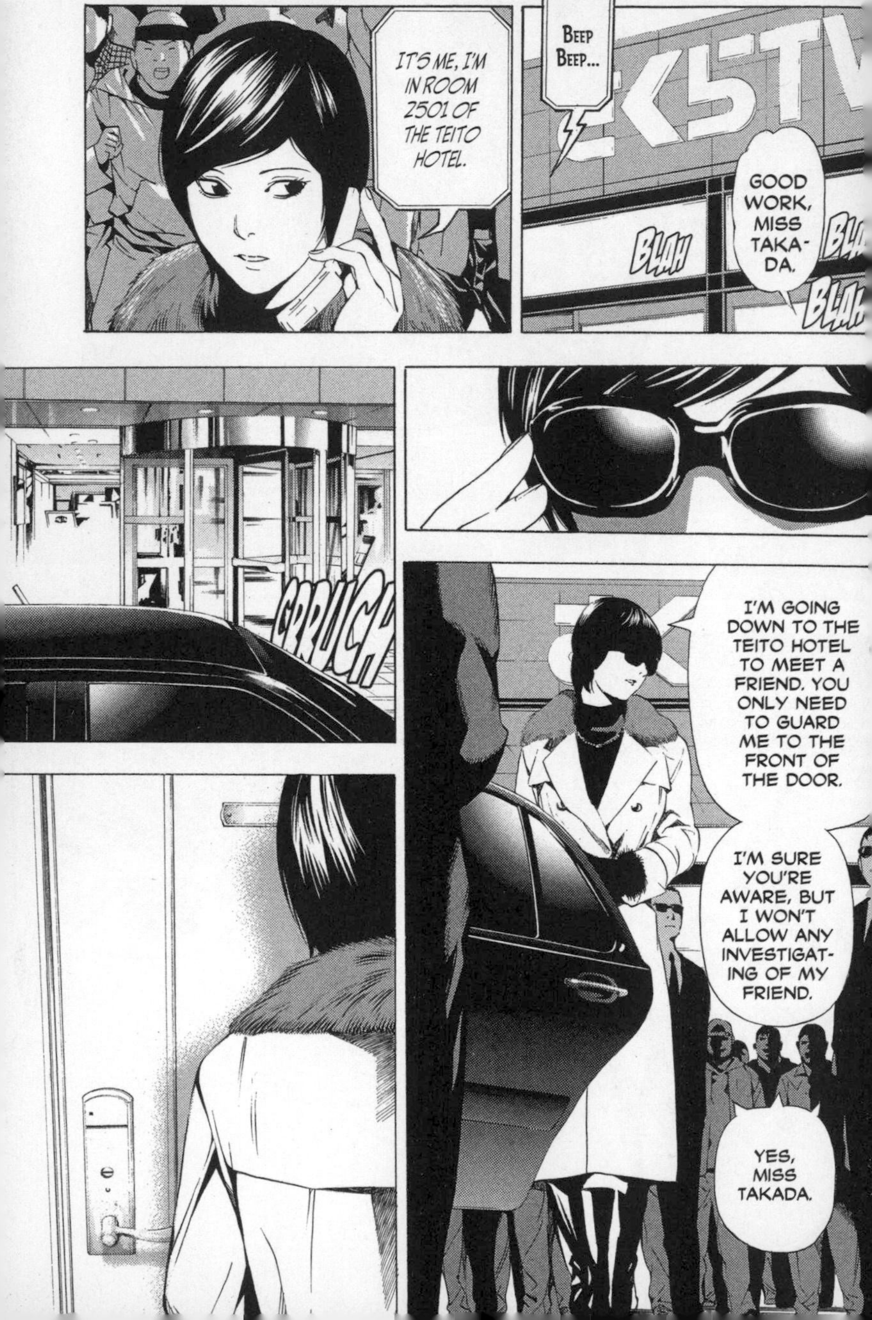
Beep Beep...
GOOD WORK, MISS TAKADA.
BLAH
BLAH
BLAH
IT'S ME, I'M IN ROOM 2501 OF THE TEITO HOTEL.
I'M GOING DOWN TO THE TEITO HOTEL TO MEET A FRIEND. YOU ONLY NEED TO GUARD ME TO THE FRONT OF THE DOOR.
I'M SURE YOU'RE AWARE, BUT I WON'T ALLOW ANY INVESTIGATING OF MY FRIEND.
YES, MISS TAKADA.
CRRUCH

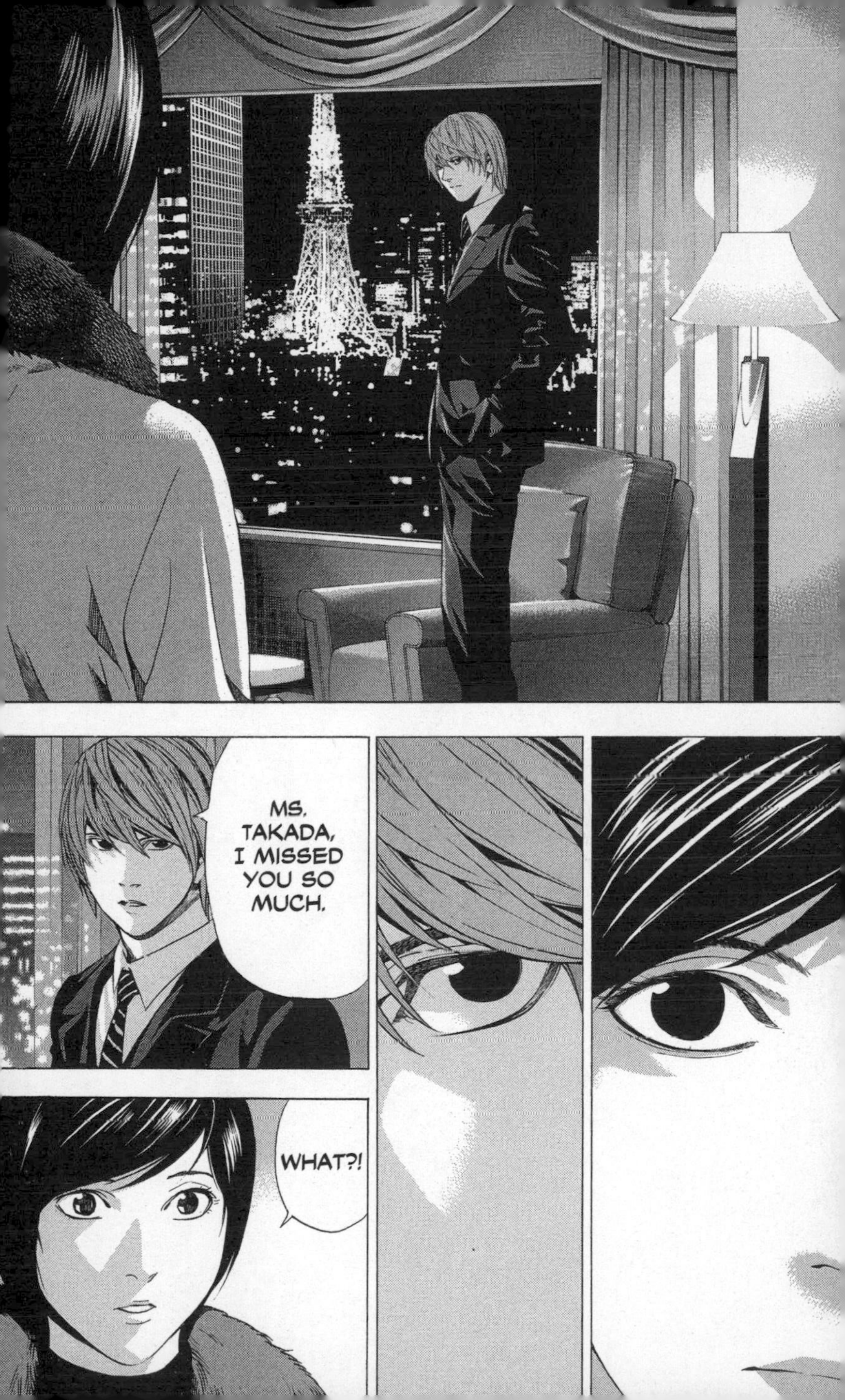
MS. TAKADA, I MISSED YOU SO MUCH.
WHAT?!

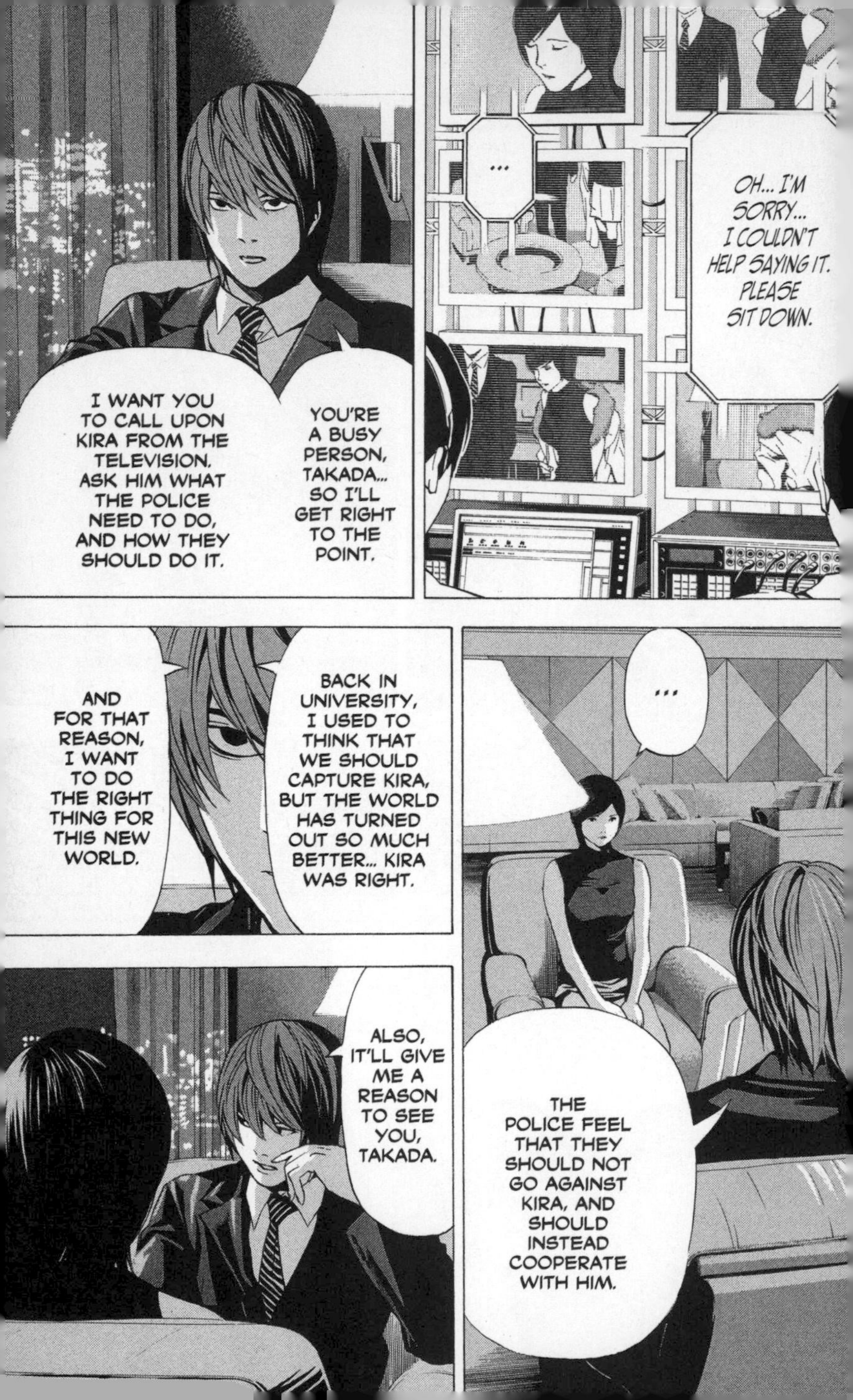
...
OH... I'M SORRY... I COULDN'T HELP SAYING IT. PLEASE SIT DOWN.
YOU'RE A BUSY PERSON, TAKADA... SO I'LL GET RIGHT TO THE POINT.
I WANT YOU TO CALL UPON KIRA FROM THE TELEVISION. ASK HIM WHAT THE POLICE NEED TO DO, AND HOW THEY SHOULD DO IT.
...
THE POLICE FEEL THAT THEY SHOULD NOT GO AGAINST KIRA, AND SHOULD INSTEAD COOPERATE WITH HIM.
BACK IN UNIVERSITY, I USED TO THINK THAT WE SHOULD CAPTURE KIRA, BUT THE WORLD HAS TURNED OUT SO MUCH BETTER... KIRA WAS RIGHT.
AND FOR THAT REASON, I WANT TO DO THE RIGHT THING FOR THIS NEW WORLD.
ALSO, IT'LL GIVE ME A REASON TO SEE YOU, TAKADA.

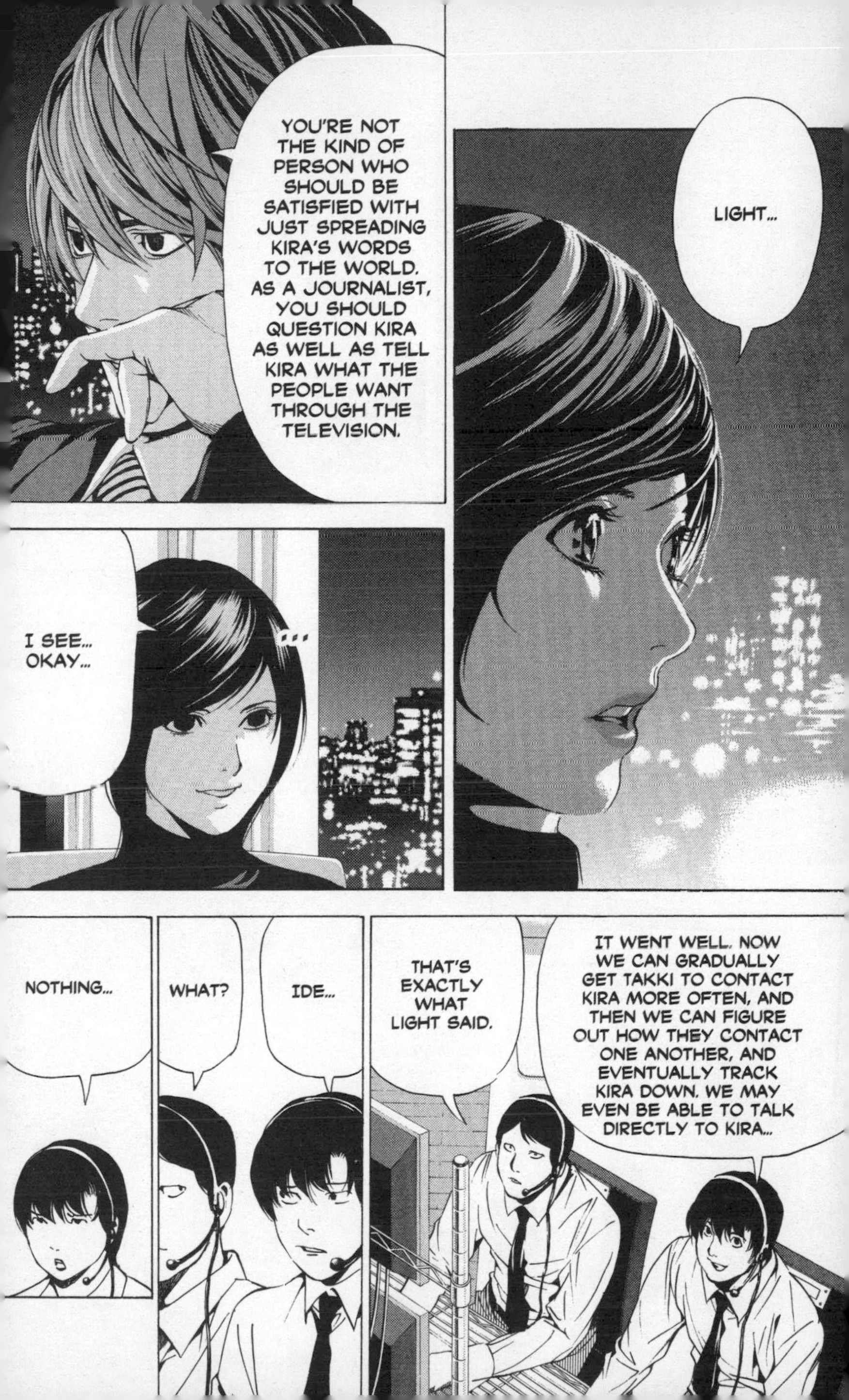
LIGHT...
YOU'RE NOT THE KIND OF PERSON WHO SHOULD BE SATISFIED WITH JUST SPREADING KIRA'S WORDS TO THE WORLD. AS A JOURNALIST, YOU SHOULD QUESTION KIRA AS WELL AS TELL KIRA WHAT THE PEOPLE WANT THROUGH THE TELEVISION.
...
I SEE... OKAY...
IT WENT WELL. NOW WE CAN GRADUALLY GET TAKKI TO CONTACT KIRA MORE OFTEN, AND THEN WE CAN FIGURE OUT HOW THEY CONTACT ONE ANOTHER, AND EVENTUALLY TRACK KIRA DOWN. WE MAY EVEN BE ABLE TO TALK DIRECTLY TO KIRA...
THAT'S EXACTLY WHAT LIGHT SAID.
IDE...
WHAT?
NOTHING...

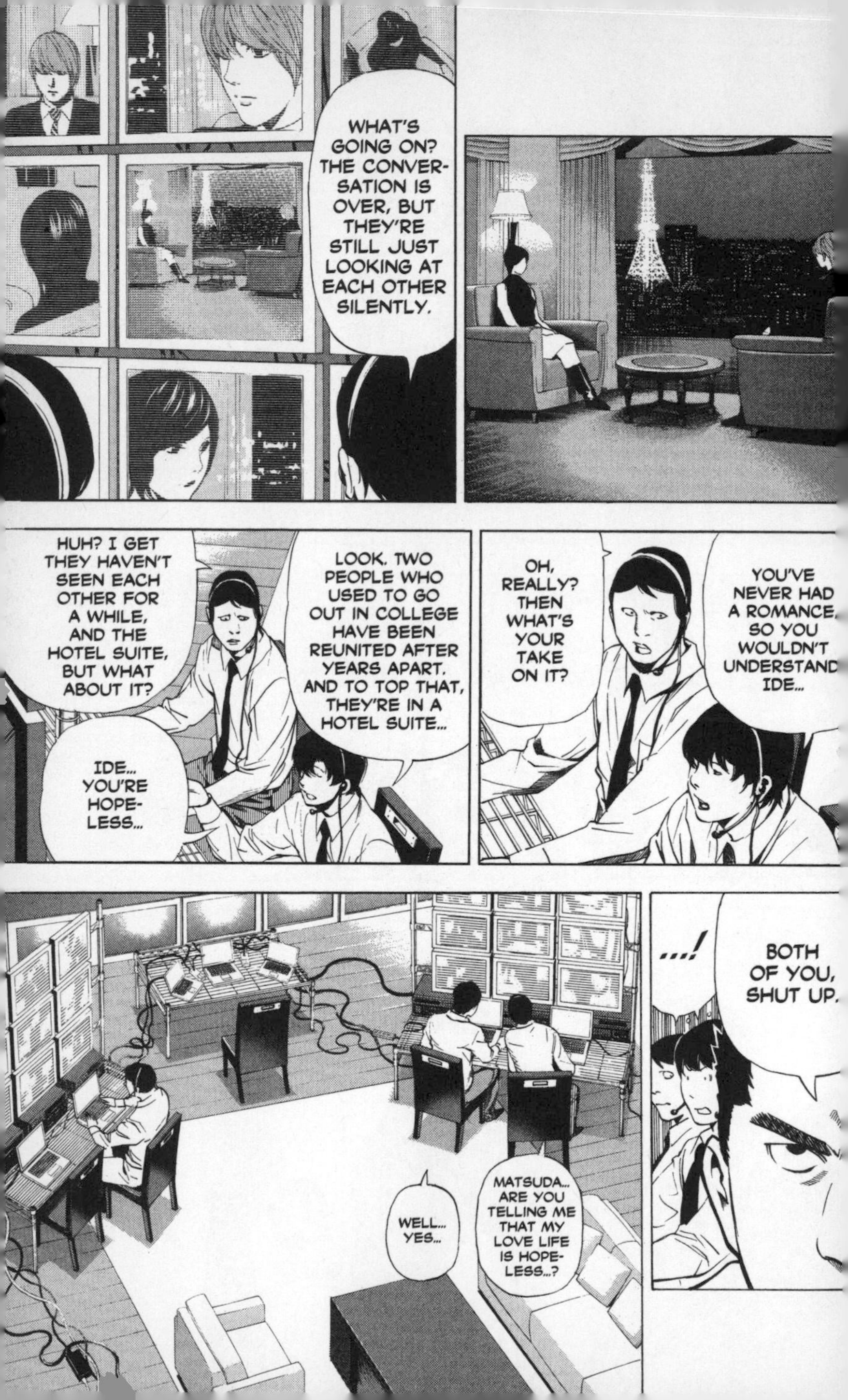
WHAT'S GOING ON? THE CONVERSATION IS OVER, BUT THEY'RE STILL JUST LOOKING AT EACH OTHER SILENTLY.
YOU'VE NEVER HAD A ROMANCE, SO YOU WOULDN'T UNDERSTAND IDE...
OH, REALLY? THEN WHAT'S YOUR TAKE ON IT?
LOOK. TWO PEOPLE WHO USED TO GO OUT IN COLLEGE HAVE BEEN REUNITED AFTER YEARS APART. AND TO TOP THAT, THEY'RE IN A HOTEL SUITE...
HUH? I GET THEY HAVEN'T SEEN EACH OTHER FOR A WHILE, AND THE HOTEL SUITE, BUT WHAT ABOUT IT?
IDE... YOU'RE HOPELESS...
BOTH OF YOU, SHUT UP.
...!
MATSUDA... ARE YOU TELLING ME THAT MY LOVE LIFE IS HOPELESS...?
WELL... YES...

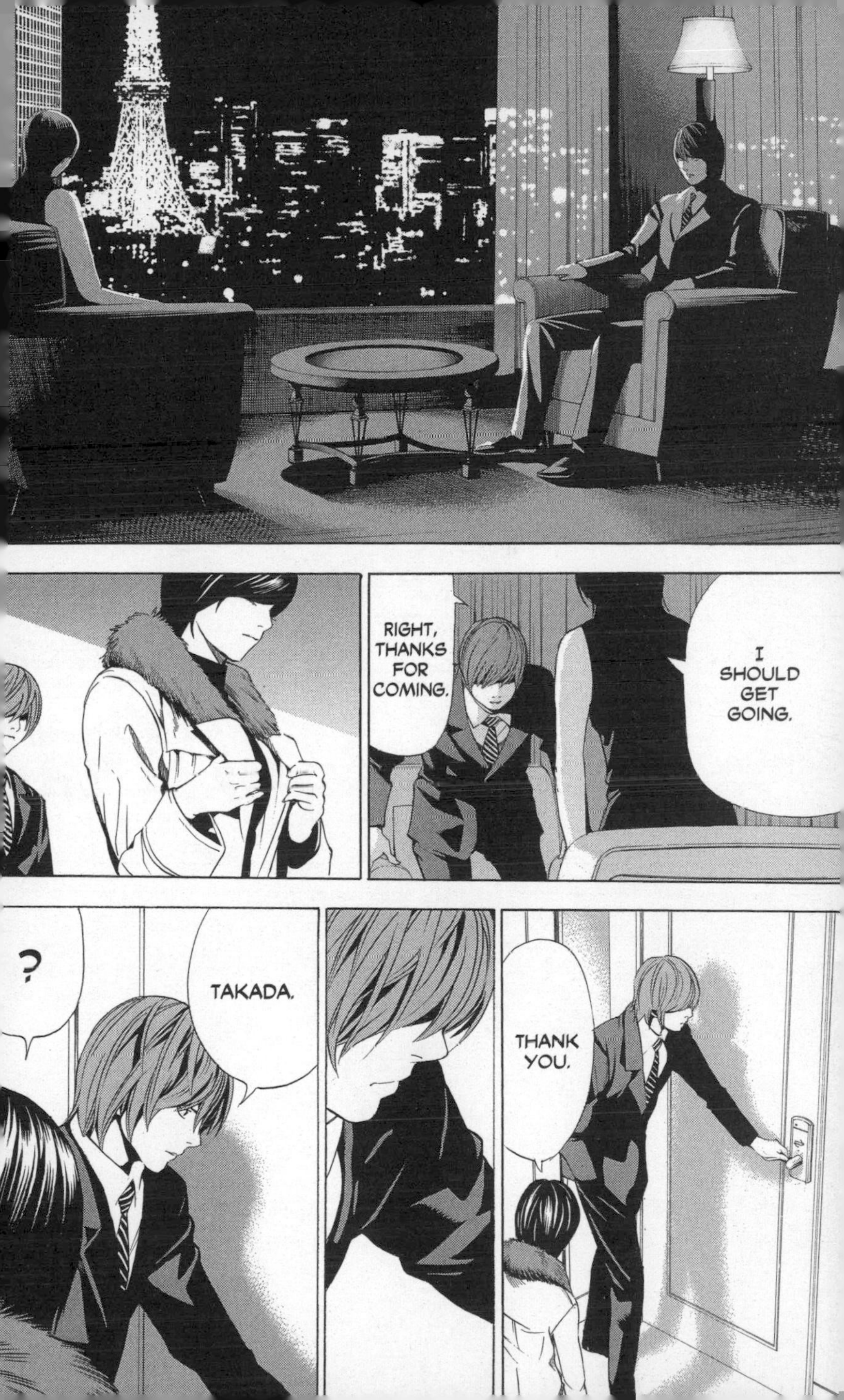
I SHOULD GET GOING.
RIGHT, THANKS FOR COMING.
THANK YOU.
TAKADA.
?

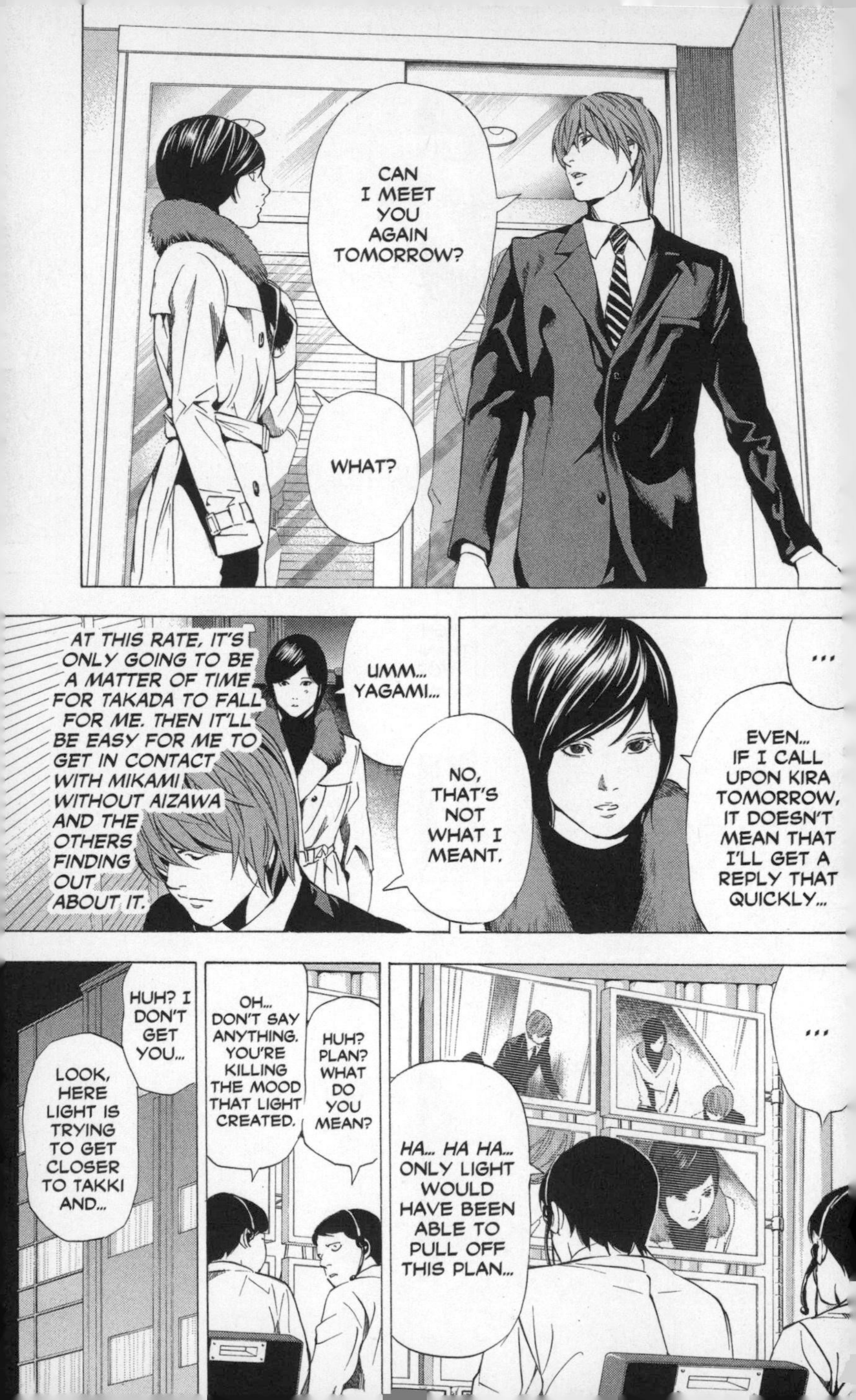
CAN I MEET YOU AGAIN TOMORROW?
WHAT?
...
EVEN... IF I CALL UPON KIRA TOMORROW, IT DOESN'T MEAN THAT I'LL GET A REPLY THAT QUICKLY...
NO, THAT'S NOT WHAT I MEANT.
UMM... YAGAMI...
AT THIS RATE, IT'S ONLY GOING TO BE A MATTER OF TIME FOR TAKADA TO FALL FOR ME. THEN IT'LL BE EASY FOR ME TO GET IN CONTACT WITH MIKAMI WITHOUT AIZAWA AND THE OTHERS FINDING OUT ABOUT IT.
...
HA... HA HA... ONLY LIGHT WOULD HAVE BEEN ABLE TO PULL OFF THIS PLAN...
HUH? PLAN? WHAT DO YOU MEAN?
OH... DON'T SAY ANYTHING. YOU'RE KILLING THE MOOD THAT LIGHT CREATED.
HUH? I DON'T GET YOU...
LOOK, HERE LIGHT IS TRYING TO GET CLOSER TO TAKKI AND...

DEATH NOTE
How to use it
Lv III

- By manipulating the death of a human that has influence over another human's life, that human's original life span can sometimes be lengthened.

その人間の生死に関わる他の人間の死を操る事で、
人間界での本来の寿命が変化し延びる事はある。

- If a god of death intentionally does the above manipulation to effectively lengthen a human's life span, the god of death will die, but even if a human does the same, the human will not die.

上記を死神が、結果として寿命が延びる人間に好意を持って行うと
死神は死ぬが、人間がこれをしても死なない。

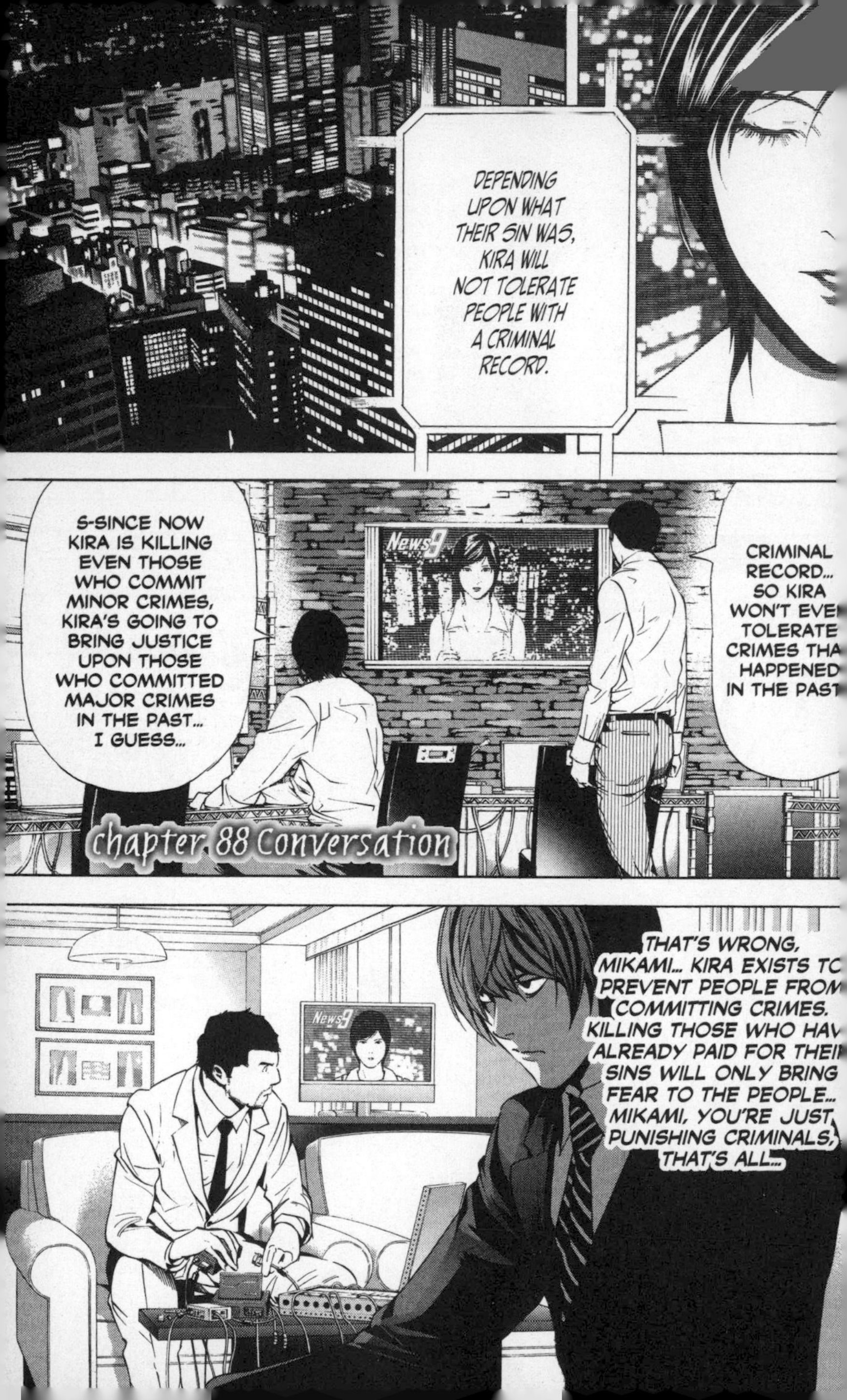

DEPENDING UPON WHAT THEIR SIN WAS, KIRA WILL NOT TOLERATE PEOPLE WITH A CRIMINAL RECORD.
CRIMINAL RECORD... SO KIRA WON'T EVE TOLERATE CRIMES THA HAPPENED IN THE PAST
S-SINCE NOW KIRA IS KILLING EVEN THOSE WHO COMMIT MINOR CRIMES, KIRA'S GOING TO BRING JUSTICE UPON THOSE WHO COMMITTED MAJOR CRIMES IN THE PAST... I GUESS...
chapter 88 Conversation
News9
THAT'S WRONG, MIKAMI... KIRA EXISTS TO PREVENT PEOPLE FROM COMMITTING CRIMES. KILLING THOSE WHO HAV ALREADY PAID FOR THEI SINS WILL ONLY BRING FEAR TO THE PEOPLE... MIKAMI, YOU'RE JUST PUNISHING CRIMINALS, THAT'S ALL...

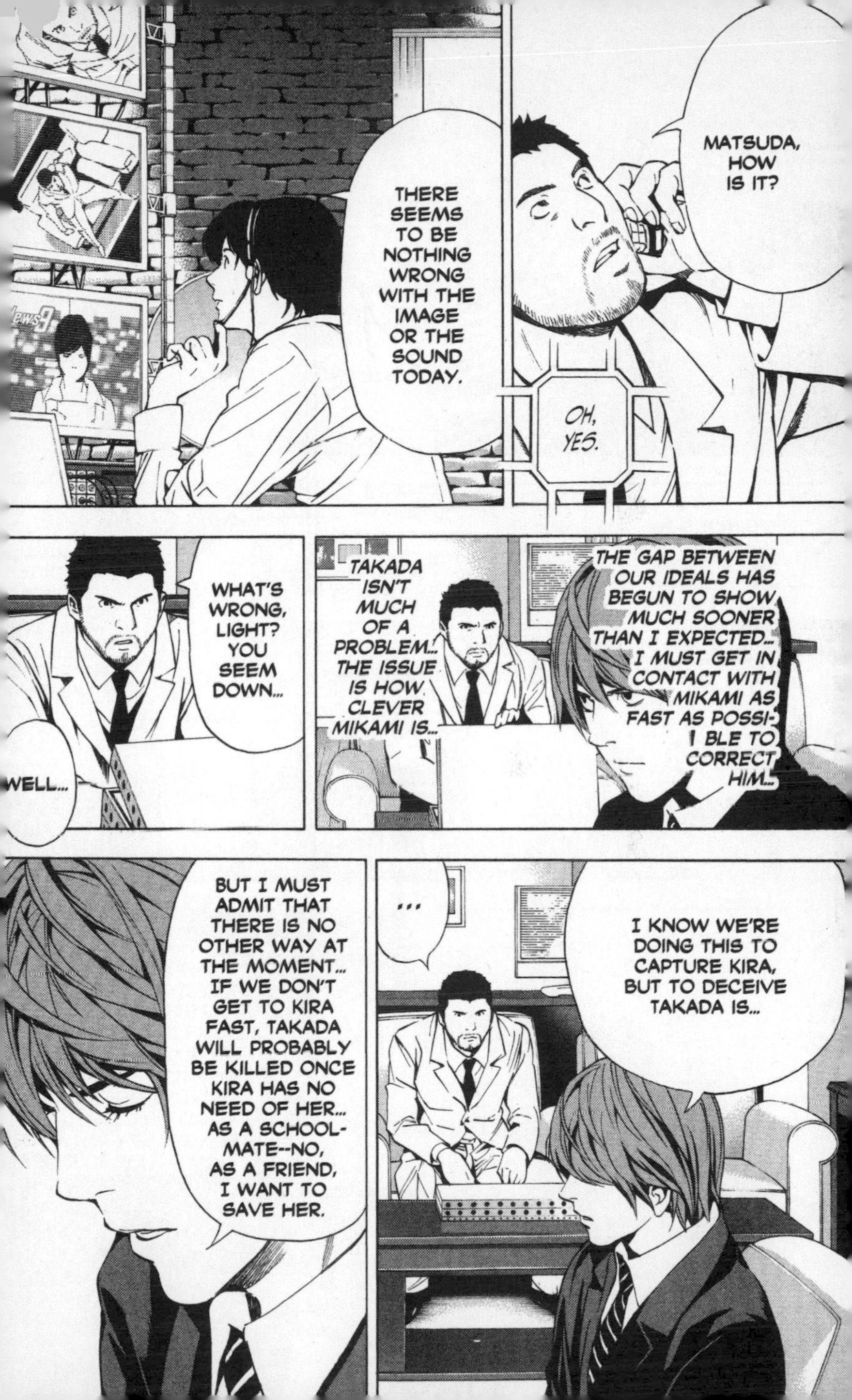
MATSUDA, HOW IS IT?
THERE SEEMS TO BE NOTHING WRONG WITH THE IMAGE OR THE SOUND TODAY.
OH, YES.
THE GAP BETWEEN OUR IDEALS HAS BEGUN TO SHOW MUCH SOONER THAN I EXPECTED... I MUST GET IN CONTACT WITH MIKAMI AS FAST AS POSSI-BLE TO CORRECT HIM...
TAKADA ISN'T MUCH OF A PROBLEM... THE ISSUE IS HOW CLEVER MIKAMI IS...
WHAT'S WRONG, LIGHT? YOU SEEM DOWN...
WELL...
I KNOW WE'RE DOING THIS TO CAPTURE KIRA, BUT TO DECEIVE TAKADA IS...
...
BUT I MUST ADMIT THAT THERE IS NO OTHER WAY AT THE MOMENT... IF WE DON'T GET TO KIRA FAST, TAKADA WILL PROBABLY BE KILLED ONCE KIRA HAS NO NEED OF HER... AS A SCHOOL-MATE--NO, AS A FRIEND, I WANT TO SAVE HER.

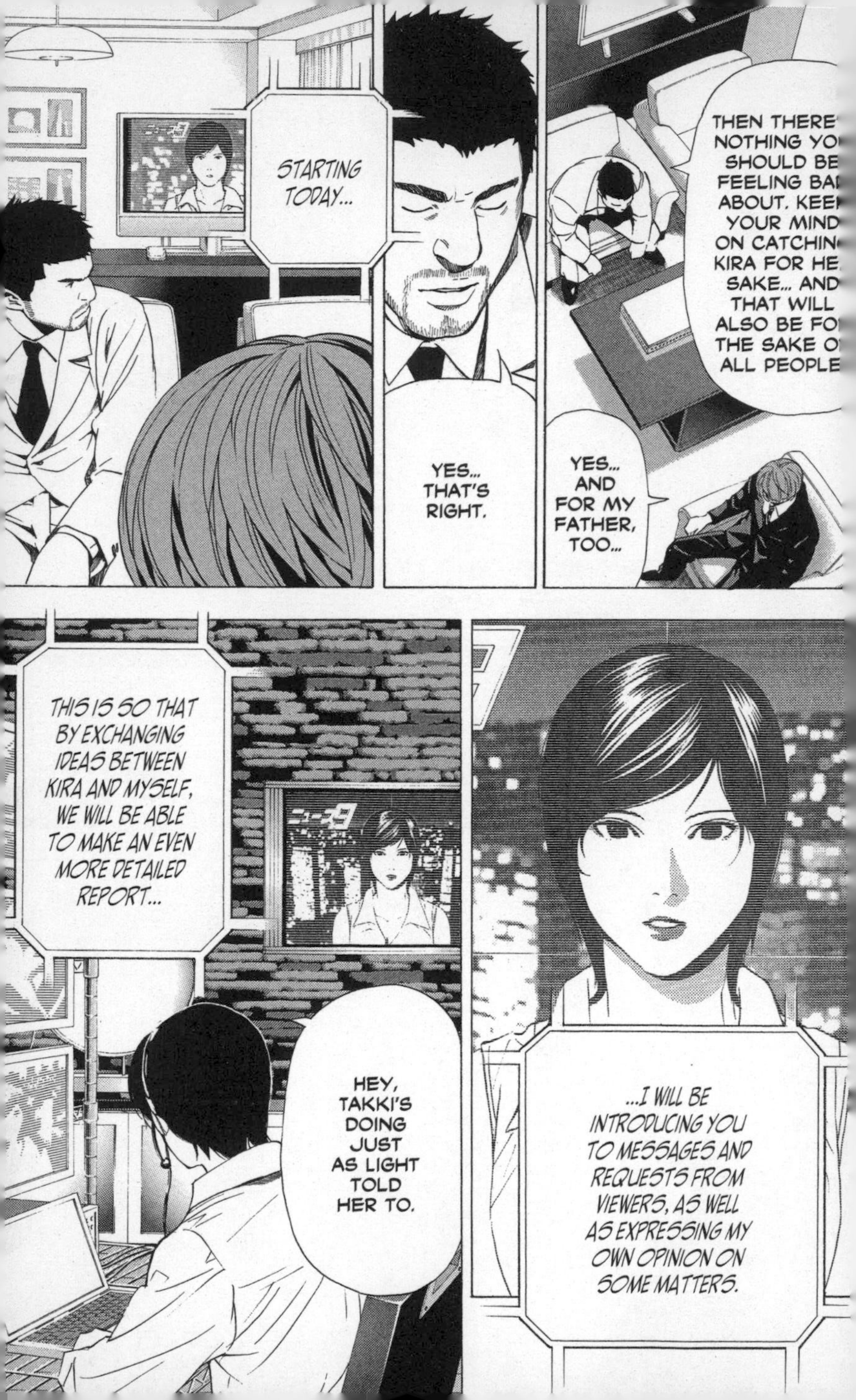
THEN THERE NOTHING YO SHOULD BE FEELING BA ABOUT. KEE YOUR MIND ON CATCHIN KIRA FOR HE SAKE... AND THAT WILL ALSO BE FO THE SAKE O ALL PEOPLE
YES... AND FOR MY FATHER, TOO...
YES... THAT'S RIGHT.
STARTING TODAY...
...I WILL BE INTRODUCING YOU TO MESSAGES AND REQUESTS FROM VIEWERS, AS WELL AS EXPRESSING MY OWN OPINION ON SOME MATTERS.
THIS IS SO THAT BY EXCHANGING IDEAS BETWEEN KIRA AND MYSELF, WE WILL BE ABLE TO MAKE AN EVEN MORE DETAILED REPORT...
HEY, TAKKI'S DOING JUST AS LIGHT TOLD HER TO.

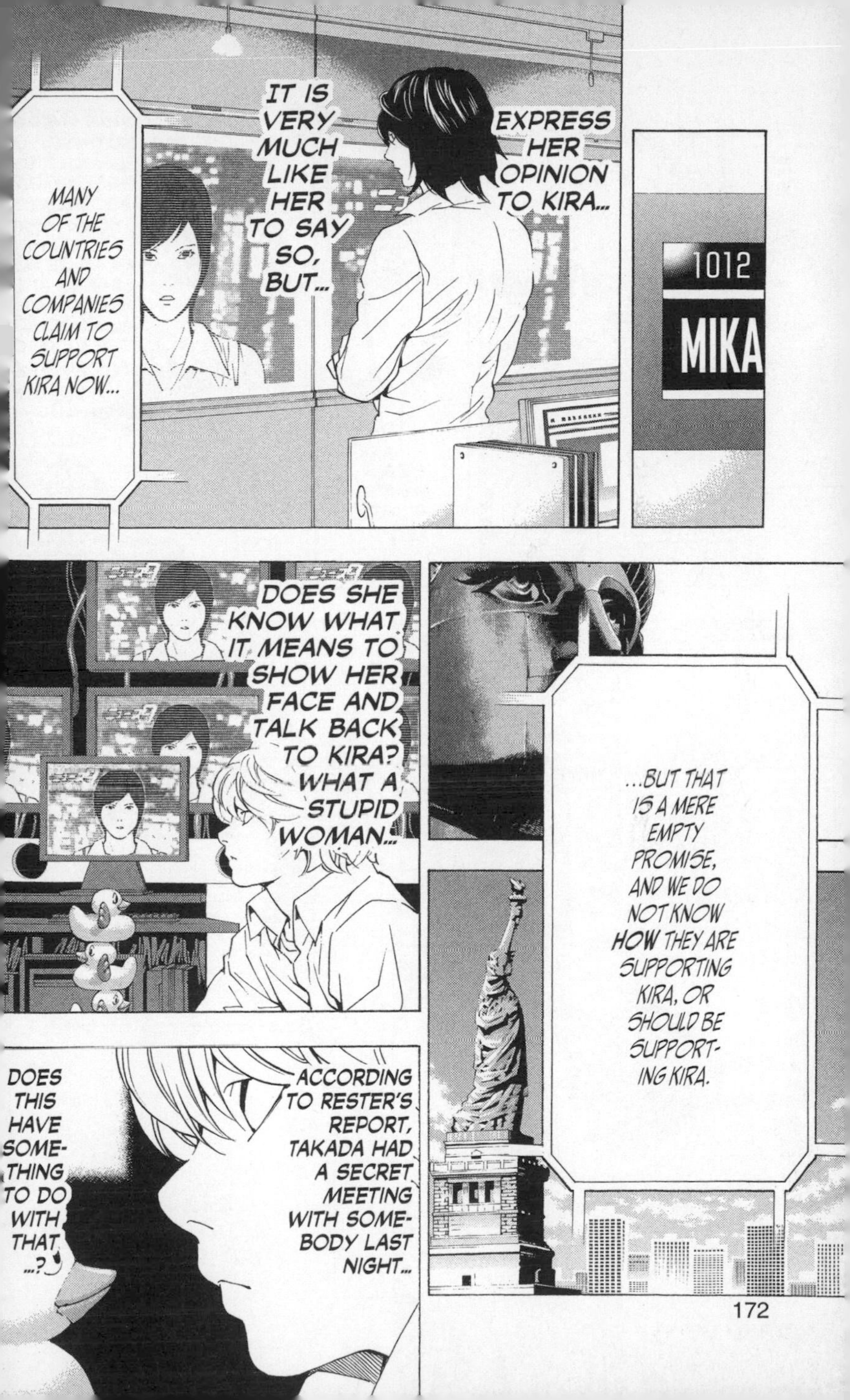
1012
MIKA
EXPRESS HER OPINION TO KIRA...
IT IS VERY MUCH LIKE HER TO SAY SO, BUT...
MANY OF THE COUNTRIES AND COMPANIES CLAIM TO SUPPORT KIRA NOW...
...BUT THAT IS A MERE EMPTY PROMISE, AND WE DO NOT KNOW **HOW** THEY ARE SUPPORTING KIRA, OR SHOULD BE SUPPORT-ING KIRA.
DOES SHE KNOW WHAT IT MEANS TO SHOW HER FACE AND TALK BACK TO KIRA? WHAT A STUPID WOMAN...
ACCORDING TO RESTER'S REPORT, TAKADA HAD A SECRET MEETING WITH SOME-BODY LAST NIGHT...
DOES THIS HAVE SOME-THING TO DO WITH THAT ...?

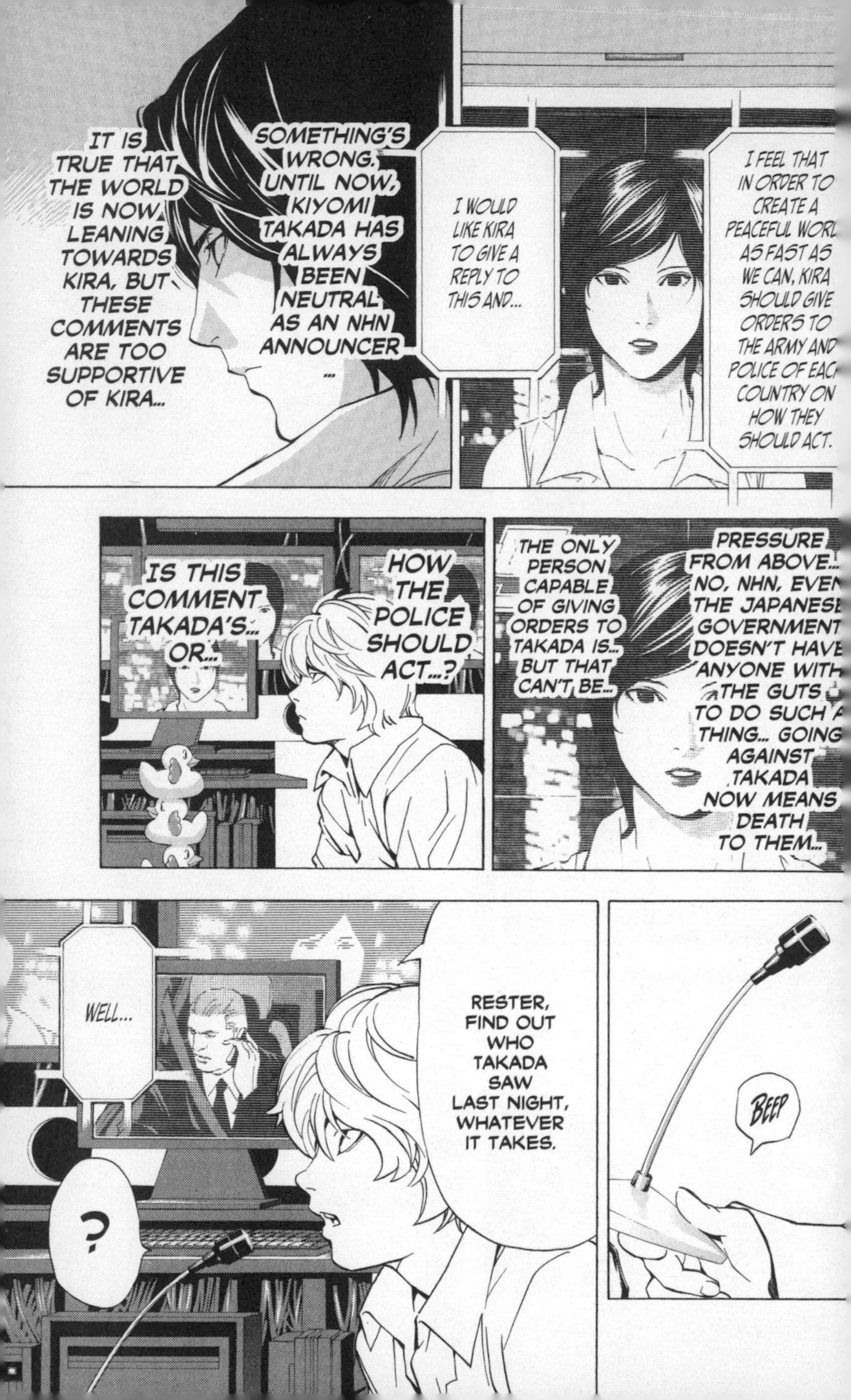
I FEEL THAT IN ORDER TO CREATE A PEACEFUL WORL AS FAST AS WE CAN, KIRA SHOULD GIVE ORDERS TO THE ARMY AND POLICE OF EAC COUNTRY ON HOW THEY SHOULD ACT.
I WOULD LIKE KIRA TO GIVE A REPLY TO THIS AND...
SOMETHING'S WRONG. UNTIL NOW, KIYOMI TAKADA HAS ALWAYS BEEN NEUTRAL AS AN NHN ANNOUNCER ...
IT IS TRUE THAT THE WORLD IS NOW LEANING TOWARDS KIRA, BUT THESE COMMENTS ARE TOO SUPPORTIVE OF KIRA...
PRESSURE FROM ABOVE... NO, NHN, EVE THE JAPANES GOVERNMENT DOESN'T HAV ANYONE WITH THE GUTS TO DO SUCH A THING... GOING AGAINST TAKADA NOW MEANS DEATH TO THEM...
THE ONLY PERSON CAPABLE OF GIVING ORDERS TO TAKADA IS... BUT THAT CAN'T BE...
HOW THE POLICE SHOULD ACT...?
IS THIS COMMENT TAKADA'S... OR...
BEEP
RESTER, FIND OUT WHO TAKADA SAW LAST NIGHT, WHATEVER IT TAKES.
WELL...
?

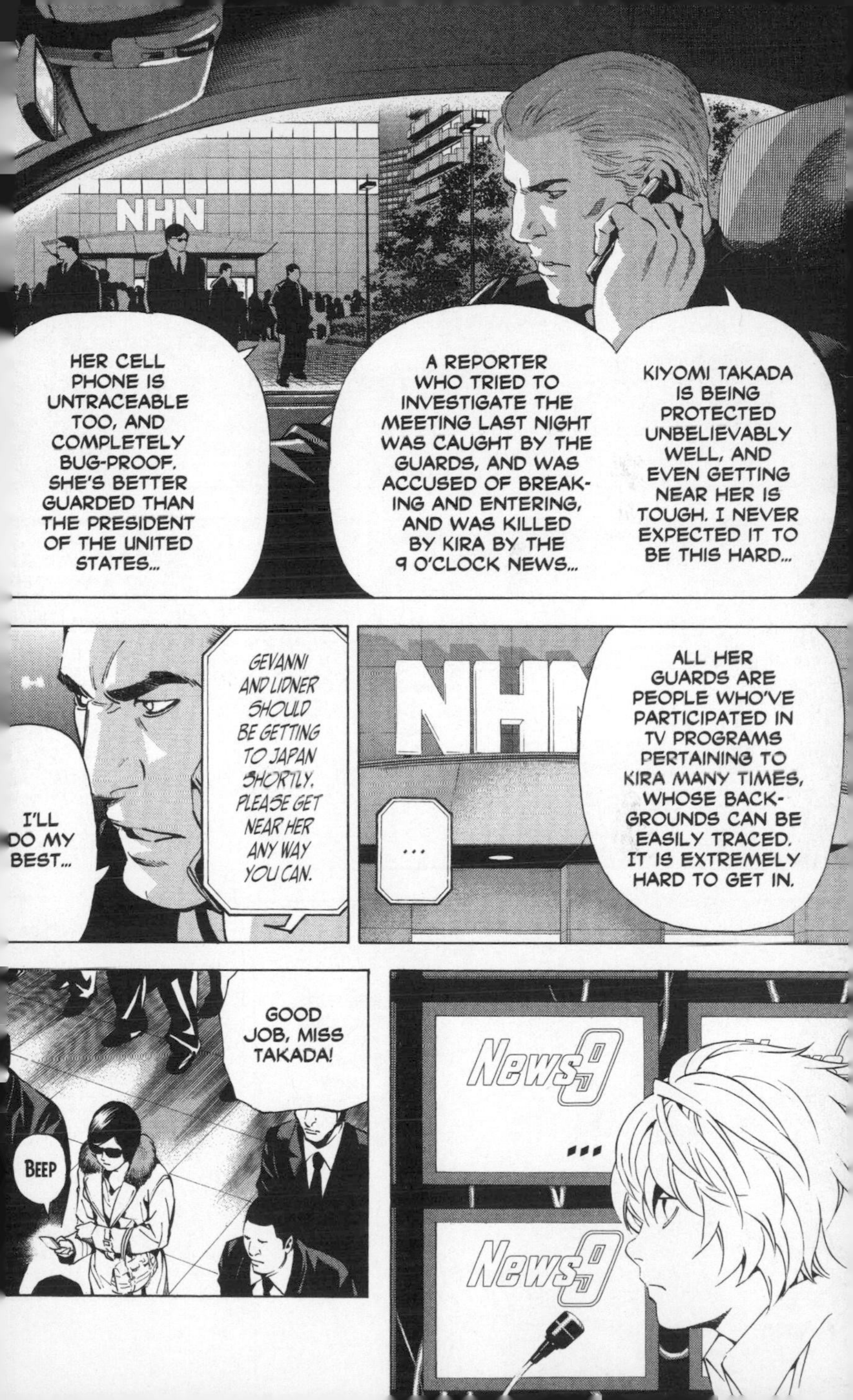
NHN
KIYOMI TAKADA IS BEING PROTECTED UNBELIEVABLY WELL, AND EVEN GETTING NEAR HER IS TOUGH. I NEVER EXPECTED IT TO BE THIS HARD...
A REPORTER WHO TRIED TO INVESTIGATE THE MEETING LAST NIGHT WAS CAUGHT BY THE GUARDS, AND WAS ACCUSED OF BREAK-ING AND ENTERING, AND WAS KILLED BY KIRA BY THE 9 O'CLOCK NEWS...
HER CELL PHONE IS UNTRACEABLE TOO, AND COMPLETELY BUG-PROOF. SHE'S BETTER GUARDED THAN THE PRESIDENT OF THE UNITED STATES...
NHN
ALL HER GUARDS ARE PEOPLE WHO'VE PARTICIPATED IN TV PROGRAMS PERTAINING TO KIRA MANY TIMES, WHOSE BACK-GROUNDS CAN BE EASILY TRACED. IT IS EXTREMELY HARD TO GET IN.
...
GEVANNI AND LIDNER SHOULD BE GETTING TO JAPAN SHORTLY. PLEASE GET NEAR HER ANY WAY YOU CAN.
I'LL DO MY BEST...
News9
News9
...
GOOD JOB, MISS TAKADA!
BEEP

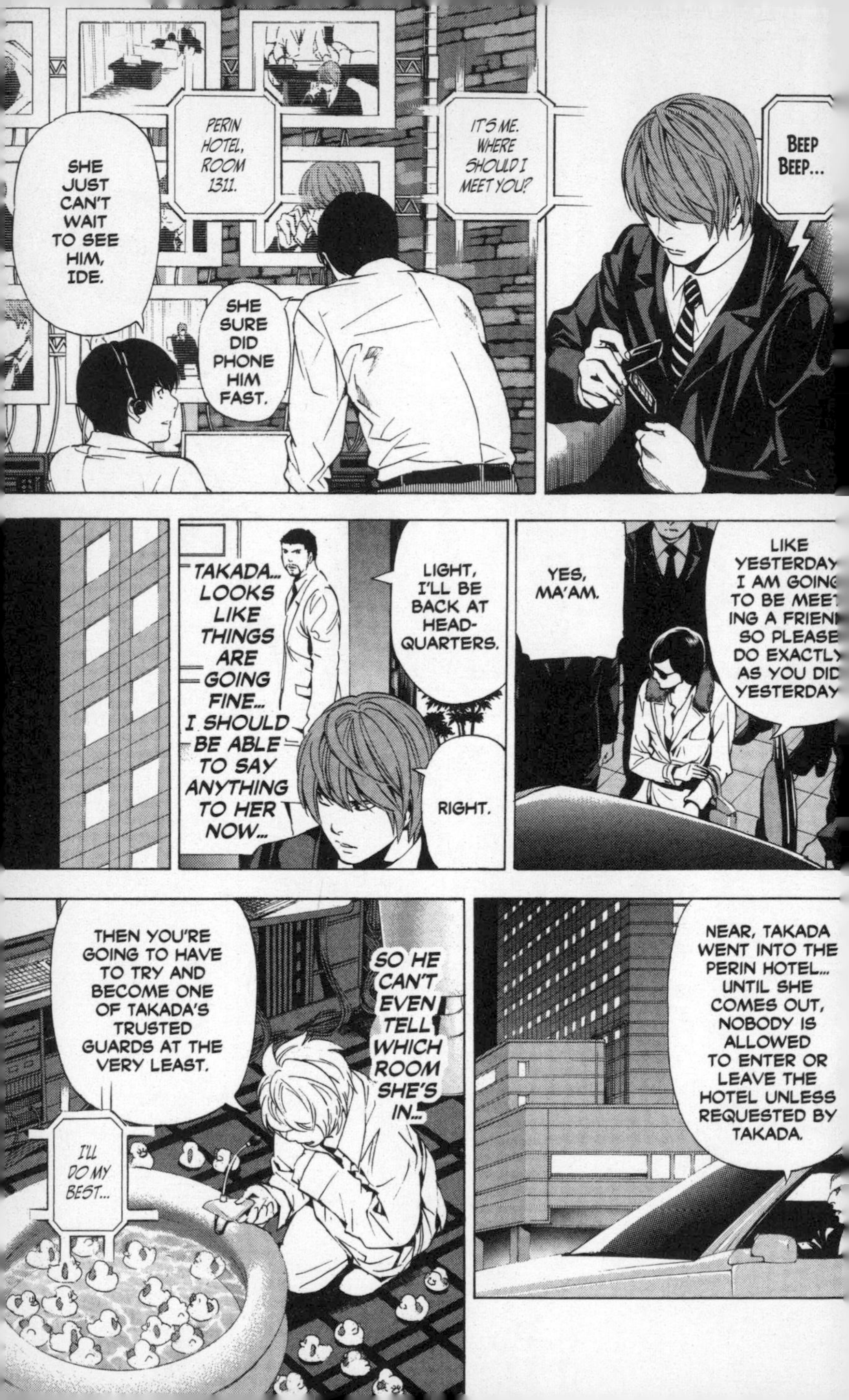
BEEP BEEP...
IT'S ME. WHERE SHOULD I MEET YOU?
PERIN HOTEL, ROOM 1311.
SHE JUST CAN'T WAIT TO SEE HIM, IDE.
SHE SURE DID PHONE HIM FAST.
LIKE YESTERDAY I AM GOING TO BE MEETING A FRIEND SO PLEASE DO EXACTLY AS YOU DID YESTERDAY
YES, MA'AM.
LIGHT, I'LL BE BACK AT HEADQUARTERS.
RIGHT.
TAKADA... LOOKS LIKE THINGS ARE GOING FINE... I SHOULD BE ABLE TO SAY ANYTHING TO HER NOW...
NEAR, TAKADA WENT INTO THE PERIN HOTEL... UNTIL SHE COMES OUT, NOBODY IS ALLOWED TO ENTER OR LEAVE THE HOTEL UNLESS REQUESTED BY TAKADA.
SO HE CAN'T EVEN TELL WHICH ROOM SHE'S IN...
THEN YOU'RE GOING TO HAVE TO TRY AND BECOME ONE OF TAKADA'S TRUSTED GUARDS AT THE VERY LEAST.
I'LL DO MY BEST...

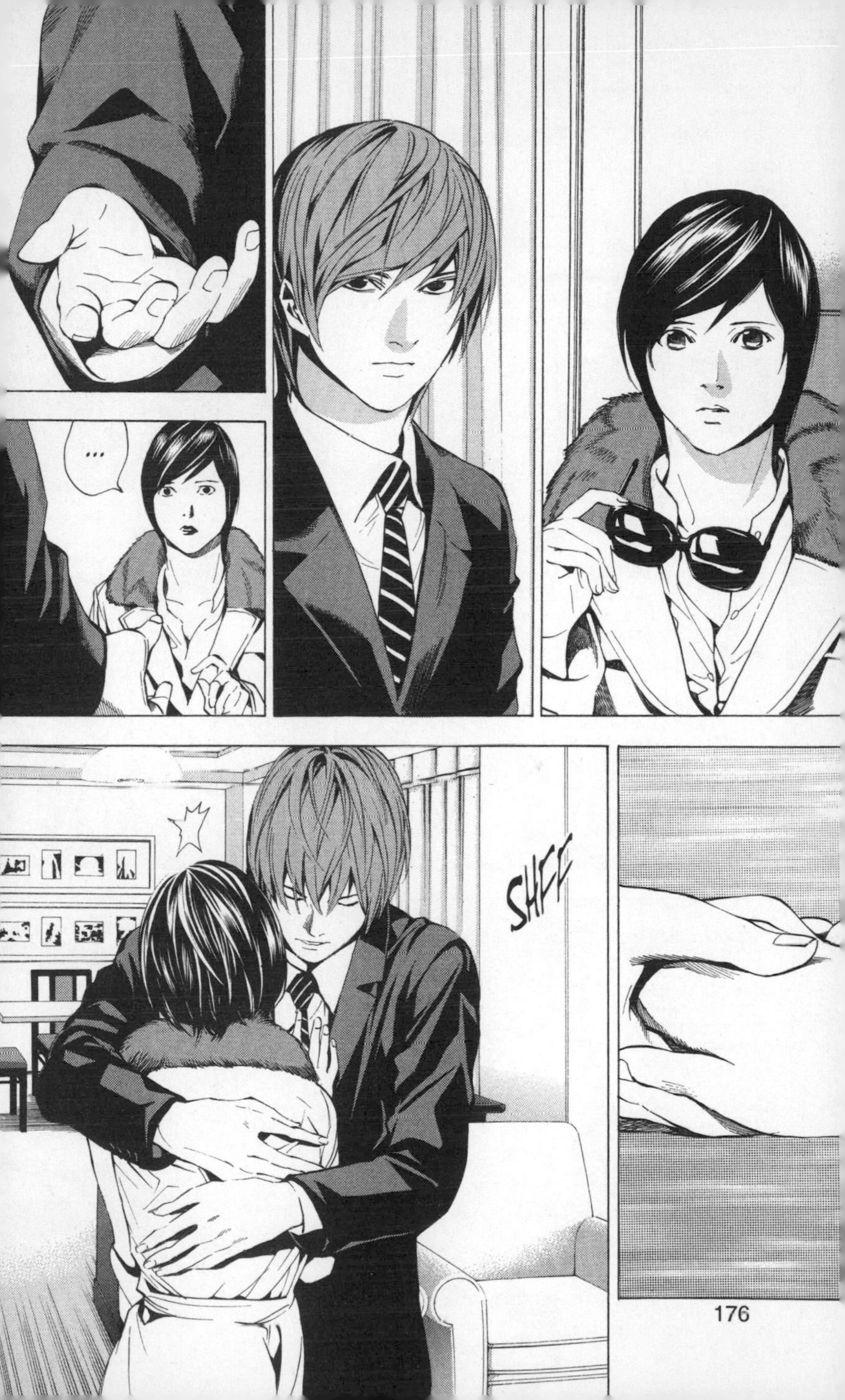
...
SHFF

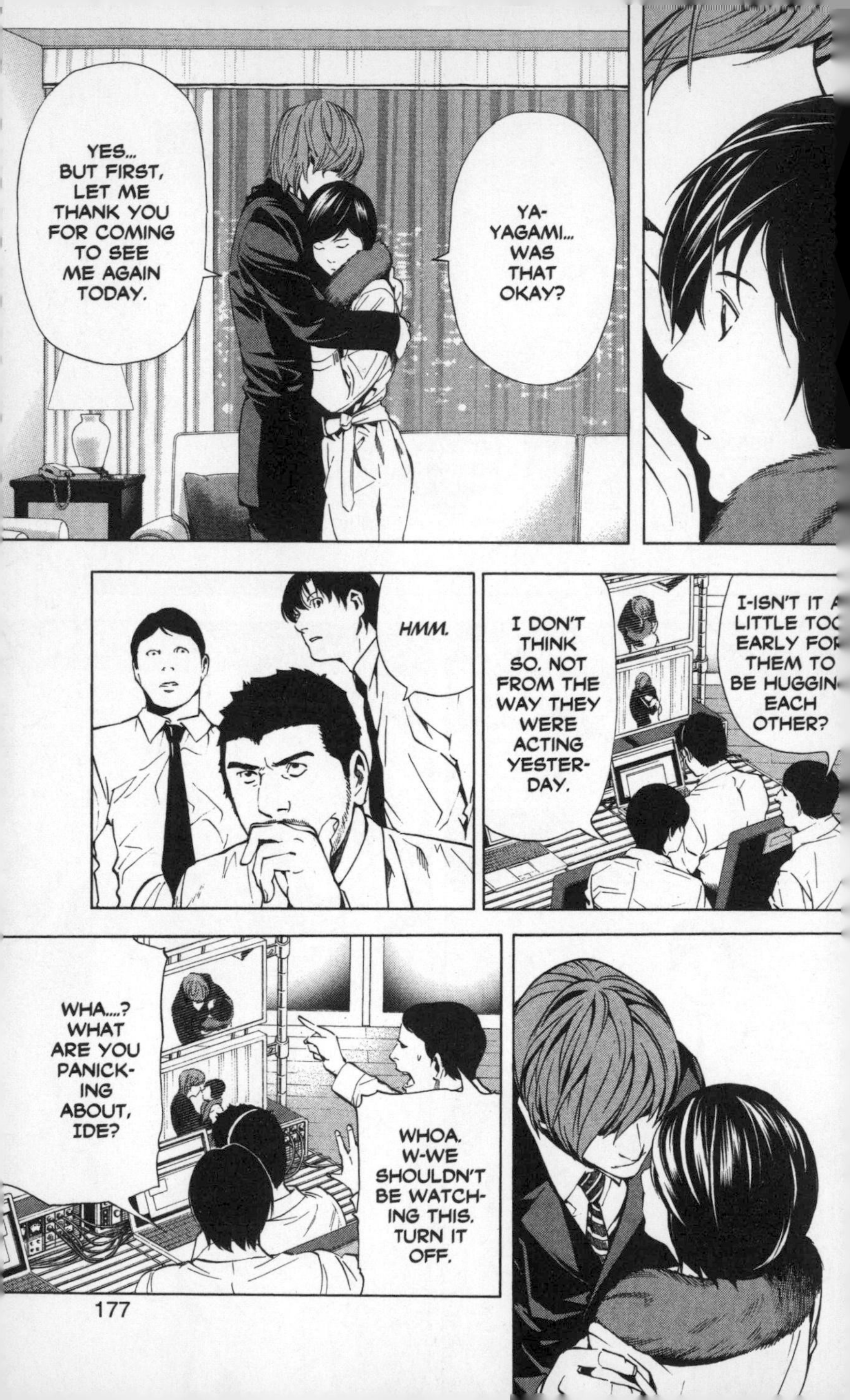
YA-YAGAMI... WAS THAT OKAY?
YES... BUT FIRST, LET ME THANK YOU FOR COMING TO SEE ME AGAIN TODAY.
I-ISN'T IT A LITTLE TOO EARLY FOR THEM TO BE HUGGING EACH OTHER?
I DON'T THINK SO. NOT FROM THE WAY THEY WERE ACTING YESTERDAY.
HMM.
WHOA. W-WE SHOULDN'T BE WATCHING THIS. TURN IT OFF.
WHA...? WHAT ARE YOU PANICKING ABOUT, IDE?

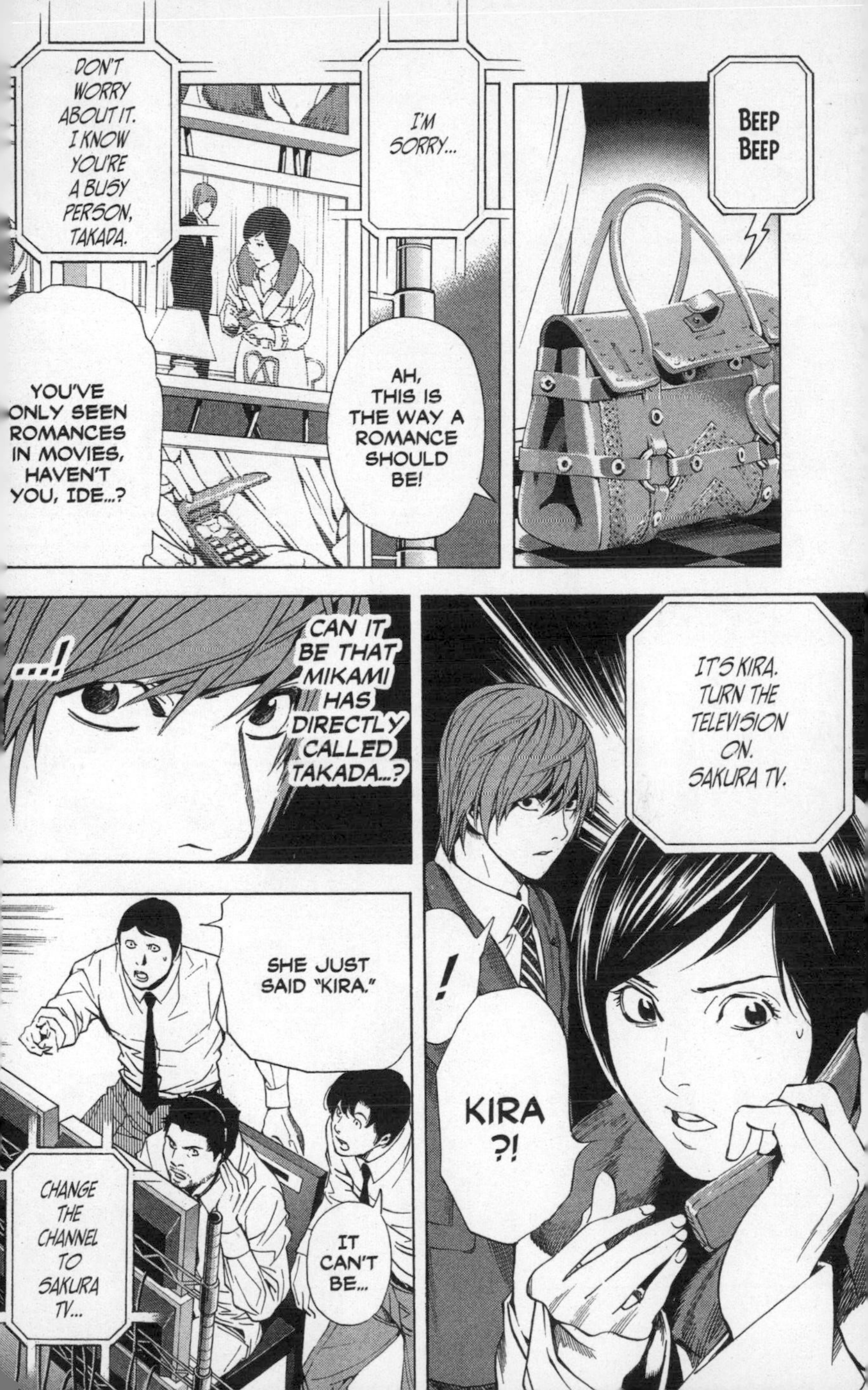
BEEP BEEP
I'M SORRY...
AH, THIS IS THE WAY A ROMANCE SHOULD BE!
DON'T WORRY ABOUT IT. I KNOW YOU'RE A BUSY PERSON, TAKADA.
YOU'VE ONLY SEEN ROMANCES IN MOVIES, HAVEN'T YOU, IDE...?
IT'S KIRA. TURN THE TELEVISION ON. SAKURA TV.
!
KIRA ?!
...!
CAN IT BE THAT MIKAMI HAS DIRECTLY CALLED TAKADA...?
SHE JUST SAID "KIRA."
IT CAN'T BE...
CHANGE THE CHANNEL TO SAKURA TV...

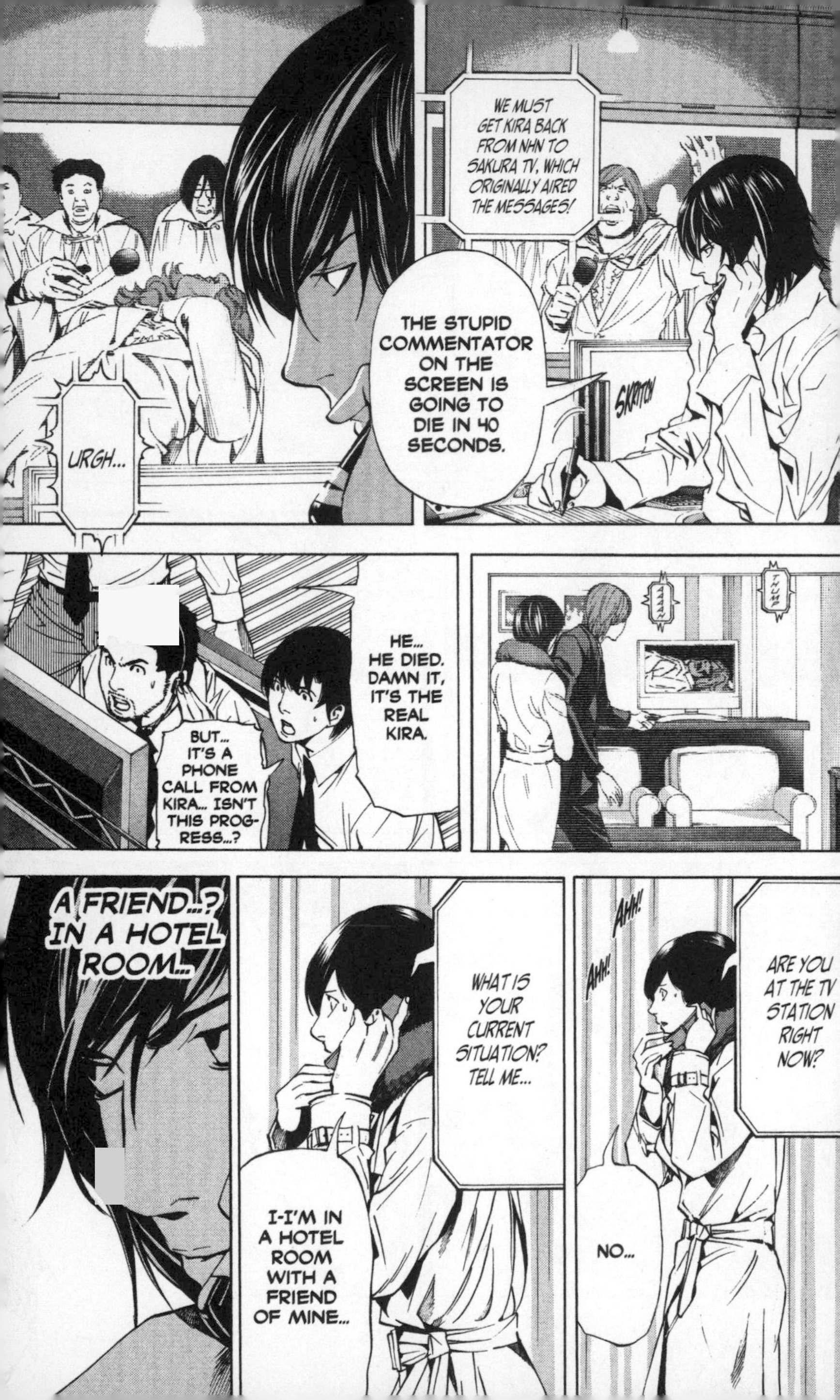
WE MUST GET KIRA BACK FROM NHN TO SAKURA TV, WHICH ORIGINALLY AIRED THE MESSAGES!
THE STUPID COMMENTATOR ON THE SCREEN IS GOING TO DIE IN 40 SECONDS.
SKRITCH
URGH...
THUMP
HE... HE DIED. DAMN IT, IT'S THE REAL KIRA.
BUT... IT'S A PHONE CALL FROM KIRA... ISN'T THIS PROG-RESS...?
ARE YOU AT THE TV STATION RIGHT NOW?
AHH!
AHH!
NO...
WHAT IS YOUR CURRENT SITUATION? TELL ME...
I-I'M IN A HOTEL ROOM WITH A FRIEND OF MINE...
A FRIEND...? IN A HOTEL ROOM...

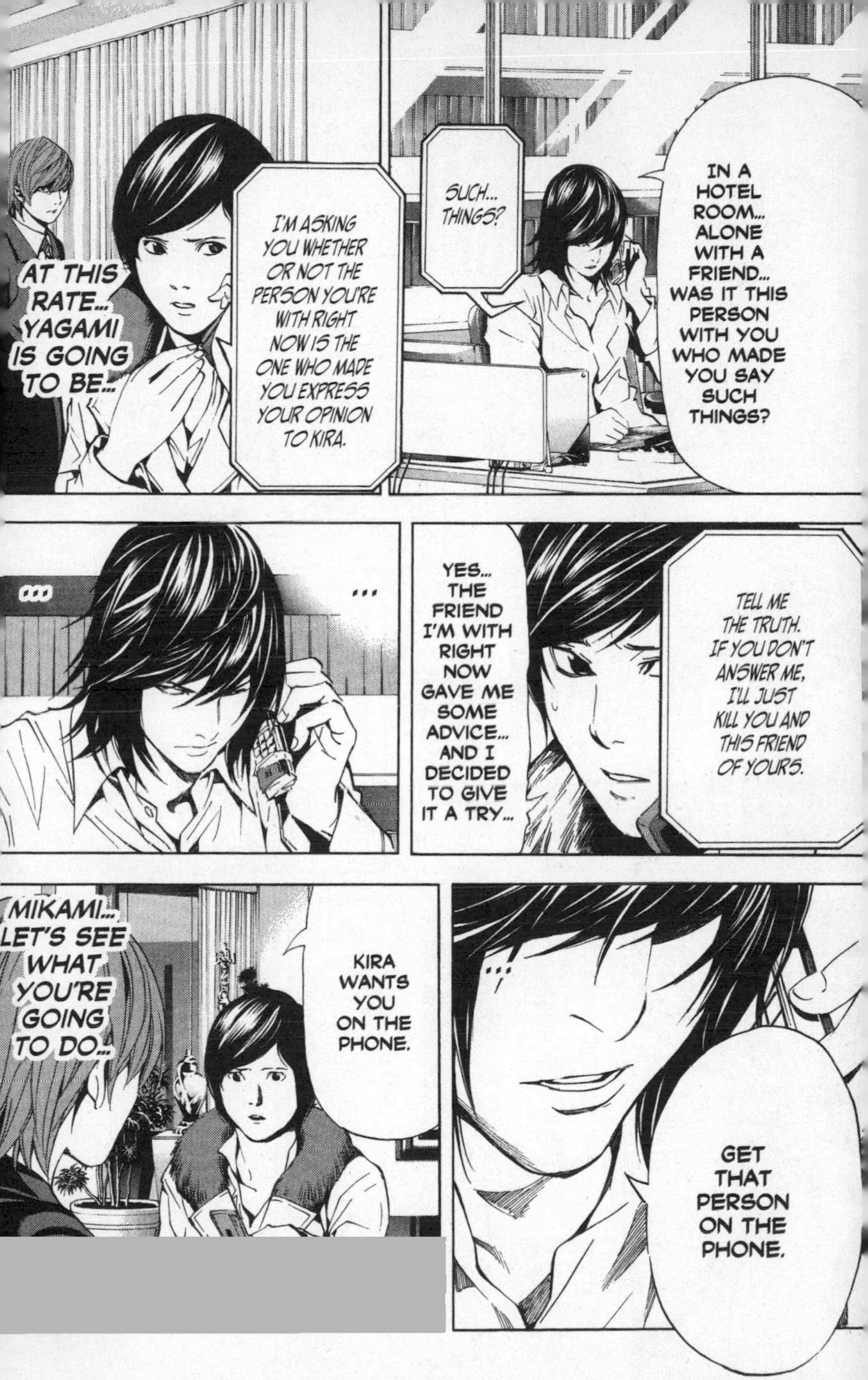
IN A HOTEL ROOM... ALONE WITH A FRIEND... WAS IT THIS PERSON WITH YOU WHO MADE YOU SAY SUCH THINGS?
SUCH... THINGS?
I'M ASKING YOU WHETHER OR NOT THE PERSON YOU'RE WITH RIGHT NOW IS THE ONE WHO MADE YOU EXPRESS YOUR OPINION TO KIRA.
AT THIS RATE... YAGAMI IS GOING TO BE...
TELL ME THE TRUTH. IF YOU DON'T ANSWER ME, I'LL JUST KILL YOU AND THIS FRIEND OF YOURS.
YES... THE FRIEND I'M WITH RIGHT NOW GAVE ME SOME ADVICE... AND I DECIDED TO GIVE IT A TRY...
...
...
...
GET THAT PERSON ON THE PHONE.
KIRA WANTS YOU ON THE PHONE.
MIKAMI... LET'S SEE WHAT YOU'RE GOING TO DO...

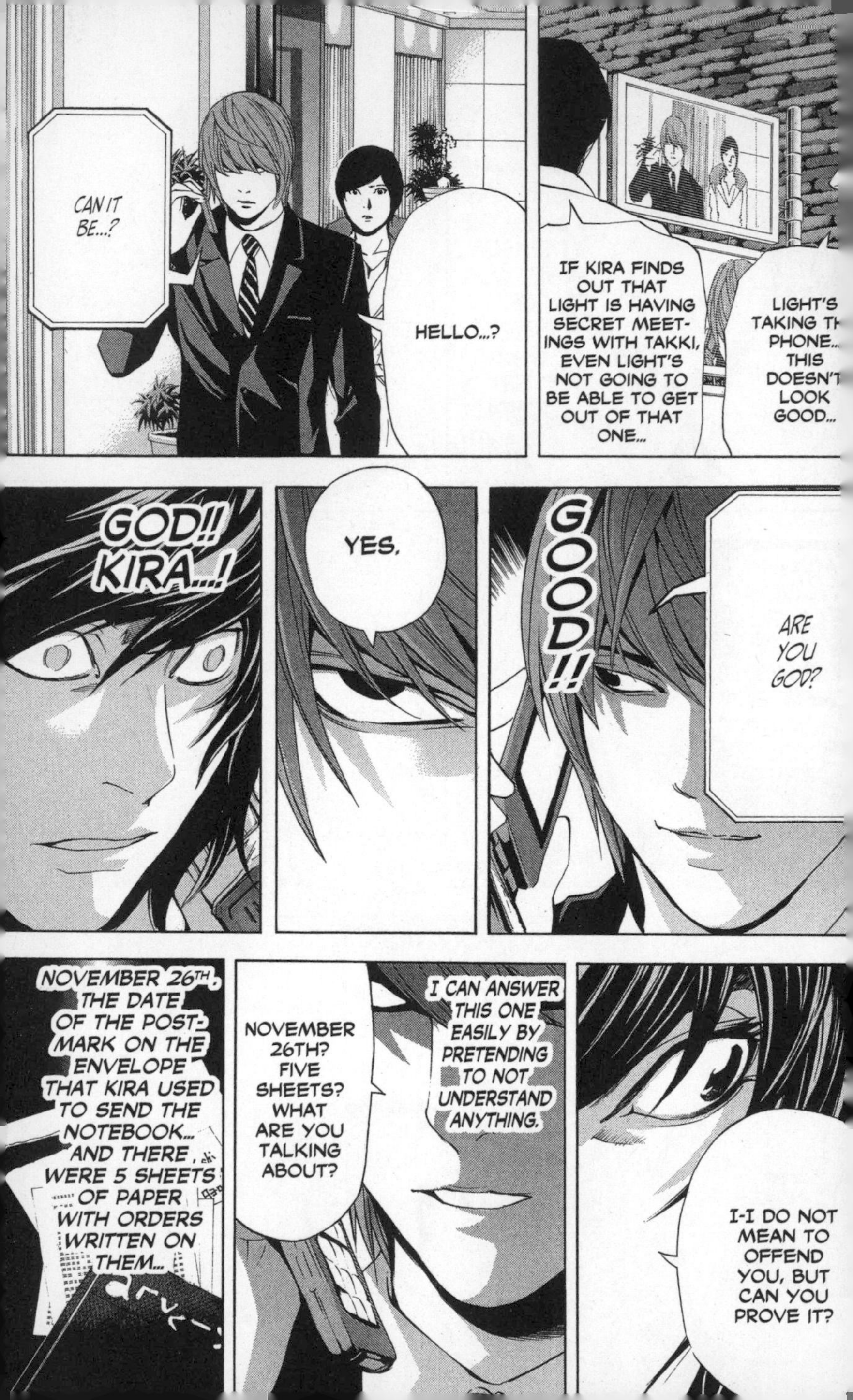
LIGHT'S TAKING TH PHONE... THIS DOESN'T LOOK GOOD...
IF KIRA FINDS OUT THAT LIGHT IS HAVING SECRET MEET-INGS WITH TAKKI, EVEN LIGHT'S NOT GOING TO BE ABLE TO GET OUT OF THAT ONE...
HELLO...?
CAN IT BE...?
ARE YOU GOD?
GOOD!!
YES.
GOD!! KIRA...!
I-I DO NOT MEAN TO OFFEND YOU, BUT CAN YOU PROVE IT?
I CAN ANSWER THIS ONE EASILY BY PRETENDING TO NOT UNDERSTAND ANYTHING.
NOVEMBER 26TH? FIVE SHEETS? WHAT ARE YOU TALKING ABOUT?
NOVEMBER 26TH, THE DATE OF THE POST-MARK ON THE ENVELOPE THAT KIRA USED TO SEND THE NOTEBOOK... AND THERE WERE 5 SHEETS OF PAPER WITH ORDERS WRITTEN ON THEM...

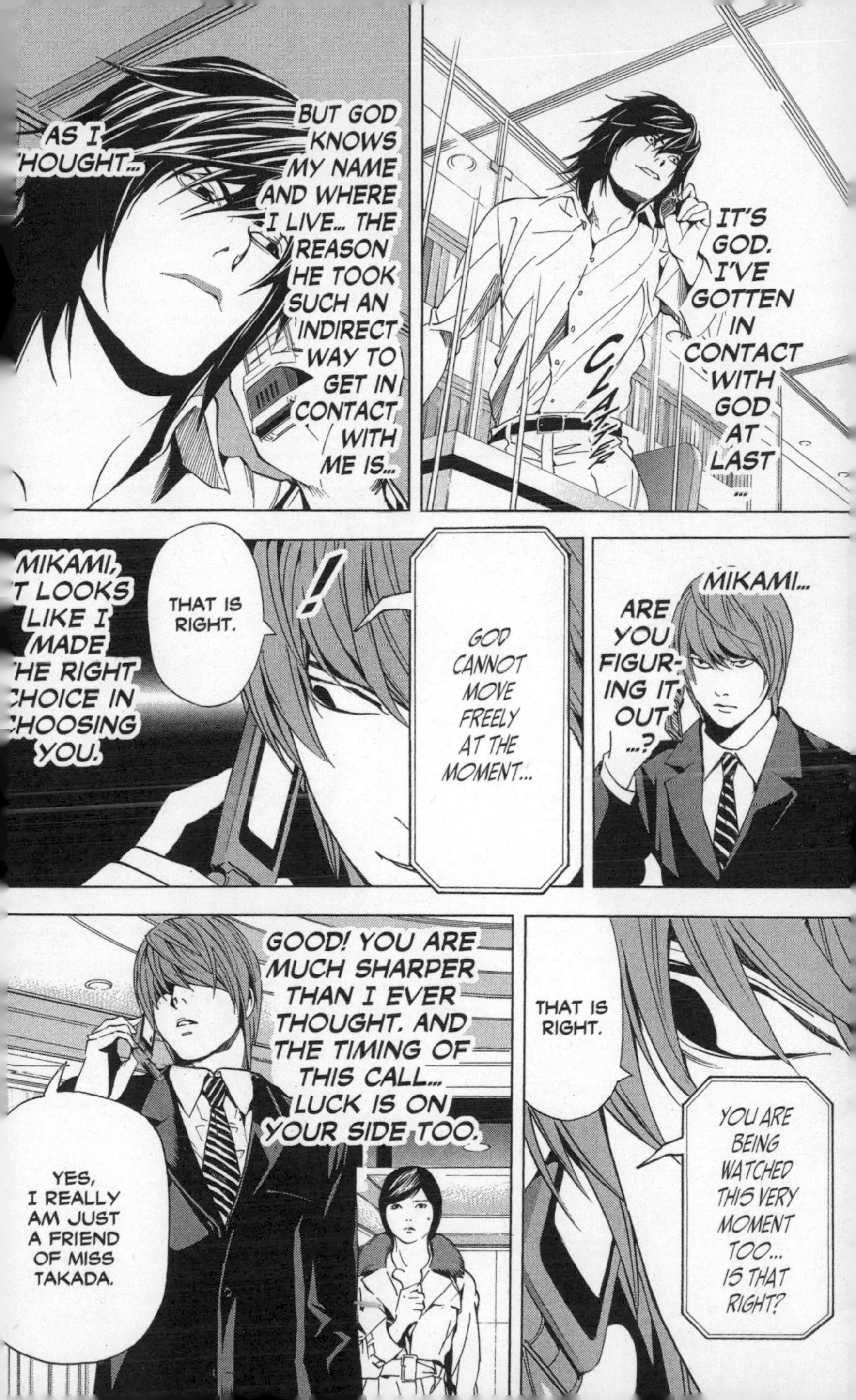
IT'S GOD. I'VE GOTTEN IN CONTACT WITH GOD AT LAST...
BUT GOD KNOWS MY NAME AND WHERE I LIVE... THE REASON HE TOOK SUCH AN INDIRECT WAY TO GET IN CONTACT WITH ME IS...
AS I HOUGHT...
MIKAMI...
ARE YOU FIGUR-ING IT OUT ...?
GOD CANNOT MOVE FREELY AT THE MOMENT...
!
THAT IS RIGHT.
MIKAMI, T LOOKS LIKE I MADE HE RIGHT HOICE IN HOOSING YOU.
YOU ARE BEING WATCHED THIS VERY MOMENT TOO... IS THAT RIGHT?
THAT IS RIGHT.
GOOD! YOU ARE MUCH SHARPER THAN I EVER THOUGHT. AND THE TIMING OF THIS CALL... LUCK IS ON YOUR SIDE TOO.
YES, I REALLY AM JUST A FRIEND OF MISS TAKADA.

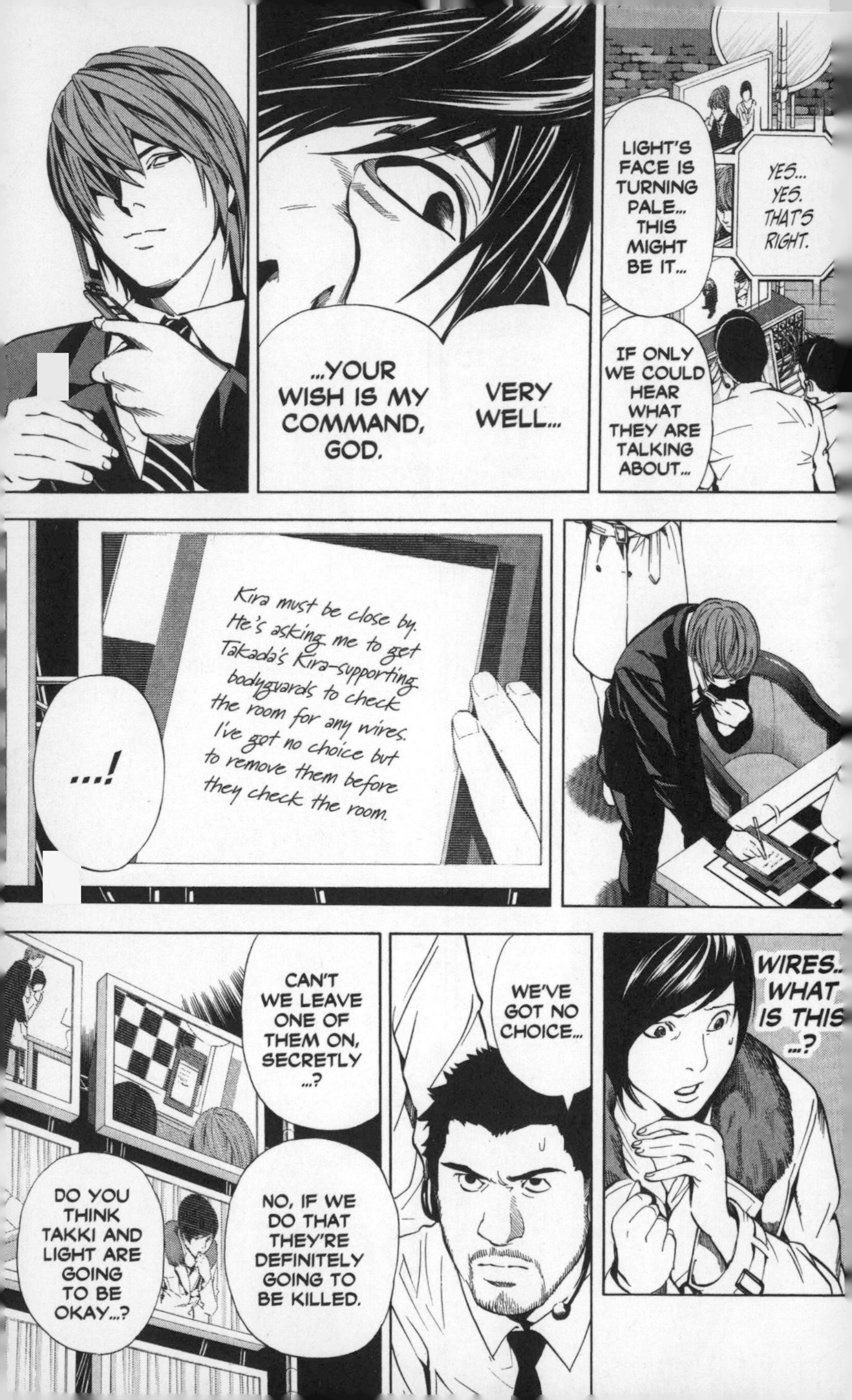
YES... YES. THAT'S RIGHT.
LIGHT'S FACE IS TURNING PALE... THIS MIGHT BE IT...
IF ONLY WE COULD HEAR WHAT THEY ARE TALKING ABOUT...
VERY WELL...
...YOUR WISH IS MY COMMAND, GOD.
Kira must be close by. He's asking me to get Takada's Kira-supporting bodyguards to check the room for any wires. I've got no choice but to remove them before they check the room.
...!
WIRES.. WHAT IS THIS ...?
WE'VE GOT NO CHOICE...
CAN'T WE LEAVE ONE OF THEM ON, SECRETLY ...?
NO, IF WE DO THAT THEY'RE DEFINITELY GOING TO BE KILLED.
DO YOU THINK TAKKI AND LIGHT ARE GOING TO BE OKAY...?

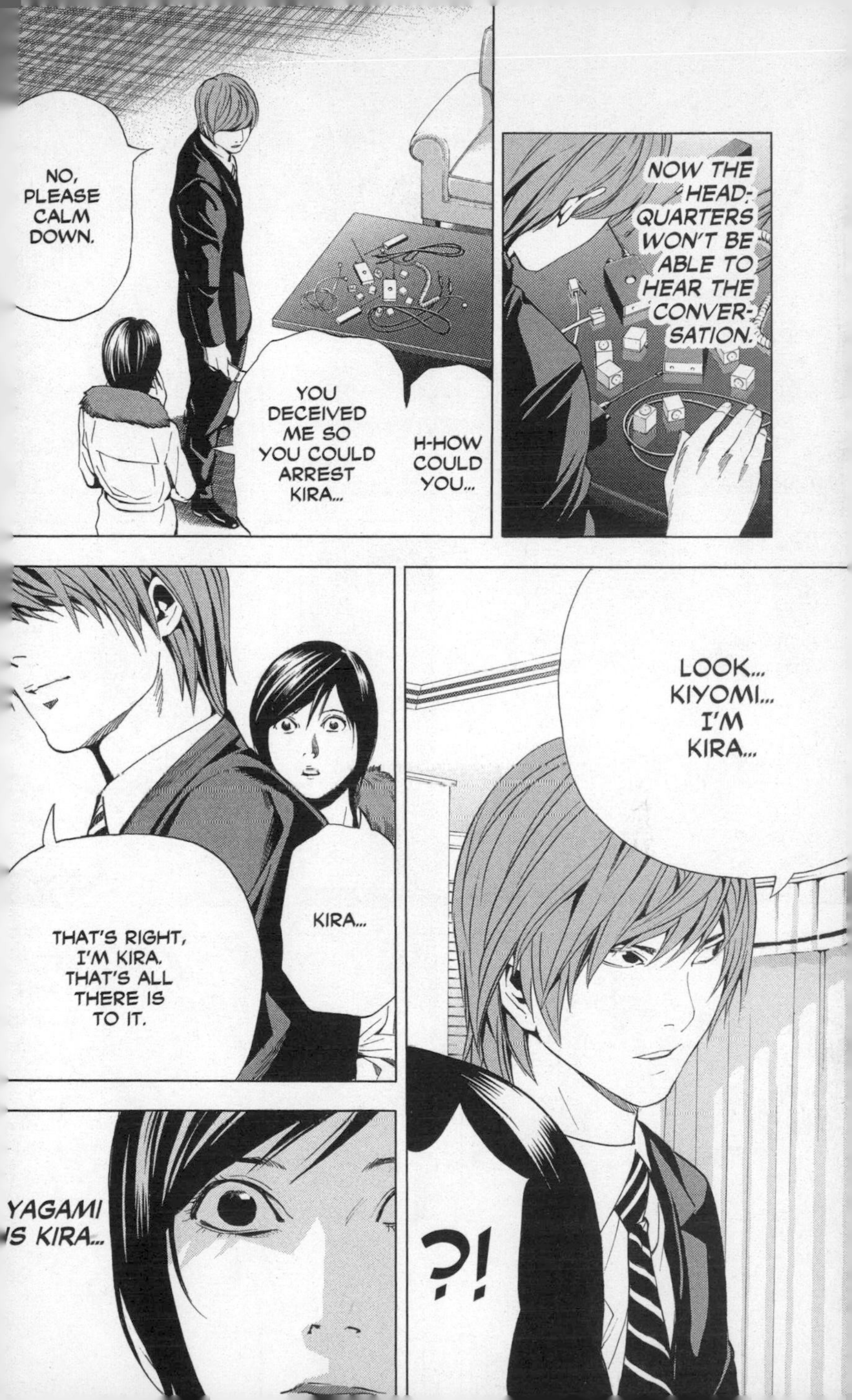
NOW THE HEAD-QUARTERS WON'T BE ABLE TO HEAR THE CONVER-SATION.
H-HOW COULD YOU...
YOU DECEIVED ME SO YOU COULD ARREST KIRA...
NO, PLEASE CALM DOWN.
LOOK... KIYOMI... I'M KIRA...
?!
KIRA...
THAT'S RIGHT, I'M KIRA. THAT'S ALL THERE IS TO IT.
YAGAMI IS KIRA...

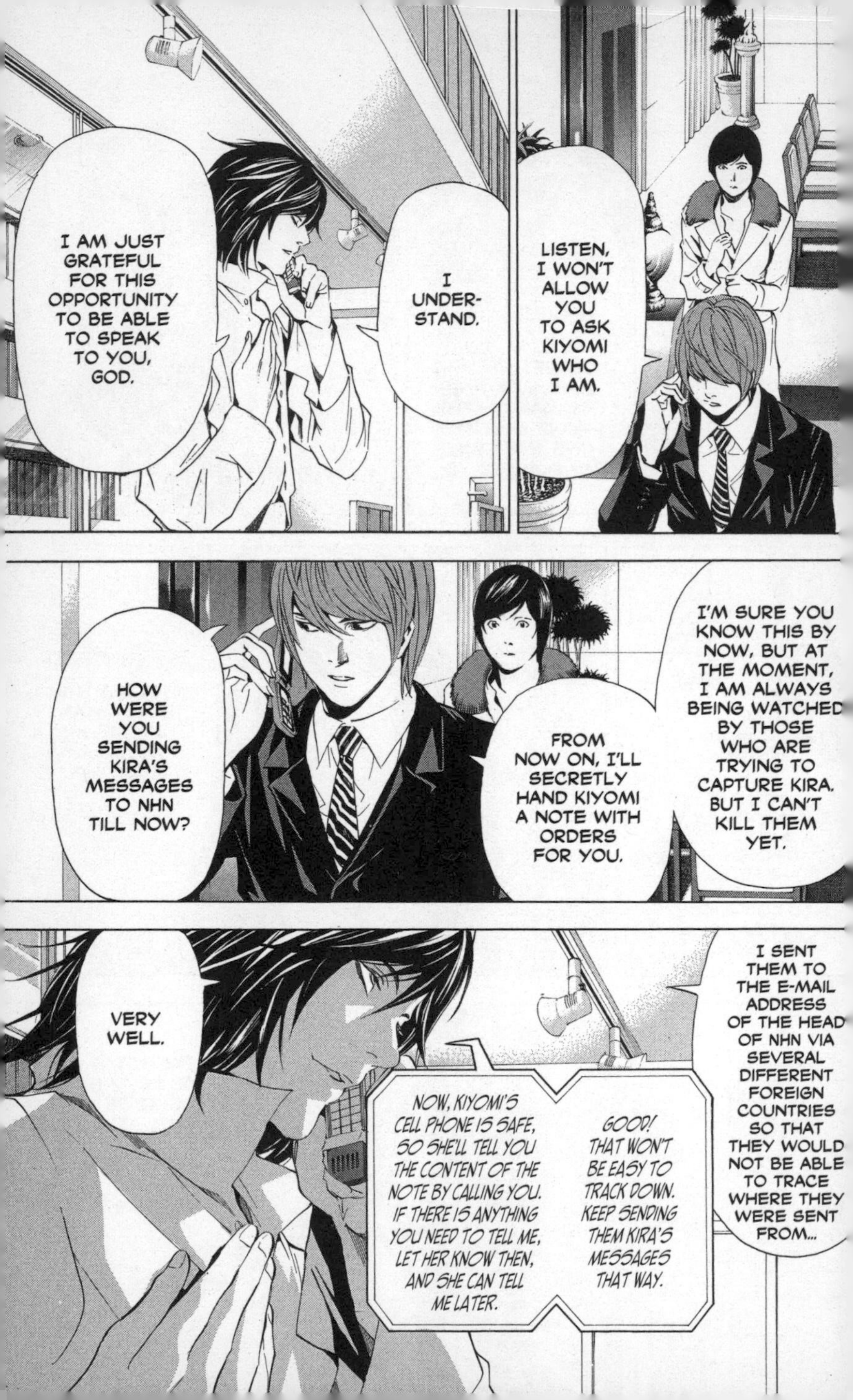
LISTEN, I WON'T ALLOW YOU TO ASK KIYOMI WHO I AM.
I UNDERSTAND.
I AM JUST GRATEFUL FOR THIS OPPORTUNITY TO BE ABLE TO SPEAK TO YOU, GOD.
I'M SURE YOU KNOW THIS BY NOW, BUT AT THE MOMENT, I AM ALWAYS BEING WATCHED BY THOSE WHO ARE TRYING TO CAPTURE KIRA. BUT I CAN'T KILL THEM YET.
FROM NOW ON, I'LL SECRETLY HAND KIYOMI A NOTE WITH ORDERS FOR YOU.
HOW WERE YOU SENDING KIRA'S MESSAGES TO NHN TILL NOW?
I SENT THEM TO THE E-MAIL ADDRESS OF THE HEAD OF NHN VIA SEVERAL DIFFERENT FOREIGN COUNTRIES SO THAT THEY WOULD NOT BE ABLE TO TRACE WHERE THEY WERE SENT FROM...
GOOD! THAT WON'T BE EASY TO TRACK DOWN. KEEP SENDING THEM KIRA'S MESSAGES THAT WAY.
NOW, KIYOMI'S CELL PHONE IS SAFE, SO SHE'LL TELL YOU THE CONTENT OF THE NOTE BY CALLING YOU. IF THERE IS ANYTHING YOU NEED TO TELL ME, LET HER KNOW THEN, AND SHE CAN TELL ME LATER.
VERY WELL.

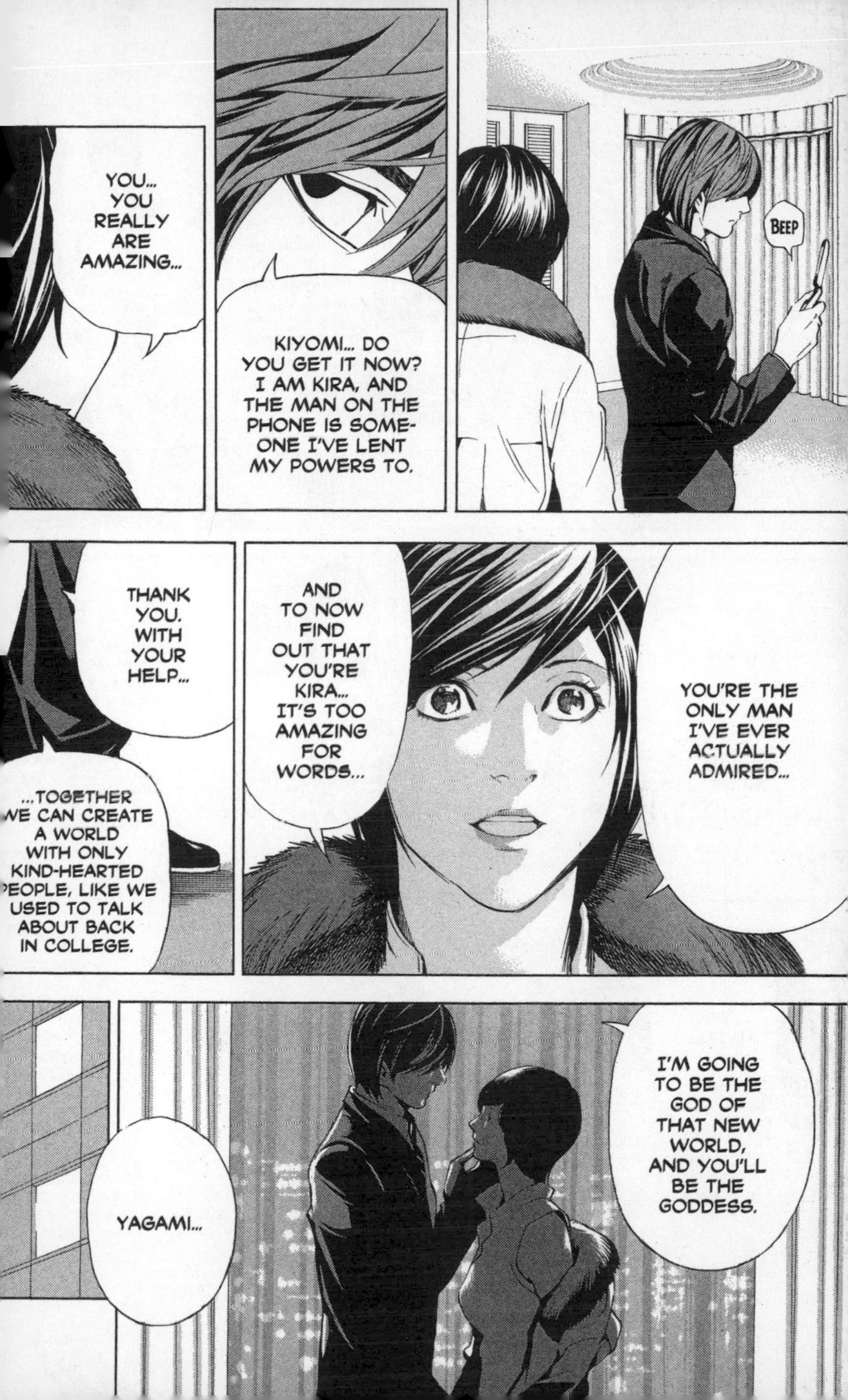
BEEP
KIYOMI... DO YOU GET IT NOW? I AM KIRA, AND THE MAN ON THE PHONE IS SOMEONE I'VE LENT MY POWERS TO.
YOU... YOU REALLY ARE AMAZING...
YOU'RE THE ONLY MAN I'VE EVER ACTUALLY ADMIRED...
AND TO NOW FIND OUT THAT YOU'RE KIRA... IT'S TOO AMAZING FOR WORDS...
THANK YOU. WITH YOUR HELP...
...TOGETHER WE CAN CREATE A WORLD WITH ONLY KIND-HEARTED PEOPLE, LIKE WE USED TO TALK ABOUT BACK IN COLLEGE.
I'M GOING TO BE THE GOD OF THAT NEW WORLD, AND YOU'LL BE THE GODDESS.
YAGAMI...

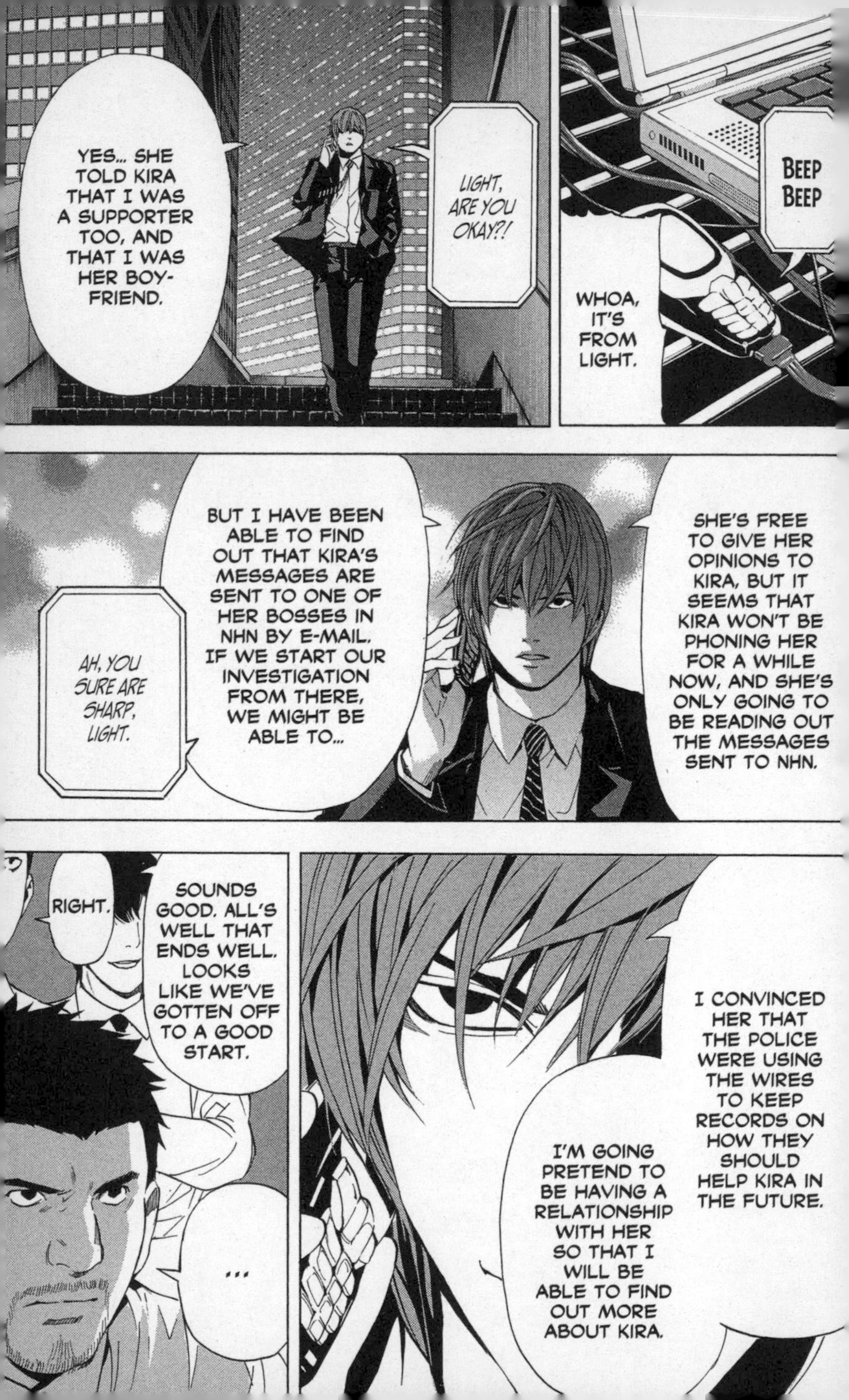
BEEP BEEP
WHOA, IT'S FROM LIGHT.
LIGHT, ARE YOU OKAY?!
YES... SHE TOLD KIRA THAT I WAS A SUPPORTER TOO, AND THAT I WAS HER BOY-FRIEND.
SHE'S FREE TO GIVE HER OPINIONS TO KIRA, BUT IT SEEMS THAT KIRA WON'T BE PHONING HER FOR A WHILE NOW, AND SHE'S ONLY GOING TO BE READING OUT THE MESSAGES SENT TO NHN.
BUT I HAVE BEEN ABLE TO FIND OUT THAT KIRA'S MESSAGES ARE SENT TO ONE OF HER BOSSES IN NHN BY E-MAIL. IF WE START OUR INVESTIGATION FROM THERE, WE MIGHT BE ABLE TO...
AH, YOU SURE ARE SHARP, LIGHT.
I CONVINCED HER THAT THE POLICE WERE USING THE WIRES TO KEEP RECORDS ON HOW THEY SHOULD HELP KIRA IN THE FUTURE.
I'M GOING PRETEND TO BE HAVING A RELATIONSHIP WITH HER SO THAT I WILL BE ABLE TO FIND OUT MORE ABOUT KIRA.
SOUNDS GOOD. ALL'S WELL THAT ENDS WELL. LOOKS LIKE WE'VE GOTTEN OFF TO A GOOD START.
RIGHT.
...

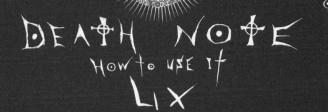

DEATH NOTE
How to use it
LIX

• A human death caused by the DEATH NOTE will indirectly lengthen some other human's original length of life even without a specific intention to lengthen a particular person's original life span in the human world.

特定の人間の人間界での本来の寿命を延ばす為の死と意識していなくても、デスノートによる人間の死で、間接的に人間界本来の寿命が延びる人間は発生してくる。

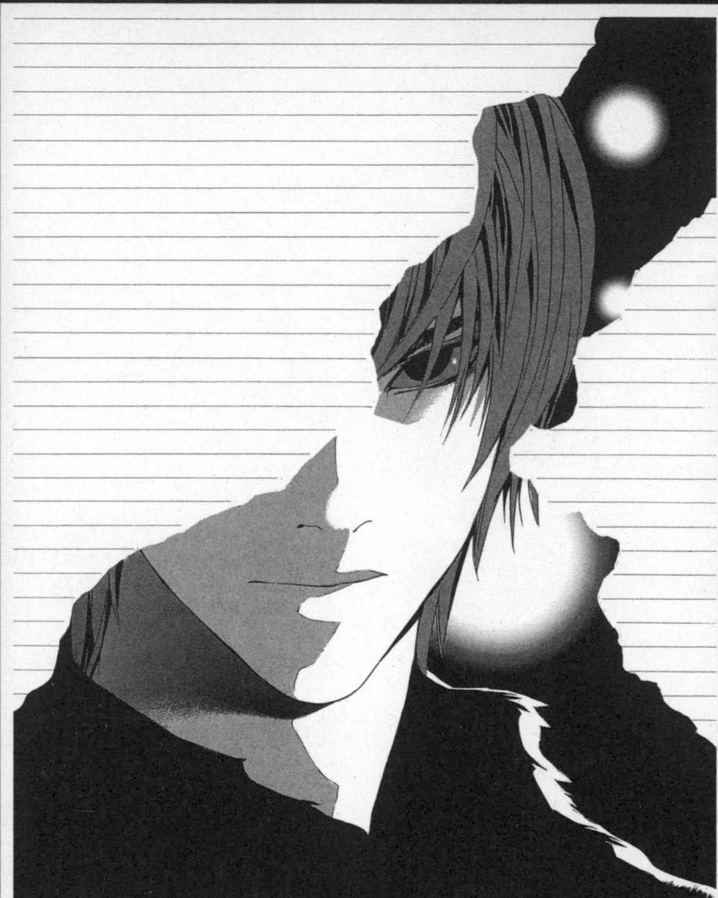

In the Next Volume

Near returns to Japan, determined to out Light as Kira. With the pressures of a fiancée, a new girlfriend, and an heir to balance, can Light maintain his fighting edge?

Available Now

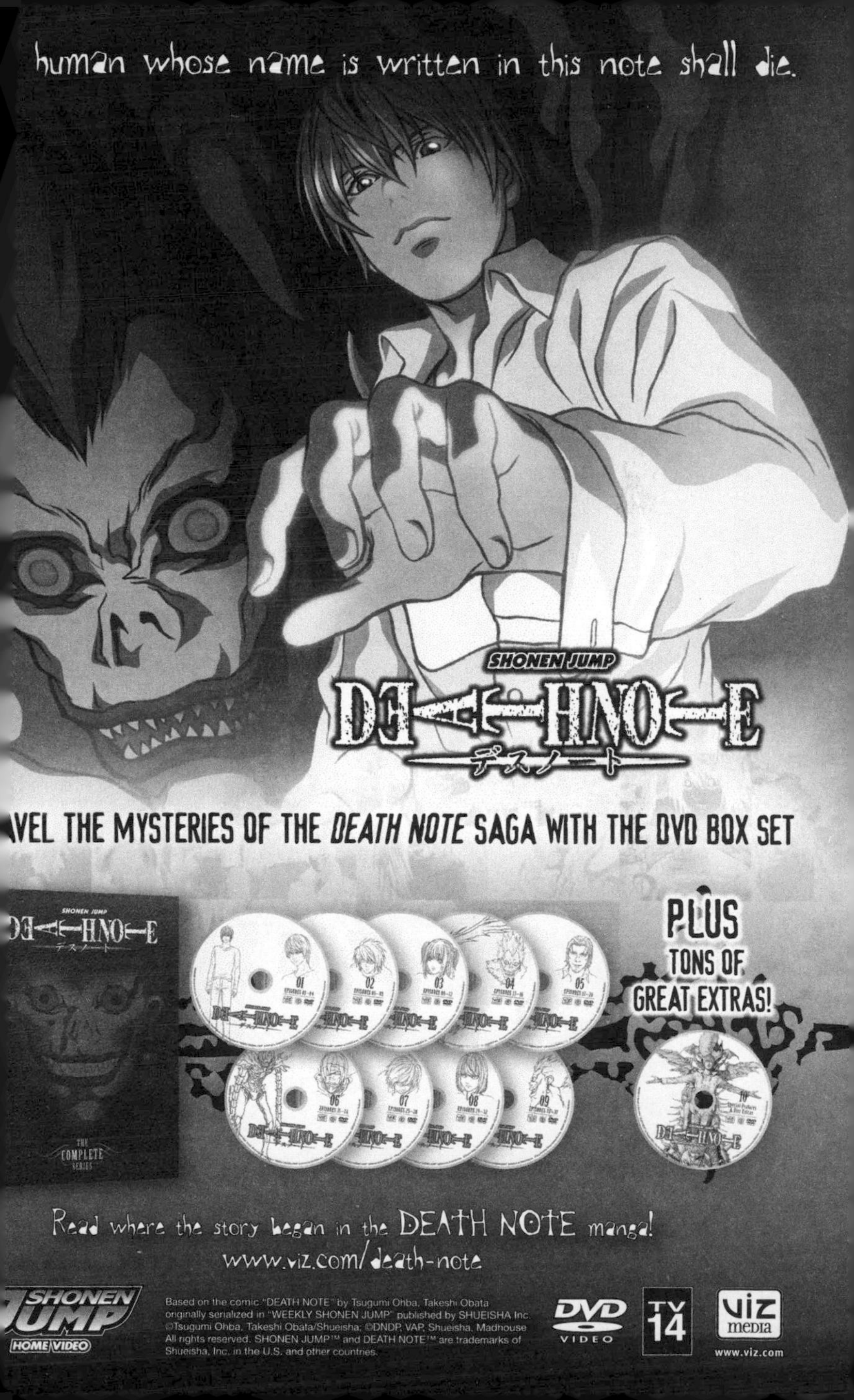

human whose name is written in this note shall die.
SHONEN JUMP
DEATH NOTE
デスノート
VEL THE MYSTERIES OF THE *DEATH NOTE* SAGA WITH THE DVD BOX SET
PLUS
TONS OF
GREAT EXTRAS!
Read where the story began in the DEATH NOTE manga!
www.viz.com/death-note
SHONEN JUMP HOME VIDEO
Based on the comic "DEATH NOTE" by Tsugumi Ohba, Takeshi Obata originally serialized in "WEEKLY SHONEN JUMP" published by SHUEISHA Inc. ©Tsugumi Ohba, Takeshi Obata/Shueisha, ©DNDP, VAP, Shueisha, Madhouse All rights reserved. SHONEN JUMP™ and DEATH NOTE™ are trademarks of Shueisha, Inc. in the U.S. and other countries.
DVD VIDEO
TV 14
VIZ media
www.viz.com

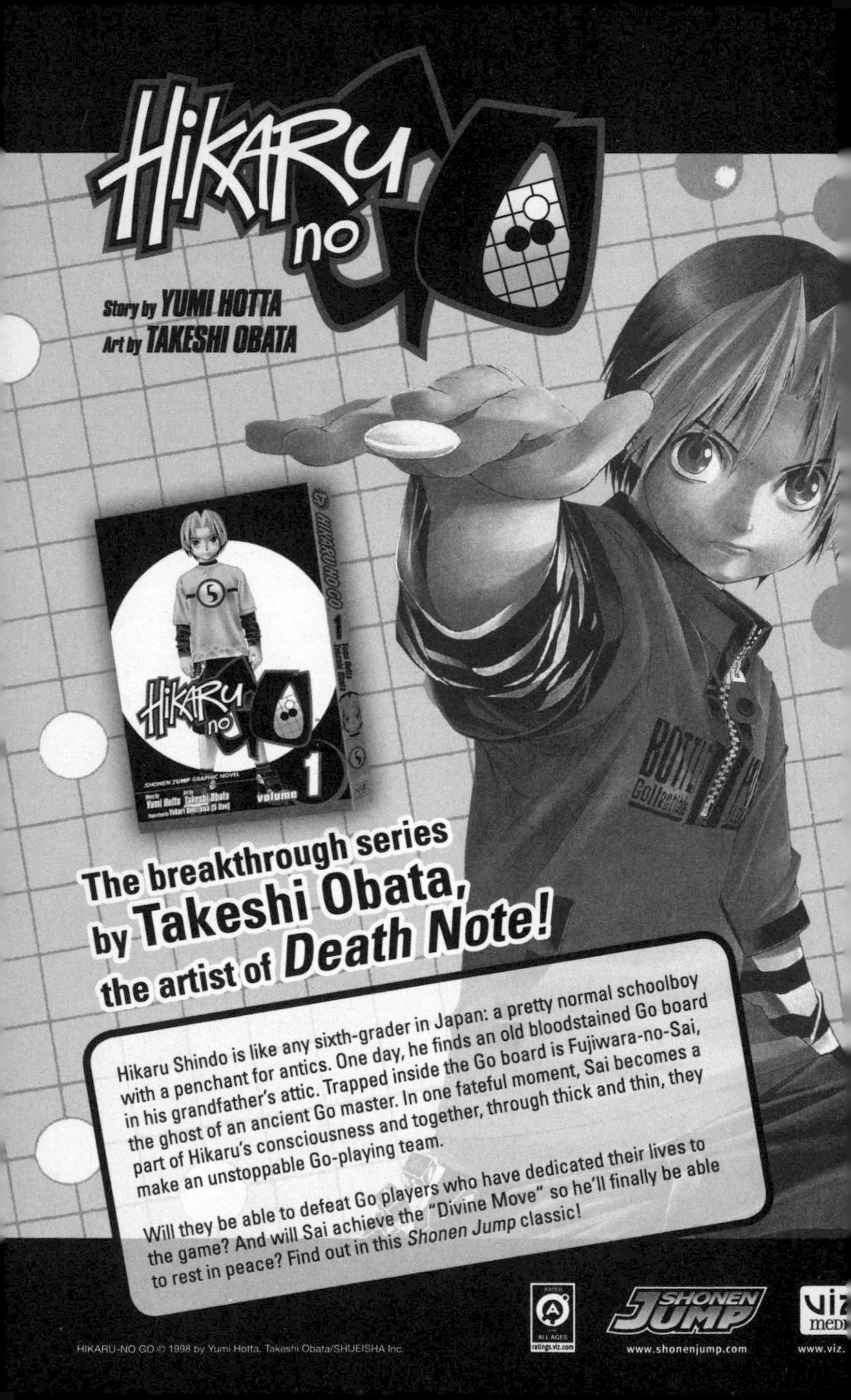
HIKARU no GO
Story by YUMI HOTTA
Art by TAKESHI OBATA
SHONEN JUMP GRAPHIC NOVEL
HIKARU NO GO
volume 1
The breakthrough series by Takeshi Obata, the artist of Death Note!
Hikaru Shindo is like any sixth-grader in Japan: a pretty normal schoolboy with a penchant for antics. One day, he finds an old bloodstained Go board in his grandfather's attic. Trapped inside the Go board is Fujiwara-no-Sai, the ghost of an ancient Go master. In one fateful moment, Sai becomes a part of Hikaru's consciousness and together, through thick and thin, they make an unstoppable Go-playing team.
Will they be able to defeat Go players who have dedicated their lives to the game? And will Sai achieve the "Divine Move" so he'll finally be able to rest in peace? Find out in this Shonen Jump classic!
RATED A ALL AGES ratings.viz.com
SHONEN JUMP
www.shonenjump.com
viz media
www.viz.
HIKARU-NO GO © 1998 by Yumi Hotta, Takeshi Obata/SHUEISHA Inc.

You're Reading in the Wrong Direction!!

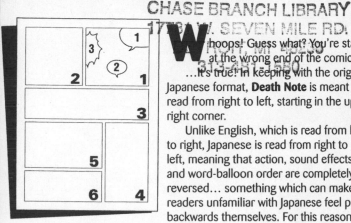

Whoops! Guess what? You're starting at the wrong end of the comic!

...It's true! In keeping with the original Japanese format, **Death Note** is meant to be read from right to left, starting in the upper-right corner.

Unlike English, which is read from left to right, Japanese is read from right to left, meaning that action, sound effects and word-balloon order are completely reversed... something which can make readers unfamiliar with Japanese feel pretty backwards themselves. For this reason, manga or Japanese comics published in the U.S. in English have sometimes been published "flopped"—that is, printed in exact reverse order, as though seen from the other side of a mirror.

By flopping pages, U.S. publishers can avoid confusing readers, but the compromise is not without its downside. For one thing, a character in a flopped manga series who once wore in the original Japanese version a T-shirt emblazoned with "M A Y" (as in "the merry month of") now wears one which reads "Y A M"! Additionally, many manga creators in Japan are themselves unhappy with the process, as some feel the mirror-imaging of their art alters their original intentions.

We are proud to bring you Tsugumi Ohba & Takeshi Obata's **Death Note** in the original unflopped format. For now, though, turn to the other side of the book and let the quest begin...!

–Editor

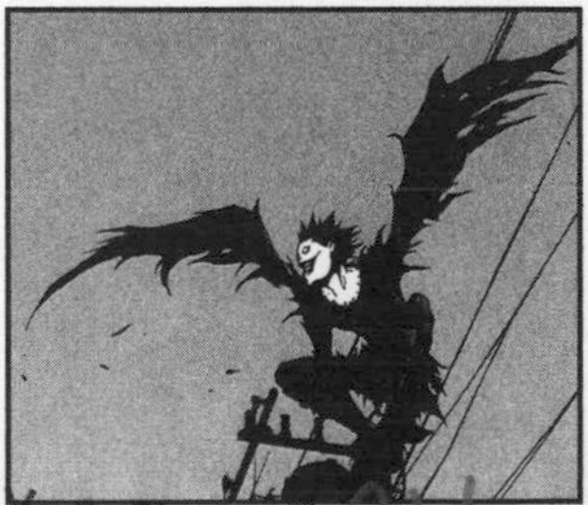